GW00468149

# *Sir* HAROLD WILSON
## YORKSHIRE WALTER MITTY

# *Sir* HAROLD WILSON
## YORKSHIRE WALTER MITTY

*Andrew Roth*

Macdonald and Jane's · London

Dedicated to
the memory of Dick Crossman,
who was generous in his help

First published in Great Britain in 1977
by Macdonald and Jane's Publishers Ltd
Paulton House 8 Shepherdess Walk
London N1 7LW

ISBN 0 356 08074 9

Printed in Great Britain by
Richard Clay (The Chaucer Press) Ltd, Bungay, Suffolk

# Contents

# Introduction

'Andy, you're in serious trouble,' was the warning with which R. H. S. Crossman began our dinner conversation a few weeks after I had gone into high gear on the research and writing of this book.

'I had dinner last night with Harold's "kitchen Cabinet",' Dick Crossman went on, 'and in the middle of it Marcia leaned across to Harold and said: "Andy Roth is trying to seduce your new research assistant!" You are in serious trouble if Marcia is against you,' he added.

My immediate reaction was to laugh because, despite the undoubted attractions of the tall, blonde and trendily-dressed Miss Jane Cousins, then Harold Wilson's research assistant, I knew how innocently professional had been my intentions. As soon as the contract for this book was agreed I wrote a letter informing Mr Wilson, as he then was, and a covering letter to Joseph Haines, his press secretary and a long-time professional colleague and friend. When Joe Haines replied, asking what he could do to help, I explained that the first thing I wanted to do was to secure the full texts of those speeches of Mr Wilson of which I only had brief newspaper reports. Joe Haines urged me to get on to Jane Cousins, who had then taken over as Wilson's research assistant and was in charge of the files.

Repeated telephone calls were unsuccessful in reaching Miss Cousins – not surprisingly, since it turned out that she was on holiday in Turkey. Finally, at the eighth or ninth attempt the House of Commons telephonist put me through to Wilson's office. A man answered – Tony Field, Marcia's brother and Wilson's office manager at the time. I gave my name and explained that I was after some documentation on Mr Wilson from Miss Cousins. This piece of information, passed on to Marcia by her brother, was presumably the basis of her accusation over dinner to Mr Wilson. I asked Dick Crossman whether Joe Haines, who was also at the dinner, had explained that it was he who had suggested I contact Miss Cousins. Crossman said Haines had remained silent. (Joe, I later learned, had been asked by Wilson how to handle my approach. He told him that, on past form, I would go ahead whether or not I had cooperation. The result would be more favourable to Wilson, Joe urged, if cooperation were offered.)

I explained to Crossman how I assumed Marcia Williams – later Lady Falkender – had allowed her suspicions, particularly of the press, to get the better of her. At his urging I decided that I should speed my intention to see her. I had known her long enough to realize that, second to his wife, she was the most knowledgeable person about Harold Wilson. But I also knew that she was spending much of her time working at home in order that she could be more often with her two children by my colleague, Walter Terry, previously political editor of the *Daily Mail* and then political editor of the *Daily Express*. Although I already knew about their love affair, it was not then public knowledge that they had had children and that this was keeping Marcia at home. Since Fleet Street, on the 'dog doesn't eat dog' principle, had not then publicized the affair, I was uncertain how to handle myself. When I met Marcia again, was I to pretend innocence? In interviews with Mr Wilson could I discuss his life after 1956 without particular regard to allegations about his close relationship with his political secretary? I knew that many anti-Marcia allegations were politically-inspired slanders. I also knew that he had been informed of them, especially of the allegation spread by Marcia's enemies in the Parliamentary Labour Party that Harold Wilson was the father of her children. How could I write an objective and honest biography without trying to find out why Mr Wilson was willing to risk so much to protect his undoubtedly able and super-loyal political secretary? Had one of the Conservative-inclined national newspaper editors, privy to the information, published early in 1970 that Mrs Williams had had two illegitimate children after her 1961 divorce, the June 1970 general election might well have turned into a rout rather than a mere defeat for the forces led by Harold Wilson. I knew that this question had been raised with the then Prime Minister by an aide, who insisted that the matter be clarified to avoid the overhanging threat. But the only answer this associate could elicit from Mr Wilson was: 'But she loved him . . .'

No biographer really expects the fullest cooperation of living politicians who are still active on the political scene. My first major effort in the field of political biography – a dual biography of Aneurin Bevan and Hugh Gaitskell – came adrift because Jennie Lee – later Baroness Lee – wanted only flattering comments made about her husband, Aneurin. Hugh Gaitskell wrote to all possible personal contacts to block my access to them. I was surprised and disappointed but noted that he tied a later biographer to a contract which enabled Gaitskell to bring the book to a halt when the author showed signs of being too critical. I later discovered that Gaitskell had feared that an uncontrolled biographer might find out about an innocuous premarital indiscretion, and that the publication of this information might preclude his becoming Prime

Minister. In my later biography of Edward Heath, which *was* published, Mr Heath withdrew the help promised, presumably to give a fairer wind to a competing biography which depicted him as a romantic figure marred by an early unrequited love.

Even the trepidations arising from these experiences did not prepare me for the comedy of my 'reconciliation' with Marcia Williams. When I wrote to tell her what I was doing and asked for her help and a telephone number at which to reach her, she replied promptly. But she declined to give her telephone number, which she kept ex-directory and changed frequently. Instead we arranged an appointment at the Churchill Hotel, not far from her mews home, a hotel in which her friend Eric Miller had an interest. When I asked whom to contact if I were delayed I was told to inform Bill Housden, Mr Wilson's genial chauffeur, who would in turn tell Marcia. On the appointed day, a Thursday, there was an extra briefing and a transport strike, so I telephoned Mr Wilson's office asking that Mrs Williams be told I would be an hour late. By the time I arrived she had come and gone; her elaborate arrangement, worthy of a pair of spies in an enemy-occupied country, had broken down. We did meet again, after someone in Wilson's office had had the rough side of Marcia's tongue. It was a very pleasant and lengthy conversation. The main conclusion of our talk was that Mrs Williams would recover and transcribe the tapes of Wilson's conversations with the kindly, unpolitical BBC producer, Leslie Smith, conversations which formed the basis of his book *Harold Wilson*, published in 1964. Although its naïve and uncritical approach aroused the disdain of experienced and somewhat cynical political reporters, the materials put at Mr Smith's disposal were very revealing, perhaps more so than Wilson realized. I was naturally very much interested in reading a transcript of the original tapes. Mrs Williams succeeded in getting them back and having them transcribed, but repeated appeals for a copy of the transcription fell on deaf ears.

Limited cooperation was also extended by the subject himself. A lengthy interview on his early life resulted in a revised draft of a chapter on this period. A chance meeting resulted in Mr Wilson's comments that there were a few 'adventitious errors' in the chapter. But these were never disclosed. One could not escape the feeling that my approach was not sufficiently adoring, as indicated in criticisms made in my book, *Can Parliament Decide?* (We did, though, have a friendly meeting in July 1977.)

Luckily I had access to more objective observers who could add an additional dimension to the self-flattering picture which Sir Harold, as he subsequently became, has been inclined to present in countless speeches and interviews. In his typically generous way Dick Crossman offered me access to his then still unpublished diaries, which he had started in 1950, and from which his literary executors have kindly allowed me to quote for the years 1951 to 1953. Reading them from the beginning in his Vincent Square study, in the company of their editor, Dr Janet Morgan, I soon came to the conclusion reached by most critics after the post-1964 diaries were published: that these were the most brilliant political diaries of our time, outstripping even the unpublished *private* diaries of Hugh (later Lord) Dalton, on which the expurgated published diaries were based. Like Roy Jenkins, I think that Dick Crossman reached a very high level of accuracy. Indubitably, like all of us, he saw the events in which he participated through his own eyes, but those were the sharp ones of a trained journalist whose brilliant mind was that of a well-honed academic intellectual. What is more, Crossman was always willing to reassess a situation once he had discovered a new factor in the equation – a trait which his colleagues, having less intellectual flexibility, often found very distressing.

The vividness of Crossman's diaries of the 1950s helped to rekindle for me the smouldering embers of my own recollections and interviews of that period. Since I had arrived from Asia on the day the Korean War broke out, my interest in the impact of that war on Anglo–American relations and British politics and politicians was intense. I was in the Press Gallery of the House of Commons for the resignation speeches of Aneurin Bevan and Harold Wilson, which brought these behind-the-scenes pressures out into the open. I attended the meetings in the country of the so-called 'Bevanites'. I interviewed many of the members of this 'party within a party', as their opponents tagged them. Going back to the writings, notes and cuttings of the time, it was particularly instructive to have not only Crossman's diaries but also the private Minutes of the 'Keep Left' and 'Bevanite' Groups – later renamed the 'Tribune Group' – lent to me through the courtesy of Jo Richardson, now an MP.

Fascination with behind-the-scenes conflicts and intrigues had gradually transformed me from a foreign correspondent writing for North American, French and Asian papers into a domestic political correspondent and biographer. Since I have wound up as a fully-fledged Lobby or political correspondent for the *Manchester Evening News*, I am bound by the rules of the Lobby. One of the key rules is that one does not disclose the source of political information unless this has been provided for the record. As a result I have been somewhat inhibited in giving due credit in this book to the many politicians, particularly on the Labour side, who have helped to make this account as accurate and objective as possible. As someone originally trained to be an academic, it grieves me not to be as generous in my attributions in reference notes as I would have liked. If my notes are less than generous I trust my direct access to politicians has made up for the lack. I should, however, repeat my gratitude to the late R. H. S. Crossman for allowing me access to his early political diaries; also to Michael Foot, who put his collection of cuttings on Aneurin Bevan at my disposal; and to the L.S.E. Library for access to the unpublished private diaries of the late Lord Dalton.

At the end of three years of research and investigation, the problem arose as to how to encompass in one volume a study of a man who had packed so much into sixty fast-moving years, half of them in politics, thirteen of them as leader of the Labour Party and eight of these as Prime Minister. A straight, descriptive biography, however attractive to one trained as a historian, was clearly out of the question; it would have required a minimum of three large volumes and full access to the documents at Sir Harold's disposal.

In the case of Sir Harold people have long been interested not so much in *what* he has done as in *why* he has done it. *Daily Mirror* columnist Keith Waterhouse reported that, in the wake of Wilson's 1976 resignation, everyone was asking: 'What is Harold up to?' Puzzlement about the mainsprings of Wilson's political actions has been constant since his earliest days, even among those who thought they knew him best. Nobody was more surprised at Wilson's joining the Oxford City Labour Party in 1938 and his adoption for Ormskirk in 1944 than his closest university friend, Teddy Jackson, who had tried unsuccessfully to recruit him earlier into the Oxford University Labour Club. Equally surprised, when Wilson turned up in 1945 as an MP, and a Labour one at that, was Frank Byers, who had no idea that Wilson had ceased to be a Liberal.

The inability of those close to him to read his mind and anticipate his actions has often been a real threat to Wilson. On the very eve of his 1963 elections as Leader he almost lost the support of a large number of left-wingers who feared he would inflict divisive revenge on those right-wingers who had been most scathing about him; instead, within months, he brought a hitherto unknown peace to Labour ranks. The inscrutability of his motives has sometimes brought division. George Brown committed political suicide in 1968 because, in his own insecurity, he misread Wilson's failure to involve him in a fairly routine Privy Council meeting and resigned as Foreign Secretary. The greatest misreading of any living politician occurred when none of his Cabinet colleagues, including those few like Callaghan who had been forewarned, believed Wilson's many references to the need for politicians to retire when they lost their flexibility around the age of sixty. On top of that, the greatest blow to Wilson's reputation, second only to the resignation Honours list uproar, came when his super-loyal press secretary, Joseph Haines, published his unexpectedly 'disloyal' *Politics of Power* early in 1977. Nobody could have been more of a hero-worshipper than Joe Haines, who had almost destroyed his reputation with his professional colleagues by treating them insultingly when they refused to worship at the same altar as he did. But Joe, I am convinced, emerged from his period of worship when he gave up trying to understand why his hero allowed his term of office to be made into a battleground – and to be unnecessarily foreshortened – by the activities of Marcia, Baroness Falkender. The honours awarded to Sir James Goldsmith and other Tory tycoons particularly distressed him.

This political biography is therefore mainly an effort to lay bare the roots of Wilsonian behaviour, which has so disturbed friend and foe alike. In some fields I must unhappily admit defeat. Thus I cannot fully explain why a man who has been so generous with his personal and unsung kindnesses should have the reputation of being 'a cold fish' and 'a cat who walks alone' even among fellow Labour politicians. I cannot explain why so intelligent a man should have remained culturally so utterly philistine, despite all his opportunities. Although he boasts of having seen *Swan Lake* a score of times, it has always been as a guest of the Russians. He has remained unashamedly a Radio 1 and Radio 2 listener, unlike his wife Mary, who has a taste for concerts and art galleries. The only possible explanation is that, once he had been programmed to get to the top as an academic swot, he so suppressed any cultural distractions that his capacity to imbibe culture shrivelled like an arm kept permanently in plaster.

Wilson may well emerge, in a few years' time, as a more considerable figure than he now appears to many. Like Lloyd George, Stanley Baldwin and Neville Chamberlain he has lost stature with the loss of office. The public regard him as they did Lloyd George, a mixture of dubious style and indubitable political talents and public achievements. If he did not win a world war, he did succeed in preventing civil war in the Labour Party. He also succeeded in bridging the dangerous social divisions caused by the Tories' 1973–74 confrontation with the miners. And his 1975 referendum on remaining in the EEC largely healed the wounds caused by that controversy. Perhaps his Walter Mitty pretensions and whirling dervish style were necessities of the time. Like Harold Macmillan in the wake of Suez, Harold Wilson may have helped both to assure and to ease Britain's transition from an Imperial power to a European state.

The difference between Macmillan and Wilson may well emerge as that between a cynical realist and a role-player. Macmillan *sounded* like a militant imperialist early in 1957 because he wanted to scupper the chances of R. A. Butler and knew that he needed such an oratorical smokescreen to cover Britain's withdrawal from its disastrous invasion of Egypt. Wilson talked Left and anti-Market in Opposition and then became pro-EEC and moderate in office. One can accept that this was imposed on him by the pressures that Labour traditionally puts on its Leader. But why, like a political Walter Mitty, did he require adoration and approval in each successive and contradictory role?

# I. Last Performance on the Tightrope

'He has earned very high marks indeed for the astonishing *coup de théâtre* with which he has brought his reign to an end – a coup that, partly because of its personal modesty and partly because of its sensitivity to the long-term needs of the party, already promises to lead to the most ordered transition of power in recent British history.'

*New Statesman*, 20 March 1976

'How typical of Harold that, after making such a graceful exit, he had to do this on the doorstep.'

Roy Jenkins, *Sunday Times*, 13 February 1977

Except for one crucial touch, nothing became Harold Wilson so much as the manner of his going; even his bitter critic the *Daily Mail* conceded, 'The timing is impeccable. No other Prime Minister in this century has bowed out with such political finesse.'[1] It was as though the country's greatest artist on the tightrope had announced – to a full house, with all the spotlights on him – that he was giving up the world he loved.

The announcement had come as a shock and a surprise because everyone thought he would only leave the political arena kicking and screaming. Whenever he had pointed out to fellow politicians that it was important to retire before age made one respond automatically, like Pavlov's dogs, to recurrent crises, this had been greeted with some scepticism. Although he was a 'poor butcher' even with his ageing colleagues, none of them expected him to commit political *hara-kiri* when he himself reached three-score: least of all his designated successor, James Callaghan, whom he had promised a fair wind. Wilson had told Callaghan his plan in December, along with the Queen, Lord Goodman and the future Speaker and Callaghan's Cardiff colleague, George Thomas. But Callaghan was doubtful. 'The Prime Minister has been saying he will retire shortly,' he told a colleague early in January 1976. 'He told me so again last week. But you know, I look at the calendar and see the Queen's Jubilee coming and the Commonwealth Prime Ministers' Conference, and the first European summit in London. And I say to myself, "Surely the little b - - - - - won't pass up those."'[2] Most top-level observers shared Callaghan's view.

Wilson's plan to retire around sixty had been greeted with a scepticism which was unprecedented since the boy who cried 'Wolf!' and which stretched from the highest in the land to constituency activists in the Liverpool suburb of Huyton. When he resumed office in March 1974, accepting the seals of office from Queen Elizabeth II, Wilson had confided to Her Majesty that he only intended to stay on the job for about two years. Since he took office on that occasion without a majority the Queen may have thought that he was being unduly optimistic about lasting that long as Prime Minister. But even her most sceptical advisers may have noticed that he had changed his style on his return to 10 Downing Street, chairing the Cabinet as though it were a team instead of trying to play all the positions himself.

The cold which he caught during his February 1974 election campaign made the job seem more of a physical strain than it had ever been before. 'This is a young man's game and I'm getting too old for it,' he told a friend in the regions[3] during that campaign, a remark which seemed significant only after he retired just two years later. When he reached fifty-nine, a year before he retired, he confided his plans to Arthur Smith, his agent for eleven years at Huyton. At the end of a 'surgery' with his constituents one cold night in March 1975, Wilson was in a confiding mood. 'I think I have done enough. I have worked hard for a long time. It would be pleasant to sit on the back benches, observe the scene and do a little writing ... I don't intend leading the party into another General Election.'[4] But the subject was not mentioned for the next year.

Wilson toyed for a time with going in September 1975 just before that year's annual conference at Blackpool. This would enable him to do an imitation of his politician-hero, Harold Macmillan. A dozen years before, at that same Lancashire seaside resort, Macmillan's need to resign as Prime Minister had been announced. The surprise disclosure had converted the 1963 Conservative conference into a sharp-elbowed scramble for the succession. Macmillan, although hospitalized in London with a painful prostate, had tried first to foist on the party Lord Hailsham, *alias* Quintin Hogg, and then Lord Home, *alias* Sir Alec Douglas-Home. Wilson thought he could do better than his model, Macmillan. By announcing his resignation at Blackpool he could hope for the party's pats on the back while he gave a leg-up to his own first choice, James Callaghan. Their relationship had altered considerably since he had excluded Callaghan from his 'inner Cabinet' in 1969 because Jim had insisted that the trade unions would not wear Labour's Bill to reform them as outlined in Barbara Castle's 'In Place of Strife'. Because Callaghan had proved that a Labour Government could not fall out with the trade-union movement, when Labour returned to office in March 1974 Callaghan *was* Wilson's 'inner Cabinet'. But Wilson accepted the perceptive argument of Lady Falkender, his political secretary, and Joe Haines that a Prime Minister's resignation should be a *national* rather than a party affair.

During that September 1975 party conference, Wilson asked his Principal Private Secretary, Kenneth Stowe, and his Press Secretary, Joe Haines, to draw up a 'scenario', as he described it, for his resignation. The first draft was made by Stowe. It was amended by Haines, for newsworthiness. Wilson, Stowe and Haines then agreed a final draft. In order to maintain secrecy, Haines typed the three copies needed. Stowe took two, one for the Prime Minister, and Haines put the other one in the safe of the Private Office in November 1975. Although Wilson almost certainly informed Marcia very soon, she was not officially involved because the matter was treated as a governmental function rather than a party one.

## ALMOST A SLIP

Wilson's elaborate plan for a surprise resignation almost collapsed through premature disclosure when he decided at the beginning of December 1975 to retire around the time of his sixtieth birthday on 11 March 1976. This, he thought, was a suitable time because it would be at the beginning of the next round of talks on wage ceilings, which were a key to Labour's chances of victory in the next General Election. If, as Wilson hoped, Callaghan won the ensuing contest in the Parliamentary Labour Party, it would give him a minimum of eighteen months in which to play himself in before the first suitable date for such an election – from *Labour's* point of view. The timing was not as good from the viewpoint of Denis Healey, since it would come just before the unveiling of the Budget. But Healey was young enough to take a second bite at the leadership cherry next time around, when he had learned more about politics. There never was any question in Wilson's mind of helping a left-winger become Prime Minister, even apart from his conviction that this would lose Labour the next election. He could not abide Anthony Benn, either for his near-disloyalty or his politico-economic judgment; he had demonstrated this publicly by signalling from Jamaica his intention to downgrade Benn from Secretary for Industry to Secretary for Energy in the columns of the *Daily Telegraph*. Although he found Michael Foot more pleasant as a person he had kept him at arm's length, dodging both private discussions on the problems Foot wanted to raise as Secretary for Employment and excluding Foot from social events at 10 Downing Street. Wilson had liked Peter Shore, one of his original 1956 'band of four', the others being R. H. S. Crossman, Thomas (later Lord) Balogh and Marcia Williams. But in the last couple of years Shore had identified himself with Benn in the Cabinet arguments.

Wilson showed his loyalty to those colleagues who *had* stood by him when he staged a reshuffle in the Department of Energy to take care of Lord Balogh, a Wilson-loyalist since 1952. Balogh had made a come-back as Minister of State for Energy because he had specialized in how to extract more revenue from international oil companies active in the North Sea. But Wilson knew that Budapest-born 'Tommy' was not everyone's favourite and would not long survive Wilson's departure from office. Balogh was moody, persistent and very outspoken. He had a bad tendency of referring to Jack Jones and Hugh Scanlon as 'animals' – a direct translation from the Hungarian word 'allatok', which has the connotation of brutishness – because these trade-union chiefs did not share Balogh's belief in wage control. Wilson used the excuse of Balogh's seventieth birthday and the need for better representation of Scotland's interest in Energy for his December reshuffle. But he named Balogh as Deputy Chairman of the British National Oil Corporation as a way of rewarding the Hungarian economist while he still could.

The Queen's advisers were struck by Wilson's jauntiness on 9 December 1975, after he had informed Her Majesty of his intention to give up office around the middle of March 1976. It was a courtesy to let her be the first to know his plans officially, and Wilson had always shown himself to be deeply conventional in respect to the Monarch. In fact, he had always shown such boyish delight in his conversational intimacy with Queen Elizabeth II that her advisers had thought that his Tuesday evening audience was one of the weekly 'perks' of the job he would be most loath to lose.

Harold Wilson was certainly anxious to retain Her Majesty's regard, because his retirement plans were modelled on those of the late Sir Winston Churchill. He was anxious to be dubbed a Knight of the Garter by Her Majesty, though he might have preferred the more prestigious and less socially snobbish Order of Merit. However, he knew that Harold Macmillan had deeply offended the Queen by refusing the KG, and he did not want to do the same when she offered him the honour accepted by Sir Winston Churchill. He also wanted the honour of her attendance at the ritual final dinner for the Cabinet at 10 Downing Street – something she had accorded Sir Winston in 1955. This was all part of the elaborate plan he was putting into operation for an event still four months ahead. To anticipate all the problems that might arise in March 1976 was a challenge to him as an experienced politician, a former civil servant and a news manager of some talent.

There were three or four other people to be informed officially that day, including his designated successor, James Callaghan, and George

Thomas, then Deputy Speaker but scheduled to succeed Selwyn Lloyd as Speaker as soon as Selwyn Lloyd's retirement pension could be arranged. On the night of 9 December 1975 Wilson went to a party at the home of Lord Goodman, at the top of Portland Place. Lord Goodman, a long-time friend, adviser and confidant from Profumo days, if not earlier, had played both 'Mr Fixit' and organizer of office finance to Wilson when in Opposition. He was privy to the Prime Minister's desire to resign around his sixtieth birthday but not yet to whether 'Operation Resignation' had been given the green light. Wilson could not wait to inform him. 'By the way, Arnold,' he said to the consternation of his companion, Joe Haines, who feared that other ears might understand, 'I spoke to the Queen about *that matter*.'[5]

Haines felt that Wilson was risking everything by being overheard. Wilson, however, was afraid that, when he came to announce his retirement in March 1976, his reason for doing so – that he had reached the age of sixty – would not be believed. By talking elliptically within earshot of a number of Fleet Street publishers three months ahead of time, he hoped to be in a position later to remind them of his remarks. Such a reminder, Wilson hoped, would disabuse them of the notion that he was deserting the ship of state because he feared economic storms looming.

Harold Wilson's elaborate plan almost crashed on the rocks because, within days, a whisper of his intentions reached the receptive ears of Nigel Dempster, then running the *Daily Mail*'s diary, or gossip column. On 16 December, a week after the Prime Minister had opened just a corner of his secret resignation plans to a handful of people, Nigel Dempster splashed the story that Harold Wilson had told close Cabinet colleagues that he was 'feeling tired and unwell' and that he considered '1976 is the right year in which to make way for another person to take up the reins'. Except for the word 'unwell' and the 's' on the end of the word colleagues, it was a remarkably accurate story.

There was consternation on the part of the Prime Minister and his handful of intimates privy to the plan. If the report were widely accepted it would mean that he would be a 'lame duck' Prime Minister for the three months to March. It was decided to sledgehammer the story into the ground, taking advantage of the fact that the *Daily Mail* was politically antagonistic to Wilson. 'No such conversation has taken place,' said a statement from Joe Haines. 'Rumours of his retirement have been current since 1964 and there are other aspects of the story which are being looked at by lawyers.'[6] Two days later Wilson sued Nigel Dempster and the *Daily Mail*[7] for libel as part of the plan to prevent anyone from giving further currency to the largely accurate story – and also because of the implication in the Dempster story that Wilson was drinking heavily.

Having suppressed disclosure from a hostile source the Prime Minister gave a teasing performance in an interview on Yorkshire TV with his favourite interviewer, Austin Mitchell, later the Labour MP for Grimsby. 'I think that while I have a job to do, I'll stay,' he said, giving no intimation that this would only be for another two months. What he did explain was his intention to imitate the late Sir Winston Churchill. 'I shall always be a Parliamentarian,' he insisted. 'I would like to write and I'd like to think about the problems facing the country. But when [my resignation] finally comes, I shall not interfere. I have a good team for them to choose another captain from.' To hammer home how hard he had to work as a Prime Minister Wilson pointed out that he had been able to take his labrador dog, Paddy, for a walk only twice since the previous October.[8]

Wilson's interview with Austin Mitchell was a token of the way in which he had mapped out his post-resignation 'redeployment'. He had spent his Christmas recess of 1975 reading *The Office of Prime Minister* by Lord Blake. This was in preparation for a working dinner at the home of David Frost on 8 January 1976 with Frost, Anthony Jay and Stella Richmond to discuss a series for Yorkshire TV on 'The Prime Ministers', which was to be made after his resignation. Frost and his colleagues were therefore privy to the knowledge that Wilson's resignation was not too far off – before the overwhelming majority of his Cabinet colleagues had been informed. Through Frost, Yorkshire TV had the inside track. When the resignation was announced and the BBC's Brian Wenham approached the outgoing Prime Minister about doing some post-resignation broadcasts, Lady Falkender managed to misplace the BBC letter for a fortnight.

Wilson's impending resignation began to shade his attitudes on Government decisions. Thus, in November he had told Industry Secretary Eric Varley to stand up to Chrysler in defence of British Leyland, 95% of whose shares had been purchased by the Government. In December, about the time he informed the Queen that he would be leaving the following March, he suddenly weakened, asking the ingenious Harold Lever, Chancellor of the Duchy of Lancaster, to find a formula by which Chrysler in Britain could be saved. The main factor in his weakening was the threats by Scottish Secretary William Ross and his Minister of State (and successor) Bruce Millan to resign if the company's Scottish plant at Linwood were closed. Wilson did not want his last months in office to be disfigured by a Cabinet crisis and arguments over factory closures and increases in unemployment. When Eric Varley, initially a Wilson protégé, protested at having had the rug pulled out from under him, Wilson gave him a tongue-lashing, urging him to grow up and stop being the tool of his civil servants.

## LAST HITCHES

Last-minute hitches made it advisable not to announce the resignation on his sixtieth birthday, 11 March 1976, however symbolic that date might have been. Because of the sterling crisis that particular Thursday had to be abandoned. In Wilson's 'Operation Resignation' it was thought vital to carry out the action either on a Tuesday or a Thursday because both were normal Cabinet days as well as being days on which the Prime Minister appears on the Government front bench in the Commons to answer questions addressed to him. This made it possible, on either a Tuesday or a Thursday, to compress the impact of resignation into one day. The Prime Minister could inform his Cabinet colleagues in the morning and the Commons in the afternoon, following up with a televised press conference to tell the country and the world at large.

The chance of announcing the resignation on 11 March was also lost because of the left-wing revolt on 10 March against the cuts planned in Government expenditure. This made it necessary to hold a vote of confidence on 11 March. The Government readily won the vote, since the Left preferred even a parsimonious Labour Government to a general election which the Tories might win. But the excitement over whether the Labour Government could survive was bound to distract attention from the elaborate scenario of a Wilson abdication.

In the event, when Wilson acted out his plan on 16 March not even his sharpest critics could fault him for the manner in which he managed to concentrate the spotlights on himself for a full 24 hours. 'True to form,' wrote the usually splenetic Frank Johnson in the *Daily Telegraph*, 'Mr Wilson the Great News Editor had made known his departure by means of a Shock Bombshell Sensation.'[9] As anyone who took part in the news coverage on that frenetic 16 March can testify, it was one Wilson story after another from 11.30 a.m. when Joe Haines informed startled pressmen that his chief Harold Wilson had just astonished his Cabinet by disclosing his resignation intentions. Wilson's resignation got more coverage than any abdication since that of Edward VIII. Even his worst enemies in the press, like the *Daily Mail*, felt compelled to devote whole pages to the end of the Wilson era.

The outgoing Prime Minister had, of course, the advantage of complete surprise. When he left 10 Downing Street that morning just before 10 a.m. there were no press photographers on hand to record his discreetly scheduled audience with her Majesty at nearby Buckingham Palace at 10.15 a.m.

## ASTONISHED COLLEAGUES

Even James Callaghan, then Foreign Secretary, was somewhat surprised at Wilson's disclosure, despite three intimations of what was to come.

The most recent assurance that Wilson would make way for him had been given in the back of the Prime Minister's car returning to Number 10 from the House of Commons the previous Thursday, 11 March. 'I don't want to stand in the way of your chance,' he had said, without specifying the exact day. But now, on 16 March, he was pinning it down. As Ministers assembled for the Cabinet meeting the Prime Minister took Callaghan to one side in the annex to the Cabinet Room. 'I will be informing colleagues at the Cabinet this morning of my resignation as soon as arrangements can be made to find my successor,' he confided.

Wilson was also anxious to give the other moderate candidate for the succession, Denis Healey, some advance warning. When he arrived, just before the Cabinet was due to start, he found Wilson signalling to him. 'Denis, I want a word,' he said, looking round for a place to talk privately. Finally they went to the men's lavatory for Wilson to impart the momentous news.[10] For Healey, with a Budget to present in three weeks' time, the news could hardly have been less welcome. Only a few days before he had cursed out left-wing rebels against his cuts in the vocabulary of a Bradford bar-room brawler rather than a Chancellor of the Exchequer.

It was unwelcome for another reason to Edward Short, the Deputy Leader of the Parliamentary Labour Party, Lord President of the Council and Leader of the Commons. As Roy Jenkins's successor as Deputy Leader he had found that he could work closely with Wilson as a fellow northerner who found southern English ways faintly foreign. At sixty-three he could see that he would be particularly vulnerable in any reshuffle after Wilson's departure. He did not get on at all well with Jim Callaghan, Wilson's likely successor.

'Before we come to Parliamentary business,' the outgoing Prime Minister addressed his Cabinet colleagues, 'I want to make a brief statement. I should be grateful if there were no interruptions.' He asked his colleagues not to leave the Cabinet Room for any reason, apparently in recollection of the time when Manny (later Lord) Shinwell left the Cabinet Room to tip off newspapers in a self-glorifying way. He also told his colleagues that there was no point in trying to persuade him to stay since the news of his resignation would be released before the Cabinet meeting was concluded. He then read the lengthy statement he had laboriously prepared as a historical document designed to be accurate technically while patting himself on the back. 'My period as Prime Minister has been longer than that of any of my peacetime predecessors in this century,' he claimed. (In fact, both Asquith and Churchill had served longer, and only two years of Asquith's service had been in the First World War.) 'I shall not go into industry or take paid employment,' he promised.[11] But that did not exclude lucrative fees for

TV performances with the fulsomely friendly David Frost on receptive Yorkshire TV, or commissions for other books like his political memoir of the 1964–70 Labour Government which had earned him over £215,000.

Wilson's basic message was that he was mentally tired after having been an MP for thirty-one years, Leader for thirteen and Prime Minister for almost eight. This had led to 'a danger to which I have been alerted all my working life. It is that, in times of rapid change, you may be faced with a decision which, perhaps in different conditions, you have faced before. If on the earlier occasion you considered and rejected a particular course of action, there is a tendency to say you have been into that, so that you do not give the fresh consideration the circumstances may require. I am determined not to succumb to this danger.' Was he thinking of the three occasions he had resisted devaluation in 1948, 1964 and 1966? He made no reference to the impact on him of emotional exhaustion from being pulled away from politics by the gentle but implacable Mary Wilson and from being subjected to the shrewish outbursts of Marcia, Lady Falkender.

Thinking back, Wilson's Cabinet colleagues realized there was, perhaps, something in his theme that things were getting too much for him. Until recently he had been a brilliant Cabinet chairman. No matter how diverse the contributions of Cabinet Ministers, he had been able to knit together some common theme. But about a fortnight before his retirement there had been a marked exception in the case of Cabinet discussions on the Official Secrets Act. Home Secretary Roy Jenkins had prepared well for the discussion, partly by consulting all his Cabinet colleagues in advance. This had not guaranteed unanimity because, for one, of Jim Callaghan's attitude of conservative traditionalism. But what had struck Wilson's colleagues was his inability to pull the discussion together at the end. 'He must be losing his touch!' said one.

Barbara Castle now broke the silence of Wilson's colleagues by crying out, 'Oh God!',[12] as though she had guessed her fate at the hands of Wilson's successor. Ted Short tried to pay the Cabinet's tribute but broke down. Callaghan then paid a warm and gallant tribute. 'The whole Cabinet wishes to place on record immediately its sense of loss and its profound gratitude to Harold Wilson for the unique service he has given to his country and his party over the past thirteen years,' was the motion he presented and the Cabinet accepted.[13] Two of his colleagues were so impressed by Jim's ability to take command that they decided then and there to vote for him as Harold's successor. When a rival, presumably Denis Healey, was told this, he exploded: '"Spur of the moment"? The bugger was given six months to practise!'[14] In fact, of course, it was only three months.

After so much forethought Harold Wilson's plans went well. Knowing that the 'old women' in the City would read the worst interpretation into the resignation of their old critic he had a courier sent to the Governor of the Bank of England to warn him to support sterling.[15] But even then, with the support of the Bank of England, a penny was knocked off the pound's value in dollars. And £1,000m was wiped off share prices. The Chairman of the Parliamentary Labour Party, Cledwyn Hughes, was brought in as soon as the Cabinet was wound up. Never before had a Labour Prime Minister departed in the midst of office and a new procedure had to be worked out. Hughes left Number 10 almost in shock and explained to the newsmen, who by then were waiting: 'We have no rules. This is the first time a Labour Prime Minister in office has retired. We're calling a meeting to discuss drafting rules of procedure.'[16]

Newsmen were loitering with intent in Downing Street because Harold Wilson and Joe Haines suddenly defrosted their 'cold war' with the press as part of their plan to dominate all the news media for the next twenty-four hours at least. At 11.30 a.m., well before the Cabinet meeting came to an end, the prepared text of the outgoing Prime Minister's statement to the Cabinet was rushed to the Press Gallery of the House of Commons, from which news spread like wildfire, as intended. The news dominated the BBC's 1 p.m. bulletin and the front pages of all the evening newspapers. To give TV a full opportunity, the long-planned press conference took place in the late afternoon in the long concourse of the Mussolini-style headquarters of the Department of Defence. 'I am happy to have been among friends,' Prime Minister Wilson said after a rather cosy, cracker-barrel performance for the cameras and radio, 'I forgive you all.' To many present he seemed to strike the wrong note, as though trying too hard to seem 'one of the boys' and to translate into the vernacular what he had already said better in the Commons after his Cabinet statement. Thus, he tried to imitate the old Macmillan flippancy of a 'little local difficulty' when asked about the left-wing revolt on the expenditure cuts which had lost the Government a vote the previous Wednesday and forced a vote of confidence on Thursday. He played it down because otherwise it might seem he was deserting a sinking ship cut in half by a doctrinal disagreement. So he dismissed the left-wing rebellion, saying: 'Yes, there were headlines last week. But it was all old news by Friday. After Thursday' – when the Government won its vote of confidence – 'it was quite peaceful again. I don't really see any problem there. They don't need me to stay on as a doctor or healer.' He then added: 'We have had much less quarrelling of late. We are much more united. We are a broad church. We have theologians and they sometimes assert that the only socialism is the one that they preach.'[17] He had the right to claim that he was leaving the Labour movement less divided than he had found it; left-wing MP Doug Hoyle spoke for many when he said: 'I wish to put on record my tribute to Mr Wilson for the way he has held the party together since 1964.'[18]

An hour before, he had shown off his many talents much more successfully in the Commons. Like a performer with varicoloured spotlights playing on him, he was alternately courteous and rude, generous and savage, witty and vicious. It was one of those setpiece occasions which the British do so well and some might think faintly hypocritical in its politeness between foes. Mrs Thatcher, the steely new Tory Leader, said: 'In spite of the political battles, we wish you well personally in your retirement.' Not able to sheathe her sword entirely, she added: 'But this has come at a time of great financial difficulty and unprecedented parliamentary events. The best way to resolve the uncertainty and give the new Prime Minister the authority required would be to put the matter to the people for their verdict.' Wilson thanked her for her 'kind words' but suggested that, in reality, 'I am not sure that she is all that keen' on a general election. 'Will you try three weeks on Thursday?' retorted Mrs Thatcher acidly. 'We will be ready.'[19] Of course Wilson was not interested in such a suggestion, since he wanted his successor to have eighteen months in office before holding an election.

His former adversary, Edward Heath, was very charming in view of Wilson's attempts to destroy him, particularly in his first year as leader. Heath paid tribute to Wilson's talents and then added: 'I congratulate you after your retirement on joining the party [of ex-Prime Ministers still in the Commons], the only party which has doubled itself in a year.'[20] The gushy William Molloy, a Labour MP with both Welsh- and Irish-speaking foibles, proclaimed: 'You go without any knives in your back whatsoever.'[21] 'The Old Magician,' wrote the *Financial Times*'s parliamentary correspondent, 'it was felt, had gone out in style. His manner of leaving was his best trick yet.... Within hours Mr Wilson had been installed in the pantheon of "all-time greats" as a kind of hybrid between Baldwin the Healer and Lloyd George the Guileful.'[22]

But the Old Magician had a number of further curtain calls to take before his successor could take over, even with the speeded-up election procedure the Parliamentary Labour Party adopted that first night after his announcement. While the voting was going on he enjoyed his remaining days in power to the full. Thus, he showed his Yorkshire 'brussen' (or brazenness) by attending the EEC 'Summit' at Luxembourg with James Callaghan only three days before he was due to hand over power. An admiring German diplomat said: 'That man can make shit taste like caviare – and he can persuade people to eat it.' An equally admiring French diplomat replied: 'And Mr Heath could make caviare taste like shit!'[23] Wilson seemed to enjoy basking in some of the last of the limelight, including the news photographs showing his wax effigy being carried away from the Cabinet table at Madame Tussaud's.[24]

The House of Commons filled for Thursday, 30 March, which was due to be his last day answering questions as Prime Minister. He showed that, however tired he was of facing crises, his verbal wit had not dulled a whit. This emerged when Andrew Faulds described himself as having 'always been 150% a Harold man' when asking a question. This amused many who knew how often the pro-Arab Faulds had clashed with the pro-Zionist Wilson and how bitter Faulds had been about Wilson's sacking him as spokesman for the arts. But Wilson, quick as a flash, replied that, with Faulds's reference to 150%, 'for the first time I begin to understand what inflation means.'[25]

As part of his technique of using his knowledge of news management to milk the media for the utmost publicity, the outgoing Prime Minister made sure there was a 'photocall' out to press and TV cameramen when he and Mrs Wilson and their labrador made a farewell call at the Bernard Arms pub at Great Kimble, near Chequers. This made the TV news bulletins that evening and the newspapers the following day, which also saw the last ballot between James Callaghan and Michael Foot for the leadership and premiership.[26]

When James Callaghan, as expected, was elected above Michael Foot on 5 April, Harold Wilson was ready with a speech of congratulation. He also praised the Parliamentary Labour Party for carrying out his prediction 'that this brief election period will be comradely and not divisive'. He then added a promise to Callaghan: 'In particular, I shall be guided by the letter and spirit of the undertaking which a prewar predecessor gave when he stood down for a successor,' without mentioning that the man he was quoting was Stanley Baldwin, to whom he had often been compared. He then quoted: ' "Once I leave, I leave. I am not going to speak to the man on the bridge, and I am not going to spit on the deck." '[27]

Unfortunately for this prediction Wilson already had a gob in his throat in the shape of half-a-dozen names to be included in his Resignation Honours list. The premature emission of these names was to produce widespread disgust.

# II. Wilson's Lords –
# An Unintended Parody

'It is true we cannot boast of any delegates representing some of the parasitic growths of Tory freedom – the Amalgamated Society of Share Pushers and Company Promoters is not an affiliated organization, nor have constituency Labour Parties thought fit to send up representatives of property speculators, takeover bidders, dividend strippers or bond washers.'

Harold Wilson's Chairman's speech to Labour Conference,
Brighton, 1 October 1962

'There is nothing of itself wrong, still less illegal, about an Opposition Leader's officially-incurred expenditure being eased by (reportedly) such business types as the millionaire chairman of a major firm of bookies, a multi-millionaire property developer, a showbiz and boxing impresario, a London-based big wheel in a Swiss bank, and several other persons who could not be said to be in the direct line of descent from Keir Hardie.... There is nothing wrong, that is, provided the Opposition Leader concerned has not founded much of his career on abusive chatter about the "candyfloss society" of the Tories, about sundry "speculators", and about the rest of the Wilsonian rogues' gallery.'

*Daily Telegraph* editorial, 19 February 1977

'Hadn't he a wonderful knack of gathering around him chums with a capacity for getting into the financial news? ... There was the late Lord Brayley, who died with just a little matter of £200,000 of Canning Town Glass money and a pending trial for fraud separating him from socialist sainthood. Now there is Sir Eric Miller, who according to one report borrowed £300,000 of Peachey Property Corporation cash and who is in dispute over what happened to a further £282,000.'

John Junor, *Sunday Express*, 24 April 1977

Sir Harold Wilson, long the best stand-up comic in politics, was not amused at the joke at his expense at the Variety Club luncheon held in his honour on 18 June 1976. His favourite mimic – and newly-promoted OBE – Mike Yarwood had raised an easy laugh with his first words, 'My lords, Sir Harold's lords...' Sir Harold had provided, quite unintentionally, widespread merriment. At the Mermaid Theatre, according to Ned Sherrin, the phrase, 'Sir Harold Wilson's Honours List', was one of the three top laugh-provokers.[1]

Sir Harold pretended it was all a plot by the press and directed at professional entertainers and not, as it really was, at tycoons. 'My constituents and everyone's constituents – and I am talking about *real* people – enjoy being entertained, entertained well and entertained professionally. And my constituents, in their innocence, prefer the ladies and gentlemen of show business to the sanctimonious and pontificating commentators.'[2] The commentators, of course, had criticized the peerages to the show-business tycoons and brothers, Lew Grade and Bernard Delfont, and *not* the OBE for mimic Mike Yarwood or the knighthood for the dying actor, Stanley Baker. The *Guardian* had been kindest: 'Perhaps Sir Harold – good socialist to the last – is executing a macabre...plan to bring the whole system toppling amid guffaws.'[3]

Although Sir Harold made the press his immediate target his bitterness was a by-product of a gnawing suspicion. The effectiveness of the press attacks on the most vulnerable of the honours had been multiplied a hundredfold by a 'leak' from within 10 Downing Street which had provided newspapers with vulnerable names to investigate and criticize over a period of five solid weeks. Sir Harold did not then share the suspicions of Lady Falkender that the 'leak' had come from one or two of those closest to him.

Sir Harold knew that his former Press Secretary, Joe Haines, had in 1974 led a delegation, which included Dr Bernard Donoughue, his policy adviser, and Albert (later Lord) Murray, his office manager, to warn him against elevating his political secretary, Marcia Williams, to the peerage. They warned that it would attract press attacks, harm his reputation and dismay Labour Party supporters in the forthcoming October 1974 general election. Joe Haines, in particular, warned that it would reawaken interest in the land deal in which her brother had been involved and in which the *Daily Mail* and others had tried to involve Prime Minister Wilson in April 1974. But Wilson, who had already promised the peerage to Marcia, would not be dissuaded. He tried to appease Haines, Donoughue and Murray as well by telling them that Marcia, after becoming Lady Falkender, would become an executive in the firm of their friendly publishers, Weidenfeld and Nicolson, headed by George Weidenfeld. Wilson had known Weidenfeld since 1944 and had been published by him since 1945; he had already knighted him in 1969 (and was to make him a peer in 1976); since, on top of this, Sir George was a frequent escort of Marcia's, the three protesters accepted this false prediction. 'We had been disarmed and the battle was lost,' Haines was later to write.[4]

Sir Harold also knew, by the time he made his Variety Club speech in June 1976, that Joe Haines had rejected his offer of a peerage with typical Bermondsey disdain. Moreover, Haines, Donoughue and Murray had reacted with hostility to the inclusion in his Resignation Honours List, belatedly published in May 1976, of a number of middle-class entrepreneurs, some hostile to the Labour Party and others indifferent. He himself could not believe that this 'insider' criticism could lead to 'leaks' to the hostile press outside. But Marcia, Lady Falkender, was convinced that the attacks were directed mainly against her alleged friends on the Resignation Honours List. Sir Harold asked his successor as Prime Minister, James Callaghan, to institute an inquiry into who had 'leaked' the controversial names on his Resignation Honours List. The task was given to Sir Philip (later Lord) Allen, a former Permanent Secretary at the Home Office. But, according to Joe Haines, while *he* was interrogated, 'neither Lady Falkender nor any other members of his Political Office staff were interviewed by Sir Philip.'[5] In the end the source of the 'leak' was not confirmed.

## VENDETTA?
For weeks Sir Harold had been livid about what he described as an 'orchestrated vendetta' of 'deliberate misrepresentations' and the 'campaign of innuendo' in the press. So much so that he broke with precedent 'to nail the lies' about his Resignation Honours List, particularly about the vital role of Lady Falkender in having suggested the more controversial names, such as that of Conservative tycoon, James Goldsmith, who had been awarded a knighthood. Since Sir James had contributed to Tory funds and advised Edward Heath, his knighthood was linked with his hospitality to Lady Falkender and his remark that Marcia was talented enough to be a Director of Cavenham Foods, his mammoth French-based company.[6] Sir Harold kept insisting, much too flatly, that Lady Falkender had nothing to do with it. It was, he insisted, 'by tradition a personal list ... I still have the original names, substantially as published, written down by myself after consultation with no one else. The list was processed under the direction of the Principal Private Secretary at Number 10, together with the Downing Street Honours Section – who jointly have an unbroken record of complete discretion over all the years. Anyone else claiming to have seen the list, or to know its contents, must by some means have got access to it without authority and against all precedents.'[7]

Sir Harold's statement, typically, was intended to reinforce the letter to *The Times* two days before by Lady Falkender. 'Perhaps behind this whole affair lies some other story,' she had written, 'some other motive for it, where frustration, malice and envy are being expressed in a final attack upon a man who has contributed so much to our national life, to the lives of ordinary people, though not necessarily to the lives of those living within certain select circles in Metropolitan London.' This attack by a peeress who lived in a three-storey mews house in select Wyndham Mews was clearly directed at the men she felt she had worsted in the 'battle for Harold's ear'.

What was hilarious was Lady Falkender's decision to deplore the 'leaks' by showing her new-found security-consciousness. 'This is unprecedented in respect of any previous Honours List,' she insisted, 'and represents a series of leaks within the machine on a subject which I understand is kept as tightly secure in No. 10 as matters affecting state security. Clearly someone in public service, in whatever capacity, has broken the trust placed in them by leaking a secret and confidential document to a newspaper.'[8] She insisted that she had been consulted only on the arts and sports sections of the honours lists, together with Joe Haines and Dr Bernard Donoughue – two names which she had tried unsuccessfully to introduce into a letter to the *Sunday Times*.[9] 'At no time during Sir Harold Wilson's Premiership was the Honours list, or lists, dealt with through the Political Office of which I was head ... As far as I am aware, no one in the Political Office has ever seen an Honours list before publication, and nor have I myself.'[10] She was promptly called a liar by George Caunt, seven months before the publication by Joe Haines of his story of having seen the Resignation Honours list on lavender paper in her handwriting. 'This is just not true,' retorted Caunt, formerly the Committee Secretary to the Parliamentary Labour Party, who had helped Wilson during his election campaigns. 'I saw Mr Wilson's 1970 [Dissolution] Honours list on her desk in the House of Commons. It was there for eight days before it was published and obviously she must have seen it several times.'[11] 'Anyone walking into the office could see it.'[12] He had noted an error on it – or one he had considered an error. He had been promised an OBE by Wilson but had only been awarded the lower MBE, a downgrading he attributed to the influence of Marcia. They had fought like cats and dogs every time they had worked together. When Marcia-baiting became a public sport after the publication of Joe Haines's *The Politics of Power*, Caunt regaled *Sun* readers with tales of having thrown her on a couch to settle an argument about where Wilson's staff were to eat in their hotel at the height of the 1966 general election campaign.[13]

Caunt's attack on Lady Falkender's claims of security-consciousness was applauded by his employer, Lord Wigg, another loser of battles with Marcia. His peerage had been Harold Wilson's kind way of 'burying' him. After having been one of those most instrumental in rounding up enough votes to make Wilson Labour's new leader in February 1963, Colonel Wigg had been rewarded with the title of Paymaster General, in charge of security (or 'Spymaster General' as the popular press dubbed him). Wigg had been aligned against Marcia Williams on two counts. First, he was a rival in the 'battle for Harold's ear': on subjects like the Vietnam war he was more likely to be on the pro-American side than Marcia. He was also, as an old soldier and anti-feminist, against allowing her to be privy to secrets to which she was not entitled. He had refused to discuss with the Prime Minister Government secrets which he thought she was not cleared to know, apparently not realizing at the time that Wilson had instructed his Principal Private Secretary, Derek Mitchell, that she be shown all secret domestic papers which came to him, including Cabinet papers.[14] Wigg was also suspicious of her as a source of some of the stories of Walter Terry, then Political Editor of the *Daily Mail*, who was her lover between 1967 and 1970. Wigg suspected her of 'leaking' to Terry information which would stiffen Wilson against giving in to the blandishments of President Johnson. On the eve of Wilson's trip to see President Johnson in June 1967, Wigg was tipped off that the Americans were worried about a precipitate British withdrawal from Asia. 'I informed the Prime Minister accordingly,' Wigg wrote in his autobiography. 'Judge my surprise when, on Friday, 2 June [1967] the front page "splash" of the *Daily Mail*, written by its Political Editor, Walter Terry, carried these headlines: "CLASH OVER VIET NAM POLICY. WILSON AND LBJ: IS THIS THE SPLIT?"... Was this just another example of irresponsible journalism? Or was it, as I feared, a well-informed disclosure of an irresponsible leak from No. 10?'[15] Wigg lost that battle and was pensioned off with a life peerage and the job of Chairman of the Horserace Betting Levy Board. Like many of Marcia's victims, he brooded on his defeat and exploded into print in his autobiography five years later. In the original version of this Wigg had justified his wariness about the liaison between the Prime Minister's political secretary and the political editor of a Conservative-inclined newspaper by a more direct accusation and by including the photostats of the birth certificates of the two children born to Marcia Williams and Walter Terry, showing the Prime Minister's doctor, Dr Joseph (later Lord) Stone, in attendance. Wilson was dismayed when he saw the proof version of the book. 'I have never seen him more hunched and battered-looking,' said an associate. Typically the Prime Minister sought the intervention of another peer he had created, the solicitor Lord Goodman, who was also Lord Wigg's closest friend. Through the mediation of Lord Goodman the birth certificates and the revelation of the Williams–Terry liaison – then still a Fleet Street secret – were removed from Wigg's autobiography.

## REPAYING FAVOURS

In its top layers Britain's Honours system has long been a way of repaying favours done for the Prime Minister, whether in personal service or in work for the party he heads or in financial facilities offered either to the Prime Minister or to his party. What was different about Harold Wilson's departure from office was that a double 'leak' at the time, followed by others later, gave the press and the public much greater opportunities for insight into Sir Harold's idiosyncratic style of leadership.

On top of the 'leak' of controversial names from 10 Downing Street, the Political Honours Scrutiny Committee's Chairman, Lord Crathorne, became unprecedentedly garrulous. A seventy-eight-year-old Tory Yorkshire squire of great charm and uprightness, he had resigned – when Sir Thomas Dugdale – as Agriculture Minister over his civil servants' misdeeds at Crichel Down (when there had been a refusal by civil servants to return to its original landowner land seized in wartime). In the spring of 1976 he clearly felt there was something 'off' about some of the names recommended by Sir Harold and submitted to the Political Honours Scrutiny Committee, which he had headed since 1961.

Lady Summerskill, who was much more discreet in April 1976 than her Tory colleague, Lord Crathorne, disclosed over a year later what had happened in a letter to *The Times* of 27 May 1977: 'Lord Crathorne and I attended the meeting of the Political Honours Scrutiny Committee on April 5 [1976], and we were both astounded when we read the list of proposed honours. We told the civil servant present [Sir Stuart Milner-Barry] that we could not approve of at least half of the list, and would he see that this was conveyed to the Prime Minister. Our only other resort was to ask the Queen to intervene and we felt, at this stage, that this would have been highly injurious to these people. However, we expressed ourselves so strongly on the subject that it astonished us to find that, with one exception, the original list of recipients was published unchanged. We were in fact faced with a *fait accompli* which we had no power to upset.' There is some indication that the Palace had raised an eyebrow discreetly by returning the Wilson list for second thoughts.

The former Prime Minister did not enhance his reputation for truth-telling after the *Sunday Times* had disclosed on 2 May 1976 that his Resignation Honours list had 'run into difficulties' because the Political Honours Scrutiny Committee had raised 'questions on some of the names'. Wilson immediately insisted this was 'totally untrue ... I have had no questions whatsoever from the Political Honours Scrutiny Committee ... and I have been informed that their certificate was issued in respect of all the recommendations which fall within their jurisdiction.' Although he may have been technically correct about the Committee's 'jurisdiction', most people in Westminster knew whom they would believe if it were a choice between Wilson and Lord Crathorne.

Lord Crathorne's indiscretions, particularly to the *Daily Express*, focused public attention on his long-somnolent Committee. It had been set up in 1926 on the recommendation of the Royal Commission established to investigate and prevent a repetition of Lloyd George's lucrative sale of Honours between 1916 and 1922. For the half-century before that Honours had been made available to generous contributors to party funds by successive Conservative and Liberal Governments, but in the discreet and subdued style of the Establishment. Lloyd George had been cruder and less discreet in 'milking' the war profiteers and others through Honours touts operating a fixed scale of fees, with knighthoods starting at £10,000. What had aroused Conservative fury was that Lloyd George, with the complicity of a corrupt and simpleminded Tory, had diverted almost the whole of this lush revenue into his own personal Lloyd George Political Fund rather than split the loot equally with the Tories, as agreed when the Coalition Government was established under his leadership in 1916.[16] To prevent a repetition, Honours-touting was made illegal and the Political Honours Scrutiny Committee established, manned by three peers who are Privy Councillors from the leading parties. Normally they had worked in secrecy, without any minutes being published and without MPs, peers or – much less – journalists being able to ask about their activities. Their job has been to ascertain whether men put up for political or public Honours have really done significant service in that area rather than merely making a contribution to the funds of the party or its leader. 'The Committee reacted very violently to the non-political backgrounds of some people,' Lord Crathorne told the *Daily Express*. 'These fellers have never done anything, we said.'[17]

Lord Crathorne had his way in blocking a knighthood for Jarvis Astaire who, though long a Labour supporter and possibly a contributor to the Trustee Fund established in 1970 to finance Wilson's private office in Opposition, was better known as an entrepreneur; he had interests in betting (William Hill), sporting events (Viewsport) and finance (Anglo-Continental Finance, where he linked up with Jimmy Goldsmith). Astaire's name disappeared from view, despite Sir Harold's careful denial 'that names proposed for life peerages have been "stalled" by Whitehall and by the Political Honours Scrutiny Committee'.[18] In fact, of course, Jarvis Astaire's name had only been submitted for a knighthood. It was also alleged at the time that Sir Harold had decided not to formalize his original intention of recommending David Frost for a knighthood, anticipating that this might be linked with Sir Harold's £100,000 contract for a TV series on Yorkshire TV. This did not prevent Wilson from recommending a knighthood for James Hanson, Chairman of Trident which controls both Yorkshire and Tyne-Tees TV. Hanson, like Wilson himself, served as a Trustee of the D'Oyly Carte Opera Company.

The spotlight of press attention focused on the Wilson Resignation Honours list in April–May 1976 gave the Political Honours Scrutiny Committee much more to work with than normal, and more time in which to do it. Ordinarily, it had looked little beyond the Establishment network when inquiring as to whether the nominal reason for an Honour was the real one. Certainly no special attention was paid to the 1975 peerage which transformed Sir Rudy Sternberg, whose knighthood he had received from Wilson in 1970, into Lord Plurenden. The stated reason – that he had formed and chaired the British Agricultural Export Council from 1968 on – was less than complete. A German-born entrepreneur, Sternberg had started as a button-manufacturer using bakelite, a German plastic-type material. He first entered the big time in 1953 when he won monopoly rights to import potash from East Germany and to export from Britain to East Germany. Since the East German Communists were then even more in the West's dog-house than other East Europeans, Sternberg was forced to get involved in politics because he imported via West Germany, where some of the profits were creamed off. He worked hard to free East German imports and exports from such inhibitions, putting both right-wing Tories like Brigadier Terence Clarke and Burnaby Drayson and left-wing MPs like Will Owen on his companies' payrolls to serve him as 'front men', particularly at international conferences.[19]

The Political Honours Scrutiny Committee may not have known in 1975 that for the four years that Wilson had been in Opposition (from 1970 to 1974) Sir Rudy had contributed £2,000 a year to the Trustee Fund to finance the Labour leader's office.[20] In 1973 he had been deeply involved in organizing and, probably, financing Harold Wilson's contentious trip to Czechoslovakia. 'In 1972 and early 1973,' according to Joe Haines, 'the Czechoslovak Government was pressing Harold Wilson to visit Prague as part of its campaign to rehabilitate itself in Western eyes after its collaboration with the invading Soviet armies in August 1968.'[21] Although Wilson was then in Opposition the Czechs were particularly anxious to get a clean bill of health from him because, from 1938 on, Czechoslovakia had been the most popular East European country among British socialists. But the Soviet crushing of Dubcek's effort to establish 'Communism with a human face' had resulted in virtually every Labour MP, including some very far to the left, turning his back on the new collaborationist regime in Prague. 'Harold Wilson turned them down, or postponed a decision, more than once, because he needed a reciprocal gesture of some kind from them. Eventually, he agreed to go to Prague, subject to the Czechoslovakian Government agreeing to release the Rev. David Hathaway, a Nonconformist minister from Yorkshire, who had been imprisoned by the Czechs for the bourgeois crime of smuggling Bibles into the country,' recalled Joe Haines. In fact, Haines also recalled, the plot was agreed so far in advance that the Czechs released the Rev. Hathaway from prison 'an hour before Harold Wilson actually got round to asking formally for his freedom'. The Foreign Office, then headed by Sir Alec Douglas-Home, tried to take credit for the Hathaway release and, to demonstrate that Wilson was only trying to cash in on the publicity, 'leaked' the telegram from Wilson's office manager, Tony Field (the brother of Marcia Williams), asking Joe Haines to organize a press conference at London Airport in order that he could take credit for the operation. The whole effort was further soured by Wilson's comment to a group of education correspondents who travelled back with him on the same plane that it was time to 'forget' what had happened in Czechoslovakia in 1968.[22] This aroused a storm of protest among indignant Labour back-benchers, who confronted a deeply embarrassed leader in a private meeting, no longer feeling like a modern-day Scarlet Pimpernel. At the time the only person in Britain apart from the Rev. Hathaway who came out ahead was the inspirer, and apparently the financer of the trip, Sir Rudy Sternberg, who won himself a place in the good books of the Czech government. Despite the embarrassment caused to his squeamish supporters in 1973, Wilson later decided that the widespread publicity had been useful in convincing people that, even in Opposition, he could make things happen.

## NO CLOSE LOOK

Although a 'leak' in 1975 might have turned up more information on the origins of Lord Plurenden's peerage, the 1976 'leakage' of Sir Harold's Resignation Honours list was wholly exceptional. The scrutiny given to the controversial names on that list would have found paydirt in virtually any Honours list, even that of the least tactical or cynical of Prime Ministers. Thus a 'leak' in 1951 could have revealed that ex-Labour MP Valentine McEntee was belatedly receiving the peerage promised him for yielding his Walthamstow West seat in 1950 to Labour leader Clement Attlee. When the latter's Limehouse seat disappeared in the 1948 reapportionment of constituencies, the then Chief Whip, William Whiteley, had proffered a peerage to McEntee if he made way for Attlee. But Whiteley then found himself unable to make good his promise, possibly because Attlee himself was scandalized. After two Honours lists had passed without the peerage McEntee complained and his constituency party threatened, in private, to drop Attlee and restore McEntee as their candidate if the promised peerage were not forthcoming. The eighty-year-old McEntee duly appeared on the June 1951 Birthday Honours list but did not live to take his seat in the Lords.

Had Honours lists been available well in advance, as in April–May 1976, their increasing role in encouraging Conservative activists during the 1951–64 period might have become more apparent. Under Sir Winston Churchill six per cent of the CBEs, OBEs and MBEs went to party workers. Under Sir Anthony Eden, later Lord Avon, the figure rose to eight per cent. Then, under Harold Macmillan, probably the most cynical exploiter of the Honours system in postwar politics, fully nine per cent of the lower Honours went to party activists.

Prime Ministers have hardly been involved in these lower Honours; their attention has been focused on peerages for senior politicians and others and on knighthoods and baronetcies for MPs who have served loyally for between twelve and eighteen years. Each of the four Tory Prime Ministers had his own style. Sir Winston tended to reward wartime buddies with peerages: Lords Woolton and Leathers, for example. Sir Anthony Eden, the longtime 'pin-up boy' of Conservative womanhood, tended to create relatively more Dames of the British Empire than knights. But Harold Macmillan utilized the Honours system to its full to restore cohesion and discipline to the divided Conservative Party he inherited in 1957 in the wake of the frustrated Suez operation. Macmillan also used the Honours system as a well-greased 'honourable exit' for superannuated politicians like Dr Charles (later Lord) Hill or Sir David (later Lord) Eccles. But he showed the disdain he had for these baubles by refusing both 'the Earldom which ⠂ my right' – which had been accepted by Attlee and Eden – and the Knight of the Garter – accepted by Churchill and, later, by Wilson. It was only in April 1976 that Macmillan accepted the more prestigious and select Order of Merit.

Harold Wilson, initially a great admirer and imitator of Macmillan's style, never shared his cynicism towards Honours. He tended to show the lower-middle-class provincial outsider's envy rather than the insider's cynical realism demonstrated by the crofter's grandson who had married a Duke's daughter. When more radical Labour Ministers urged him to scrap the Honours, the stock Wilson reply was: 'I do not see how Members of Parliament, who like to see "MP" after their names, have a right to deny similar privileges to those who value them.' He may, of course, have been looking forward to his own knighthood. This meant enough to him for him to pay roughly £650 for his Gilbert-and-Sullivan-style costume, which he bought instead of renting, and another £590 to the College of Arms for his coat of arms and supporters; one of the mottoes on his coat of arms was 'Honi soit qui mal y pense'.[23]

To Wilson, the Honours system meant several things, as it had to previous Prime Ministers. It was Britain's own 'gilded escalator', speeding the movement up the Establishment pyramid of four over-lapping types of people. One was a group to whom Wilson wanted to say 'thank you' for some special favour to himself or his party. Another included those raised to the peerage to do a special job for the Government in the Lords. Another were the 'high achievers' – often in industry or the arts – who were made knights or peers in order to recruit them into the governing class as a way of invigorating it. But by far the largest group were those for whom a set of initials after their names was a prized but inexpensive way of saying 'well done'.

Wilson began in 1964 as a new and fairly stiff broom. He named only *life* peers to the Lords, thus making it difficult for the Tories to revive hereditary peerages thereafter. He also stopped the Conservative practice of offering a knighthood or the more prized and hereditary baronetcy to obedient MPs after a dozen to eighteen years of loyal service; he made the offer only to MPs with a record of exceptional, often outside service, as in the Inter-Parliamentary Union. When William Hamilton, a Wilson-baiting Labour MP, later accused him of having fondled his patronage as 'a bridegroom fondles his bride', Wilson was able to retort with statistics. In the seven and a half years he had been Prime Minister, six knighthoods had been conferred on MPs compared with fifty-seven such knighthoods during the last seven and a half years of Tory rule.[24]

Wilson had also taken much credit for halting the award of CBEs and MBEs to local party worthies. This, Wilson felt, had the dual advantage of appearing quite a good reform while hitting at a crucial source of Conservative funds and activism. In the previous decade representatives of the Conservative Central Office's Board of Finance had told well-heeled, Honours-hungry businessmen: 'If you contribute generously to our party funds, and are active locally, this will be deeply appreciated by us.' Commented one south-coast Tory MP: 'I have known busy tycoons to motor ninety miles to an unimportant Tory meeting, hoping that this will prove a shortcut to a knighthood or other honour.'

There was some argument about Wilson's initial idea of banning Honours for local politicians and professionals, according to the Diary entry of R. H. S. Crossman for 22 September 1966: '... we had a meeting at No. 10 about political Honours. Harold again repeated his determination to get rid of political honours. I had thought this a good idea at first but after I'd talked to [the Labour Party General Secretary]

Len Williams at Transport House I realized that excluding political Honours really meant excluding party agents and regional organizers and virtually no one else. When Harold heard this he replied: "We'll include them all under public Honours." But of course once you do this your announcement is merely a gimmick because you *haven't* cut out political Honours.' In the end it was decided to give most of such Honours to Labour men when Labour was in Government, but to include about a third of such Honours for Tories and Liberals – to make them less anxious to contribute to their own party funds.

Wilson's first batch of elevations to the peerage in 1964–65 reflected well on his judgment and the popularity of the Labour Party in certain unexpected places. These elevations also did much to restore some vitality to the Lords, particularly on the Labour side. During the thirteen years of Tory rule support in the Lords for Labour had sunk to about forty members, mainly aged peers in an Upper House at which almost 1,000 hereditary peers could attend. Wilson's first priority was for peers willing 'to do a job of work' there. The famous Labour QC, Gerald Gardiner, became Lord Gardiner and Lord Chancellor. The Principal of the Institute of Science and Technology at Manchester University became Lord Bowden and, briefly and ineffectively, Minister of State for Education and Science. Famous novelist/scientist C. P. Snow became Lord Snow and Parliamentary Secretary for Technology. *The Times*'s military correspondent and friend of George Wigg became Lord Chalfont and Minister of State at the Foreign Office. Wilf Brown, the Chairman of Glacier Metals and a leading management intellectual, became Lord Brown and Minister of State at the Department of Trade in 1965. Wilson elevated other entrepreneurs at the time, almost all of them native-born with a strong toehold in either the Labour Party or the Establishment. Thus Roger Makins, Director of A. C. Cossor, Raytheon and other companies and former Economics Minister at the Washington Embassy, where he had worked with Wilson on the launching of the FAO in 1946, became Lord Sherfield in 1964. Among Wilson's first elevations to the peerage was a Welsh mining engineer, Arwyn Davies, whose friendship with Marcia Williams's brother, Tony Field, was later much mentioned; but Lord Arwyn, as he became, had been a socialist of long standing, friendly with Aneurin Bevan and, during the war, with Wilson's father, Herbert, in Cornwall, long before he became Deputy Chairman of the Bath and Portland Group. Sir Christopher Hinton became Lord Hinton in 1965 largely for his work as Chairman of the Central Electricity Generating Board. The new Baron Cole was a Director of the Commonwealth Development Finance Company and had been Chairman of Unilever. Baron Sieff, the first of the Jewish entrepreneurs to reach the Lords with the help of Wilson, was then President of Marks and Spencer, with an extensive record of charitable activities. Baron Campbell, elevated in 1968, was the former 'Jock' Campbell, sugar tycoon of Booker Brothers and then the Chairman of the *New Statesman*.

These entrepreneurs, who seldom attended and seldom spoke in the Lords, were outshone by the 'Labour luminaries' – those who had made their names at the tops of their professions. These included: Baron (Richard) Llewellyn-Davies, the topflight architect and planner; Baron (Ted) Willis, the popular TV dramatist; Baron (Noel) Annan of King's College; and Baron (John) Fulton of Sussex University, all named in 1964–65. During that same period Wilson showed his own undoubted kindness, on the inspired advice of his political secretary, Marcia Williams, by naming five 'worthy widows': Baroness (Dora) Gaitskell, widow of Hugh; Baroness (Norah) Phillips, widow of Morgan; Baroness (Beatrice) Plummer, widow of former Labour MP, Sir Leslie; Baroness (Clementine) Spencer-Churchill, widow of Sir Winston; and Baroness (Audrey) Hylton-Foster, widow of a former Conservative Speaker.

By the time of his Resignation Honours list in May 1976 Wilson had been responsible for over two-thirds of the almost 150 peers taking the Labour Whip. Some of these were outstanding choices, like Baroness (Patricia) Llewellyn-Davies who became Labour's Chief Whip after having been a civil servant, a Labour candidate against Enoch Powell, and the longtime Secretary of the Labour Parliamentary Association of Candidates.

After an initial good start Wilson seemed largely to lose interest in manning the Lords properly. His drive to improve the Labour performance in the Upper House by providing more effective and younger life peers petered out after the frustration of his 1968–69 efforts to reform the Lords. This was stopped largely by the resistance of the 'unholy alliance' of Michael Foot, Robert Sheldon and Enoch Powell, who spearheaded the fight against the Parliament (No. 2) Bill, a compromise measure to reform the Lords which R. H. S. Crossman had agreed with the Tory and Liberal peers. The Bill proposed a House of Lords in which hereditary peers would no longer have a right to vote but instead there would be 230 salaried 'voting peers'. These would be divided into 105 peers on the side of the Government of the day, eighty for the principal Opposition party and fifteen for the other (meaning Liberal) Opposition Party, with about thirty cross-benchers – those without fixed party loyalties. Among those resisting the Bill, apart from traditionalists like Foot and Powell, there were many who were against it because it would have given the Prime Minister too great a power of patronage. It would enable him to name scores of salaried 'voting peers'.Opposition was so marked that the Government feared to allow a free vote on the reform and finally had to abandon the Bill in April 1969. When Wilson rose to jettison the Bill he tried to gallop through his statement to minimize the pain of eating humble pie. 'Eat it slower!' called out Enoch Powell.[25]

After this setback the Labour Leader of the Lords, Lord Shackleton, repeatedly urged on Wilson that he substantially increase the Labour contingent in the Upper House. In fact he worked up a list of over twenty names of suitable Labour peers for Wilson to elevate, but he could not get the Prime Minister interested in this transfusion of new blood: not, at any rate, until he suffered the trauma of his June 1970 defeat.

When Wilson left 10 Downing Street in June 1970, the Dissolution Honours list he recommended immediately thereafter was still very much in the tradition of departing Prime Ministers. It had long been normal for a departing Prime Minister to use an Honours list to thank those leaving with him. In December 1964 Sir Alec Douglas-Home had named a viscount, six hereditary barons, two life peeresses, three baronets and five knights. In comparison with this Wilson was modest. He named only two life peers: George Brown, who had lost Belper, and Harold Davies, who had lost Leek. It had also been a tradition for a departing Prime Minister to thank his own doctor. Churchill had been exceptional in making his outstanding doctor, a famous consultant with an MC from the First World War, a Lord (Moran). Macmillan had made a baronet of his personal physician. Wilson gave a knighthood to his general practitioner and golf partner, Dr Joseph Ellis Stone, brother-in-law of Lord Bernstein. Wilson also gave a knighthood to his former press secretary, Trevor Lloyd-Hughes, a lesser award than the baronetcy awarded by Macmillan to his press adviser. Whereas Macmillan had enabled his political secretary to revive the famous title of Lord Egremont, Wilson limited himself to a CBE for Marcia Williams.

Possibly because it was not 'leaked' prematurely not much attention was paid to Wilson's knighthoods for entrepreneurs. That for successful publisher George Weidenfeld, of Weidenfeld and Nicolson, was readily understood because of their personal link since 1945, when Wilson's *New Deal for Coal* was a first book for both of them. There was also a knighthood for his Gannex-maker and long-time financial supporter, Joseph Kagan. Had there been more time to dig, newsmen might have connected the knighthood for John Brayley, then Chairman of Canning Town Glass, with his generous contribution of company shares to the Labour Party. Some curiosity might also have been expressed about the knighthood provided for Kenneth Selby, the accountant who was Chairman of the Bath and Portland Group, of which Lord Arwyn was Deputy

Chairman. The knighthood which should have aroused interest in Fleet Street was that for Rudy Sternberg, the highly successful East–West trader who had made such controversial use of right-wing Tory and left-wing Labour MPs in East European trade fairs. But, in retrospect, the interesting point about Wilson's relatively restrained 1970 Dissolution Honours list lay in its foretaste of the later much-attacked Resignation Honours list. Five of the 1970 knights became 1976 peers as Wilson's generosity to entrepreneurs turned into travesty.

In 1970 Wilson was still relatively restrained, as his last-minute decision not to elevate Leslie Lever to the peerage demonstrated. Leslie, a rotund solicitor with little of the suave brilliance of his brother Harold, had long been the MP for Ardwick, a seat which he held by extravagant cultivation of its dominant Roman Catholic population, leading to his being made a papal knight. But the honour he had long sought, almost openly, was a British peerage. When he decided to step down, Leslie Lever made it clear that he would help Wilson's aide, Gerald Kaufman, succeed him in exchange for a peerage. Lever kept his side of the bargain, introducing Kaufman to all of the Catholic organizations active in the Ardwick Labour Party, assuring them that Kaufman would be a worthy successor – which turned out to be an understatement. When Kaufman was elected and Labour was defeated in June 1970 he went to see Wilson to ask about Lever's peerage. Wilson told him that, with the defeat, all bets were off. Wilson made Lever a knight in 1970. But, for the peerage, Lever had to wait until Labour returned to office in 1974. By that time it was impossible for him to take his seat in the Lords, because of ill health. He died in July 1977.

## THE TRAUMA OF DEFEAT
The defeat of 1970 was a trauma for Wilson, not only in its immediate impact but in its aftermath. When Edward Heath moved in by the front door of 10 Downing Street and Harold Wilson moved out by the back, Wilson not only had no home to call his own but no real resources with which to begin to fight back against the Government apparatus, now in 'hostile' hands. Transport House only offered £6,000 to finance the office of the Leader of the Opposition, or enough for two secretaries. Wilson felt he required upwards of £20,000 for his political secretary, Marcia Williams, his new press secretary, Joe Haines, and three or four other secretaries. This was a bare minimum, a fraction of the £150,000 which the Wilson Government later made available to the Conservative Opposition Leader's office after 1975.

The need for money caused Wilson and his political secretary to become heavily preoccupied with the raising of additional finances for their office. This need was filled by a dozen or so entrepreneurs who contributed up to £2,000 a year to a Trustee Fund. Among these were the new Sir Rudy Sternberg, Sir George Weidenfeld and Sir Joseph Kagan, and a slightly older, 1967-vintage knight, Sir Samuel Fisher, Vice-President of the London Diamond Bourse and Chairman of the London Labour Mayors Association. One of the few unknighted contributors was Arieh Handler, the London Managing Director of the International Credit Bank of Geneva, a shell manipulated by some Israeli financiers. Some of those who contributed were asked to do so by Baroness Plummer, the widow of Labour MP Sir Leslie Plummer and herself a fervent Zionist. The deeds of the fund were drawn up by Lord Goodman's firm (Goodman had been made a life peer in 1965). The first Chairman of the Fund was Lord (Wilfred) Brown. 'It was low-profile,' he later explained in answer to the question why the Fund's existence had been kept secret. 'We did not want the Labour Party to know about it because they would have wanted to get their fingers into it. It was for Harold Wilson as Opposition Leader. If it had gone through Transport House, we could not have been sure it would have got to him.'[26] 'It was not especially secretive,' added Lord Goodman, 'indeed, it was above board and open in every respect short of actual disclosure to Fleet Street.'[27] Lord Goodman was then Chairman of Fleet Street's Newspaper Publishers' Association. The reason for the secrecy was that Wilson did not want to move as far left as the Labour Party wanted and knowledge of the sources of his revenue could have been used against him. 'At that time,' Lord Brown later recalled, 'Harold Wilson was having trouble with the National Executive.'[28]

Subsequently this fund, which was paralleled by the Industry Group, was joined by a research fund established with the backing of Sigmund Sternberg, a Vice-Chairman of the Industry Group and a 1939 refugee from Hungary. He had made a fortune in scrap metal through his firm Mountstar Metal, which he had sold to British Amalgamated Metal Corporation. In 1973 he contributed £20,000 to set up a research fund to service Wilson and other Labour front-benchers. With the advice of Dr Norman Hunt, later Lord Crowther-Hunt, three or four graduates were hired at £2,000 a year.[29]

Wilson was not satisfied to have outside entrepreneurs doing all the work of supporting his office. He himself made arrangements to sell the rights of his book, *The Labour Government, 1964–70*, to the *Sunday Times*, who sold rights to hardback publishers Weidenfeld and Nicolson and Michael Joseph. The sum he received, as a result of Lord Goodman's negotiating ability, was something over £215,000. But Wilson was always very touchy about this subject. When David Dimbleby unexpectedly asked him about it on the BBC-TV programme 'Yesterday's Men', a year after his defeat, Wilson exploded and stopped the recording. He was furious because inclusion of this question had not been agreed in the months of negotiations for the programme which had preceded the recording and because the BBC had never asked Edward Heath similar questions. 'Ask *him* where he got the money to pay for his boat!', Wilson demanded angrily, referring to Heath's yacht *Morning Cloud II*, thought to have cost upwards of £40,000.[30] But even if Heath's source of funds had compelled Wilson to be more forthcoming it would have been easier to disclose the total earned by his book than to make available the names of those providing sources of revenue for his private office.

## BEHIND THE 'BAR-MITZVAH CIRCUIT'

Harold Wilson and Lady Falkender later attacked the 'anti-Semitic implications' of newspaper articles which called attention to the high proportion of Jews, particularly foreign-born entrepreneurs, among those he had honoured. But for years before that a number of close observers, including those of Jewish origins, had been astonished at the extent to which Harold and Marcia tended to restrict themselves socially to the 'Bar-Mitzvah circuit', as some civil servants unkindly described it. It was not commented on publicly, largely because of commentators' fear of being called anti-Semitic. Had almost all of Wilson's financial supporters at a crucial period been papal knights, this fact would have been noted more publicly, despite the fact that his Huyton constituency is predominantly Roman Catholic. Even with this inhibition there might have been some publicity had it been known that of the trustees of his 1970–74 office fund – Lord Brown, Sir Samuel (later Lord) Fisher, Sir Rudy Sternberg (later Lord Plurenden), Lord Goodman and Arieh Handler[31] – four out of five were of Jewish origin. Wilson's dependence on foreign-born Jewish entrepreneurs recalled the dependence of Edward VII and Bismarck on Jewish bankers.

Although the Israeli Embassy and Zionists in general were, of course, delighted, Wilson's pro-Semitism puzzled them and other close Jewish observers. This tendency to mix so largely with Jews is expected, say, of gentile professional musicians, because a large proportion of composers and serious musicians are of Jewish origin; so too in the case of gentile politicians deeply involved in the anti-Fascist movement of the 1930s or in the battles of the infant Israeli state in 1948–49. But Wilson had stood apart from both of these. The fervour of his Zionism only became apparent in the days immediately before the June 1967 'Six-Day War'.

Wilson's pro-Semitism, as documented in his Honours awards, had three origins. The first lay in his own social-religious upbringing. Although Congregationalist by background the Wilsons belonged to the Baptist church in Milnsbridge, on the outskirts of Huddersfield. In that

Nonconformist church worshipped the 'producers of wealth' – the workers, foremen and working owners of small factories – in contrast to the less worthy 'owners of wealth' who tended to be Church of England in Huddersfield. This was later to make him feel more at home with 'hard' Northern and Jewish pursuers of 'brass' than with 'soft' southerners seeking refinement.

Secondly, Wilson's preference for 'producers of wealth' was to take a new turn when he joined the Board of Trade in 1947, first as its Secretary and then as President. His job was to rebuild Britain's foreign trade after a punishing war while the Empire was dismantled. He found a contrast between comfortable British businessmen and more energetic immigrant entrepreneurs, who were then mostly Jews uprooted by Hitler before the war. Wilson had contact with these small firms largely through Lord Piercy, a Labour peer who headed the semi-official Industrial and Commercial Finance Corporation which helped them to expand. In Piercy's circle were Tom Horobin, a Labour MP who had a consultancy with the Welsh mining and explosives expert, Arwyn Davies, later Lord Arwyn, and also Harry (later Lord) Kissin, a Liberal lawyer of Russian-Jewish origins specializing in commodity trading.

Typical of Wilson's links was that with Austrian-Jewish Frank Schon and Marchon Products. Wilson helped get ICFC financing to expand Marchon's detergent plant in Cumberland, with Arthur Creech Jones, former Colonial Secretary, put on its board as Government 'watchdog'. When Americans hoarded sulphuric acid after the outbreak of the Korean War Wilson also helped get Treasury backing for a new plant in Cumberland to derive sulphuric acid from local anhydrates. Later, after Wilson had resigned as President of the Board of Trade and was serving as a consultant on East European trade, Schon went to him when he wanted to sell detergent plant to the Russians in 1958. After Wilson's intervention with Mikoyan had helped clinch the deal he went on the Marchon payroll as an unpublicized consultant, receiving about £1,000 annually in retainers and expenses. This discreet deal, which lasted until he became leader in 1963,[32] enabled Wilson to make a great show in 1959 of giving up his publicly-known consultancy with Montague L. Meyer, the multi-million-pound timber importers. It was perhaps indicative of Wilson's greater admiration for immigrant entrepreneurs that he was later to give Schon a life peerage while John Meyer, Chairman of Montague L. Meyer, was only to receive a CBE, despite the essential support he provided for Wilson between 1951 and 1959.

The third reason for Wilson's preference for foreign-born Jewish entrepreneurs probably lay in terms of his appreciation for what he considered to be their kindness. Coming from his sort of Yorkshire family, Harold Wilson has always put a high premium on personal kindness. What he may not have understood adequately is that the kindness of some of his immigrant entrepreneur friends has a different background. Jews brought up in Central and Eastern Europe have always felt very vulnerable and therefore very sensitive to the advantages of having a highly-placed 'protector' sympathetic to their interests and problems. Thus it was typical that George Weidenfeld cultivated Wilson and his menage from 1944 on. Some sceptics thought he overpaid Marcia Williams for her book, *Inside Number 10*. It was Sir George who staged Wilson's sixtieth birthday party on the eve of the latter's resignation and who was able to enjoy his own peerage six weeks later. Certainly Wilson did not have with foreign-born entrepreneurs the trouble he had with Cecil King. When he had offered King a life peerage, the *Daily Mirror* tycoon and nephew of Northcliffe had insisted on a life earldom to reflect his eminence in comparison with the other press lords, Viscounts Northcliffe and Rothermere. The previous life earldom had been awarded two centuries before to the mistress who serviced both George I and his father.

## MONARCHICAL KINDNESS

There is inevitably a type of monarchical quality about the honours bestowed by a Prime Minister, particularly a kind and isolated one who places heavy importance on the loyalty of his courtiers. On the simple level there was the peerage in 1970 for Harold Davies, his cheerful former Parliamentary Private Secretary whom he had sent to Hanoi in 1965 in the forlorn hope of breathing life into his effort to bring peace to Vietnam. By deciding to hold the 1970 general election during Wakes Week in June, when all factories closed for a vacation in Staffordshire, Wilson had ensured that Davies would lose the marginal seat he had held in Leek since 1945. So he transformed the exuberant Welsh left-winger into Lord Davies of Leek.

Wilson could also be slightly Machiavellian in his elevations to the peerage. When he recommended John Harris for a life peerage after Labour returned to office in March 1974, this was widely misinterpreted as being at the request of Roy Jenkins. (Harris had been Jenkins's aide and PR man and, while on the *Economist*, Jenkins's link with that Euro-fanatical publication.) According to intimates, the elevation was Wilson's own idea. It was a way of embarrassing Jenkins and depriving him of a link with the *Economist*. At the same time it provided Wilson with a balance for his intended appointment of one or more of his intimates: Marcia Williams, Terry Pitt and Joe Haines. Neither of the last two agreed to be immolated in the Lords.

Inevitably Wilson's relations with his real inner circle or 'kitchen cabinet' were more complex. He had started out with only two intimates in 1952; R. H. S. Crossman, politician and journalist, and Dr Thomas Balogh, Hungarian economist and Fellow of Balliol. Wilson had conferred with Balogh almost every week for the next dozen years. Once Labour had won office in 1964 Dr Balogh was able to take three years' leave from his duties at Oxford to serve as Economic Adviser to the Cabinet. When his leave was over he had to return to Oxford. Wilson first tried appointing him Consultant to the Prime Minister in 1968. But an Oxford colleague denounced this to the Visitorial Board as illegal, so Balogh was made a Hungarian-accented peer to enable him to travel to London to confer with Wilson. In fact, this was an example both of Wilson's kindness and of Marcia's tendency to intervene on behalf of an ally. At that point Balogh, having been defeated by the Treasury on devaluation and other subjects, had little influence – though he was later to make a comeback on North Sea oil.

The role of the Honours in demonstrating the kindness of a Prime Minister was very much in evidence when Crossman, who was dying of cancer, lunched with Wilson at 10 Downing Street a week after Labour returned to office in March 1974. The Prime Minister offered a peerage to Crossman, who had given up his Coventry seat because of his terminal illness. According to Joe Haines, Crossman accepted the offer.[33] The significance of that offer and the seriousness of the acceptance were indicated by Crossman's death several days later. This was not the first time that Wilson had made kind offers on which he did not expect to have to deliver. When George Brown was in hospital in July 1968, after he had resigned as Foreign Secretary, Wilson visited him and encouraged him to believe that he would yet be back in the Labour Cabinet. By some circuitous route, perhaps telephonic, this information appeared on the front page of the *Daily Mail* in an article by Walter Terry, who had been 'exiled' to Washington because of the embarrassment of his editor over his affair with Marcia Williams. But, of course, this Brown comeback never took place.

Although the offer and acceptance of the Crossman peerage aroused no storm, because it was never realized and did not 'leak' at the time, another Wilson offer caused almost as much of a storm behind the scenes as in public. This was the surprise elevation which transformed his political secretary Marcia Williams into Lady Falkender. When Wilson returned from his Easter holiday in the Scillies in 1974 to tell his press secretary that he was elevating Mrs Williams, Joe Haines was indignant. He had recently been at his most devastating in denying a *News of the World* story that the Prime Minister would make Marcia a peer and Minister for the Arts. Joe Haines, who had long been Marcia's rival in the 'battle for Harold's ear', tried to warn the Prime Minister off. 'He was not, however, to be moved by argument,' Haines later recalled, 'which meant that he was committed to going ahead with the honour.'[34]

The Prime Minister was determined to elevate Marcia Williams in part because he wanted to extend two fingers in defiant contempt at the newspapers which had tried to attack him through Marcia and her brother, Tony Field, who had been his office manager. Tony Field, a geologist by training, had been involved in land reclamation near Wigan from 1968 onwards, and had cut in his sister on one of the companies involved. A local Conservative began 'leaking' details of these deals just before the 1974 general election. First the *Guardian* investigated reports that Wilson had been involved because of special road facilities the Field companies had received. Both the reporter and his editor accepted the assurances of Joe Haines and Wilson himself that there was no involvement by the Prime Minister. Then the *Daily Mail* made an approach to Marcia Williams just before the election. Joe Haines was frightened that they were going to 'blow' the story of her illegitimate children. But they too were interested in the Wigan land deal. Joe Haines did what he could to keep newsmen away from Marcia. Wilson's friend and adviser, Lord Goodman, who was then Chairman of the Newspaper Publishers Association, persuaded the *Daily Mail*'s owner, Vere Harmsworth, that an election-eve stunt would do neither the *Mail* nor the press any good. It was this sort of activity which led to Wilson's attack on 'hordes of journalists' scavenging for material against him.

Two weeks after Labour formed the new Government on 4 March 1974, the *Daily Mail* published its story about Tony Field's sale of land to Ronald Milhench. After a fortnight's lull the *Mail*'s circulation rival, the *Daily Express*, picked up the story. The *Daily Mail*, learning of this in advance, released a story which tried to connect Wilson to the Field–Milhench land deal by disclosing a letter on his official stationery with a Wilson signature which was clearly a forgery. This started an unpleasant inundation of publicity – 6,000 column inches between 3 April and 11 April, according to Joe Haines's count – linking the Prime Minister through his political secretary with the land deals of her brother and the forger and confidence trickster, Ronald Milhench. Wilson was livid as reporters laid siege to Mrs Williams's Wyndham Mews house, sending various members of his staff to help fend off boarders. But two of those he sent, Joe Haines and Dr Bernard Donoughue, his policy adviser, were overruled when they advised against his getting involved in transactions which were not his concern. Their advice only resulted in the toning-down of his Commons statement of 8 April which defended Marcia Williams and her brother against charges of 'land speculation' by insisting it was only 'land reclamation' – which brought ribald laughter, not only from Tories.[35]

As we have seen, Wilson faced another confrontation with his closest advisers when he insisted on going ahead with a peerage for Marcia Williams. 'So strongly did we feel about it that in the early afternoon of 23 May 1974 – only a few hours before I was due to give the information, under embargo, to political correspondents – we decided that I should lead a small deputation of four to the Prime Minister urging him, even at this late stage, not to go ahead with the ennoblement.' The delegation included Joe Haines, Dr Bernard Donoughue and Albert Murray. They warned that news of the peerage would serve as a new excuse for anti-Wilson propaganda in the predominantly Conservative popular press in the period leading up to a general election. 'What is more,' Joe Haines warned, 'I do not see how I can protect her any longer.' As a peer, she would become a legitimate object of public interest, he felt.[36] But Wilson would not be dissuaded, hoping partly to 'do a Harvey Smith' at the press, as he told the Queen, according to Marcia Williams.[37] He was also trying to prepare a political platform for her once he had passed from the political stage, as planned, in a couple of years' time.

## EXCEPTIONS AND THE RULE

Just as Marcia Williams's name on the list to be ennobled in the 1974 Birthday Honours dominated reaction to that list, so too did a dozen names dominate Wilson's Resignation Honours list under two years later. This was largely because, as we have seen, these names were 'leaked' by someone at 10 Downing Street in April 1976, giving the *Sunday Times* and others plenty of time to focus on them.

When the list was published in full in May 1976 there was no criticism of the two life peerages for Terence Boston and Albert Murray, ex-MPs who had lost their Faversham and Gravesend seats respectively and subsequently assisted in Wilson's office. There was only applause for the long overdue knighthood for 'Freddie' Warren, the key civil servant in the Chief Whip's office, who had long kept Chief Whips and Commons Leaders on the rails. Nobody challenged the elevation to the Privy Council of Len Murray, the General Secretary of the Trades Union Congress, nor the Companion of Honour awards to the Lord Chancellor, Lord Elwyn-Jones, and the retiring Deputy Leader, Edward Short (whom James Callaghan subsequently ennobled as Lord Glenamara). Much of the rest of Wilson's Resignation Honours list was also in line with the prior lists from Macmillan, Douglas-Home and Heath. There were CBEs for his veteran constituency agent, Arthur Smith, and for Labour's National Agent, Reg Underhill. There was an MBE for Peggy Field, Marcia's sister, who had served as personal secretary to Mrs Wilson. There were also lesser honours for Bill Housden, Sir Harold's popular personal driver and messenger, for his housekeeper, for the senior Wren steward at Chequers, and for his senior cleaner at Number 10. The newspapers duly photographed the veteran constable at the door of Number 10, also honoured, in company with the lady cleaner.

The names which provoked the most rigorous attack were the handful to which Joe Haines strongly objected as a Bermondsey egalitarian and an opponent of the dominating influence of Marcia Williams, now Lady Falkender. Haines was at least half right. Lady Falkender had been responsible for some of the most inspired Honours in the various Wilson lists since 1964. This was her last opportunity to use her influence on Wilson to push the names of people in her circle. Eric Miller, who was to receive a knighthood, was her generous friend and frequent host; she had virtually insisted that everyone use the Churchill Hotel in which he had an interest. Sir George Weidenfeld, who was ennobled, was her publisher and a frequent escort and host; he had dangled the possibility of a post within his publishing company. John Vaizey, the Brunel University economist and Wilson critic, had been helpful in opening the doors of private schools to her two sons.

In his loyalty to Lady Falkender Sir Harold insisted that all these names had been recommended by him alone. The result was that he was roundly abused. Arthur Blenkinsop, a self-effacing Labour back-bencher of many years' standing, collected a hundred signatures to a letter of protest directed to the Parliamentary Labour Party. Lord Shinwell attacked as a 'stupid error' the Wilson peerages for people like Sir Lew Grade and his brother Bernard Delfont,[38] neither of whom had a record of support for Labour objectives or even, as yet, for Wilson. Why the honours for Conservatives like James Hanson and James Goldsmith? Was it because of Hanson's work for the D'Oyly Carte company, to which he had been appointed together with Sir Harold, or for his chairmanship of the holding company controlling Tyne-Tees TV and, of course, Yorkshire TV, which was to broadcast a lengthy series on British Prime Ministers featuring Sir Harold? Of these questions raised, the most biting concerned James Goldsmith, who seemed due for a peerage until newspaper disclosures elicited protests from Lord Longford and others. A very wealthy entrepreneur who had served as adviser to Edward Heath on European affairs – his Caven-ham Foods was French-based – he was acknowledged to be a heavy contributor to Conservative Party funds. What was he doing on the Resignation Honours list of a departing Labour Prime Minister, supposed to give recognition to those who had helped him? Because the newspapers had been forewarned of this nomination, their investigations turned up the information that he had lunched twice with Lady Falkender and that he had considered her to have directorship potential. These rumours circulated in April 1976, long before Joe Haines's book quoted Wilson on the subject ten months later. Unhappily for Wilson, Goldsmith survived the Political Honours Scrutiny – unlike Jarvis Astaire, the boxing impresario who was a genuine Labour supporter. This did Wilson's reputation with his Labour colleagues little good because Goldsmith was very much in the public eye with his criminal libel suits against *Private Eye*. His use of his great wealth as a legal sledge-hammer and his personal style – redolent of the very 'William Hickey society' Wilson had so often attacked – made him a highly unpopular figure with Labour backbenchers and supporters. Even the *Daily Mirror*, from among whose executives Sir Harold had contributed five peerages to the Lords, was scathing. The only one of those ennobled who was unperturbed by the storm of criticism was Lord Kagan, Sir Harold's long-time financial supporter and host and the manufacturer of the Gannex raincoats which were the Wilson trademark. 'Those who mind don't matter,' he snorted, 'and those who matter don't mind!'[39]

Virtually the only serious defence of Sir Harold's Resignation Honours list came from an unexpected source – Austen Albu, a former Labour MP of distinctly pro-Gaitskell, anti-Wilson sympathies who had no reason to be grateful to Sir Harold, although he had served as a Minister. He wrote a letter to *The Times* replying to its criticism of Wilson's list as 'one of unrepentant Darwinism, of the business survival of the fittest and of nature red in tooth and claw':[40] 'There is no evidence that Sir Harold's ennobled industrialists were ruthless employers or broke any recognized commercial code; their only faults are that they were immigrants, like so many of our successful business leaders in the past, and so the distaste for entrepreneurship which permeates British social values, but on which the material standards of all classes depend, easily turns into anti-Semitism and there are signs appearing that the commercial success of the new immigrants is creating a similar prejudice against Asians. Is it not time that we recognized that an outdated aristocratic traditon, extended by a couple of centuries of imperial rule, is a serious obstacle to our economic recovery and so to the maintenance of those very values of our society which are most worth preserving?'[41]

To those who understood the Honours system, this telling blow in Sir Harold's defence was wide of the mark. Nobody was arguing against honouring industrialists for contributions to the export drive, wherever they were born or whatever God they worshipped. What was being asked was: why had particular men (about a dozen at most) been honoured in the highly-personal list of the departing Prime Minister? The controversy was revived ten months later with the publication of Joe Haines's book, *The Politics of Power*, in which he blamed all the controversial names on Lady Falkender even to the point of recalling a list written on 'lavender paper', which caught the fancy of headline writers. Hard on the heels of that claim, vigorously denied by Wilson as a 'farrago of twisted facts'[42], came more damaging information.

On 18 February 1977 the *Daily Mail* headlined: 'WILSON HAD A SECRET FUND'. The story told of a 'syndicate of wealthy businessmen' who contributed to the Opposition Leader's office between 1970 and 1974. This 'Trustee Fund', as it was sometimes described, had been known to a handful of people earlier and had been written about briefly on several occasions. What made it newsworthy now – apart from the specific indication that the former Sir Rudy Sternberg had contributed £2,000 a year for four years – was the fact that five of the six trustees of this fund had been ennobled by Sir Harold. This aroused the spectre of Lloyd George.

A Conservative MP, John Cope, suggested to the new Prime Minister that Sir Harold's ennoblements might have contravened the Honours (Prevention of Abuses) Act passed in 1925 to prevent a repetition of Lloyd George's sale of honours. He asked 'whether a payment to a fund to provide a political office for a Prime Minister constitutes a payment to a party or political fund for the purpose of the certificate given to the Honours Scrutiny Committee when someone is to be recommended for an honour to Her Majesty'. Prime Minister James Callaghan replied: 'Yes, if such a payment is directly or indirectly associated with any recommendation made in any list.'[43]

This year-long campaign against at most a dozen of the honours he had recommended was very hurtful to Sir Harold, who had now taken to sitting on the back benches as Sir Winston Churchill had done. In the weeks after the publication of his Resignation Honours the coolness amongst his colleagues was discernible. On at least one occasion they refused to move up to make space for him on the 'Churchill seat' on the front row just below the gangway. As more and more revelations emerged, more and more Labour MPs were heard to say, 'That's finished Harold for me!'

Any tendency to let bygones be bygones on this score was retarded repeatedly by front-page news about some of the entrepreneurs Wilson had honoured. Thus, Sir James Goldsmith was kept in the public eye in 1976–77 by his criminal libel action against *Private Eye* and his subsequent effort to take control of Beaverbrook Newspapers. Sir Eric Miller, who had lent Wilson the Peachey Corporation helicopter for the general election campaign in 1974, was ousted from control of Peachey

Corporation in May 1977 amidst a welter of publicity about his alleged misuse of Peachey assets for personal purposes. And Lord Brayley, whom Wilson's chiefs in the Lords had urged him to drop as a Minister for incompetence, died in 1977 before he could clear his name of charges that he had misused *his* company's assets. This publicity about a handful of those honoured by Wilson exaggerated the impression that too often his honours went to the wrong people.

# III. Walter Mitty
## and Muhammad Ali

'You're having another of your Walter Mitty fits!'
> Mrs Marcia Williams to Prime Minister Harold Wilson aboard
> HMS *Fearless* at Gibraltar, 1968[1]

'I would have said that if the film of Walter Mitty hadn't come first, Harold Wilson must have been the prototype on which that mythical character was based. His fantasies are endless. The roles he allots himself are breathtaking. His capacity for rewriting events would do credit to Edgar Wallace ... The pity was that if only he had been able to persuade himself that he was secure – and that the more successful the team worked together, the better for everybody – then the greater would have been his success and his place in history.'

> Lord George-Brown[2]

'His India-rubber resilience is linked, of course, with self-deception. No man can be the kind of Boy Scout Harold is and read aloud Kipling's "If" as often as he reads it to me without a great deal of self-deception in his makeup.'

> R. H. S. Crossman[3]

'Fantasy is a defensive or tension-relieving mechanism offering either solace or an illusionary release from unsatisfying reality or an imaginary satisfaction of wishes, any actual gratification of which has been forbidden.'

> Arthur Noyes and Lawrence Kolb, *Modern Clinical Psychiatry*[4]

'Among political leaders a high degree of narcissism is very frequent; it may be considered an occupational illness – or asset – especially among those who owe their power to their influence over mass audiences. If the leader is convinced of his extraordinary gifts and of his mission, it will be easier to convince the large audiences who are attracted by men who appear to be so absolutely certain. But the narcissistic leader does not use his narcissistic charisma only as a means for political success; he needs success and applause for the sake of his own mental equilibrium. The idea of his greatness and infallibility is essentially based on his narcissistic grandiosity, not on his real achievements as a human being.'

> Dr Erich Fromm, *Anatomy of Human Destructiveness*[5]

There was little chance for others to congratulate Harold Wilson adequately in March 1976 when he startled everyone by announcing his resignation. He was too busy congratulating himself. Thus, not for the first time, he described himself as 'the longest-serving peacetime Prime Minister' on the day he surprised his Cabinet and the Commons.[6] The word 'peacetime' had been inserted to eliminate Asquith and Churchill, who had served longer but whose service had included bits of the First and Second World Wars. It was as though the East Germans had boasted after the 1976 Olympics at Montreal that they had been its 'non-super-Power' winner, thereby excluding the Russians and Americans.

Typically, in his last interview with Arthur Williamson, chief political correspondent of the Press Association, Sir Harold said: 'I know more than anyone else about how Britain's Government works.'[7] This was typical of Sir Harold imitating Muhammad ('I am the greatest!') Ali or the Graeco–Roman youth, Narcissus, who fell in love with his own image. Sir Harold had acquired the habit of trying to use the press to create his self-image and then getting angry with it if it did not oblige. This particular boast was typically unnecessary. Certainly he must have been among the top half-dozen in knowledgeability. But why did he feel compelled to boast? Why did he write *The Labour Government, 1964–70* as if it had been a one-man-show? Why did he give so little credit in the book to fellow Cabinet Ministers? Why was there no mention of Dr Thomas Balogh or Mrs Marcia Williams? This preening was no new trait. Civil servants who worked with him in wartime recall many conversations which began: 'When I got my First...' One of the first substantial references to Wilson in the 1952 section of Crossman's still unpublished diary for that era records with some amusement the length at which Wilson told his fellow-Bevanite MPs how clever he had been when President of the Board of Trade. He rose to new heights of self-congratulation in his authorized biography by Leslie Smith. With a straight face Wilson claimed that Aneurin Bevan had canvassed senior colleagues with the proposition that Harold Wilson replace Clement Attlee in 1947, at the time of the Dalton–Cripps plot against Labour's then Prime Minister. 'To appoint a relatively unknown newcomer, however brilliant and capable, as Leader of the Government seemed completely idiotic to all of them – as it did also to Wilson himself, when he later heard of it,' wrote Wilson's gullible biographer.[8] The only thing more idiotic was to believe that Bevan could have suggested it, if at all, as anything more than a leg-pull to ridicule the whole idea of a palace revolution.

Sir Harold's need to talk almost non-stop about himself has long ignored the receptivity of his audience. In his last months in office he embarrassed his staff by long boastful speeches to increasingly in-attentive audiences. In his last days in office he asked Ian Mikardo, the

veteran left-winger to whom he had never offered office, for a briefing
on the Socialist International. Mikardo warned that, on the day prescribed, he could only fit in twenty minutes. During the twenty minutes
in which they met Mikardo never got in a word because Wilson spent
the whole time telling him how he had kept Labour united.

It is this sort of repetitious 'I am the greatest!' that has led to Sir
Harold's being tagged 'the Muhammad Ali of British politics' by the
hostile popular press. And, unlike the case of the black American
heavyweight boxer, these boasts are no publicity-stirring 'gimmick', as
can be seen by Sir Harold's tendency to surround himself by those
willing to chant, 'Yes, he's the greatest,' and to denounce those who did
not speak up for him, particularly when he was under attack. In 1972 he
complained bitterly to one right-wing ex-Minister that none of the
people he had promoted had come to his defence when, during the
previous eighteen months, he had been subjected to an unprecedented
barrage of attacks over his opposition to entering the EEC on the terms
acceptable to Edward Heath. 'It's not only Roy Jenkins and his lot that
have not come to my defence. But not even you and Shirley Williams!'
He set his PPS, the late Will Hamling, to write letters to the press in his
defence.[9]

For a politician of long standing Sir Harold proved how thin-skinned
he could be. Sir Tom Williams, QC, one of the topflight barristers on
the Labour benches, who had been at Oxford and in the Bevanite
movement with Sir Harold, tried to enliven a speech with a witticism.
'We have been ruled for thirty years by economists,' he joked. 'And we
are no further forward than if we were ruled by witch doctors!' When
he learned that Wilson had felt wounded by the remark, Williams went
to see him to explain that it was interjected for light relief and that he
had Tommy Balogh and Roy Harrod in mind. Wilson explained his
anger: 'I have spent all my life doing things for other people, going out
of my way to help them. And then I find, so often, that they act as if I
have no feelings!' Williams, although among the highest-paid QCs in the
1960s, was bypassed for others when Wilson named his Attorney Generals
and Solicitor Generals. He was finally knighted in 1975 for his work for
the Inter-Parliamentary Union rather than for his loyalty to Harold
Wilson.

Sensitive about disloyalty, Wilson has rewarded loyalty generously.
Thus, if he paved the way for James Callaghan as his successor, this
was partly because Callaghan had never exploited his opportunities to
oust Wilson after his 1970 defeat. Callaghan had warned Wilson against
trying to discipline the unions in Barbara Castle's 'In Place of Strife'
legislation, and had been excluded from Wilson's inner counsels in
retaliation. When enough trade-union activists refused to vote Labour

in 1970 and brought about the party's defeat, Wilson became vulnerable. This vulnerability increased as a result of Wilson's somersault on the EEC in 1971–72. Because Callaghan threw his support behind Wilson then, he earned a crack at the top job. This did not, of course, mean that Wilson was always 100% sure – as illustrated early in the 1974 Parliament when the name of James Callaghan went up on the internal TV in the Commons. Knowing that Jim was not scheduled to speak a glowering Wilson stormed into the Chamber. But then a smile broke out when he saw that it was the newcomer of the same name, the Labour MP for Middleton and Prestwich, making his maiden speech.

To an incredible degree, while Sir Harold was on the Front Bench and particularly when he was at Number 10 there was a simple criterion for evaluating attitudes. Anything which was Harold-enhancing was good. Anything which was Harold-depreciating was bad. This was particularly true of the press. Thus, Crossman recorded in his diary how Wilson had complained to him about the 'misbehaviour' of Douglas Jay in leaking to the press the story of the import surcharge. Crossman went on to recount how Wilsonian complaints about leaks to the press exasperated the Cabinet because 'ninety-nine per cent of the so-called leaks' came from Wilson at Number 10 or from Callaghan, then at the Treasury, or George Brown, then at the Department of Economic Affairs.[10]

This same ambivalence towards the press was demonstrated at Sir Harold's departure. For months the Lobby of political correspondents had been in Number 10's 'dog-house' deprived of their daily 'bones' of briefings. Then, suddenly on the day Sir Harold's resignation was announced, they were inundated with information.

In the press assessments of Sir Harold's career, which appeared on his sixtieth birthday and on his announcement five days later of his impending 'redeployment', the phrase 'Walter Mitty' recurred. Walter Mitty, of course, is the character created by James Thurber and made more famous on the screen by Danny Kaye: a hen-pecked little man who sought escape from his impotence and frustration by day-dreams and fantasies about his role as a superman – RAF flier, world-famous barrister, brilliant surgeon, sharpshooter, spy who 'faced the firing squad; erect and motionless, proud and disdainful, Walter Mitty the Undefeated, inscrutable to the last'.[11]

This Wilsonian quality of fantasizing was emphasized by Anthony Shrimsley, then Political Editor of the *Daily Mail*, who had started out a dozen years before as sympathetic to Wilson. This is evident from his book *The First 100 Days of Harold Wilson*,[12] which recounted the efforts of Labour's new Prime Minister to set a Kennedy pace in 1964–65. But, summing up Sir Harold a dozen years later, Shrimsley made the point that what 'in others would pass for cynicism ... in Wilson is simple self-delusion.'[13]

What particularly widened the gap between the new Labour Prime Minister of 1964–65 and the political correspondents, who often started off as admirers, were his efforts to involve them in his Mitty-style fantasies. Between 1965 and 1967, when Britain's power base was shrinking because of recurrent economic crises, he tried fruitlessly to solve many of the world's problems.

It had been difficult to avoid noticing Wilson's role-playing fantasies, partly because he was so open about it. When he first became Prime Minister in October 1964 he could not quite decide whether he was 'MacKennedy' or 'Kenmillan'. Certainly he was trying to emulate the youthful pace of Kennedy. At the same time he tried to emulate the shrewd political tactics of his favourite model among British Prime Ministers, Harold Macmillan: particularly his airborne pursuit of peace. Sometimes he seemed to be playing the pipe-smoking, avuncular 'healer' in imitation of Stanley Baldwin. And then, finally, he retired somewhat in the style of an earlier Knight of the Garter who remained in the Commons, Sir Winston Churchill.

The difficulty Wilson had in distinguishing between what *was* demonstrable fact and what he *believed* to be true was dramatically illustrated during his transition from Prime Minister to back-bencher. He used one of his last question times as Prime Minister to assert that South African interests were responsible for the blackguarding of Jeremy Thorpe and for his consequent retirement as Leader of the Liberal Party. He repeated this insistently at his farewell speech to the Parliamentary Press Club at luncheon. Quite naturally, political journalists assumed that he made his allegation on the basis of secret intelligence sources. In fact British Intelligence had been quite unable to find evidence to underpin his suspicions. Once he was no longer Prime Minister, Sir Harold encouraged the BBC to give a contract to two freelance journalists on the promise that he would participate in uncovering the 'South African connection' in the dethronement of Jeremy Thorpe as Liberal Leader. Despite months of expensive investigation the suspicion which Sir Harold had presented as a reality remained only a suspicion. It was not the first time that he had blurred the boundary between reality and his doubts or hopes in Southern Africa. His fury about their failure to prove his suspicions produced suggestions of MI5 'plots' against him.

Although many later laughed at his prediction that the embargo on Rhodesia would topple the regime of the white supremacist Ian Smith in 'weeks rather than months'[14] his efforts there were more realistic than most. He bent quite far in his attempts to reach a compromise with the slippery Ian Smith, even risking the resignations from his

Government of Shirley Williams, Edmund Dell and others. He may have been over-optimistic of the possibility of Ian Smith freeing himself from the hold of the white supremacists who dominated him. But Wilson did not, on Rhodesia, quite fall into a Suez-style fantasy of thinking that Britian had the military capacity to overthrow the Smith regime by airborne intervention.

It was his efforts to save President Johnson's scorched bacon in Vietnam which showed Prime Minister Wilson in his most Mitty-like role. Britain, of course, had no status in that crisis apart from the diplomatic technicality that in 1954 the then British Foreign Secretary, Sir Anthony Eden, had convened with the Russians the Geneva Conference which enabled the French to pull out their defeated troops from Vietnam. But on his first official meeting with President Johnson in December 1964 Wilson turned down the President's request for a token number of British troops for Vietnam, using the excuse that Britain already had 54,000 of its men in Malaysia resisting an incursion by the Indonesian President Sukarno. When Johnson ordered the first heavy bombing of North Vietnam in retaliation for the Vietcong attack on the US base at Pleiku in February 1965, Wilson attempted to 'do an Attlee'. He wanted to repeat the role played by the Labour Prime Minister in December 1950 when he flew to Washington to warn off President Truman from allowing General MacArthur to expand the war in Korea. But when Wilson telephoned Johnson on 11 February 1965 to invite himself to Washington the President almost burned the insulation off the 'hot line' in his fury. President Johnson was not interested in Wilson crossing the Atlantic with his 'shirt-tails flying' every time there was a crisis. 'If one of us jumps across the Atlantic every time there is a critical situation, next week I shall be flying over when Sukarno jumps on you and I will be giving you advice ... I won't tell you how to run Malaysia and you don't tell us how to run Vietnam ... If you want to help us some in Vietnam send us some men and some folks to deal with these guerrillas. Now if you don't feel like doing that, go on with your Malaysian problem.' After all, Johnson pointed out, Attlee had a right to give advice to Truman in 1950 because Britain had troops fighting in Korea.[15]

Johnson's brutal lesson in the realities of power politics did not stop Wilson from seeing himself as playing the role Sir Anthony Eden had played in 1954. In June 1965, without consulting his full Cabinet, he decided to launch a famous lead balloon, the Commonwealth Peace Mission, intended to bring peace to Vietnam. Since it had the backing of President Johnson, Sir Robert Menzies and other pro-Americans, it was sure to be rejected by the other side, particularly since it would stabilize the division of Vietnam just when the Northern revolutionaries thought they had the South and the Americans on the run. But the Prime Minister bulldozed the plan through the Commonwealth Conference, revelling in the compliments of the *Daily Mail* ('It is a bold and imaginative stroke'). But China's Prime Minister, Chou En-lai, described it as 'a manoeuvre in support of the United States' "peace talks" hoax' and refused to receive Wilson's former Foreign Secretary, Patrick (later Lord) Gordon Walker.[16] Hanoi rejected the plan and Moscow refused to receive the mission. President Nkrumah of Ghana, the only person not pro-American in the Commonwealth Mission, which was to be headed by Wilson, bombarded him with the proposal that he be allowed to go on his own, since he was *persona grata* in the Communist capitals. But Wilson rejected this. He preferred, instead, to send as his personal door-opener Harold Davies, later Lord Davies of Leek. Davies, a Welsh left-winger who was then Parliamentary Secretary for Pensions, had long had an interest in South-East Asia, which he had visited twice and about which he had written pamphlets. He was one of the very few Labour MPs who had kept in touch with Hanoi's journalistic representatives in London, a very inarticulate pair. The Prime Minister, consulting President Johnson on the project, asked Davies to use his Vietnamese contacts to get to Hanoi. Davies succeeded in arriving there because the Vietnamese Communists did not like turning down an old friend. But nobody would see him. It should have been apparent to an old specialist in dealing with the Russians, as Wilson was, that no Communist regime at war with the Americans would touch with a barge-pole a mission which every major Communist Power had tagged as an example of London's 'consistent effort to serve as errand boy to the US'.[17] But Wilson, even in retrospect, insisted that 'whatever hopes the Davies visit might have justified were dashed by a serious, indeed disastrous, leak in London, while he was on the way.'[18] He blamed this leak for grounding in Pnompenh the Foreign Office expert on Vietnam who was to have accompanied Harold Davies. But the mission was foredoomed because the Vietnamese Communists were committed to winning a military victory and to avoid giving their Southern opponents any breathing space in which to recover.

Curiously enough, Asia had a special attraction for Wilson in playing out his neo-Kiplingesque role. This comes out most vividly in an astounding speech he made from a prepared text to the Parliamentary Labour Party and then distributed to the press, but which he later managed to leave out of his mammoth, 836-page, 400,000-word book *The Labour Government, 1964–70*. He made this speech on 15 June 1966 to beat off a combined attack by left-wingers and pro-Europeans, both of whom were demanding arms cuts 'East of Suez'. In trying to fight off the demand Wilson portrayed Britain as about to emerge as the saviour of peace in the Commonwealth, operating from inexpensive bases on islands in the Indian Ocean. 'Does anyone think India wants us to leave her to become a cockpit, forced to choose between Russia and America to protect her from China?' He then sneered: 'Perhaps there are some Members who would like to contract out and leave it to the Americans and the Chinese, eyeball to eyeball, to face this thing out ... It is the surest prescription for a nuclear holocaust I could think of.'[19] This picture of a Britain strong enough to serve as a referee-mediator was so far-fetched that the *Observer* described him as living in a 'fantasy world'.[20]

Unlike most fantasies, which serve the purpose of relieving tensions, this one had a more practical purpose. Britain had, in fact, accepted a request by America to allow it a base in the vast Indian Ocean in which the Russians were becoming more active. Without a refuelling base US fleets had to rely wholly on fleet tankers. Diego Garcia was selected because it was centrally located, because it was largely uninhabited except for contract labourers, and because, unlike Gan, its British sovereignty was not disputed. This concession was kept secret for years – even from the readers of Wilson's political memoirs. To have disclosed this at the time would have exposed the Prime Minister and Britain to the charge of being helpmates of the US Navy, then engaged in flattening large parts of North Vietnam with its heavy guns and naval aircraft. By oratorical fantasies that this new island strategy was designed to give Britain a new capacity for an independent neutral strategy in Asia, Wilson provided an effective, if temporary, smoke-screen.

The political effectiveness of his Mitty-like fantasies was emphasized in his sudden dash to Salisbury, Rhodesia, after Ian Smith had indicated a willingness to talk about his intention of proclaiming a Unilateral Declaration of Independence. The Prime Minister made his decision only four days after the Cabinet's Defence and Overseas Policy Committee had discussed Rhodesia for almost a whole day, without his once raising the possibility of his personal intervention. Then, although Parliament – in which Labour had a majority of only three – was about to open, he suddenly flew 6,000 miles to try to solve what he later privately described as 'my Cuba' – again playing the Kennedy role. When he failed to talk Ian Smith and his white supremacists around and felt he had to impose sanctions, he spoke of their succeeding in 'weeks rather than months'.

This role-playing represented much more than the energetic acting out of Wilson's personal fantasies. By his whirling dervish attack on international problems Wilson managed to concentrate the attention of the media on one after another of his foreign trips: to Moscow,

Washington and Ottawa as well as Salisbury. In doing this he was emulating the feat of former Conservative Prime Minister, Harold Macmillan, who transformed the Tories from a divided and battered party in January 1957 – after the Suez fiasco – to the victorious possessors of a majority of 100 in the October 1959 general election.

Like Macmillan's many foreign trips Wilson's forays produced few results, except in bridging the Indo-Pakistan difficulties over the disputed territory of the Kutch and keeping at bay Sukarno's raiders into Malaysia. Rhodesia stayed under white minority rule. Vietnam remained locked in bloody warfare. But Wilson's capital-hopping transformed him from a partisan political leader in October 1964 into a national leader able, in March 1966, to duplicate Macmillan's 1959 electoral victory with a Labour majority of 100 seats. This victory stilled for a matter of weeks the complaints of MPs like George Brown who did not like his 'gimmicky style' or his preoccupation with tactics.

Those who complained about Wilson's boastfulness did not seem to realize that this was a tradition of political leadership. Lloyd George's promises of 'a home fit for heroes', Chamberlain's promises of 'peace in our time' or Churchill's threats of what unarmed Britons would do to Nazis landing on the beaches and sundry other places were similarly boastful, and often for similar reasons. Leadership almost requires the type of boastfulness which derives from emotional deprivation. Recent biographical studies have demonstrated to what extent Sir Winston Churchill came from an aristocratic version of a broken home, with a father who died insane from syphilis and a mother who played fast and loose all over the world.

In her fascinating book, *The Fiery Chariot – A Study of British Prime Ministers*,[21] Lucille Iremonger, the wife of a former Tory MP, has demonstrated the curious drives which have moved many Prime Ministers. In a close study of the first two dozen Prime Ministers she has shown symptoms of emotional deprivation to have been general, with five-eighths of them having lost a parent early in life. 'Deprivation of love in childhood ... set up the drives in certain gifted boy-children which were to take them to the heights of achievement.' Such men showed 'abnormal sensitivity, isolation ... ultra-normal drives for attention and affection, subjugation to the inspirational teaching and unbending discipline of a stern but transparently admiring mentor, marked interest in religion in one form or another, passionate need for an ecstatic and total relationship with one self-immolatory and adoring woman ... and suicidal, astounding, recklessness there and elsewhere.'

## CONDITIONAL LOVE

Harold Wilson did not suffer emotional deprivation in the sense that his parents were not sufficiently loving. His deprivation lay in the fact that their love was conditional. It was always 'We love you but. . .' And the condition was that to satisfy them and be truly lovable he had to be top of his class, top of the school, earn the best First-Class degree in his university. Because of this implicit condition in his parents' love he had to go through life saying, in effect, 'See, folks, how clever I am!' He was really trying to win his parents' unconditional love when he set on edge the teeth of MPs and other colleagues by his perpetual boasting.

James Harold Wilson was born on 11 March 1916, the first son and second child of Herbert Wilson, industrial chemist, and his wife, Ethel, who had trained as a teacher – as had the mother of Enoch Powell. Ethel Wilson was 'placid', Harold Wilson told me. 'She was very placid. I hardly ever saw her cross.' But she was implacably ambitious for her son, as was her husband. They saw him as restoring the family's fortunes. Their son was to be not only the kindest and most polite little boy, but also the best dressed, the most clever and most successful ever. It was the sort of programming which loving and ambitious ex-teachers tend to implant in their sons.

'There seems every reason to suppose that self-confidence in later life is based upon the infant's earliest experience of his mother; if such that he has not acquired the conviction of his essential "goodness' or lovability, [he] will possess no inner sense of self-esteem on which to rely,' wrote psychologist Anthony Storr. 'However successful he may be in later life, he will remain intensely vulnerable to failure, rejection or disappointment, which will seem to him the end of the world, and throw him into profound depression.'[22]

The first time a Wilson fantasy burst upon the great British public was on 3 July 1948, when he claimed: 'The school I went to in the North was a school where more than half the children in my class never had any boots or shoes to their feet.'[23] He was instantly rebutted by Alderman Oliver Smith, his former teacher but then a Labour Mayor of Huddersfield: 'I was a teacher in Huddersfield at the time Mr Wilson was a pupil. I cannot recall ever seeing a single child walking the streets without boots or shoes.'[24] Wilson, then President of the Board of Trade, wrote an apology. 'I am not blaming the reporter who got my words down very accurately and fairly . . . I referred to this in terms of the slums of Liverpool and other big cities . . . I did not say or suggest that that was at all the case in Huddersfield . . . I never suggested that my school friends had to go to school barefoot.'[25] He then explained the origins of his fantasy: 'I well remember how I felt "out of it" at school in that my leather boots meant I could not join in a slide in the school yard so successfully, or strike sparks out of the school yard'[26] as those who wore wooden clogs with metal cleats could. So much did he envy those carefree schoolchildren sliding on the school playground that, over twenty years later, he had to fantasize them into barefoot children. A fantasy like that had roots in his early insecurity.

His more carefree, scruffier schoolmates had envied his toys, particularly of the 'educational' sort. (He was a Meccano addict before he was four.) They enjoyed his magazines, the *Meccano Magazine* or the *Children's Newspaper*; they also had access to his sister's *Children's Encyclopaedia*.

What they did not envy him was the way in which 'Willy' – as they then called him – always had to have his nose to the grindstone. When *he* returned from school, he was allowed to play outside with his school chums only *after* he had done his homework. 'Herbert Wilson was fifty years ahead of his time in his confidence that his child could go to university,' one of Harold's schoolmates emphasized to me.

Herbert Wilson supported his wife in pointing his son's nose towards the academic heights because he too felt that was the only way to achieve full professional attainment and avoid the insecurity of unemployment. A highly intelligent man and a brilliant mathematician, Herbert Wilson felt he had not had his due because he was the product of Manchester Technical College rather than a university. As one of five in a draper's family of limited means, he could only have gone to university on a scholarship. But only his mathematics had been up to scholarship standards. He later felt at a professional disadvantage in competing with men holding university degrees. Until the First World War expanded the Institute of Chemistry he had even been barred from having after his name the professionally-important AIC – for Associate of the Institute of Chemistry. This was important for securing and keeping jobs. Just before Harold was born, Ethel and Herbert Wilson had had to move from Manchester, where both of them had been born, back to Yorkshire, where the Wilson family came from originally, in pursuit of an industrial chemist's job making picric acid for the shells being produced in the Royal Arsenal at Woolwich.

Harold's conditioning started very early, even earlier for him than for his sister, Marjorie, seven years his elder, who was encouraged to become a teacher. There was an amusing incident in 1920, when Harold was four and his eleven-year-old sister was awarded a county Minor Scholarship to Huddersfield Girls' High School. 'I've won a scholarship!' she proclaimed triumphantly. 'I want a "ship" too!' squealed little Harold in tears. When the term was explained to him he opted for that target too, abandoning his previous ambition of becoming a carpenter and undertaker.[27]

Although he came from a loving home, the joint determination of his parents that he should 'get on' made them somewhat too ready to encourage him to grow up too soon. Theirs was a generation in which parents believed that if boys were to 'get on' they had to learn to fight their own battles and be 'manly'. Young Harold's parents did nothing to protect him against a teacher who caned him when he was six or to comfort him afterwards. Coming from a home in which moral disapproval was considered a major punishment, being beaten with a cane was genuinely traumatic. But little Harold had been so conditioned by his parents' stoicism that he never complained at home. And his parents never indicated that they knew of his ordeal or that they sympathized with him. Harold even thought of jumping off his father's motorcycle on the way to school to play truant. Could this brusque douche of isolation have helped his later tendency to be 'the cat who walks alone' – as he was to describe it?

With his first-class brain and supercharged motivation Harold scored tops at Royds Hall, the grammar school a mile and a half from his home. 'In all academic subjects, Wilson was brilliant,' recalled a teacher. 'He excelled at French, Latin and Greek and displayed more than a passing interest in Esperanto while at school.'[28] And he kept up the family standards which fellow-pupils had noted at primary school, of never wearing darned socks or hand-me-downs. A contemporary photograph showed him as a pleasant-looking, chubby youngster – the only one in his group to wear the authorized school uniform of brown and Eton blue.[29]

Amidst surface respectability, the emphasis was very much on the need for success. This showed itself in an amusing incident. Young Harold's favourite book was *Engineering for Boys*. On one occasion he entered a Meccano bridge-building competition. He had intended to build a model of the Forth Bridge, but on discovering that he did not have enough pieces, he changed the name of his entry to the shorter Quebec Bridge.

## ROLE-PLAYING FOR RESPECTABILITY

It was at this stage, when he was fourteen, that young Harold had a vivid lesson in the family's belief in the need for role-playing to preserve respectability. He had just come close to death from typhoid fever after drinking milk on a Scouts' outing. Six of his fellow Scouts died, while six survived, including Harold. He spent over three months in Meltham Isolation Hospital before being allowed home in January 1931.

'When I came back from hospital,' Harold Wilson recalled to me, 'I slept in my parents' room, because I had to be watched and fed every two hours during the night. When I woke up the first morning, I was surprised to find my father still there, instead of at work. "Shall we tell him?" he asked my mother, who agreed. He then explained that he had lost his job.'

The blow had fallen a month earlier, before Christmas 1930, but nobody outside the family knew. It was impressed on young Harold that nobody outside the family was to know that the head of the family had, at forty-eight, been sacked again. In 1930–31 more than a third of the workers in the Colne Valley were unemployed. But the Wilson family's lower-middle-class ideas of respectability compelled them to behave as though unemployment were some sort of disgrace.

Although kept from the neighbours, the impact of the loss of salary every month eroded the family's savings. It was reluctantly decided that if Herbert Wilson were still unemployed when Harold reached the age of sixteen in March 1932 and the top of the fifth form, he would be compelled to leave school then instead of going on to university as they all desired. 'I had a job all fixed up for me when I was sixteen – with my uncle, a merchant in Manchester,' Harold Wilson told me. 'Unemployment, more than anything else, made me politically conscious.'

Getting to university became even more precious when, in the nick of time, a job for his father saved Harold from becoming a shop assistant in Manchester. His father had finally found a job as chief chemist with Brotherton Ltd, a chemical firm in Bromborough in the Wirral, Cheshire, just across the Mersey from Liverpool. With the appointment went a lovely company house in a beautiful garden surrounded by trees on pleasant Spital Road. Having been twice saved – from death by typhoid and from a premature end to his studies by economic necessity – Harold might understandably have concluded there was some special Nonconformist deity protecting him.

He also had the advantage of moving to a better grammar school. Wirral Grammar School had only been opened the year before. All masters but the headmaster were under thirty. Harold was the first youngster to enter its sixth form. As a result he had individual tuition. 'If your school and staff can make their name with my son,' Herbert Wilson told the headmaster, 'good luck to both sides.'[30]

'Young Wilson was a remarkable lad,' recalled the deputy headmaster, O. Wilson. 'He could start with Sir Robert Walpole in 1721 and recite the entire list of Prime Ministers of England with the dates of their appointments. Wilson was far above average, both in class and in outside activities. He was the first Captain of the school.'[31] He was also a bit of a prig. At one point he was disturbed that boys in the fifth form were spending their lunch hours exchanging dirty jokes. Harold secured the approval of the headmaster to organize lunchtime soccer matches. This, he felt, helped evaporate his fellow pupils' preoccupation with sex.[32]

## HOPING FOR JESUS

Perhaps because the school lacked academic traditions or connections, the Head, Mr Moir, gave Harold one less-than-brilliant piece of advice. He urged Harold, at seventeen, to try for a history scholarship at Jesus College, Oxford – a half-Welsh college without great academic distinction. Harold worked hard through the summer of 1933 in preparation for the examination the next winter. He missed winning a full scholarship, perhaps because he was a year younger than average, but he won an Exhibition, which gave him £60 (instead of the £80 for Scholars) and entry to Jesus College. It was hoped he would secure the rest of the money by winning a county Major Scholarship, but he failed because, he felt, of a weak English paper. His Head unsuccessfully sought a special county grant for him. The Director of Education thought Harold too young and urged that he should try again next year, but he finally gave in and Harold was awarded a county grant. This left him only £50 short of his needs, a sum which his father agreed to make up.

If Harold seemed to be breaking all records for swotting at Oxford between 1934 and 1937 it was because he recognized that he was not there on his own, as an individual. He had the whole family's hopes invested in his success.

Harold started as he meant to go on. During his very first visit to Oxford he spoke to *all* the history dons in his college. He found he could settle in at Jesus because few of its undergraduates came from monied homes or from public schools. Most were Nonconformists from grammar schools, like himself. It had its own division – between its rough rugby players and its serious students. Harold was quite popular with the rugby types because, while very studious and competitive, he was generous in his help to less studious college mates. One of his contemporaries, turning out his university mementoes years later, found an essay in Harold's handwriting: 'Economic History – 1760–1900' marked 'J.H. Wilson, Jesus, Trinity Term, 1935'; it had been widely used by others as well.

As a northern Nonconformist Harold found it easier to adjust to ex-grammar school Welsh Nonconformists like the plumber's son with whom he shared a room at Jesus than to the products of southern public schools. Even in prewar Oxford the idle, noisy and free-spending sons of the rich were a minority compared with the quieter sons of the professional middle classes. But to a Northerner all glib Southerners sound alike. 'You cannot over-estimate the inferiority complex of the Northerner when he arrives at university and comes into contact for the first time with the trendy articulate, middle-class Southerners,' recalled a ministerial colleague of Harold's from a similar northern background.

'Because of his limits of speech and background, the Northerner tends to feel inferior and incapable of competing. He therefore tends to become more competitive out of desperation, thinking the Southerner's surface glibness a reflection of greater academic ability.'

Wilson soon won the regard of his tutors because of his combination of high intellectual ability with a capacity to work which was regarded as phenomenal in a university where hard work was considered rather degrading by the fashion-setters. It was regarded as phenomenal even by other grammar-school scholarship types. 'If you work eight hours a day,' Harold told a college mate on the train from Cheshire to Oxford, 'you'll do alright.' But he did not limit himself to eight hours. 'He worked all the hours that God gave,' recalled this contemporary at Jesus.

To help keep himself up to the mark he set for himself, Wilson made a compact with another Nonconformist undergraduate to check up on one another's use of time. They each wrote into a Boots' diary the number of hours of study they put in. When eight hours were totted up, the day was circled in red. When more than ten were chalked up, a blue circle was added. The one who worked the longest could retain the red-and-blue pencil for the duration of his supremacy. Harold retained it longer. On one occasion his co-competitor, Eric Clarke – who later became a Baptist Minister – worked eleven hours in one day. To recapture it Harold had to work twelve hours.[33]

The extent to which he considered himself to be his family's candidate at Oxford was demonstrated initially a few months after he had arrived. He telephoned his father. 'There's a new degree course here called Modern Greats. It's Philosophy, Politics and Economics. Do you think I should take it?' Herbert Wilson discussed it first with Harold's favourite former masters and then with his tutor, Goronwy Edwards, before giving his permission.[34] 'It was perfectly obvious that his interest was in economics,' Sir Goronwy later told the author. 'I said it would be a mistake not to let him change over.' So Harold changed from historian to economist, altering his future in so doing.

Soon the high opinion in which Harold was held by his tutors was taken up by his college mates. 'That's the man who will put Jesus on the map,' said a fellow-Welshman to Tom Williams, then at St Catherine's and later a colleague in the Commons. 'He will get one of the best Firsts of the century and wind up a Professor.'

This opinion was strengthened when Harold began winning prizes. His only failure came in his first year when he missed winning the Cecil Peace Prize with his essay on the private manufacture of armaments. In March 1936, in his second year, he won the Gladstone Memorial Prize with an 18,000-word essay on 'The State and the Railways, 1823–63'. In his researches at Gladstone's old home, Hawarden, he unearthed a draft Bill for nationalizing the railways drawn up by Gladstone when President of the Board of Trade. Harold, accoutred in white tie and tails, had to read a page from his winning essay at the degree ceremony of June 1936 under the proud eyes of his parents and in the presence of Sir Anthony Eden, who was awaiting an honorary degree.

Harold then spent the summer vacation of 1936 preparing material for the Webb–Medley Junior Economic Scholarship, worth £100 a year. He won it in October 1936, largely because he did very well in the field of economic organization, where his knowledge of the Colne Valley Cooperative movement proved a great strength and incidentally appealed to one of his examiners, G. D. H. Cole. This prize enabled him to become independent of his father's financial contribution.

While awarding him the prize, Cole warned Maurice Allen, Harold's tutor in Economics, that Harold had shown himself weak in economic theory, thus imperilling his chance of a First-Class Honours degree. As a practical Northerner Harold found economic theory both pointless and frustrating. So it required a particular effort for him to study even the assigned economists, much less those not assigned like Keynes or Marx. 'Although Keynes' *General Theory* came out in his second year, he did not read it and was not influenced by it,' insisted a close colleague. 'I've never read *Das Kapital*,' later boasted Wilson. 'I only got as far as page two – that's where the footnote is nearly a page long. I felt that two sentences of main text and a page of footnotes were too much.'[35] He was to repeat this boast, in almost identical terms, after retiring as Prime Minister.[36] But had either book been on the PPE reading list he undoubtedly would have read it.

He certainly approached Kant's *Critique of Pure Reason* differently. He worried about his ability to master it for his final examinations in Philosophy. So he decided to boil it down. First he compressed it to 150 foolscap pages. He then cut it to thirty, then twelve, and finally to four pages. He then committed the four-page summary to memory, and he gave the twelve-page summary to Teddy Jackson, an Oxford friend who was his closest rival for a First-Class degree in PPE. Both got the top mark, an Alpha, in Philosophy, and Harold had done a kindness without sacrificing his competitive edge. (Edward Jackson later became Director of the Oxford University Institute of Economics and Statistics.)

Finally, Harold's industriousness, his spectacular memory for facts and his unusual ability to marshal them paid off. He took nine papers for his degree, each of which was marked twice, independently. On one he even won an insufferable Alpha-plus, which some Oxford men have never encountered. On top of that he secured seven Alphas and one Beta treble plus. It was perhaps the best First-Class degree of the century.

Harold was proud. His tutors were pleased as Punch. His parents and girlfriend, Gladys Mary Baldwin, whom he'd met just before going up to Oxford, were bursting with pride. His graduation ceremony was a high spot in their lives.

Yet one cannot escape the feeling that he was something of an emotional cripple at the end of his Oxford ordeal of swotting; he had hardly allowed himself any time to enjoy the opportunities Oxford afforded outside the PPE syllabus. Contemporaries remember him going for solitary walks on Christ Church Meadow, swinging the cane he then affected. When Teddy Jackson and his girl-friend (and later wife) Anne Cloake came out of the cinema they knew that if they went to a particular snackbar for coffee after 10.30 p.m. they would find Harold there having his evening's sausage and mash. Although they were then 'going steady', Harold never thought that they might want to be alone and would draw up a chair to join them.

The extent to which Harold still felt in emotional bondage to his family was illustrated by a confrontation when he emerged from Oxford with the flying colours of probably the best First-Class degree recorded in fifty years. He wanted to go into journalism, an idea which he had been nursing since a trip with his mother to visit relations in Australia as a ten-year-old, as a result of which he had tried unsuccessfully to place articles in the *Scout Magazine* and elsewhere.

As he approached the end of his three years at university he approached R. B. McCullum, a leading Liberal who was his tutor in politics, about the possibility of getting a job on the *Manchester Guardian*. Although Dr McCallum thought of Wilson as a potentially highly-professional civil servant or academic, probably rising to Vice-Chancellor level, he agreed. He wrote to W. P. Crozier, Editor of the *Manchester Guardian*, who offered Wilson a three-month trial as a member of the paper's editorial writing staff in Manchester.[37]

When Harold disclosed this to his parents, they were dismayed. How could he go into so insecure a profession as journalism when his brilliant academic attainments opened up to him such secure professions as university teaching or the civil service? This argument was a telling one, because Harold's father had just lost his third job, at Brotherton's in the Wirral. Harold himself had helped him apply for (and secure) another, quite modest post as works manager of an explosives factory in Cornwall. Harold heeded his family's advice and wrote to W. P. Crozier to decline the leader-writing post. Instead he became Senior Research Fellow in Economics at New College, Oxford, soon upgraded to lecturer and tutor. The achievement of becoming a don at twenty-one was said to have been unequalled since the time of Cardinal Wolsey.[38]

## PROBLEMS OF A 'BEVERIDGE BOY'

Even for so ambitious and fast-rising a young man his next step further speeded his abnormal tempo. In May 1938 he was lured away from New College to University College, where the new Master was Sir William (later Lord) Beveridge. Sir William had brought to an end his stormy career at the London School of Economics, which he had expanded fairly ruthlessly, sacking people like Kingsley Martin, who became Editor of the *New Statesman*. Sir William was a Victorian reformer for whom the goal was more important than the manners used in attaining it. 'Such a despot needs a confidant on whom he must rely too much for his subordinate's liking,' wrote Kingsley Martin in his obituary of Beveridge.[39]

For two years Harold Wilson was that confidant and slave. Beveridge had asked John (later Lord) Fulton, then Fellow of Nuffield College, for a research assistant. Fulton asked Maurice Allen, Harold's ex-tutor, who recommended him. What Harold did not realize in advance was that becoming research assistant to Beveridge was more like joining a religious order – or the Communist Party. 'Beveridge was a difficult man ... difficult to get on with and intolerant of inefficiency or sloppy thinking. In a way it was best to keep working with him – engrossed and extended he was easier to get on with,' Wilson later recalled. 'Beveridge had a lot of influence on me. For instance, he taught me to work hard. I thought I knew what hard work was long before I met him, but I found I hadn't really started. One thing I learnt from him was that a great man does his own work. His own essential work, at any rate.'

'I was, of course, tremendously keen to work with him and equally keen to work on the subject which he had made his own, namely the statistical and administrative aspects of unemployment, which ... was and had been one very close to my heart as well as my head for years before I met Beveridge.' Beveridge was convinced that unemployment was mainly due to 'frictional' reasons – the inability of the unemployed to find the job which awaited him perhaps in another part of the country. Since Harold's father had had to move his family four times in pursuit of a job, this was naturally of personal interest. But he had a much earthier approach to the problem than Beveridge. 'I remember his face, very puzzled, one day after he had visited a camp for unemployed men. He said he couldn't understand why decent, able-bodied men like the ones we had seen *could* be out of work. He didn't want to face the real problem. He wanted to think in terms of frictional unemployment ... He didn't realize – until much later – that there was a fundamental problem of under-demand in the economy,' recalled Wilson later.[40]

Wilson soon found that Beveridge was ruthless in his pursuit of knowledge 'and drove me as hard as he drove himself in his work'.

Wilson was expected to work eighteen hours out of twenty-four, often using primitive but enormous wooden slide-rules for calculations. Although academics normally take long vacations neither Beveridge nor his assistant did so. Beveridge took Wilson down to 'Green Street', a lovely house on the Wiltshire Downs near ancient Avebury, site of the famous stone circle. Beveridge and his wife-to-be had first come there when he was Director of the LSE. Beveridge would rise at 6 a.m. and take a swim in the pool erected by what he called the 'free labour' of LSE students. 'From my experience of that labour,' Wilson later recalled, 'by other guests including myself, I think that "free labour" was a euphemism for "forced labour".

'I did not join him in this early plunge, but he followed it by making himself a cup of tea and kindly making me one. We then did two hours' work on the old faithful slide-rule. After breakfast again we worked solidly together till half past twelve when we had a viciously competitive game of deck tennis followed by a plunge into the still-cold, but now more tolerable, water.

'After lunch we did work of a more strenuous and less intellectual character – usually involving digging, painting – until about teatime. We then worked from tea to dinner on the trade cycle and after dinner – the part of the day I dreaded most – I was conscripted for bridge until fortunately the number of guests grew and I was able to escape ...

'He could sometimes be quite childish – childishly affectionate to those around him and childishly petulant. One day, Mrs Maire, later Lady Beveridge, allowed her motor mower to get out of control and it ran over Beveridge's beloved tweed jacket, turning the whole of the front of it into a very neat pattern of inch-wide brown ribbons. After a short and characteristic outburst, Beveridge sulked the whole afternoon and throughout tea, insisting on wearing the tweed jacket in its ruined state. Nor was there ever any forgiveness.

'Beveridge was "abrasive" to a degree. I was one of many close colleagues who sustained the abrasions, and in that role he had qualities which made the modern forms of carborundum look a pretty soft material ... An old LSE associate commented that I had stayed with him much longer than any other research assistant he had had and that I must have had unsuspected qualities of toughness. In fact, what I learned then ... was that the only way of dealing with downright rudeness was to ignore it, knowing that it would pass.'[41]

Young Wilson put up with this rudeness because he was learning not only statistical skills but also Beveridge's insights into how British Governments really work. Beveridge had joined the Board of Trade in 1910, having been recommended to Winston Churchill as 'a young man of ugly manners' but ability by Beatrice Webb. He had helped to set up the national network of Labour Exchanges. By the end of the First World War he was Permanent Secretary of the Board of Trade.

'Beveridge's conversation, fascinating to any young economics colleague, tended to go back to his early years in the civil service, with Churchill at the Board of Trade ... and his war years.... He told us with great excitement how food rationing was introduced in World War I on a basis, perhaps unusual for Beveridge, of total decentralization.... He was very anti-Treasury, because the Treasury had originally blocked his appointment to Permanent Secretary.... He had a number of theories about administration. One was that all problems were soluble, given enough staff. Having decided how the problem could be solved, you then had to decide whether its solution was worth that amount of staff...'

Young Wilson was worried because Beveridge, who was then past sixty, was getting fixed, rather potty ideas about how depressions started. 'He ... discovered that the downturn in almost every depression back to 1815 occurred at the same time of the year, the autumn, and this set him off, to my horror, on a new theory. I was not worried that he started looking to world agriculture for the explanation, but when he revived the sixty-year-old Jehovian theory of sun-spots I really got worried.'[42] Then Beveridge fell ill and this gave Wilson a chance to produce an alternative theory.

The last time they worked together was the summer of 1939. Young Wilson was working on a paper he was due to give to the British Association in September 1939 on the relationship between exports and imports in trade cycles, and how that affected employment. Harold had discovered that when certain Imperial raw materials collapsed in price, the British textile industry tended to start to buy less cotton in expectation of further falls, and also to produce less in expectation of a smaller market overseas.

'In the last days of August 1939 I drove North from Wiltshire to Dundee for the meeting of the British Association,' Beveridge later wrote, leaving out that his assistant Harold Wilson was travelling with him. 'The Soviet agreement with Hitler had been announced a few days before. In passing through a Scottish village, as I heard the baker on his round ringing his bell, I wondered how long the established simple life which his daily visit typified would go on.'[43]

The news of war itself came just after Harold had read his paper. 'It was, in fact, during the discussion on my paper on September 1, 1939,' Wilson later recalled, 'that a message was brought that Hitler had invaded Poland.'[44] Then came Neville Chamberlain's statement that Britain was at war with Nazi Germany. 'In Dundee, the British Association, after one night, decided to postpone the rest of their meeting and I drove back to Oxford to be at my post,' wrote Beveridge.

Beveridge could hardly wait for his country to call upon his administrative genius, which it did, reluctantly and belatedly.

For two years, then, Wilson had been exposed to the activities of what lay persons might call an 'egomaniac' and psychologists a 'narcissist'. Beveridge certainly fitted into Dr Erich Fromm's description of narcissism as 'a state of experience in which only the person himself, *his* feelings, *his* thoughts, *his* property, everything and everybody pertaining to *him* are experienced as fully real, while everything and everybody that does not form part of the person or is not an object of his needs is not interesting, is not fully real, is perceived only by intellectual recognition, while *affectively* without weight and colour.' Because Wilson served him, he had an importance to Beveridge.

'When the war came,' Wilson recalled, 'Beveridge was utterly frustrated by the fact that, as he felt a young man of sixty, he was not called upon. He stayed at Oxford with a high degree of frustration, snorting at the appointment of top administrators, many of whom had been his juniors in World War I.'[45] Beveridge's self-centredness was such that he even interrupted the Wilsons' brief honeymoon in January 1940. Harold and his bride, Gladys Mary, had spent a week at a small hotel in the Cotswolds walking in the snow by day and nursing their colds before an open fire in the evening, when a telegram came from Beveridge. This reminded Harold that urgent academic work awaited his attention at Oxford. Harold and Mary meekly returned to Oxford.

## HELP INTO WHITEHALL

Although Beveridge himself was not immediately called upon to return to Whitehall he was of considerable help to Harold, who had volunteered for military service. However, the Oxford University Military Recruiting Board pointed him in the direction of the civil service, which was expanding enormously with the demands of wartime mobilization.

Harold's first appointment in March 1940 was at the Ministry of Supply. His performance there was more sparkling than the job itself. The Director of Statistics asked him whether he had read an article on the mobilization of the war economy in that week's *Economist*, and how he would summarize. Wilson did this so well that the Director looked startled; he then admitted that he had helped Beveridge write it. Wilson was taken on.

His two years with Beveridge had convinced him that Whitehall was not just a group of buildings but an endless arrangement of what C. P. Snow later tagged 'the corridors of power'. He soon discovered that such corridors can have dead ends. Finding his job boring he accepted the offer of a more interesting post at a higher grade in the Ministry of Food from John Maude (later Baron Redcliffe-Maud), who had been a

Fellow and Dean at University College. Two months later, still waiting to transfer, he discovered that his superiors had told Food that he did not want to move – without consulting him.

In the end his Beveridge connection enabled him to escape. One evening Harold was invited out by three members of the Cabinet Secretariat. One of these, Lionel (later Lord) Robbins, he knew through Beveridge, the other two he had met at the British Association the previous summer. He agreed to join their new staff. He was made Joint Secretary of the Anglo-French Coordination Committee, whose job it was to report on supply routes to endangered France.

With the emergence of Churchill as Prime Minister in May 1940 a new chance was given to Beveridge and others who had hunted with Winston in the First World War. 'In fact,' Beveridge wrote later, 'the change of Government brought all the "old dogs" sooner or later into some kind of harness again.' Beveridge turned down the first offer, from Ernest Bevin, to organize factory welfare. Instead he wanted to do a survey of manpower available for war mobilization. By August 1940 a Manpower Requirements Committee had been set up with Beveridge as its Chairman. 'They allowed me to have as Secretary of the Committee,' Beveridge wrote, 'my first-class research assistant from Oxford, Harold Wilson.'[46] Frank Pakenham (later Lord Longford) was named Joint Secretary with Wilson. In December 1940 Wilson was transferred to the Cabinet Office Secretariat.

At times it seemed as though the whole university world had been dumped into Whitehall, where they had unprecedented opportunities to commune. 'By day we worked, by night we slept in a shelter below Scotland Yard,' Wilson later reminisced. He found Lionel Robbins a great asset because of his fund of anecdotes. One was about how he learned that he was to become a Professor at LSE in a letter from Hugh Dalton after the latter had spent a weekend walking with Beveridge on the Wiltshire Downs. 'Beveridge and I went for a long walk,' Dalton had written. 'He fiddled with his cock and said: "I am going to make Robbins a Professor."' Wilson found this amusing because he was so familiar with the gesture Beveridge made as a result of wearing too tight underwear.

Although he seldom has referred to this, Wilson's rapid initial rise in the wartime civil service owed not a little to the influence of Beveridge and others from Oxford. 'At Christmas 1940,' Beveridge recalled later, 'I found myself summoned hastily to the Ministry of Labour. One of the Under Secretaries had fallen ill. I was asked to fill the gap.'[47] As a result of this unexpected switch by Beveridge, Wilson emerged as chief of the Manpower Statistics Branch of the Ministry of Labour, at the incredibly young age of twenty-four.

But the Minister of Labour, tough trade-union boss Ernest Bevin, did not enjoy the aggressive egotism of Beveridge. He resisted in particular Beveridge's insistence on the need to conscript women. By June 1941 Bevin had squeezed Beveridge out of his Department. This made it advisable for Wilson to look elsewhere.

Oxford again provided, with Beveridge urging him on towards John Fulton, former Balliol tutor, who was then serving as Assistant Secretary of the Mines Department of the Board of Trade. In June 1941 Sir Andrew Duncan, a Scottish company director and Tory MP, became President of the Board of Trade. He discovered, on going into a conference on the critical coal situation, that the statistics provided him by his own Mines Department were hopelessly out of date. He discussed this with John Fulton. 'There is a good chap who used to work with Beveridge,' suggested Fulton. 'How old is he?' 'About twenty-five.' 'Why isn't he in the Army?' 'Because the Oxford University Recruiting Board assigned him to the civil service.'[48] As a result, Wilson joined the Mines Department as chief of its Statistical Department in the autumn of 1941 at the age of twenty-five.

Although his Oxford friends had given him a leg-up, Wilson knew that it was now up to him to demonstrate what he could do by showing the usefulness of statistics in the battle for more coal production during the war. His weapons to hand were incredibly primitive. 'The Mines Department's prime weapon was a cylindrical wooden slide-rule, too heavy to hold in the hand, mounted at an angle on a spiky base, like a Crimean War mortar, and equivalent to a flat rule eighty-three feet four inches long. My chief of staff one day produced a departmental minute from World War I showing that not one, but two had been ordered at that time, and one of the two was not accounted for. An air-raid, which caused some confusion, unearthed it – it was in a box propping up my desk,' Wilson later recalled.[49]

Yet statistics were crucial for the battle to increase coal production, which had suddenly slumped. The coal industry had been in a crisis which the war had intensified by disrupting its overseas markets and stripping it of its most active miners. The collapse of France and the entry of Italy into the war in 1940 lost these additional markets, resulting in the closing of an additional hundred mines. Low wages in the mines resulted in the drift of miners into better-paid war production. By the spring of 1941 a shortage in the supply of coal needed for war production began to show itself. Miners were ordered to register and then ordered back to the mines, although for many it meant a cut in wages.

Wilson's position as the Mines Department's chief statistician put him in conflict with the mine-owners as soon as he began to get a flow of correct figures moving. 'Up to that time, in accordance with the Government's purely passive role in coal matters,' he later recalled, 'the collection of figures of absenteeism was left to the owners, and these were presented in a way which was, to say the least of it, misleading and contentious.' Wilson discovered some of the statistical tricks the owners got up to in order to discredit the miners. Thus, they concentrated attention on the growth of shifts lost through absenteeism without pointing out that many more shifts were being worked. The mine-owners, he discovered, were trying to prove that 'the only way to get coal from the mines is to keep wages as low as possible.'[50] 'Coal, even in wartime, was an intensely political issue,' Wilson later recalled. 'Coalowners and unions, MPs, even in a Coalition Parliament, fought it out on a naked basis of class war. But the coalmasters, grouped in the Mining Association, dominated by the veterans of [the general strike of] 1926, had the figures.'[51]

Fortunately for the war effort this attitude did not affect the President of the Board of Trade, Sir Andrew Duncan, who was the Tory MP for the City and had been a Director of the Bank of England and of ICI. He had learned the realities of the industry as Coal Controller in the wake of the First World War.

'I was closest to Sir Andrew,' Harold Wilson later told me. They got on very well because Sir Andrew greatly admired the efficiency of Harold's work. 'Every Monday morning he would get on the telephone and reach every mine in the country, securing their latest statistics,' John Fulton told me. 'By teatime on Monday he would provide Sir Andrew with the up-to-the-hour statistics which he could take into the Coal Production Council.' 'I've lived through three generations of statisticians,' Sir Andrew told Fulton. 'But Wilson represents the new generation – one that can see the administrative significance of accurate statistics.' Sir Andrew, Wilson later recalled, 'was a smooth operator. Still more, he was a statistical operator. One meeting a week on Monday at five – hence my time-table – gave him control. He operated through [me as] the Director of Statistics and [the Assistant Secretary of the Mines Department] John Fulton, now Lord Fulton. And control was complete.'[52]

Wilson was at his best in negotiations and meetings where, according to a fellow civil servant, he counted on his superior information to steam-roller results. Consequently he had no great liking for competitive brainy operators. After a meeting he would tear back to his office, order the other people out and then dictate like mad. Outside work he showed no cultural interests and, as at university, he did virtually no reading that was not connected with his work. His wife, Mary, seldom appeared on the scene; she was very much the little housewife who did not want to be involved in Whitehall battles. What distinguished Harold from other academics turned wartime civil servants was that he had political 'feel', an instinct for the key issue at the core of the problem faced.

By February 1942, when Sir Andrew made way for Hugh Dalton, Wilson's reputation had been established. Dalton, the son of the Canon of Windsor, had been both a Labour MP and a lecturer at LSE, and had met Wilson at Beveridge's bungalow at Avebury. Dalton wrote in his diary about the Board of Trade he was taking over: 'Among the junior officials at the Mines Department was Harold Wilson, a don at University College, Oxford, who had worked with Beveridge, and was now showing a gift for forecasting, with quite uncanny accuracy, our monthly coal output.'[53]

Harold Wilson became increasingly fascinated by Whitehall in-fighting, in which personalities, policies and economics became interlocked. When he met Oxford friends in Westminster he would regale them with the manoeuvres of 'big Hugh' (Dalton) and 'little Hugh' (Gaitskell, Dalton's *chef du cabinet* or Principal Private Secretary).

Dalton's own unpublished diaries – more intimate and detailed than the three volumes of extracts published – make clear that Wilson himself was involved in the battle over personalities and policies. Thus, in March 1942, Deputy Prime Minister Clement Attlee told Dalton that the Prime Minister, Winston Churchill, wanted to drop Dai Grenfell, his ineffective Secretary for Mines, whose sole qualification was that he had been a miner and miners' agent. Dalton had lunch with Sir Andrew Duncan to get his opinion. Sir Andrew was against dropping Grenfell but in favour of strengthening the department's civil servants. He urged Dalton to 'ask H. Wilson for some bright new No. 1 from outside. For No. 2 he would move up Fulton. He would also promote Wilson to be Director of Programmes.'[54]

Wilson was able to observe closely the activities of Dalton, his chief, in bringing in fuel rationing. Dalton could use people even if he disliked them personally. Thus he called in William Beveridge to draw up a fuel rationing scheme, at the suggestion of Gaitskell and Fulton. But Dalton grew irritated by his 'daily dose of Beveridge'. 'He is very troublesome.' 'It all lasts a very long time and B[everidge] is very difficult and feminine ... full of egoism and petulance ... He is a most tiresome man ...' '"Not really a very nice human being," says H[ugh] G[aitskell].'[55] Despite this, Wilson observed, 'Hugh Dalton ... was prepared to take strong measures with the problem'[56] of fuel rationing, along the lines recommended by Beveridge.

Wilson developed an increasing respect for his new chief as an effective 'operator'. 'He immediately accepted the need for coal rationing,' Wilson wrote.[57] Dalton squared Sir Stafford Cripps, then

Leader of the House, on the publication of Beveridge's Report on fuel rationing. He then saw the Report through two meetings of the War Cabinet's sub-committee on coal. Then, in the War Cabinet meeting of 27 April 1942, he had the support of the Prime Minister for rationing. 'Don't let them form up on you,' said Churchill, '... we must all stand together.' When the Report on Fuel Rationing came out next day, Beveridge himself handled the briefing of Lobby journalists. Dalton helped: 'I spent some time and a number of drinks in squaring the D[aily] H[erald] – [its Editor, Percy] Cudlipp and [its Political Correspondent] M[aurice] Webb.'[58] 'The Government's decision to introduce rationing forthwith was announced in the House [of Commons] and was loudly cheered,' recorded Wilson.[59]

Suddenly the atmosphere changed. 'A word with Rab [Butler] who says the Tories are against fuel rationing because they are afraid that it will mean that they won't get enough for their country houses,' Dalton recorded.[60] But Wilson found deeper motives. 'It was rumoured inside and outside Parliament that [Dalton] felt the only hope of solving the coal problem was to take over the mines for the duration.'[61] 'It is clear that the coal-owners are spending a lot of money trying to get rid of me,' Dalton confided to his diary.[62]

The coal-owners had indeed persuaded a lot of the Tory MPs – who had two-thirds of the seats in the Commons – of the danger of fuel rationing leading to the wartime requisitioning and ultimate nationalization of the mines. In the Cabinet meeting of 12 May 1942 Churchill switched his position and resisted coal rationing. A week later Sir Stafford Cripps told Dalton that Churchill, whom he now described as 'most reactionary' on coal, was against introducing rationing until December to avoid upsetting the coal-owners or the Tory Party. Sir Andrew Duncan took the same viewpoint.[63]

A confrontation was avoided when the Cabinet meeting of 29 May 1942 set up a new Ministry of Fuel and Power to handle coal, petroleum, gas and electricity. Its Director of Economics and Statistics, with the civil service rank of Principal, was twenty-seven-year-old Harold Wilson. Wilson discovered, to his surprise, that he had been recommended for the job by Hugh Gaitskell, then Dalton's chief aide. Wilson had feared that he would be out of favour in the Dalton menage because of the increasing irritation that Dalton had displayed towards Beveridge, Wilson's sponsor. Dalton had hardly been able to disguise his glee when he had heard from Beveridge a fortnight before 'the not unwelcome news' that he wanted to 'regain his freedom to speak and write ... With an appearance of reluctance and broken-heartedness, I acquiesced.'[64]

Wilson was able to give himself and his new Ministry 'a good send-off', as he has described it, by serving as Joint Secretary of the Board of Investigation into Miners' Wages. This Board after only ten days' deliberation, produced the first ever national minimum wage for miners – of £4 3s – and a flat-rate wage increase and output bonus, which, Wilson complained, was 'generally but incorrectly described as the "Greene Award"'[65] He meant that the Board's Chairman, Master of the Rolls Lord Greene, was a nonentity with little knowledge of the mining industry. Wilson did all the real work, as was appreciated by his old boss, Hugh Dalton, and his new chief at Fuel and Power, Gwilym Lloyd-George, the National Liberal son of the 'Welsh Wizard'.

It was on this Board that Harold first got to know the miners' leaders, including Will Lawther of Durham, Sam Watson of Yorkshire, Jim Griffiths of South Wales and Tom Swain, then Vice-President of the Derbyshire Miners. Some found Wilson a 'college boy' and rather 'academic'. Swain even found him 'intellectually arrogant' with a tendency to talk down to men who had gone to work from elementary school. Jim Griffiths, by then a Labour MP, found that Harold, because of his wartime exposure to the mine-owners, was moving towards the need to nationalize the mines. 'Wilson is pre-eminently a pragmatist,' Griffiths told me in 1972, 'and he came to coal nationalization pragmatically rather than out of ideological conviction.' The late Sir Will Lawther was more blunt: 'He did a helluva good job. I think Lord Greene told him to get to know us. Harold used to meet with us and talk. He got his socialist outlook then.'

This friendly reception from some mineworkers' leaders did not guarantee a friendly reception in the newly-formed Ministry, particularly from older and more conservative civil servants. To be appointed a Director of Economics and Statistics with the rank of Principal at the age of twenty-seven got up the noses of older permanent civil servants. One of these was Reuben Kelf-Cohen, twenty years his senior and Principal Assistant Secretary for Gas and Electricity in the new Ministry. When Harold started to produce monthly fuel statistics limited to coal, Kelf-Cohen telephoned him from his Bloomsbury office to complain that he had ignored gas and electricity. 'I will be glad to include gas and electricity, if you will let me have your statisticians in the field down here on the Millbank,' Kelf-Cohen recalls Wilson replying. Kelf-Cohen declined, complaining that he needed the statisticians for day-to-day work. When this dispute was taken up with the Permanent Secretary, Michael Tribe, the latter allowed Kelf-Cohen to retain his statisticians and Wilson's statistics remained limited to coal. But Kelf-Cohen, a right-wing Conservative if one is to judge by his subsequent writings in the *Daily Telegraph*, concluded that Wilson was 'a first-class intriguer' who kept himself in 'the good books of [Gwilym] Lloyd-George', the Minister. Wilson does not deny that he had an inside track. 'Perhaps I was the only [civil servant] who was instructed to report direct to the Minister, Gwilym Lloyd-George, bypassing the Permanent Secretary and the Director General. I was sufficiently house-trained to send carbons to their private offices. And it helped that I shared an air-raid shelter with the then Principal Private Secretary.'[66]

Wilson was refining the knowledge acquired from Beveridge about how to operate in the 'corridors of power' in Whitehall. 'I found that experience of the civil service invaluable.... I learned that for about three months the civil servants study a new Minister to see where he is vulnerable, so that they shall be able to play on it whenever they want to break him down, get control of him when any issue comes up in which he is particularly interested.'[67]

But Wilson did not limit himself to accumulating desiccated statistics or practising Whitehall in-fighting. By investigating complaints he discovered the realities behind the statistics. 'One of the most respected of miners' leaders ... told me that this [absenteeism] occurred in the last war' due to the absence of goods worth working for in local shops. 'Absenteeism for a cold or a headache was quite common in his own family. After the war, when there were goods in the shops again, it would have taken a broken leg for him or one of his brothers to have the day off,' Wilson recorded after talking to Will Lawther.[68]

## THE TURN TOWARDS POLITICS

Some time in 1943 Harold Wilson decided he would prefer to take the risks of becoming a politician rather than stay on the secure path toward the top of the civil service or the academic profession set for him by his parents. 'I saw that, in spite of the importance of the civil service, the role of the Minister was crucial. Under a strong Minister, things got done ... I worked very closely with four Ministers. Two of them – one was Labour [Hugh Dalton], one was Conservative [Sir Andrew Duncan] – got things done. Two of them, one Labour [Dai Grenfell], one Tory [Gwilym Lloyd-George] didn't. They were all getting the same quality advice and information from their civil servants but, as I say, two got things done, two didn't.... If you wanted to be sure of getting things done, you had better go into politics.'[69] 'What I learnt in those days ... was this: you can always get someone to find the answers to the questions, what you need in Government ... is the man who knows the questions to the answers.'[70]

In December 1943 Harold decided to discuss his possible future as a politician with Sir William Beveridge, who was facing a similar problem. By this time Beveridge had been converted from an angry wasp buzzing in the ears of impatient Ministers into a national hero, as a result of his Beveridge Report on the need for postwar social security. 'The Report,' Wilson later commented, 'produced with exemplary speed, characteristic clarity and launched with something of Beveridge's not inconsiderable gifts for showmanship, hit Britain at the moment when it was most needed, when a nation determined to win a war, capable of bearing the sacrifices of war, was beginning to ask to be reassured about the kind of Britain that would follow the war ... What it did was to make Beveridge overnight a national figure, no longer the possession of the administrative cognoscenti or of a small radical sect, but a figure, a symbol of something new.... But I think those closest to him at this time would feel that the heady wine of popular acclaim had in some ways proved too much for him. Once again he had shown that he – and in this context it could be said he alone – had found the answer to one of our great problems.' It is so much easier to be objective about the narcissism of others.

Wilson found that he and Beveridge were thinking in similar ways. 'It was at this time – as he told me when I met him in December 1943 – that he was thinking of entering Parliament, though as late as that month his expectations, following discussions with [Labour political boss and Home Secretary] Herbert Morrison, were that he would be fighting the next general election as a candidate for London University on the Labour ticket, or as Beveridge would have hoped, a radical ticket.'[71] Wilson was able to tell Beveridge that his own name was being put forward for the Labour Party's list of potential Parliamentary candidates, perhaps the first time he had disclosed to Beveridge his formal Labour allegiance. He was being sponsored by James Parker, Labour MP for Dagenham and General Secretary of the Fabian Society, and Tom Smith, the ex-miner who was Parliamentary Secretary for Fuel and Power, the Ministry in which Wilson worked. Beveridge expressed himself as delighted. But Wilson kept this a secret from other friends and colleagues, particularly in the civil service, which was supposed to be non-political.

Wilson was so anxious about his new career that, having been selected for Ormskirk – between Liverpool and Manchester – in September 1944, he made an unusual blunder. He allowed himself to be adopted formally on 1 October 1944. When he returned to London the civil service authorities were bleak. It was pointed out to him that it was a rule that once a civil servant had been adopted formally – as distinct from being selected – it was incumbent on him to resign from the non-political civil service. Other wartime civil servants – like Hugh Gaitskell – had been selected but not formally adopted. So, much against his will, Wilson was compelled to resign from the civil service forthwith. His resentment boiled up in a lecture to naval officers at Greenwich in January 1945, attended by J. P. W. Mallalieu, then an officer but later to be a colleague on the Labour benches. Wilson, who was lecturing brilliantly to the officers on the coal industry, in order to support his family, described himself as having been 'sacked' from the civil service.

It was not easy for a relatively well-paid senior civil servant of twenty-eight, with a dependent wife, a small son (his first son Robin had been born in 1943) and a father in Cornwall who needed help, suddenly to finance himself whilst awaiting a still uncertain election for an uncertain seat. Harold therefore applied to return to University College, from which he had obtained leave for the duration of the war. There was some objection to his returning, since he wanted to become an MP. In fact, the College had enacted a rule in 1944 that no MP could hold a position in the College. This was directed against Sir William Beveridge, who had just won a seat at Berwick as a Liberal. But Harold claimed that he was not likely to win Ormskirk from the widely-popular journalist–author Commander Stephen King-Hall. This was accepted and he became Domestic Bursar, responsible for the College's catering finances. He sank his humiliation into working on *A New Deal for Coal*.

Wilson's success at the 1945 general election and his immediate appointment as a junior Minister drew a veil over his unusually clumsy mistake. All that he had had to do was to avoid formal adoption proceedings, as all the other Labour candidates in the wartime civil service had done. By making that mistake he had put paid to any hope of a professional career in the upper reaches of the civil service and severely damaged his academic career possibilities as well.

Psychologists tell us that there is no 'immaculate conception' of such catastrophic errors. A psychologist might find this action typical of a 'narcissist', so preoccupied with *his* need to find expression as a politician that the normal rules of the very civil service he could ordinarily manipulate so skilfully lose their weight and colour in his perception. 'A person, to the extent that he is narcissistic, has a double standard of perception,' writes Dr Erich Fromm. 'Only he himself and what pertains to him has significance, while the rest of the world is more or less weightless or colourless, and because of this double standard, the narcissistic person shows severe defects in judgment and lacks the capacity for objectivity.'

Or was it more simple? Had it simply been Wilson's secretiveness about his new Labour enthusiasm, even with Labour supporters among his old Oxford colleagues, that led him astray? Could it have been that, because he did not confide in them, they could not set him right on the need to avoid the pitfall of formal adoption?

# IV. Right, Left, or Flexible Centre?

'D'Arcy: I'm in politics. I'm a ruddy MP.
'Lt. Commander Peter Fraser: God help our native land! Which side, if any?
'D'Arcy: Socialist, of course ... Wormskirk ... It's in Lancashire, near
   Liverpool.
'Fraser: Why "of course"?
'One has to keep in with the ruling classes, old man.'
   *Off The Record*, a comedy by Ian Hay and Stephen King-Hall (whom
   Wilson defeated at *Ormskirk*)[1]

Few politicians who have been on the political stage for over thirty years
and at or near the centre of it for over twenty-five have so confused
observers as to where they stand as Sir Harold Wilson. As he handed
over the lead part in the spring of 1976 newspapers which had long
accused him of being the 'tool of the union bosses' suddenly decided
that his Resignation Honours list demonstrated that he was a pal of the
tycoons.

This uncertainty arose in part because Sir Harold, like most politicians, could orate on one level and act on another. Thus, six months
after he retired as Prime Minister he boasted to Terry Coleman of how
he had frustrated the proposals of Labour's National Executive to
nationalize some insurance companies and banks. He sent for a 'garden
girl' – one of the typists on the garden floor of Number 10 – and
dictated first a letter to himself and then its answer. He sent these to the
insurance companies and the banks, making it clear that if they sent him
the same sort of inquiring letter they would get the same sort of
reassuring answer in reply. In this way he publicly repudiated the
decision of the party's National Executive.[2]

Sir Harold, like most serious politicians, has a complex of attitudes.
Thus, he is as strongly pro-NATO and pro-US on defence issues as he
is pro-Russian on trade matters. This sort of conflict is not unusual.
Gaitskell's fervent opposition to the EEC put him out of step with most
of the other 'Gaitskellites'. Sir Winston Churchill was in advance of his
Conservative colleagues on resistance to fascism but behind them on
resistance to Indian and other colonial nationalisms.

Where Sir Harold has sometimes surprised even those closest to him has been in the layer of secrecy or half-truth which has overlain the conflict of political attitudes within him. A revealing incident occurred in Whitehall just after he was adopted as the prospective Labour candidate for Ormskirk in October 1944. Wilson ran into Teddy and Anne Jackson, who were then working as civil servants. At Oxford, where Teddy had – like Wilson – earned First-Class Honours in PPE, he had tried without success to persuade Wilson to leave the Liberal Party and join Oxford's Labour Club, then very left-wing. Now Wilson, bursting with pride, told Teddy and Anne that he had been adopted as a candidate. 'For which party?' was their immediate query. Jackson did not know that, shortly after he failed to get Harold into the Labour Club, Wilson had joined the more moderate Oxford City Labour Party. Not once during their many wartime encounters in Whitehall had Harold disclosed his political convictions or ambitions.

This reaction was almost identically duplicated in July 1945, just after the general election had swept Labour into power. Wilson ran into Frank Byers, coming off a bus. They too had been friendly at Oxford, particularly when Harold was active in the Liberal Party there. In the normal way Byers asked Wilson what he was doing. Harold replied that he was an MP – like Byers. 'For which party?' asked Byers, knowing he was not part of the small Liberal contingent in the Commons.

One or both of these encounters clearly reached Commander Stephen King-Hall, the Independent journalist whom Wilson had defeated at Ormskirk in the 1945 general election. He satirized Wilson as 'D'Arcy', the opportunist Labour MP for 'Wormskirk', in his comic play, *Off the Record*.

Yet neither Wilson's secrecy nor his friends' subsequent surprise should have been necessary. The movement of Northern Non-conformists from the Liberals to Labour had been going on for over twenty years, and it was particularly marked in areas like Lancashire and Yorkshire, where the Wilson family had its roots. Harold Wilson's grandparents were pillars of the Liberal and Nonconformist movements in Manchester. Harold's paternal grandfather, James, had moved to Openshaw, near Manchester, from York after marrying Eliza Jane Thewlis, the daughter of a Huddersfield mill-owner. James Wilson started very modestly, first as a warehouseman, then as a draper. He had four children, including Herbert, Harold's father, who was born in 1882.

Mrs James Wilson's more prosperous brother, James Herbert Thewlis, a local umbrella manufacturer, became Lord Mayor of Manchester in 1906. He was also Chairman of the Liberals in the Northwest Manchester constituency, where Winston Churchill was fighting as a famous new convert from Toryism to Liberalism. A radical Liberal himself, James Wilson unsuccessfully fought the 1906 election. Rumbustious political controversy became a family tradition. Harold's father and uncle were thrown out of a Conservative meeting in Manchester because they kept raising points of order about the right of a Tory brewer to drape the platform with a Union Jack.

Harold's grandfather, James, also became a Vice-President of the Nonconformist brotherhood called the PSA for 'Pleasant Sunday Afternoon'. In Manchester, Liberalism and Nonconformism tended to be almost interchangeable. 'The day after the 1906 election results came out,' Harold later recalled, 'my grandfather – he was a Sunday school superintendent – chose for the hymn, "Sound the loud timbrel o'er Egypt's dark sea! Jehovah has triumphed – his people are free".'[3]

Herbert Wilson, Harold's father, was as enthusiastic a radical Liberal as his father. From the age of ten he had participated in anti-Tory activities by distributing Liberal handbills. At twenty-six, in 1908, he was given a chance to show his mettle when he became Sub-Agent of the Northwest Manchester constituency association of which his uncle, James Herbert Thewlis, was Chairman. His trial by fire came in the famous by-election lost there by Winston Churchill in 1908. This took place because Herbert Asquith, in forming his new Cabinet, offered Churchill a post in it. According to the practice of the time a Cabinet appointment required the endorsement of a by-election. Churchill lost his seat in a stormy campaign enlivened by the activities of local suffragettes. Churchill himself went off to represent Dundee.

By that time Herbert Wilson had been married for two years to Ethel Seddon, the schoolmistress daughter of William and Elizabeth Seddon, whom he had first met in chapel while she was still a pupil teacher. Her folk, the Seddons, were Lancashire railway employees – engine drivers, fitters, coalmen and clerks.[4] Most of these Seddons later migrated to Australia because of the bronchitis suffered by Harold's uncle.

The young Wilsons, Herbert and Ethel, both worked for a time. But when Ethel was expecting her first child, daughter Marjorie, she gave up her job as a teacher in 1909 and they relied on Herbert's pay as an industrial chemist. It was therefore all the more of a blow when he lost his job in Manchester in 1912. Unable to find another locally he moved with his family some thirty miles away over the Pennines into Yorkshire, where he found a job as a works chemist in Milnsbridge, a drab suburb of attractive Huddersfield. 'Huddersfield is the handsomest by far of all the factory towns of Yorkshire and Lancashire, by reason of its charming situation and modern architecture,' wrote Manchester-based Friedrich Engels in his book, *The Condition of the Working Class*.

Although there was no doubt about Herbert Wilson's continuing

Liberal allegiance, he was not active locally in the Liberal cause in Milnsbridge or in Huddersfield, where Harold was born in 1916. This was partly because Herbert Wilson was very busy manufacturing and safely transporting picric acid for the millions of shells consumed in the First World War. But it was also because, with a young family, he had no desire to incur the wrath of the Conservative factory-owners.

It was not as though the area itself, the Colne Valley, was inhospitable to Herbert Wilson's form of radical Liberalism. No Conservative had ever represented the Colne Valley in the House of Commons. As long ago as 1895 it had given 1,500 votes to Labour's Tom Mann. In 1907 it had shocked the country and set itself alight by returning the controversial left-wing socialist Victor Grayson at a by-election. But having lost one job already Herbert Wilson preferred to keep his political opinions within the family.

'I was profoundly affected by my father's political views and education of me,' Harold Wilson recalled later.[5] On a visit to Stirling, the former seat of the radical Liberal Prime Minister, Sir Henry Campbell-Bannerman, Herbert Wilson enthralled his young son with the story of how the Liberals had massacred the Tories in 1905.[6] But Harold Wilson was born in 1916, the year when David Lloyd George became wartime Prime Minister of the Liberal-Conservative coalition government. He therefore quickly began to experience his father's disappointment with Lloyd George's Government, in particular with its brutalities against the Irish and the Indians, the betrayal of its promises of a 'land fit for heroes', and its refusal to help the unemployed who multiplied with the end of the war.

Harold Wilson has tended to play down his family's basic commitment to radical Liberalism by playing up the exceptional circumstance of the Philip Snowden candidacy in the Colne Valley in 1923. 'The first time I can remember thinking systematically about politics was when I was seven. I was in hospital with appendicitis,' Harold Wilson emphasized to a biographer. 'My parents came to see me the night after my operation and I told them not to stay too long or they'd be too late to vote – for Philip Snowden.'[7] The family was leaning towards voting for this persuasive Labour moderate contesting the Colne Valley, because Wilson senior was dismayed by the split in the Liberal Party which took place after the Conservatives had dumped Lloyd George in 1922. The woollen mills in the valley were on short time and it was thought that Snowden and Labour might bring pressure for help. Although the Wilsons were willing to deviate from their basic Liberal allegiance on this occasion they were delayed by fog on their return from seeing Harold in hospital and so did not contribute to the re-election of

Snowden, who served as Chancellor of the Exchequer in Ramsay MacDonald's first Labour Government.

In fact, of course, the moderate, non-Marxist wing of Labour was adapting itself to the chapel culture of the northern working and managerial classes. This adaptation was very important for families like the Wilsons. 'I was impregnated with Nonconformity,' is the way Harold Wilson has summed it up. 'I have religious beliefs, yes. But I'm no theologian ... I'd always taken my own religious views for granted.... I'd never had any emotional or intellectual crisis which made me think them out.'[8] He later insisted that, at the age of forty-four, his religious views were the same as they had been when he was in the chapel Scout Group thirty years before.

Chapel-going – with its Scouts, dramatics and operatics – had no relationship to the once-a-week or four-times-a-year lipservice of more sophisticated Anglican types. Grace was said before meals. Church and Sunday school were attended every Sunday. After the Sunday evening service friends would come in for hymn-singing. During the week his parents were deeply involved in the chapel's many activities. His mother was a founder and organizer of the Women's Guild, a Guide Captain as well as a Sunday School teacher. His father once more became a Sunday School teacher after his period of war-induced overtime. Herbert Wilson also became the chapel's 'Rover Scout Leader' and eventually District Commissioner for the Scouts. Mrs Wilson became Secretary of the chapel's Amateur Operatic Society, and Harold's sister, Marjorie, became a Guide, a Guide Captain and, eventually, a District Commissioner.

This chapel activity was nothing new for either of Harold's parents. They had both been staunch Congregationalists in Manchester, where they had been Sunday School teachers in the Lees Street Congregational Chapel in Openshaw. The Reverend Robert Sutton there had married Ethel's parents, christened Ethel and married Ethel and Herbert. Therefore, although Harold himself was born in Milnsbridge, Huddersfield, he was taken back to Openshaw to be christened. There was no Congregational Church in Milnsbridge, so the focus of the Wilson family's religio-social activities became the Milnsbridge Baptist Church which, they felt, was the closest in its Nonconformism.

One feature of the Baptist Church's activity obviously had a big impact on young Harold: its Amateur Operatic Society, which paid a two-guinea royalty annually to the D'Oyly Carte Company. His liking for Gilbert and Sullivan was to be the high spot in his musical taste. 'By the age of six,' he later mused, 'I was word-perfect in *Pirates* – Major-General's song and all.'[9] One of his first jobs was as call-boy. 'With

Wilson as call-boy,' reminisced the Operatic Society's producer, 'there was never any fear of the performers missing their cue.'

## POLITICAL AMBITIONS

Partly because of his father's interest, partly because of the time and area in which he lived, young Harold began expressing political ambitions very early. The fact that he was photographed in front of Number 10 Downing Street at the age of eight shows more of his father's thinking than Harold's at that point. 'You know, in 1923, when Harold was eight and a half, I took him to London to see the Wembley Exhibition. We travelled up from Huddersfield by motorbike and sidecar. His mother had a party of Girl Guides at the Exhibition. Well, I took him to Westminster Bridge, and Harold had threepennyworth peering at the face of "Big Ben" through the telescope there. Then we went to Westminister. I took him round to Downing Street. At that time there was a great craze among Americans for knocking on the door and running away. Ramsay Mac was PM, you know. Well, I took this picture of young Harold standing on the steps of Number 10. I had my folding "Brownie".'[10]

When Harold was twelve the local Education Officer, Mr Thornber, asked the bright young student at Royds Hall: 'What do you want to be when you're older?' 'Chancellor of the Exchequer,' replied Harold. 'Where does he live, at 9 or 11 Downing Street?'[11] He then wrote an essay, 'Myself in Twenty-five Years'. In this he imagined himself as the Chancellor, being interviewed on his Budget. 'All I remember of that Budget is that I intended to put a tax on gramophone records. We didn't have a gramophone, so I felt strongly about it.'[12] But the Wilsons did have one of the first wireless sets in their neighbourhood.

His sights may have been altered slightly a couple of years later, in 1931. One of Ramsay MacDonald's Cabinet Ministers, A. V. (later Lord) Alexander spoke to the boys in one of those encouraging/patronizing lectures which urged them to think high. 'There is no reason why one of you should not be a Cabinet Minister some day.'[13] This may have persuaded Harold to up his sights slightly to Number 10 rather than the Chancellor's home at Number 11. 'The prediction was made while we were walking the one and a half miles to school and discussing our ambitions,' recalled schoolfriend Raymond Gledhill. 'Three of us made our modest forecasts, then it was Willy's turn. After some thought he said he intended to enter the Diplomatic Corps or the Consular Service. When asked what this could lead to, young Wilson ... replied without a smile: "One day I might be Prime Minister".'[14] But no prediction as to whether he would be a Labour Prime Minister, like Ramsay MacDonald, then in office, or a Liberal

Prime Minister, like Lloyd George, who had started his six years in office in the year of Harold's birth.

There was, of course, some dissatisfaction in the Wilson family with the Liberal Party's apparent disregard of the economic problems of ordinary people. The Government's effort to cope with the crisis by cutting the salaries of its employees began to hit at sister Marjorie, just then beginning her teaching career. This helped launch Harold on a new career as a political heckler. There was considerable political turmoil in the Colne Valley in 1931, with its Labour MP, Philip Snowden, following Ramsay MacDonald into the National Government. Harold and some of his mates attended a meeting held by the Liberal candidate for the Colne Valley in 1931, E. L. Mallalieu, supported by Dingle Foot, then still a Liberal too.

Young Harold rose and asked the speakers what they thought of the Department of Education circular cutting wages. Neither lawyer had heard of it, but both were put in the picture by the chairman. Mallalieu, later the Labour MP for Brigg, started to give a 'we must all make sacrifices' reply when his speech was noisily interrupted by his wolfhound, which erupted from the room behind the stage in which it had been locked. Philip Snowden spoke in support of Mallalieu, also a member of the National Government, to the accompaniment of shouts of 'Traitor! Traitor!' Despite this, Mallalieu was elected, with the backing of the Wilson family.

## A LIBERAL UNDERGRADUATE

Against that background it was not surprising that Harold Wilson should have been a Liberal while an undergraduate at Jesus College, Oxford. He has claimed that it was class and region rather than politics which kept him out of the Oxford Labour Club. 'When, as I saw it, all these public-school Marxists, many of them Communists, most of them knowing nothing of the conditions in which we in the North were living or had been brought up, I reacted so strongly against it that I felt the Oxford Labour Club wasn't for the likes of me.'[15]

Admittedly Harold, as a practical, provincial Northerner, tended to be turned off by the foppish, extravagant ways of the middle-class Southern extroverts who tended to be prominent in the Labour and Conservative clubs and the Oxford Union. The Labour Club was dominated by a handful of fashionable middle-class Communists, preoccupied largely with Marxist theory and foreign affairs, as made clear by one of them, Philip Toynbee, in his autobiographical *Friends Apart*. 'You can hardly blame Harold for having been put off by the likes of Philip Toynbee,' reminisced a contemporary.

There was no doubt that Harold was hung up about the middle class and therefore tended to exaggerate its predominance. Thus, the contemporary who tried to get him into the Labour Club while at Oxford was Teddy Jackson, his closest rival for the top First in PPE and no 'public-school Marxist'. He had come from West Bromwich Grammar School and was the son of a schoolmaster. Another Labour Club activist at the time was Denis Healey, also the son of a principal, who had come up to Oxford from Bradford Grammar School.

Because he was a provincial and spoke like one Wilson was unusually shy of crossing verbal swords with Southerners, whom he considered more glib and polished. Therefore he almost entirely avoided the Oxford Union, where the son of a Kentish carpenter, named Edward Heath, began to make his name. Harold so feared being criticized for his provincial speech that he spoke only once at the Oxford Union, in an end-of-term debate which would not be reviewed in *Isis*, which did not publish during the vacation.

Wilson preferred to debate within Jesus College against fellow grammar-school Nonconformists with even stronger provincial accents than his own, mainly Welsh. He played a prominent part in its debating club, called the Sankey Society after the famous jurist, Lord Sankey, whose Commission first advocated nationalizing the coal mines. In his last year he was President of the Sankey Society. He was also Secretary of the Jesus College History Society and Treasurer of the Meyricke Society, which specialized in bantering, humorous debate. Thus, he read a paper on Britain's two nations – the North and the South – and the need to inform the ignorant South about the worthy North, where all the work was done.

There is no doubt where his political loyalty lay while he was an undergraduate. 'I never asked my pupils their politics,' his tutor in politics, Dr R. B. McCullum, told me in 1972. 'But I had the impression that he was neither Tory nor Labour. He had no touch of the aggression of some of the socialists ... At Oxford, he was like Asquith – he never put a foot wrong.'

Dr McCullum, who was then writing his life of Asquith, was a leading Liberal and may have gathered his impression of Wilson's politics from undergraduate Liberals like Frank Byers, who had revived the Liberal Club. 'Wilson was a regular attender,' Lord Byers told the author, 'attending most meetings. I can remember him sitting there, smoking a pipe.' Byers was attracted to Wilson because he thought of him as having a solid 'Northern approach'. Byers shared Wilson's disdain for the Oxford Union. 'It was very superficial, very lightweight, part of the after-dinner network.'

Wilson joined the Liberal Club at the beginning of his time in Oxford, in October 1934. At the end of his second term, in March 1935, he was elected to the Liberal Club Committee. At the same time he was promoted with seven other Oxford Liberal undergraduates to the Executive of the Eighty Club. This club, formed in 1880 to encourage support for William Gladstone, was helpful in financing Liberal activities at the Universities by such things as paying the expenses of Liberal speakers at university functions. Among those promoted with Wilson were Frank Byers, Honor Balfour, James Brown and Raymond Walton.

'When I was President of the Liberal Club,' recalled Honor Balfour, 'he was college secretary for Jesus. He never took any initiative or decisions, but if you wanted him to whistle up some members or subscriptions, it was always done perfectly.' Heavily committed Liberals tended to resent the fact that Harold's first commitment was to a First-Class Honours degree. 'He didn't do anything outstanding,' mused Lord Byers. 'He stood for Treasurer and became Treasurer of the Club.' 'I wiped out the Liberal deficit in one term,' recalled Wilson.[16]

Lord Byers has his explanation for the falling away of Wilson's interest in Liberalism. In his third year he failed to become President. 'Harold was very disappointed when he was defeated by James Brown, later a judge in Northern Ireland, for President.' But he continued to attend Liberal conferences, particularly in the vacation. Thus he was at a Union of University Students' vacation conference in Liverpool, 9–11 April 1935. The next time it was held, in Manchester, 8–10 January 1936, he made a speech urging moderation on a motion criticizing the League of Nations. The resolution he supported was one backed by the Oxford University Liberal Club, which took note of the 'dangers inherent in a system of private manufacture of armaments and munitions' and called on the Government 'to work wholeheartedly for the complete abolition of private enterprise in this field'.[17] In this speech Wilson was able to use some of the material prepared for his Cecil Peace Prize attempt. Harold was in the thick of Liberal activities in his third year, despite his disappointment. Another keen Liberal, Derek Tasker, got Harold's agreement to contribute a chapter on unemployment and the depressed areas for a book by Oxford Liberals.

What his Liberal friends objected to was his sense of priorities. He was interested in politics but would not let it interfere with his work. In 1935 he preferred to stick to his books rather than accompany Frank Byers to canvas for his father, C. C. Byers, who was fighting a hopeless Liberal seat in the 1935 general election. 'Oxford in the 1930s was alive with political protest,' recalls Honor Balfour. 'Crossman and Pakenham were in the thick of it, but you never heard Harold's voice. He preferred to burrow behind the scenes.'[18] This was hardly fair as a generalization because both Crossman and Pakenham were several years older and already established as dons and came from much more securely placed and better-heeled families than the Wilsons. Wilson's top priority was winning a First-Class Honours degree to enable him to secure a first-rate job after university. His colleagues found that he could only be inveigled into social activities if those activities might help him toward those targets. Thus Teddy Jackson was able to persuade him to become Secretary of the Political and Economic Group. This had been organized by a group of bright undergraduates led by Jackson, who became its Chairman. It invited professors and lecturers from various universities to address them over dinner at a local hotel. Wilson came to almost every meeting and stayed on afterwards, talking to the guest speaker. Jackson and the Treasurer exploited Wilson's interest in making these contacts to persuade him to take on the job of Secretary.

Although Wilson resisted joining the Labour Club, events pushed him to the Left. 'In my third year,' he told me, 'I was attending Labour Club meetings.' He still objected to the preoccupation of fashionable left-wingers with theory and foreign affairs. 'I think I would be right in saying that most of my passionate feelings at the time were in terms of unemployment and home affairs, rather than foreign affairs,' Wilson recalled.[19] In this he shared the outlook of trade-union leaders like Ernest Bevin and the bulk of Labour Party supporters in the country. Neither Bevin nor ordinary Labour supporters could understand, for example, the attitude of left-wing trendies at the time that the Chamberlain Government should be denied support in rearmament at a time when these same left-wingers were saying that fascism was a menace to all democratic countries, including Britain, and were actually backing the resistance of Ethiopia, Spain and China.

The extent to which Harold Wilson put his job before politics, particularly the politics of foreign affairs, was negatively demonstrated in the autumn of 1938. In September 1938 Chamberlain's appeasement of the dictators came to a climax at his meetings with Hitler at Berchtesgaden and Munich. After agreeing to the dismemberment of that 'faraway country', Czechoslovakia, Chamberlain had been welcomed back in Britain with hysterical relief as the bearer of 'peace with honour'. Anti-fascists felt that the appeasers, having betrayed Spain, were now in the process of betraying Czechoslovakia, a democratic country for which there was much sympathy.

By chance Oxford secured an opportunity to demonstrate its feelings in a by-election held in Oxford City. Quintin Hogg, later Lord Hailsham, was the candidate of the pro-appeasement Conservatives. The Labour candidate for Oxford was a don, Patrick Gordon Walker, later neighbour and Cabinet Minister under Wilson. But in October the economist Roy Harrod urged that Gordon Walker and the Liberal candidate, Ivor Davies, step down in favour of an independent anti-appeasement candidate, A. D. Lindsay, the Master of Balliol. Although there was some uneasiness among Labour supporters about Gordon Walker's being strong-armed into stepping down, Lindsay's candidacy aroused tremendous enthusiasm among anti-appeasers in Oxford and throughout Britain. 'The times are too grave and the issue is too vital for progressive Conservative opinion to allow itself to be influenced by party loyalties or to tolerate the present uncertainty regarding the principles governing our foreign policy,' wrote left-wing Tory Harold Macmillan to *The Times*.[20]

Anti-appeasers from all the parties at Oxford and indeed from the whole country rallied to the cause of A. D. Lindsay and against Quintin Hogg as the defender of Neville Chamberlain and his policies. Among undergraduates Balliol men like Tory Edward Heath, Labour supporter Roy Jenkins and Denis Healey, then a Communist, were very prominent in the campaign. Liberal undergraduates and recent graduates like Frank Byers and Honor Balfour were active. Young dons at Oxford were the mainstay of the anti-Hogg campaign. But no Harold Wilson. He was then a young don at University College, where he was being exploited unmercifully by the Master of that College, Sir William Beveridge. Like Wilson, Beveridge was not primarily interested in foreign affairs; and Wilson, while strongly anti-fascist, was not enamoured of the idea of the Popular Front implicit in the Lindsay campaign, incorporating everyone from anti-fascist Tories like Harold Macmillan and Winston Churchill to the Communists. So Harold Wilson never showed what Honor Balfour described as his 'smooth cherrystone face'[21] in the Lindsay campaign against Hogg. In the end Hogg won, but the Conservative majority had been halved.

**THE QUIET JOINING**
Just after the Oxford by-election Wilson quietly joined the Oxford City Labour Party. It was done so secretively that it seemed as if he were joining an unpopular conspiracy like the Communist Party rather than the second biggest party in the country. It was the very secrecy of this decision which led to the subsequent surprise of his Oxford friends in 1945, when he became a Labour candidate, MP and Minister.

Part of his discretion was due, undoubtedly, to the fact that he had just become a don at University College and research assistant to its Master, the famous Liberal Sir William Beveridge. This took place just as Harold Wilson was disengaging from the Liberal Party at Oxford. In February 1938 he resigned from the Liberals' Eighty Club. At the same time he was drawing closer to Labour people in his own fields of interest at Oxford. 'In 1938,' Sir Harold told the author, 'I started to join with [G.D.H.] Cole in the "Cole Group",' a discussion group largely for undergraduates. His relationship with Cole was different from that of the left-wing dons who also shared with Cole his famous 'pink lunches' on Thursdays at University College. Wilson worked with Cole on more practical matters. He agreed to help Cole with some of his work for the Fabian Research Bureau, although Wilson was not yet a member of the Bureau then. Wilson also agreed to do a chapter on public control of transport for a book on planning to be published by the Fabians. Others working on the volume were Michael Stewart and W. A. Robson. It was designed by Cole to help the next Labour Government 'lay secure foundations for a socialist economic system'.[22]

There was another factor in Wilson's joining the Oxford City Labour Party apart from his movement towards economic planning. For him it was also a small vote of sympathy with Patrick Gordon Walker, the former Labour candidate, who had been pushed to one side for the Popular Front candidate, A. D. Lindsay, 'Had I been in the [Oxford] Labour Party at the time,' Sir Harold told me, 'I would have supported the retention of Patrick as the Labour Candidate.'

Although Wilson has argued that he was alienated from the foreign preoccupations of the Marxist-orientated University people, the element of secretiveness about his Labour affiliation was already present. This was confirmed when he left Oxford for London early in 1940 to take up a series of posts in the wartime civil service. Instead of transferring his Labour Party membership from the Oxford City Labour Party to a London branch in one of several suburbs which he inhabited, Harold Wilson did something so discreet as to seem almost conspiratorial. He joined the Labour Party in Liskeard, in Cornwall, where his father lived and worked, manufacturing explosives for local mines. While visiting his father Harold walked with him from the Wilson's house to the signalbox of railwayman Jack Hubert Pitts. They stayed half the night talking politics with Mr Pitts and Harold enrolled in the local Labour Party.[23]

As a hard-pressed wartime civil servant he could hardly hope to participate in political debate in Liskeard in Cornwall, 200 miles from London; and at no time did he tell Labour supporters from Oxford whom he ran into in wartime London what he had done. This secretiveness encouraged the subsequent jibe that he had jumped on a winning bandwagon by becoming a Labour candidate in October 1944. But he had, after all, joined the Labour Party at end of 1938, when Chamberlain-style Toryism was still riding high and the Labour Party had only a quarter of the seats in the Commons. Even when he decided to stand as a Labour candidate, at the end of 1943, it was rare to find any

Labour leader who thought his party could defeat the wartime leader-hero Winston Churchill in any early general election.

Although Wilson did not, as a wartime civil servant, disclose his political affiliations to the miners' leaders with whom he dealt, he increasingly identified with them and against the coalmine-owners. As his book, *New Deal for Coal*, makes clear, he emerged from his wartime experience a wholehearted supporter of the nationalization of the coal industry. But even before this he had shown an interest in the nationalization of transport, both as an undergraduate researching on Gladstone and in writing for G. D. H. Cole and the Fabians. Early in 1945, just after his forced resignation from the civil service on becoming a prospective Labour candidate, he prepared a report on the finances of railway nationalization for the Railway Clerks Association, which became the basis of their own plea for nationalization. His intellectual conversion to Labour was a matter of fact long before he disclosed it, even to friends.

## CENTRE-LEFT CANDIDATE

When Harold Wilson finally did emerge into the open to speak to the people he was wooing in Ormskirk in May–June 1945, the people he had known in London and Oxford weren't there to hear him. The rather lovely constituency he was contesting included at that time some voters within the borders of Liverpool and stretched up the coast almost to Southport and inland almost to Preston. There were only obscure little weekly newspapers within the constituency, and the war-shrunken *Liverpool Daily Post* could hardly report him at length.

In fact, the people within the constituency were not able to follow him too well, even if they did attend his meetings. He was still accustomed to speak in the academic-intellectual jargon common among the denizens of Oxford and Whitehall, which had led some of the miners' leaders to refer to him as a 'college boy'. His agent, Arthur Waite, a Huddersfield man like himself, was in despair at first; he told me that after one of Harold's first speeches he demanded: 'Can't you talk down to the people, so they can understand what you're talking about?' He also had difficulty at first getting Harold to mix with working people in local workingmen's clubs; the constituency Chairman, F. J. Sayer, seemed to be indulging in wish-fulfilment when he claimed that Wilson had come from the working class and believed in the working class.[24]

The fact that Harold Wilson did identify with the mining vanguard of the working class was demonstrated when he persuaded both William Lawther and James Bowman, President and Vice-President of the National Union of Mineworkers respectively, to come specially to Lancashire to speak for him in the mining village of Skelmersdale. To make it clear he had friends on both extremes of the Labour movement he also had the wealthy left-winger Lord Faringdon speak on the need for the Labour Britain of the future to serve as the postwar interpreter between the USA and USSR.[25]

When Wilson was speaking for himself his arguments put him slightly to the left of the centre of the Labour Party. He was certainly no Churchill-basher like Aneurin Bevan. There was no reason to fight dirty, he told an audience. In fact, his slogan seemed to be: 'Vote Labour and save Winston from his friends.' Labour's fight was to save the economy from the incompetence which had brought the basic industries to chaos before the war. Labour was not ungrateful for the great work done in wartime by Churchill, but the Tory Party wanted to 'cash in' on his popularity to hold back social progress. The problems of postwar Britain were too great to be dealt with on the basis of a coalition with Labour as the junior partner, he argued.[26]

He was to the left of the centre of the Labour Party in the strength of his demands for nationalization, which had been incorporated in the party manifesto only as a result of a revolt by left-wingers led by Ian Mikardo, against the protests of the Morrison-Attlee leadership. Wilson insisted that it would be necessary to build eight million houses ultimately to tackle the problem of the slums. Labour wanted to nationalize the land so that landowners would not stand in the way of rehousing. By nationalizing the mines Labour would end the domination of 2,000 company directors, many of whom were amateurs at the job and had never been down a mine.

The Wilsons had three nail-biting weeks to wait before they could discover whether Harold's gamble in sacrificing his civil service career and putting at risk his academic one had paid off. After those three weeks – needed to gather in and distribute the Services' vote – it turned out that his gamble had succeeded. On 26 July 1945 he became the new MP for Ormskirk by a margin of over 7,000 votes. This recapture of Ormskirk by Labour – previously won in 1929 – had been repeated in similar seats throughout the country. Labour had secured 393 seats, a staggering majority of 146 over all the other parties in the Commons – the first full-scale Labour majority in British history.

Harold Wilson got his first glimpse of his new colleagues *en masse* on the following Saturday morning, 28 July, in the Beaver Hall in the City of London. There had been tremendous manoeuvring before the meeting, some of it in public, most of it behind the scenes. Professor Harold Laski, that year's Chairman of the National Executive Committee of the Labour Party, had been campaigning to block Clement Attlee becoming Prime Minister automatically. He felt that the man who accepted the Monarch's mandate to form the new Labour

Government should be first elected or endorsed by the new Parliamentary Labour Party which was twice as large as the prewar PLP that had elected Attlee, and was overwhelmingly different in both personnel and outlook. Laski would have preferred to see Herbert Morrison succeed Attlee and would have accepted Ernest Bevin, but he insisted that the decision should be made by the new PLP. Morrison liked the idea, but Bevin, always suspicious of Morrison, was loyal to Attlee. He urged Attlee to go immediately to Buckingham Palace to accept the King's commission to form a Government. In fact Attlee did just this on Thursday evening, 26 July, after Churchill had thrown in the towel. On Friday he announced the main Cabinet posts, with Ernest Bevin as the new Foreign Secretary and Hugh Dalton as the new Chancellor of the Exchequer. This was somewhat of a surprise, because Bevin had wanted the Treasury and Dalton the Foreign Office, to which Attlee had originally agreed. There was some objection to this by the King, who disliked Dalton and his anti-appeasement and anti-Court ideas. But Attlee made the switch largely because he thought of Bevin as a 'tank' who could be used against the burgeoning Russians but who could not be contained in the domestic field along with his old rival Herbert Morrison, who would be Leader of the Commons and, in effect, Deputy Prime Minister and co-ordinator of the domestic front.[27]

As a new boy with only the thinnest of roots in the Labour Party Wilson was hardly conscious of these cross-currents as he entered the Beaver Hall. He could hardly have witnessed one of the last tries by Morrison's friend, Ellen Wilkinson, to get Edith Summerskill's support for Herbert in the ladies' toilet at Beaver Hall. Ernest Bevin was introduced as the new Foreign Secretary, just back from the Palace with his Cabinet colleagues to collect their seals of office. Bevin promptly moved a vote of confidence in Attlee as the Leader of the party and the new Prime Minister. This was carried by acclamation, burying the last traces of the rebellion. Attlee then spoke, promising in his dry way to carry out Labour's reforming Manifesto. Attlee and Bevin then left the Beaver Hall to fly back to Potsdam for the interrupted meeting with Stalin and Truman.

Wilson was preoccupied with an insignificant trip which almost proved horrendous. He was to be the key figure at an Ormskirk Labour Party victory celebration next day. Since it was the Bank Holiday, getting a place on a train on Saturday was uncertain. He had borrowed an Austin 10 and packed in four other Lancashire MPs anxious to get home. En route the car blew a gasket. They hired another car on payment of a £5 deposit only to find after a while that the brakes were not working. Rather than go back all the way Wilson decided to crawl on slowly. He delivered one Lancashire MP, George Tomlinson, at 2 a.m. and only reached Ormskirk himself at 4 a.m.

Almost as soon as the Ormskirk celebrations were over Wilson had to turn round and set off to London for a social meeting whose importance to his personal advancement he did not underestimate. On the surface it was a private dinner given by Hugh Dalton, the new Chancellor, to a dozen 'Young Victors' at Westminster's Edwardian-style St Ermin's Hotel on Monday, 30 July. Wilson knew that Dalton, who had briefly been his wartime chief, was interested in young men partly personally, partly as the most energetic 'talent-spotter' among senior Labour politicians. Not all of those invited by Dalton were to be given jobs by Attlee, certainly not immediately. However highly Dalton rated R. H. S. Crossman, an old anti-Nazi ally, Attlee would not accept him because Attlee had been a friend of his father, Mr Justice Crossman, and had sided with him against Dick's youthful rebellions. Major Woodrow Wyatt, who was typically talkative at the meal, would have to wait because he was still thought to be under the influence of the Indian Communists who had befriended him in wartime on the sub-continent. But most of the others – Kenneth Younger, Christopher Mayhew, John Freeman, Evans Durbin and a curiously silent George Brown – were soon to find themselves in the Attlee Government – on Dalton's recommendation.

'It was my first meeting with John Freeman,' Sir Harold recalled to me. It was with Freeman and Aneurin Bevin that Wilson was to resign with a bang in almost six years' time. Sir Harold recalls a discussion led by Evan Durbin, a friend of Gaitskell's who was to die in a drowning accident three years later, about whether new MPs should go right into Ministerial jobs. Durbin favoured this. But Wilson was opposed, although he himself had had some experience observing the House from the civil servants' box there and in writing draft speeches for his Ministers. 'None of us knows anything about how to handle Parliament. It would be quite wrong to put a newcomer in such a position.' Then he added: 'But I'd make one exception – on sheer merit: Hugh Gaitskell.' He knew this would go down well with the host, 'big Hugh' Dalton, who had so clearly favoured 'little Hugh' Gaitskell during the war. Gaitskell had, of course, been invited to the dinner as the new MP for Leeds South, but had been unable to come because of the slight heart attack which had kept him out of the election campaign. Inevitably the mention of Gaitskell's name had attracted Dalton's attention. 'That's not possible!' he boomed, cutting into the conversation. Gaitskell's health would prevent his being considered for office for some months at least.[28]

Harold Wilson had still to go through the ceremonies of taking the

Oath and signing on the Register before formally becoming an MP and being able to collect his pay. He signed on 2 August, being sandwiched in the queue between Sydney Silverman, the tiny, peppery left-wing solicitor who had been elected for Nelson and Colne, and Benn Levy, the newly-elected left-wing MP for Eton and Slough and playwright husband of actress Constance Cummings. It was no indication of his own stance; he was to have no contact with the Left for almost six years.

Wilson was thrilled that week to learn that his wartime experience as a civil servant dealing with coal might give him a tiny leg-up on the promotion ladder. A Whip approached him and said that Emanuel ('Manny') Shinwell wanted him as his PPS. Attlee had sent for Shinwell: 'I want you to take the Ministry of Fuel and Power – and the job will include nationalizing the mines. You will be in the Cabinet.'[29] It was not surprising that Shinwell should have thought of Wilson, who had been Director of Statistics in that Ministry and had, in his *New Deal for Coal*, argued the case for nationalizing the coal mines. What was slightly surprising was that Shinwell should have thought of Wilson for the unpaid post of Parliamentary Private Secretary, usually a personal confidant and errand boy who serves as the Minister's liaison with other MPs in particular. But it was pointed out that this unpaid position is usually regarded as a stepping stone to a junior Ministerial position. So Wilson accepted gratefully.

He was able to take this good news back to Oxford, where his wife, Mary, and his son, Robin, were living in college. Since there was still a shortage of economists at Oxford he had agreed to teach on Saturdays and Sundays at University College while serving as an MP during the week. This enabled Mary and Robin to live on there. It was difficult for them to move to London, apart from Mary's disinclination, because Harold's father had left his poorly-paid job in Cornwall and was temporarily employed at the Ministry of Supply in London. Harold's parents were therefore living in his Richmond flat. He stayed with them during the week, spending the weekends he could spare from his constituency with his wife and son.

Returning from doing the Saturday morning shopping on 4 August Wilson was startled when the College porter told him that he had been looking for him everywhere. 'The Prime Minister was wanting to speak to you on the telephone.' After Wilson had hastened to the 'phone and got through to the Prime Minister, Attlee, quite typically, went straight to the point.'I want you to be Parliamentary Secretary at the Ministry of Works. This is a planning job. George Tomlinson will be your Minister, and he's quite happy about your appointment.' (Apparently Tomlinson had replied to Attlee's question: 'Ay, ah know him all reet. Apart from the fact he tried to kill me in a motor car, ah've nowt against him.')[30]

This was shrewd team-building because George Tomlinson, a Lancashire textile trade unionist, was as timid and benevolent in the 'corridors of power' as Wilson was determined and dynamic. Even long afterwards Attlee was curiously misleading as to how he came to know Wilson would be effective. 'I had heard of him as a don at my old College,' Lord Attlee told an interviewer almost twenty years later, 'and knew of work he had done for the party.' Since the only work Wilson had done for the Labour Party was standing for election in 1945, this reason was transparently faulty. Wilson thinks he was recommended to Attlee by two people: Viscount Hyndley, who was Comptroller-General at the Ministry of Fuel and Power in wartime and became the first Chairman of the National Coal Board, and Hugh Dalton.

Dalton's booming voice was clearly behind two helpful items of publicity for Wilson, one on the day he was forced to retire from the civil service when he became a prospective Labour candidate in October 1944, the other when he entered the House of Commons in July 1945. When he was adopted for Ormskirk, the *Daily Telegraph* forecast: 'At twenty-eight, Mr Wilson is looked on by socialists as becoming President of the Board of Trade or Chancellor of the Exchequer.'[31] On the day after his election for Ormskirk, Ian Mackay wrote in the *News Chronicle*: 'Outstanding among the really "new" men on the Labour benches I would put that brilliant young civil servant, Harold Wilson, who won Ormskirk from King-Hall. He is only twenty-eight (in fact he was by then twenty-nine) but is regarded by the Whitehall high-ups as one of the great discoveries of the war. Wilson it was who supplied the Minister of Fuel with his facts and figures, and his statistical digest of the coal industry, issued earlier this year, was such a model of clear and concise statement that even the industrial correspondents could not find any fault with it.' It is unusual for a political or industrial correspondent to be able to evaluate the work of a civil servant or know what anonymous Government publications he has written unless he has been tipped off by a Minister.

So far as the House of Commons was concerned, Wilson fulfilled his own warning that it was unwise to become even a junior Minister immediately without any back-bench experience. R. H. S. Crossman, later Wilson's closest political colleague, described Wilson of that period to me as a 'haughty popinjay'. Because he had gone from being a don and civil servant to being a junior Minister surrounded by civil servants he did not learn the realities of political in-fighting until he resigned almost six years later. Wilson worked hard, fourteen to eighteen hours a day, as he had during the war. He was fully informed but his speeches in the Commons were dull and donnish, delivered too rapidly and with neither oratory nor humour. 'If Churchill himself wrote a speech for Mr

Wilson,' scoffed one paper, 'Mr Wilson would manage to make it sound like an inscription on a tombstone.'[32] Back-benchers were also resentful that this former don and civil servant, with no record of service or seniority in the Labour movement, had been preferred to so many of his senior colleagues. This coolness melted slightly when it became clear he was self-conscious about his youthfulness – confessing he had grown his moustache to look older. In the rare times he could be found in the Members' tearoom, northern MPs were also relieved to find that he could speak, eat and drink like someone from the Yorkshire/Lancashire area, not as though fully formed by Oxford and Whitehall.

In his first Commons speech he admitted the disadvantages of 'making a maiden speech from ... an unusual part of the House' – the Front Bench. He was opening the 9 October 1945 debate on the perennial subject of improved amenities for MPs, many of whom had not been able to find rooms in war-devastated London, much less office accommodation within the bombed House of Commons. Wilson speculated on the possibility of finding some 'wartime hostel' for MPs' use, at which point the tough-minded left-winger Ian Mikardo interjected: 'If we all held the rank of colonel, I am sure that a block of offices would soon be commandeeered for us!'[33]

## MASTERY BEHIND-THE-SCENES

Wilson's better-informed left-wing critics in the Commons began to hear reports from across the 'Great Divide' separating Westminster from Whitehall that he was showing real spunk in behind-the-scenes battles in the Ministry. He had walked into a tough situation. The most pressing need facing the incoming Labour Government was to make good the damage to housing done by wartime bombs and neglect, particularly in the old working-class areas of the big cities which had borne the brunt of the Luftwaffe onslaught. Some plans, particularly for temporary housing, had been made by the wartime coalition Government, but nothing had been done to end the division of responsibility between the Ministry of Health, which supervised housing policy, and the Ministry of Works, which was supposed to provide the materials for housebuilding. Labour had campaigned on a promise to set up a separate, integrated Ministry of Housing. But on assuming office Attlee had found out that this would only delay the housing drive because it would require fresh legislation which would take months to pass. What is more, he gave chief responsibility to the new and controversial Minister of Health, Aneurin Bevan, who at forty-seven was the youngest Cabinet Minister in 1945. The Ministry of Works, with its responsibility shrunken from wartime, when Lord

Portal had a Cabinet seat, was put under timid George Tomlinson, who was not in the Cabinet.

What is more, when Wilson arrived at the Ministry of Works – where he hoped to make his Ministerial reputation – he found that its Permanent Secretary, Sir Percival Robinson, KCB, had got rid of some of the best of the temporary wartime civil servants, such as Sir Hugh Beaver, who had been Director General and Controller General, and Sir Frederick Pile, who had been brought in by Duncan Sandys, and that the old prewar slothfulness was beginning to set in again.

Wilson also found that the Ministry's statistics and progress-chasing were years behind the systems he had set up in wartime in Fuel and Power. He asked the Permanent Secretary what had gone wrong with plans for the rapid erection of prefabricated buildings. The Permanent Secretary took him to the statistical chart room. There he showed him that one basic part of the many hundreds which went into a prefab was four months behind time; other parts – the kitchen and bathroom units – were six months behind schedule; and, worse still, the Ministry of Health were ten months in arrears in providing the promised sites for prefab construction. 'Right,' said Wilson grittily. 'Now we're going to get everything on schedule.' The Permanent Secretary gave an indulgent smile and went on his planned leave for three weeks.

On his return the Permanent Secretary was astonished to find that Wilson had been interviewing everyone concerned at all levels to see how things could be speeded up. 'Parliamentary Secretary,' he told Wilson with some agitation, 'a rather serious thing has happened and I feel I ought to speak to you quite frankly about it. I gather that when I was away you had a meeting in your room?' 'I had a great many meetings.' 'I gather there were people of different ranks round the table?' 'There might have been,' Wilson retorted. 'I simply told my secretary to get hold of all the people concerned with the problems, so that we could get on quickly with things.' 'You must know this is completely contrary to Civil Service discipline!' Wilson replied he had never heard of such regulations and that he had himself attended many meetings with people of different ranks round the same table. 'Look, I must speak frankly to you,' said the Permanent Secretary, adding truthfully: 'After all, I'm twice your age, you know. I really must explain that this sort of thing simply isn't done.' 'Look here,' retorted Wilson sharply, 'you'd better get this clear. I've served in more Government departments than you. And this was how the war was won.'

'Your attitude is going to cause a lot of difficulty,' replied the Permanent Secretary. 'We've had enough trouble here already with Ministers trying to run the Department – like Duncan Sandys, for instance. As I see it, a Minister should answer in the House of Commons for the Department, but leave the decisions to the civil servants.' The interview ended in deep antagonism, with Wilson realizing he had to face the problem of getting rid of the Permanent Secretary, no mean task even for a fully-fledged Department chief, and one that was exacerbated by the deepening crisis involving building materials, which would provide more ammunition for the Tories to exploit. Wilson was able, through his participation on the Cabinet committee on Housing presided over by Aneurin Bevan, to see the whole gloomy picture owing to his special training as an economic statistician. He urged his chief, George Tomlinson, to bring in a brilliant administrator, F. W. ('Bomber') Smith, who had been in charge of bomber production at the Ministry of Aircraft Production during the war. When the Permanent Secretary learned that 'Bomber' Smith was being brought in to take charge of building materials as Director General, he threatened to put another senior civil servant above him to control him. 'In that case,' threatened Wilson, 'I must tell you that I shall answer no question in Parliament, and take no briefs for any Cabinet committee unless my advice comes directly from the man actually doing the job!' The Permanent Secretary backed down, but Wilson knew he had to go. But he also knew his Minister was too soft-hearted to have the Prime Minister sack him, unless he was forced by circumstances.

The circumstances arose as a result of a great shortage in brick production, the very occurrence Wilson had been trying to prevent. There was widespread concern, fed by cartoons in the press. Attlee had heard about the inadequacies of the Permanent Secretary from Dalton, who had been told by Wilson. But Attlee could only send for Tomlinson, who pretended that everything was in order. 'What about the Permanent Secretary?' persisted Attlee. 'I've been thinking perhaps we ought to move him. There's a good man who's at present Deputy Secretary at the Ministry of Supply – Oliver Franks. You could have him.' At that point Tomlinson still preferred to stick to his old Permanent Secretary. But after two more weeks of crisis and Tory attacks Tomlinson was back on Attlee's mat. Again the Prime Minister asked him about his Permanent Secretary. 'I'm quite happy with him, but Harold isn't. Perhaps you'd better talk to him.' Wilson was summoned with all the building material figures. He spread them before Attlee, who studied them. 'They seem all right,' Attlee commented drily. 'Why haven't they been carried out?' 'They have, mainly, but we've had some difficulties.' 'What's wrong?' snapped Attlee. Wilson replied that he should ask George Tomlinson. 'I have already done so,' Attlee replied, 'and he suggested I should send for you because your view is different from his.' 'In that case, I can speak frankly,' Wilson said. 'That department will never be any good until you get rid of the Permanent Secretary!' 'Exactly as I thought,' said Attlee. He pulled out a sheet of paper and wrote on it a simple minute to the Chancellor of the Exchequer, then still in charge of the Civil Service: 'Please find another job for the Permanent Secretary, Ministry of Works.'[34]

This story, told at length by Wilson to his first serious biographer, Leslie Smith, said a great deal about Wilson's abilities as a behind-the-scenes progress-chaser and in-fighter. They were the qualities of an efficient and dynamic Ministerial technocrat rather than those of a politician. In contrast to Aneurin Bevan, who was attracting all the Conservative attacks, Wilson's efforts were mainly to avoid giving the Tories ammunition rather than to trade verbal blows.

Winston Churchill and his colleagues were determined to get the most mileage over criticising Labour for its housing inadequacies. On 17 October 1945, two months after the war's end, the Conservatives attacked the Government for the 'existing shortage of houses', when two-thirds of the building workers had still to be demobilized and there was a shortage all over the world of building materials, particularly the softwoods that had to be imported from devastated Eastern Europe. Bevan taunted the Tories that 'only a very grave concern for the public weal could have inspired them to put down a motion on a subject so embarrassing to themselves.'

Initially Bevan was correct in his view that the shortage of housing was a result of inadequate wartime planning by the Churchill-led coalition. Now a basic divergence of approach between the two parties increasingly made itself felt. Ernest Bevin had committed Labour to gradual demobilization on a 'first in, first out' basis. Bevan helped commit the Labour Government to rehousing supervised by local authorities, with the central Government providing subsidies, materials and guide-lines. In contrast, the Conservatives insisted on a swift return to free enterprise and a rapid demobilization. They hoped somehow to recapture the building volumes of the 1930s, when uncontrolled speculative building produced 350,000 houses. To hold out this hope in the immediate wake of the war was to ignore the fact that the 1930s had been a period of cheap and available manpower and materials and low interest rates. To use the slowness of housing was a sure political 'winner' for the Tories, because everyone was anxious for early and decent housing despite wartime damage which had knocked out at least 700,000 houses.

Because their interest in housing overlapped Wilson often alternated with Bevan in answering questions on the subject. They had very differing styles, leading Bevan to the conclusion that Wilson was 'all head and no heart'. Wilson's replies tended to be dry and factual. Thus, on 3 December 1945 Wilson warned the Tories that you could not have small staffs and adequate statistics on housing: 'I am a little interested in figures,' said the professional economic statistician, 'and on going to the Ministry of Works I asked for figures, which are of very great importance in this connection – the figures of such things as the production of raw materials – but there were none available which were less than four or five months old, although we wanted much more recent figures.'[35] This reasonableness made him a difficult and uninviting target for the Tories.

In contrast, Aneurin Bevan was Churchill's favourite target, partly because Bevan had been one of the few Labour back-benchers who had been consistently critical of various alleged Churchillian wartime blunders. On one occasion Churchill had retorted by describing Bevan as a 'squalid nuisance'. Bevan was dangerous because of the power of his oratory when he fought back. But because his powerful oratory was uncontrolled, he could often stoke up an argument in a way which aroused Tory supporters.

In a riproaring censure debate on 6 December 1945 Churchill attacked Bevan and the Government for having 'already allowed four months of excellent building weather to slip away' and having constructed only one thousand permanent homes and ten thousand prefabs. Churchill also taunted the Government for not allowing Bevan, the responsible Minister, to reply to the debate, being kept 'in his dugout' by his comrades. Instead, the debate was answered by the Leader of the House, Bevan's old enemy, Herbert Morrison. Morrison carried around with him a tattered old newspaper cutting quoting Bevan as having described him as a 'third-rate Tammany hack'. When colleagues asked Bevan whether he had been quoted correctly, Bevan would correct it, smiling softly: 'No, I said he was a fifth-rate hack.'[36] On the occasion of the censure debate Wilson later recalled for Bevan's adoring biographer, Michael Foot, that he had asked Bevan: 'Did Herbert rise to the occasion?' 'No,' replied Bevan, 'he reduced it to his own level and then rode it.'[37]

Wilson has retrospectively attempted to improve his relations with Bevan in that 1945–47 period. He told his first biographer, Leslie Smith, how much he came to admire Bevan in the Cabinet committees on housing. What he did not recall, as Michael Foot has, is that Bevan tried hard to scotch the ambitions of the Ministry of Works, particularly its ambitions for a mammoth Housing Corporation, which Bevan was sure would turn into a 'muscle-bound giant'. Bevan suspected the Ministry of Works of being too much subject to the pressure of big building contractors and the building workers' unions. He also tended to look down very much on the prefabs, which were a main responsibility of the Ministry of Works.

Wilson secured respect in his own Ministry, at least, when he defended it against Tory attacks in the 25 March 1946 debate on building materials. 'I am sorry to say ... that the planning of the temporary housing programme was inadequate and amateurish in the extreme. Although [the Minister's] predecessors gave a great deal of personal time and attention to the matter, virtually no forethought was given to it. The so-called military revolution was almost totally un-planned. Promises were given at the time which a realistic study of the facts would have shown had no hope whatever of fulfilment. We have done a great deal in pulling the programme into line, and it is not in line yet. We are now bearing the brunt of the misleading promises that were made. It is just a little ironic to hear this described as a breakdown of State control and so on, since the scheme from its very beginning was under the control of Ministers from the Party opposite and was, in fact, never planned at all.... It was never realized at the beginning that producing [prefabricated] houses from so many factories and for so many sites with so many components was so involved. It was thought that somehow they would arrive miraculously on the site at the same time. No provision was made for storage.'[38]

Despite the increasingly high regard in which he was held by the knowledgeable Wilson's need to reassure himself by name-dropping was still insatiable. He ran into an old Oxford friend on Westminster underground station. When the friend made an observation Wilson could not restrain himself from saying: 'You know, that was just what I was saying to Clem only ten minutes ago!'

Although he was highly regarded by Attlee and others as an adminis-trator, his inadequacies as a House of Commons man told against him as he waited anxiously for promotion. In May 1946 Wilson was tipped off by the Chief Whip, William Whiteley, that he was to be the new Parlia-mentary Secretary at the Ministry of Fuel, whose chief, 'Manny' Shin-well, was already getting into difficulties over low coal production. Wilson was delighted at the idea of getting back to the Ministry and the problems he knew so well – and perhaps succeeding Shinwell as its chief. He even offered to cancel a trip to Portsmouth for the Ministry he thought he was leaving, but just before he left he was told the plan had changed.

On his way back from Portsmouth Wilson read that Hugh Gaitskell, now recovered from his heart attack, had been appointed in his stead as Parliamentary Secretary for Fuel. He was reassured when he was told that Attlee had made the decision because he felt that this appointment, the lowest in the Ministerial scale – then £1,500 a year – would have to last two or three years while the Bills to nationalize the coalmines and gas and electricity organizations went through Parliament. Wilson, Attlee felt, would be due for a promotion long before that.

In September 1946 it looked as though his luck would change. Hugh Dalton told him that he had been recommending him to the Prime Minister and that it looked as though he would become the Minister of Transport in succession to Alfred Barnes. But then the Chief Whip stepped in. He told Attlee, Sir Harold informed me, that Wilson could still not handle the House well enough. So Attlee kept Barnes on as Minister for Transport.

Wilson was very highly regarded by Attlee and the other Ministers as an efficient technocrat rather than a politician. Thus, Education Minister Ellen Wilkinson described him to Labour's Bournemouth conference as a man 'who gets things done when it seems almost impossible. He is one of our finest young men.'[39] The Ministry of Works had the job of providing the schools needed for the rapidly growing school population.

## WASHINGTON BREAKTHROUGH

Finally, the opportunity came. Wilson knew that something was up when Attlee summoned Tomlinson suddenly. He delayed his departure until his Minister returned. 'What's it all about, George?' he asked. 'Is it anything serious?'

'Ay, it's about thee,' replied Tomlinson. 'It's nothing serious though. It's very good. Well, it's in confidence, really. But I'll tell thee as long as when Prime Minister send for thee it comes as a surprise – tha knows *nowt* about it, see?'[40] John Boyd-Orr, the Independent MP for the Scottish Universities, had gone to see Attlee after the Copenhagen conference establishing the Food and Agriculture Organization, where Boyd-Orr had urged the establishment of a working commission in Washington to put it on a permanent basis. Boyd-Orr urged Attlee to send a young Minister rather than a 'dried-out' senior civil servant. Attlee had decided on Wilson and had then called in his chief to break the news. 'I'm going to have to borrow Harold Wilson from you for three months. I want to send him abroad on a job.' He promised Tomlinson a temporary replacement and pledged him to secrecy. The fact that Tomlinson did not keep his promise enabled Wilson to bone up a bit.

'Do you know what the FAO is?' the Prime Minister demanded of Wilson in his usual brusque manner. 'The Food and Agriculture Organization,' replied Wilson promptly. Attlee told him that he would be in Washington about three months, heading a team of officials. Wilson was delighted to accept, knowing that such a post at the age of thirty would enable him to show what he could do.

In Washington Wilson was able to demonstrate how hard work and ingenuity could overcome a weak position. Because of Britain's shortage of hard currency it could not commit itself to the generous contribution that Sir John Boyd-Orr, the FAO's Director General, would have liked. But Wilson's delegation produced alternative plans, such as multilateral commodity agreements. Wilson's team was impressive, including John (later Lord) Wall, then with the Ministry of Food but later with Unilever and EMI and Eugene Melville, then with the Colonial Office, later Sir Eugene Melville, KCMG and Permanent UK Delegate to GATT and EFTA. Every time a draft was sent to them they spent the evening drafting amendments and considerably rewriting the document. These civil servants were greatly impressed with Wilson's performance. 'He reads his documents in a way that Ministers are not always known to do, and gets to the heart of them. And that is a thing that gets to the heart of civil servants, who are not the kindest critics of their political masters,' was one summary of their attitudes.[41] 'John Boyd-Orr and I became very good friends,' Sir Harold told me, 'which resulted in his CH eventually.' However, Boyd-Orr was disappointed in Wilson for having played a 'pro-American role' in not accepting the World Food Board Boyd-Orr wanted. But this was a Cabinet decision, not Wilson's.

When he went home for Christmas at the end of 1946 Wilson had two problems to sort out. His wife Mary had been rather disturbed at being left alone in Oxford with her young son Robin for so long. He decided to bring her back to Washington with him for the last three or four weeks of the FAO conference.

The other problem was persuading the Government that it could secure timber in the USA. Before he left for Washington it was transparently clear that the house-building programme was threatened by the shortage of softwoods for building, and he had discovered that there were adequate sources of US timber for export. This had been uncovered by Tom Meyer, the son of Montague Meyer and his successor as head of Britain's largest timber importing firm. Meyer was touring the USA and Canada partly to recover from his wartime imprisonment, partly to search for new timber supplies. The Meyers were friends of Wilson's chief, George Tomlinson and of Ernest Bevin as well.

At home during the Christmas period Wilson learned how worried the Government was about the timber shortage, but he discovered from Bevan that it was accepting the Board of Trade story about no American timber being available. When he lunched with Attlee at Chequers, mainly to report personally on the progress of the FAO negotiations, he went on to the timber problem, which Attlee urged him to take up with the President of the Board of Trade. When he did so he found Sir Stafford Cripps accepting his department's verdict that there was no timber in the US available for export and that the purchasing mission due to leave for Canada would not even go the US.

Wilson then launched a scheme to get around what he considered official pig-headedness in the cunning style which was to be considered his hallmark. He had 'Bomber' Smith added to the purchasing commission as Works' Director General for building materials. He then briefed Smith about the availability of US timber and put him in touch with Tom Meyer. Smith persuaded the others to arrange their travel plans so that, despite their resistance to visiting the US, they had time left over for such a trip after completing their Canadian purchases. Once in the US they 'accidentally' encountered Tom Meyer, who enabled them to purchase US timber. This helped the housing programme to continue, even if it also helped to use up dollars when a shortage of dollars was looming.

The Wilsons returned from the booming US to a London in the grip of its hardest winter and a gathering fuel crisis. But things were looking up for Wilson. The Chief Whip called him in and told him that the Government wanted him to lead a full day's discussion on the FAO on 6 February 1947. He was thrilled because it could easily have been ignored. It was only afterwards he realized that the Chief Whip had probably devised the debate as a 'time-filler'.

Wilson attempted to show that the policies he had carried out at the FAO conference had been enlightened but realistic. He accepted that 'half the human race ... were living at a standard of life far too low to support a decent human existence and a large proportion of the other 1,000,000,000 were, even so, not properly fed.' But the British Government had had to oppose Sir John Boyd-Orr's proposal for a supra-national World Food Board, designed 'to buy and hold stocks of the more important food commodities, to provide a world famine reserve.' This was because a number of nations, and particularly the USA, would not put up the money to finance this international organization. It would be enormously expensive if the organization were to cut prices. Britain did not have the foreign exchange to help finance it. 'No one has a greater respect for [the] FAO, or a greater belief in the work that [the] FAO can do in this field, especially in the undeveloped regions of the world, than I have, but I emphasize that the greatest efforts in this respect must come from the undeveloped countries themselves,' Wilson emphasized.

He warned against allowing a return to prewar over-production, which had led to destroying surplus food when it could find no buyers. 'Even within my own small constituency ... thousands of families on the outskirts of Liverpool and in the Lancashire coal field were living on rations then far lower than those they are getting today, and this was so at a time when farmers and market gardeners within the same Parliamentary division could find no market for their produce, and when farm workers in that area were being asked to live on a standard of life which was quite simply a disgrace to our civilization. At the time when food was being destroyed ... when shiploads of fruit were being dumped into the sea off the foreshore of Formby and Southport ... there were children in Liverpool, a few miles away, who had never even tasted an orange.' He was congratulated by Labour MP Evan Durbin for 'his able and lucid explanation', and Tory Richard Law, who had been the first delegate to the FAO, agreed that Wilson's report was 'lucid' and 'reasonably objective'.[42]

Praise in Parliament and the press warmed the cockles of Wilson's heart, and hope of promotion flickered briefly. Ellen Wilkinson died on 7 February 1947 – the day of his FAO debate. It was expected that his chief, George Tomlinson, would be promoted in her place, thus leaving his job vacant. Wilson would have liked this. But Aneurin Bevan persuaded Attlee to appoint his Parliamentary Secretary, slight and silvery Charles Key, as the new Minister of Works. This would guarantee the subordination of Works to Health and the integration of their housing responsibilities. Wilson hid his disappointment. It hardly increased his admiration for Aneurin Bevan at the time.

He now threw himself into a study of the development areas, where the factory-building programme was going wrong. He was interested both as his Ministry's representative on the Cabinet Committee presided over by Chancellor Hugh Dalton and as an MP for a Merseyside constituency. He had spoken repeatedly, both in his own constituency and in Liverpool, about the Government's plans to build factories and roads to attract industry to the Liverpool area in order to overcome its built-in unemployment. Wilson had himself appointed to investigate problems of development areas. It was no sinecure that winter. Every factory site he visited seemed to be buried in snow. When his tour was over he submitted a report which was scathing of the efficiency of the Board of Trade, which controlled these projects.

## AT LAST

When a summons arrived from the Prime Minister that the Minister, Charles Key, and the Parliamentary Secretary, Harold Wilson, should present themselves at Number 10, Wilson feared the worst. He was afraid he was going to get a dressing-down for daring to attack another department. He had had a minor rebuke from Attlee over misinterpreting the Cabinet's policy on squatters. But now he expected a major rebuke, with his Minister on hand to witness it.

Attlee showed no sign of anger. 'I'm making some Ministerial changes,' he told Key. 'Hilary Marquand is to become Paymaster General to do long-term planning. I want the Parliamentary Secretary to succeed him as Secretary for Overseas Trade.' Attlee then told Wilson: 'There's a big conference over in Geneva in a month's time, so you'd better get yourself briefed.' Wilson was delighted. The pay would be the same – £1,500 – but he would be Number 2 to Sir Stafford Cripps in a big department with foreign trade ramifications. His principal local newspaper, the *Liverpool Daily Post*, was laudatory about his promotion a week before his thirty-first birthday. 'The new Secretary for Overseas Trade, Mr Harold Wilson, MP for Ormskirk, is making his mark early in politics. He is certainly one of the most able among younger Ministers.'[43] But on the Left his promotion – like that of Christopher Mayhew as Under-Secretary for Foreign Affairs and Hugh Gaitskell as the new Minister for Fuel – was taken as typical of the Attlee Government's preference for middle-class right-wingers. 'What do Messrs. Mayhew, Wilson and Gaitskell know of the trade union struggle?' demanded Communist leader Harry Pollitt in the April 1947 *Labour Monthly*.

The tall, spare and austere Sir Stafford Cripps invited him to dinner immediately to explain his methods. 'Well, my boy, I hold two morning meetings every week with my senior officials. They start at 9.30 and I look forward to your presence at the next one.' Wilson was somewhat dismayed when, arriving at his first meeting, he found on the agenda his own report criticizing the Board of Trade's role in factory-building in development areas. The official responsible was also at the meeting and attempted to defend himself, but found Wilson unyielding.[44]

The civil servants at the Board of Trade were not sure they would like this 'new broom'. So they found, from their friends at Works, what his weak spot was. 'In those days,' Wilson recalled, 'I was a glutton for detail. I'd read everything that was put on my desk. It was a very big department, one-tenth of the whole administrative civil service, and I felt I had to know all that was going on. So I was submerged in detail.'[45]

His first task was to read up on the International Trade Organization (later known as GATT) which was to have its conference at Geneva at the end of March. He only had a few hours in the House of Commons on 17 April after returning from Geneva and before taking off next day for Moscow, where he really made his reputation. Sir Stafford Cripps had explained its purpose in a Bristol speech. 'I have done my damnedest to get the Soviet Union to do a deal in industry of any kind, particularly in timber, but, unfortunately, for reasons which no doubt suit their economy, they are not able to do it.'[46] Wilson was clearer in talking to his local political correspondent: 'His job was ... exploratory in the main: to see how far the Russians were prepared to go in trade talks. Britain needed timber, and the Russians had some difficulty in supplying it. The Russians needed electrical and other heavy machinery, and

Britain had some difficulty in supplying that. It was thought high time that the subject was thoroughly explored.' Britain particulary needed a non-dollar source of animal-feed cereals and timber. Harold's secretary, Miss Eileen Lane, took a copy of 'Learn Russian in Three Months' with her. But it was hoped it would not take that long.[47]

There was not much optimism about the talks. The war-battered Russians were acting tough partly because they were still so weak economically. The talks had come about because the Foreign Secretary, Ernest Bevin, had suggested them to Stalin at the end of the fruitless Council of Foreign Ministers' meeting earlier that year in Moscow. Since Montague Meyer had suggested it Bevin had raised the question of Soviet timber exports. Stalin had replied there was not much timber available because of the destruction of logging machinery, but that there might be some cereals available. It was this that Wilson was exploring.

Wilson's delegation was housed in considerable discomfort at the National Hotel in Moscow. Food was still short, service execrable and Stalin's paranoid fear of foreigners reflected in heavy police observation. The timing of the negotiations also reflected Stalin's habit of working through the night, although the trade negotiations were conducted by his Deputy Premier and Foreign Trade Minister, the astute and tough Armenian, Anastasias Mikoyan. Meetings never started before ten at night and usually continued through until the morning.

It was an indication of the desperate need of the Russians for enlarged trade on easy terms that they agreed to negotiate with this bland-faced junior Minister of thirty-one, whose chief would have been of the right status had he been well enough to go. The Russians joked that Wilson could not be as young as he pretended. He joked that the aged Attlee Government was very vigorous, proposing: 'I'll pick a football team of British Ministers, and you pick one of Soviet Ministers, and we'll play you at the Dynamo Stadium in Moscow and knock hell out of you!'[48]

This emphasis on fitness was not misplaced because negotiations with the Russians tend to be an ordeal; they hope that tiredness and the wish to get away will lead to concessions on the part of visitors. In this field Wilson's strong constitution helped. Night after night he negotiated hard with Mikoyan, from 10 p.m. until 6 a.m. 'As soon as the [conference] door opened,' one of his colleagues recalled later, 'it was like showing the ideal pond to a very vigorous duck.' 'Mikoyan and Wilson were still collected and fresh at the end of it, but several of their followers were stretched out on the chairs and sofas.'[49] They went over forty-five different items Britain was willing to import, from building timber to the hair from the tails of Siberian ponies for making violin bows. On their side the Russians did not want to pay cash. They wanted to defer payments for twelve to sixteen years, paying interest at only

5%. They also wanted to scale down the interest on the £60m already owed Britain by Russia from the war. They also wanted to reduce their down-payment on this debt from half to a quarter. They agreed to provide timber and one million tons of cereals initially. Britain agreed to export machinery and chemicals.

Contacts between the two sides were not always hard-bargaining. There were often interludes while fresh instructions or the latest wheat prices from Chicago were awaited. Mikoyan would show his sense of humour by inventing folk sayings like: 'When an Armenian is dealing with a Yorkshireman, what chance is there of an agreement?' – which Wilson later told Attlee. Wilson displayed his own sense of humour by teasing quotations, allegedly from Marx. Since Wilson had never read past page two of *Das Kapital* these were clearly invented. There were also occasional great luncheons, one of which lasted for fully six hours. The Russians, who were generous with the vodka, were careful enough to have a doctor and nurse stand by, with twelve beds – one for each member of the British team. But only two Britons got that 'tired' – and three Russians.

After three weeks of such exploratory talks Wilson and his team flew back to London. The idea was that the Russians needed British exports so much that it was wiser to await their request. But the British Government weakened first in the face of its own economic crisis. Sir Stafford Cripps urged Wilson to go back to Moscow in June. The housing programme was threatened by another timber shortage. The big agricultural expansion planned was threatened by a shortage of animal foodstuffs. Wilson was reluctant to go so soon. But, he agreed, it would give Britain additional bargaining power against the Americans, who were proving quite tough in the Geneva negotiations for GATT, if Britain had alternative sources of raw materials. So on 20 June 1947 he took off with a bigger team, which included specialists.

The second stage of the Wilson–Mikoyan negotiations began as a market haggle between impoverished but willing buyers and sellers. Wilson made some concessions on the Russian wartime civilian debt without going as far as the Russians wanted. Wilson then sought the 700,000 tons of feeding grain the Cabinet had ordered him to get as a minimum. Mikoyan initially offered him 500,000 tons but Wilson insisted he needed two million and, when Mikoyan would not move, he telegraphed for the team's aircraft and retrieved their washing from the laundry at the hotel. On the evening before the plane was due to arrive Mikoyan invited him to a midnight meeting. There he told him that Stalin had authorized the release of 1,250,000 tons. Wilson, containing his triumph, said this was a step in the right direction which justified continuing the talks.

At one point Mikoyan lost confidence in the British team's sincerity as a result of the impossible conditions about shipping payments put up by one of the British officials. Wilson, suspecting this was being done to sabotage the talks, sent the official home and eliminated the shipping payment demand. He met privately with Mikoyan to tell him what he had done. The talks went on, but the tension was wearing. Wilson found that his cigarette-smoking was becoming too heavy. So he switched to the pipe that was to become his hallmark from that point on.

Finally, after five weeks the negotiations were caught in the first chills of what was increasingly becoming a 'cold war'. The timber agreement was agreed. The minimum grain shipments had been agreed. But the price of wheat had not been agreed when the Canadians objected to more being paid for Russian wheat than for theirs. But it was the sudden Foreign Office inflexibility over the size of the Soviet down-payment on their wartime debt for power-stations that caused the final breakdown. The Russians wanted to pay £18m of it while Britain was demanding £25m of the £60m owed. Ernest Bevin was anxious that Britain should not seem to be weakening.

Wilson, anxious to clinch his £40m trade deal, again sent for his plane, thinking that Mikoyan would again weaken. But this time Stalin let the team fly off without the agreement Wilson so much wanted. He did not allow Wilson to live up to his advance billing in his local *Liverpool Daily Post*: 'Almost singlehanded, Mr Harold Wilson, Overseas Trade Secretary, seems on the point of winning a trade pact with Russia which may lessen considerably the strain on Britain's hard currency resources.... The wheat imports in particular would materially lessen the amount of dollars at present needed for Argentine and United States grain and ... go far to make Britain's position secure.'[50]

As Wilson's returning York aircraft landed at London Airport, its brakes failed and it overran the runway. 'Then, as we were landing, there was a terrific bumping and all the lights went out. I was thrown forward in my seat,' he told the press at the airport, after he had helped the more injured from the aircraft. 'I have got to see a doctor, my ribs are hurting me.'[51] He then went home to rest in Oxford, after X-rays had shown there were no minor fractures.

Wilson reported to the Cabinet on the following Monday, 29 July. His ribs still felt painfully sore as he sat on the Front Bench waiting for Sir Stafford Cripps to make a statement on the breakdown of the talks. It was made clear in the House that Britain would have accepted a down-payment of £25m from the Russians the previous Friday, but that Mikoyan had offered only £18m. The door was still open to clinch the deal, it was emphasized, but the Russians would have to go through it first.

The failure of his two-stage negotiations ironically did much to enhance his reputation at a crucial point in his career, now that Sir Stafford's health was sagging. How the Establishment felt was re-captured a couple of years later by the *Observer*: 'Perhaps few people realize that Harold Wilson was under a special temptation during those negotiations. He was a young man just beginning his career; what a triumph to bring back an agreement after so many had failed ... the temptation must have been almost insupportable. Everything had been settled – the amounts and the prices – and only the ... payment remained ... the question for Wilson was whether he should cable for fresh instructions, urging the Cabinet to accept the Soviet terms. He absolutely refused to do so. Courage and strength of character must be added to his proved gift of a quick and brilliant mind.'[52] What those outside the Cabinet and Foreign Office did not know was that his instructions had been growing stiffer, partly to avoid alienating the stiffening Americans. After he returned to London Wilson felt it necessary to deny that the Government was 'refusing to enter into a resumption of the Anglo-Soviet trade talks ... under pressure from the USA on this matter'.[53]

By the summer of 1947 young Harold Wilson had demonstrated several qualities to Clement Attlee. He was an able and dynamic administrator with a lot of resourcefulness. He had also shown in the FAO negotiations in Washington and two sets of trade negotiations in Moscow that he could get along with the Americans and be Yorkshire tough–friendly with the Russians. He also earned a bit of a reputation as a 'know-it-all' with some of his Ministerial colleagues. 'I know how to handle these East Europeans,' he told Arthur Bottomley, the next Secretary for Overseas Trade. 'You give them one overnight session and you break the back of the negotiations.' He took over talks with the Yugoslavs in 1948 and followed his own maxim, negotiating until 7 a.m. Then he handed the talks back to Bottomley, who took fully ten months to finish the negotiations after Wilson had failed.

All politicians on the way up are like ghouls in that they cash in on the disasters of others. In this respect Harold Wilson was no exception. He won the big prize in September 1947 because of the depth of the economic crisis that year and the crass ineptitude of senior Labour leaders in handling it. The unprecedented severity of the previous winter had intensified Britain's economic crisis. Not enough was being produced and exported. Too many men of productive ages were locked up in the Services because of lingering delusions of an imperial past. Despite this the Treasury accepted the American-pressed con-vertibility of the pound sterling in July 1947, precisely when there was a shortage of dollars.

Against this dire background the leadership of Attlee was palsied. Herbert Morrison, who led the Commons and was supposedly in charge of economic planning, was away for months with a thrombosis. Wilson's boss, Sir Stafford Cripps, and a sponsor, Chancellor Hugh Dalton, spent much of their time planning a palace revolution in which Attlee would be dumped in favour of Ernest Bevin, who did not want the job. In the end the attempted *putsch* was blocked by Bevin's disinclination and Attlee's shrewd move to buy off high-minded Sir Stafford by giving him Morrison's economic planning job as Minister for Economic Affairs, leaving a slightly downgraded Presidency of the Board of Trade up for grabs.

## RECALL FROM CORNWALL

Harold Wilson was sitting on a lobster pot in Cornwall enjoying a long-delayed vacation with his family when the call came. He was told that Sir Stafford Cripps wanted to speak to him. When he called back he learned that the Prime Minister wanted to see him for lunch on Sunday at Chequers. 'Listen,' he complained to Sir Stafford's senior private secretary who passed the message, 'this is the first break I've had all year. I came here for a week only. Can't I have even five days without being recalled?' He calmed down when he realized that there was probably a reshuffle afoot and he was included. He thought he might become Minister of Fuel, Supply or Food.

Attlee received him cordially at Chequers and showed him around before lunch. After lunch he resumed his crisp Prime Minister's manner. 'I'm making some changes. The economic situation is very disturbing. It needs better control. So Stafford is going to become Minister for Economic Affairs – a new position which will give him an overall, co-ordinating and supervisory responsibility. I want you to succeed him as President of the Board of Trade.' Wilson was so astonished that he only just managed to thank Attlee.[54]

He had never expected to be promoted to Cabinet rank, heading a mammoth department manned by a tenth of the civil service. He might be able to administer the department, as the political equivalent of its top civil servant. But how could he step into the enormous shoes of Sir Stafford, or Winston Churchill or Lloyd George, who had preceded Sir Stafford? 'When I became President of the Board of Trade, after working for Stafford and seeing how high his standards were, I felt almost appalled at the prospect – but did not feel strongly enough to turn it down.'[55]

Wilson sought out Sir Stafford first thing the morning after his appointment. 'Well, my boy,' he said, 'You've seen Clem. Let me say I'm very glad indeed – and happy for you.' Sir Stafford insisted that, although he would be supreme economic co-ordinator, he would not lean on his youthful successor or diminish the importance of the post of President of the Board of Trade. Wilson raised the question of an ineffective senior official whose fuddy-duddy ways had irritated him. 'If you've decided to get rid of him,' Sir Stafford said, 'you must do so at once. I've never had time to get round to it myself, but you're probably quite right.'

Back in his Overseas Trade office, Wilson had hardly received the congratulations of his Permanent Secretary, Sir John Woods, before he raised the question of getting rid of the civil servant he considered inefficient. After warning Wilson against being too hasty Sir John saw that his mind was made up. 'Right,' he said, 'I've done my duty and stuck up for him. Can I now say to you – I think you're absolutely right.'[56]

At Cabinet, Wilson was far from being so assertive. He was not only the youngest Cabinet Minister by far at thirty-one – the youngest in the twentieth century – but the new boy with the lowest seniority in the Cabinet pecking order assigned by the Prime Minister. He was tremendously impressed by Attlee's efficient chairmanship, his detachment and fairness. He was also conscious of Attlee's sharpness when anyone, no matter how senior, submitted a poorly-argued Cabinet paper and was submitted to the Prime Minister's ruthless cross-examination.

Initially he was concerned mainly to stay out of trouble. He wanted to avoid embarrassing the Government, and also to retain the respect of non-Labour people who respected him more as an efficient 'technocrat' rather than an ideological politician. Thus, the *Economist* wrote, after his appointment: 'Mr Harold Wilson joins the Cabinet at a remarkably early age. He has given promise of great ability both as a politician and as an administrator, and he carries with him into the Cabinet Room the ardent good wishes of a whole generation.'[57] The *New Statesman*, in contrast, spoke of the September 1947 reshuffle which promoted Wilson as making it 'much more "intellectual" than its predecessor ... slightly to the Right of it, and, psychologically, considerably more remote from the Labour Movement. The country will probably be ruled more efficiently this winter than last; but there is a danger that the working class may come to think of this Government not as "us" but as "them".... As far as possible he has created a Government of public servants which will win confidence less by working-class socialism than by its respect for the Statistical Digest.'[58]

Although he did not immediately start his famous 'bonfire of controls' which later enraged the Left, he did soon talk of simplifying them. Controls were important to the Left because those wanting full-scale socialism realized it would be easier to tread that path if the wartime panoply of physical controls were retained. In one of his many speeches urging more exports to enable Britain to survive, he promised the Liverpool Institute of Export simplified controls. 'I am particularly asking our regional offices to ensure that firms who require the assistance of a number of departments should be, so far as possible, dealt with by their parent department and not bandied about from one to another in the search for materials, components, permits, essential building licences and the like.' A few days later, in Manchester, he repeated: 'It is a time when we all want to see that our controls and administrative arrangements are as simple and as streamlined as possible ... We will welcome any advice from the industries that have to deal with those controls, for their improvement, provided that their essential purposes are still carried out.'[59]

At the end of October 1947 Wilson made his third trip to the Geneva talks which produced GATT, his first as President of the Board of Trade. But that was a highly technical conference in which developed countries traded concessions. Britain's main concessions had to come in Imperial Preference.

In December 1947 he urged on Sir Stafford a resumption of the Anglo-Soviet negotiations. Cripps was willing, suggesting the dispatch of a team of officials headed by Foreign Office Under-Secretary Sir George Makins. Wilson, against the advice of all his officials, wanted to head the mission himself. 'There was a hard fight in the Cabinet before Bevin's resistance was overcome and it was possible to let Harold Wilson go to Moscow,' alleged left-winger Konni Zilliacus.[60] Wilson certainly argued that it would end left-wing criticisms if he made an honest attempt to reach an agreement.

Wilson cabled Mikoyan proposing to come for three days to secure the outline of an agreement. He refused to give Mikoyan the commitment in advance that Britain would scale down the £25m downpayment on civilian war debts previously required. He took off with a small team but all were delayed by weather. Mikoyan was sufficiently anxious to start negotiations to be waiting for Wilson at the British Embassy when the party finally arrived in Moscow on a Soviet holiday. A deadlock appeared in the shape of Mikoyan's demand for guarantees on deliveries, possibly anticipating 'cold war' embargoes; but Wilson worked out a compromise on this enabling the Russians to cut off their deliveries as well. A real Middle Eastern market bargaining session went on over the price of cattle grain. Wilson had Cabinet authority to go up only to £130 a ton but by a number of bargaining ruses he managed to get Mikoyan's price down to £111, again using the device of having his plane stand by for take-off. The whole deal was wrapped up on the morning Wilson had insisted he had to leave. A number of their advisers were so tired by the all-night negotiating that they were fast asleep. But both Mikoyan and Wilson were quite fresh.

Wilson took quite a bow in the Commons on 11 December 1947 when he reported on his Moscow success. He was repeatedly and heartily cheered, with the Front Bench beaming benevolently at their young prodigy who could turn the 'iron curtain' into velvet.

Wilson then left Westminster for a whirlwind weekend of constituency and other engagements in the area of Merseyside and Lancashire. The subject of the great achievement in Moscow came up repeatedly whether he was talking to the Lancashire and Cheshire Regional Council of the Labour Party, a trade-union rally in his constituency, his presentation of the Leverhulme Trophy in his old school Wirral Grammar, a public meeting in Blackburn, or a briefing for local reporters in his normal local lodging, the Adelphi Hotel, Liverpool. He gave away a secret to his old school: 'I am sure my Russian friends will not object to my saying this: if you go on a mission to Moscow for three months you may well take three months. If you go for three weeks, it will take three weeks. But if you say you have got to get back in three days for an important engagement in the North, they will only take three days.'[61] If Mikoyan had read the *Liverpool Daily Post* on the following day he would have discovered that Wilson had dodged his invitation to a meeting with Marshal Stalin *not* because of a meeting with His Majesty the King, as he pretended, but because of a presentation and speech at his old school.

Sir Stafford Cripps reported to Wilson that when he showed Agriculture Minister Tom Williams the telegram from Moscow in which Wilson said he had secured the needed animal feed at a low price, Tom Williams had burst into tears. Although others in the Cabinet did not show their feelings as openly there was widespread enthusiasm for Wilson's achievements in keeping agriculture and housebuilding expanding. This was the reaction as well among rank-and-file MPs, particularly those on the Left who had long asked for more trade with Eastern Europe to diminish dependence on the USA. But Conservatives showed their lack of enthusiasm even while Anthony Eden congratulated him in the Commons.

Wilson was subjected to a much harsher Tory attack during the debate on 2 March 1948, with Oliver Lyttelton (later Lord Chandos) and Brendan Bracken, Churchill's protégé and former Information Minister, leading the attack. Lyttelton charged Wilson with having returned with 'a balalaika and a bad bargain'. In exchange for the animal feeding stuffs, which he conceded Britain needed, Wilson had let the Russians have a 'large range of manufactured goods' which were 'about the hardest currency we have at our disposal'. He charged that Wilson

had agreed to use Britain's limited productive ability to make dredgers
and railway locomotives for the Russians which could better be sold for
dollars. He claimed that Wilson had agreed to pay too much for the
coarse grains and to 'lending Russia money to pay off 50 per cent of its
indebtedness'. Bracken claimed the Board of Trade's 'public relations
officers were kept well up to the mark' to 'talk at length about their
master's gifts as a negotiator, but they were silenced about their prices.'
In fact, Bracken claimed, Wilson had swallowed the very terms they had
previously rejected and Wilson's 'performance in Moscow reminds me
of the story of the hunter who shouted to his companion, "I've captured
a bear, but he won't let me go." '

Wilson declined to let Bracken know what he had agreed to pay, but
claimed: 'The prices we paid for Soviet barley, maize and oats were, on a
conservative calculation, about one half the price which [Conservatives]
would have had to pay if trading on world markets.' Had he accepted
Soviet terms in July this 'would have involved a great loss in dollars
because we should have had to pay in convertible sterling. By December
... payment was on a sterling basis.' He had no option but to offer
essential manufactures. 'The essence of a successful deal at the present
time is a provision for the importation of food or raw materials which we
would have had little hope of getting unless we were prepared to give
something of value in return ... electrical plant, locomotives, exca-
vators, machine tools and so on.' He deflected the attack on himself by
counter-attacking the Tories for their opposition to bulk-buying of food
overseas, which had produced good bargains. 'But, then, maybe the
Party opposite do not want us to get our food cheaply.' This produced
the riposte from Brendan Bracken: 'Let [Wilson] try to be a statesman
and not a "smart Alec"!'[62]

Although his anti-Tory combativeness increasingly irritated his
opponents, Wilson at this stage was very much the neutral, slightly
right-wing technocrat, who stayed out of the Right–Left,
Zionist–Arabist arguments which sharply divided the Parliamentary
Labour Party. This was amusingly illustrated in January 1949. The
Parliamentary Labour Party was deeply split over the anti-Zionist
policies of Foreign Secretary Ernest Bevin. Bevin was delaying recognition of the infant state of Israel set up by the UN with Soviet
support. He had persuaded the Cabinet to pull out the British Army in
the expectation that Jordan's Arab Legion would overrun Israel. Now
RAF planes were overflying Israeli lines to find out how far Israeli
forces had penetrated into Egypt. Attacks by the pro-Zionist Crossman
on Bevin were featured from Tel Aviv in the *Sunday Pictorial*. On
Wednesday morning, 19 January 1949, Labour MPs crowded into the
weekly meeting of the Parliamentary Labour Party in the hope of

hearing the inside story. Instead they heard Harold Wilson speaking on trade with Eastern Europe, which instantly lowered the temperature, as intended. If he was then as pro-Israel as he later showed himself to be, he certainly did not show this in a Cabinet in which Ernest Bevin was the most powerful single figure.

With a staff of over 15,000 civil servants to administer the complexities of a tremendous range of functions in the wake of the war there was little wonder that the 'new boy' kept his nose out of others' problems and his eyes focused on his own. This was a period of rationing, price controls and utility furniture, and a tremendous range of normal peacetime responsibilities, including subjects like the cinema, came within the province of the Board of Trade. Wilson worked hard all day, mainly in his large, walnut-panelled office on the sixth floor of the Board of Trade building which then overlooked Lambeth Palace and the Thames. As soon as he came home to the £5,100 Hampstead Garden Suburb house into which he, Mary and Robin had moved at the end of 1947, the inevitable red boxes began to arrive, keeping him up way into the night.

His hard work aged him prematurely. 'In repose,' wrote a former Oxford contemporary, Honor Balfour, 'his manner, his greying temples and his formal clothes give him an appearance of middle age. But once he begins to speak, he cannot restrain his liveliness nor his interest in a subject or person, and his blue eyes twinkle as he chuckles at his own jokes; with that impishness, he must sometimes have been an angelic-eyed, mischievous choir boy shooting pellets at the parson.' If Baptists had choirs!

Miss Balfour found differing opinions about Wilson's abilities among the businessmen with whom he dealt. 'It was in Birmingham recently ... that an irate and frustrated manufacturer fulminated, "Bah, the swashbuckling little pipsqueak ..." But I must record that a City friend of mine narrows his eyes when he speaks of Harold Wilson – "He's a dark horse," he says, "You watch him. He's got something – and don't underrate his ability".'[63]

The opinions of these businessmen were important to Wilson because, although he was top man in the Board of Trade, it was the businessmen of Britain who had to go out to get the foreign orders. When he had first come into the Ministry, the Chancellor had said rightly that bridging the gap between imports and exports was 'by far the greatest and gravest of the immediate economic problems to be faced', and on this depended 'the whole future of our country and the standard of life we shall enjoy'.[64]

However dramatic that challenge, Wilson's own job was limited to providing the ammunition for the battle and to ensuring that there were no blockages in the way of those who wanted to export more. He was involved in seeing through the Commons lots of Bills with titles like Export Guarantees Bill, the Cotton Spinning Bill, the American Aid and European Payments (Financial Provisions) Bill, the Patents and Designs Bill, Distribution of Industry Bill and the Monopoly (Inquiry and Control) Bill, as well as answering dozens of questions, many of them technical and of interest to few.

His speeches at luncheons of Chambers of Trade also tended to be ignored except by trade papers and the loyal *Liverpool Daily Post*. It was understandable that at the British Industries Fair lunch on 5 May 1948 he should have claimed that he was 'probably the only one of His Majesty's Ministers who has drunk a Soviet Minister under the table'. His reference was to the six-hour lunch given by Soviet Deputy Premier Mikoyan the year before. He claimed that he had avoided succumbing to the Russians' trial by endurance by eating snacks of something fatty between drinks. The heroine of the occasion, he insisted, was his young secretary who not only stayed the course but led the company in 'Auld Lang Syne' at the end. The Russians joined in, including the Soviet junior Minister, under the table.[65]

The *Financial Times*, then controlled by Wilson's critic, Brendan Bracken, MP, ridiculed this 'chapter in autobiography': 'Few politicians have made it so plain as Mr Wilson that he considers himself one of Britain's best negotiators. But the benefits to this country of what Mr Wilson conceives to be bargains are far from obvious. No perceptible advantage to Britain has yet resulted from Mr Wilson's wassailing with the Commissars.'[66] But Wilson enjoyed the publicity he had received by telling this story. When the chairman of the Food Machinery Manufacturers' luncheon told him that this had endeared him to all sections of the British public, Wilson joked back: 'I should be very glad if we could communicate on the subject to the temperance vote in my own constituency. The fact that I remained sober when others did not has not in any way secured the support of that very important section of the Ormskirk vote.'[67]

Wilson's unashamed exploitation of such publicity to glamorize himself and the Labour Government made the Conservatives and the Tory press rub their hands with glee when he stumbled in another effort a few weeks later. This was the great 'shoe' controversy referred to in the previous chapter. The issue was shoe rationing and the shortage of good-quality shoes. Wilson, after answering questions in the Commons, expanded on the problem posed by higher working-class demands for shoes in a period of still-restricted domestic production. In a Birmingham speech on 3 July 1948 he began, as we have seen: 'The school I went to in the North was a school where more than half the children in my class never had any boots or shoes to their feet.' In his script he then added: 'They wore clogs, because they lasted longer than shoes of a comparable price,' but he left out that crucial sentence in delivery, so – as he explained – 'the argument was a little compressed'.[68] Then he continued:' 'I have been up there again. The children of my old school are now running about with decent pairs of shoes because their fathers are in safe jobs and have got the social security which we promised our people.'[69] Without the key sentence referring to clogs, Wilson's speech suggested that half his schoolmates in Milns-bridge/Huddersfield had been sent barefoot to school before the war. Despite his apologies for the misunderstanding the Conservative papers did not let him live it down, even pretending that he had claimed to go to school barefoot. Labour had already been in office three years and a general election was not long off. If they could demonstrate that Labour claims of social improvement were vastly exaggerated, this could throw doubt on more realistic claims. The press attack on Wilson lumped him with Aneurin Bevan who, a day after Wilson's speech in Birmingham, had described as 'lower than vermin' those prewar Conservatives who had denied people like himself jobs or social security and forced him to live on his elder sister's earnings.[70]

Curiously enough he got no such stick from the press when a corruption scandal erupted, beginning in October 1948, which affected the Board of Trade. In August 1948 the Permanent Secretary approached Wilson about a 'very serious matter'. Sherman Pools, whom they were thinking of prosecuting for having exceeded their paper ration, had informed the department that a certain Sidney Stanley had offered to have the prosecution dropped for a fee of £5,000. He had claimed to be a friend of John Belcher, Wilson's Parliamentary Secretary, a modest and hard-working ex-railway clerk who had entered Parliament with Wilson in 1945. Wilson ordered the papers to be made available to the police and went to report the matter to Attlee that evening. The Prime Minister then referred it to the Lord Chancellor, who established a powerful Tribunal of Inquiry under the Act of 1921 which gave it certain judicial powers, including compelling a witness to attend, documents to be produced and testimony to be given on oath. John Belcher was given leave until the Lynskey Tribunal concluded its findings.

For the last two months of 1948 Harold Wilson was under considerable tension as the ruthless public cross-examination of Attorney General Sir Hartley (later Lord) Shawcross filled the press. The story which was unravelled centred upon the activities of a larger-than-life, Polish-born Jewish 'fixer' who called himself Sidney Stanley. He claimed, for large fees, to be able to get the Government off the backs of harassed businessmen through his exaggerated claims of friendship with Labour Ministers. He had never met Wilson but had befriended his Parliamentary Secretary, helped by a free holiday at Margate for the Belchers, a birthday party, a gold cigarette case and free suit for John Belcher. Stanley then introduced himself to the Sherman brothers, who ran the pools firm, and told them he could help quash their prosecution for over-using their paper quota. He introduced Harry Sherman to Belcher, who later decided to drop the prosecution. These facts slowly emerged from Shawcross's cross-examinations, including one mild one of Harold Wilson himself. In the Report, which came out in January 1949, Belcher was held to have accepted favours from Stanley and to have given some in return. Belcher apologized to the Commons and resigned his seat. Wilson felt sympathy for him but, also, relief that the corruption had been demonstrated to have been so limited and to have been originated largely by one person,[71] whose tactics were to be imitated a generation later in the Poulson affair.

Wilson derived a good deal more pleasure – if not much success – out of his contacts with the troubled British film industry. In fact, some of his Board of Trade staff thought he was slightly dazzled by his film contacts – as much with Hollywood starlets as with Hungarian-born Alexander Korda. Wilson himself took an impish delight in trying to solve the industry's problems, including 'fathering' one of his brain-children onto someone else. Despite fine actors and writers and a few good directors, the British film industry was weak and in the process of being pushed to the wall by Hollywood, which had a home market almost four times as big. In 1947, when the dollar gap yawned widest, Hollywood was earning $70m in Britain alone. At the height of the crisis, in August 1947, Chancellor Hugh Dalton slapped customs duty of 75 percent on the value of all imported films. Hollywood retaliated with an immediate embargo on the export of films to Britain. Sir Stafford Cripps, then still President of the Board of Trade, privately appealed to Joseph Rank to increase his group's film production, to which he agreed. But nobody in the Government realized at the time that there were a great many American films already in Britain, with the profits on them still bound to be repatriated.

The film crisis was one of the first tackled by the new President of the Board of Trade, Harold Wilson. 'Though I negotiated with Eric Johnston, then head of the MPAA [Hollywood's Motion Picture Association], with great difficulty a concordat between HM Government and Hollywood, I was determined not to allow Hollywood penetration to destroy our film industry – particularly the considerable number of independent producers who needed help and did not want to become fiefs of the two big distributors and organizations.'[72] Wilson agreed with Johnston that the seventy-five percent duty would be lifted and the Americans could take $17m annually out of the country. The rest would be left in Britain, mainly for producing American-financed films here. In exchange the Americans ended their embargo. Wilson did not consult the Rank Organisation, Britain's biggest film company, either on the ending of the embargo or on his next step – the sharp increase in the quota for British-made films to be shown in British cinemas (from twenty percent to forty-five percent). Since he had given Johnston no advance notice this was taken by Hollywood to be sharp practice, a feeling shared by some British specialists. 'Cries of "British double-dealing" were heard on every side of the American press,' recalled Nicholas Davenport in the *Financial Times*. 'Mr Johnston and his colleagues had not broached the question of [a] quota in the original negotiations because the Films Bill was then still before the Parliament, but he had relied on a statement by Mr Wilson in the House of Commons of 19 January 1948, that [the] British quota would be consistent with British production capacity. As we all know to our cost, a first feature quota of forty-five per cent was far more than we could sustain with the very limited number of talented producers or experienced directors we had so far bred or naturalized. As the quantity of British films went up, the quality went down. And so eventually did the quota – to thirty per cent.'[73]

By his mistimed increase in the quota Wilson dealt a severe blow to the industry. 'The Rank Organisation was already seen to be over-extended, independent smaller producers could not quickly fill the gaps, with the result that poor quality films were turned out in a hurry – then flung into the line against the best of the American films that had been stockpiling during the embargo,' records one film historian. 'Inevitably, the public preferred the latter, and one of the cruellest aspects of Rank's situation was that, as a major exhibitor, he was bound to show his own bad films in his own cinemas, to try to cut his losses, knowing that he was bound to lose patrons and so lose his profits as exhibitor. He lost on both swings and roundabouts.'[74]

Wilson was under considerable pressure, not least from the films unions. Tom O'Brien, a fellow MP, warned him: 'If the present situation even continues, let alone worsens, it is the end of the British film industry as we understand it today.'[75] 'That is why I set up the National Film Finance Corporation,' Wilson later recalled, 'which, it may be claimed, injected new life into the industry.' This was a kind of State-owned bank with £5m capital to subsidize producers who did not have Rank's millions behind them. 'When you look at the impressive list of world-beating titles financed through the NFFC over nearly thirty years, one can see the measure of its achievement,' Wilson later claimed.[76]

He was partly right. NFFC funds helped a few good films, like *The Third Man*, to see the dark of cinema halls. But, with Wilson's encouragement, the bulk of the money available went to Sir Alexander Korda's British Lion where it was squandered on costly prestige flops like *Bonnie Prince Charlie*. Wilson's critics think that either he should not have interfered in the production sector in favour of people like Korda, or the Government should have gone whole hog and set up the film equivalent of the BBC in competition with Rank to give real scope to the talented but less tycoonish producers.

Wilson took even greater pride in having fathered a new plan to replace the Entertainment Tax which, in 1948, took £39m out of the sagging industry. Wilson thought of a new form of tax, known to the industry as 'the so-called Eady Levy', as Wilson later put it, after Treasury official Sir Wilfred Eady. 'As a matter of fact,' Wilson confided twenty-seven years later, 'I thought *this* one out while on holiday in Cornwall on a particular favourite walk of mine down to the beach, and succeeded in getting it through the Treasury. I knew it would be highly controversial, and being always a prudent and uncontroversial kind of chap, I was only [too] happy to father its title on the hard-working Treasury official who turned my ideas into a detailed official scheme.'[77] It was planned to provide film producers with an additional £3m a year.

In his interventions in the film industry Wilson managed to persuade both those in the industry and his civil servants in the Board of Trade that he was an ingenious moderate with a weakness for tycoons. But his caution was re-emphasized and his judgment put under considerable strain in the great battle over devaluation which dominated much of 1949. It was a momentous battle in which, as usual, the conflict of personalities was linked with the conflict over policies.

Meanwhile Wilson gave his Ministerial colleagues the impression of being an enormously clever and talented administrator who got a tremendous kick out of cutting corners. This was reflected in his own recollection of how he ended clothes rationing by coupons on 14 March 1949: 'I found out the black market price of coupons; when they dropped from half a crown to threepence in the East End, I knew I was safe. I didn't even take it to the Cabinet. I should have done.'[78] He took advantage of the cutback in such bureaucratic curbs, symbolized in the topical phrase, 'the bonfire of controls', to become a minor press hero for a time – but not with the Labour Left by any means.

## THE BATTLE OVER DEVALUATION

The battle over devaluation in the summer of 1949 was crucial, for Wilson as well as for Britain. The relationship between the pound sterling and other currencies, particularly the dollar, was of great importance to Wilson as President of the Board of Trade. He was in charge of maximizing exports to bring in the most foreign exchange possible and to secure needed imports at the lowest prices possible. If the pound was overpriced it meant that British goods became too expensive overseas.

In April 1949 Wilson launched a new drive for dollar exports, favouring firms which won orders in the US or Canada. This was because, as a result of a recession in the US, there were fewer purchases there of British goods. In May he flew to Canada to investigate possibilities on the spot. There he found that British manufacturers would have to adapt themselves better to North American tastes, as he proclaimed publicly. Privately he came to the conclusion that Britain's prices were too high and that the pound might have to be devalued somewhat.

From the time of his return, the battle over whether to devalue and by how much dominated the top level of the British Government. Initially, in June 1949, both the current and previous Chancellors, Sir Stafford Cripps and Hugh Dalton, were against devaluation. In the first meeting of the Cabinet's Economic Planning Committee, on which Wilson sat, Sir Stafford warned that all Britain's reserves might go suddenly, leading to 'a complete collapse of sterling'. A worried Attlee spoke of '1931 all over again' to Dalton as they left.[79] But when the full Cabinet discussed the crisis at the end of June, Cripps still supported the line taken by the Treasury, the Bank of England, the City and top civil servants like Sir Edward (later Lord) Bridges, then Cabinet Secretary. This was to impose a tighter monetary policy – including higher interest rates and cuts in Government spending – but to oppose devaluation. Morrison began arguing against City-Treasury orthodoxy, insisting that devaluation was a lesser evil. He was joined by Dalton, who had been persuaded by his protégés, Hugh Gaitskell and Douglas Jay, then both junior Ministers under Cripps at the Treasury. It irritated all three of them that Wilson, who had first backed a relatively small devaluation, now seemed to be swinging behind Cripps and Bridges. Dalton, who had long considered him very promising, complained that Wilson 'trims and wavers and is thinking more of what senior Ministers – or even senior officials – are thinking of him than of what is right'.[80]

Like his colleagues Wilson could observe that the ailing Chancellor, Sir Stafford Cripps, would soon be retiring from his post. He had been working terribly hard and showing signs of overstrain in unprecedented demonstrations of impatience and irritability. On 17 July 1949 it was announced that he would retire 'temporarily' for six weeks. He was replaced by the 'Cripps team' involving Harold Wilson, Hugh Gaitskell, then Minister of State for Economic Affairs under Cripps in the Treasury, and Douglas Jay, also there as Financial Secretary. Of these three, Wilson considered himself to be the senior, as the only Cabinet Minister. This was confirmed when he was sent to Paris to represent Britain in Sir Stafford's place at the end of July. The battle for Sir Stafford's succession was on.

Wilson's hesitation about drastic devaluation to about $3 to the pound sterling did him lasting damage. 'In this situation,' recalled Douglas Jay, 'Hugh Gaitskell, who had been given part authority for Treasury policy under the PM in Cripps' absence, made up his mind clearly and decisively what needed to be done, convinced the doubters, including the Chancellor himself while abroad, and supervised all the arrangements (for which credit should also be given to the official Treasury) with remarkable efficiency and absolute secrecy. In effect, at the moment of crisis, he took charge as the man who knew what needed to be done and was able to do it. It was this chapter which left no doubt in the minds of those few who knew the facts that, if Cripps' health failed, Hugh Gaitskell was the only possible Chancellor.'[81] Wilson, as the senior Minister in the 'Cripps team', had the dreary responsibility of signing all the chits for the sale of gold reserves, as the run on sterling pushed Britain inevitably towards devaluation. 'It's like watching yourself bleed to death,' he told friends subsequently.[82]

Wilson finally fell in line with Gaitskell, Dalton and others pressing for devaluation. When Attlee consulted him he agreed it was inevitable, although he was not enthusiastic about dropping so low as $2.80. Atlee, knowing that Wilson was shortly to have a Continental holiday with his sister Marjorie after stopping in at the GATT talks in Geneva, gave him the task of informing Cripps of the Cabinet decision. At the beginning of August Wilson and his sister set off to the GATT meeting at Annecy in France. He did not take with him the letter signed by Attlee for fear of its contents being disclosed in the event of a car crash. Instead, Wilson's Private Secretary, Max Brown, was despatched from London to Zurich with the letter. Meanwhile Wilson made his way slowly. He stopped off first in Evian-les-Bains, where Foreign Secretary Ernest Bevin was resting. There he brought him up to date on the decision made on devaluation in his absence from London. This was necessary because it had been decided that the Foreign Secretary should accompany Cripps to the September dollar talks in Washington, after which devaluation was to be announced. Then Wilson went on to Annecy, where the GATT talks were proceeding; he found the Americans resisting the British plan for commodity agreements to support prices for Commonwealth raw materials like rubber and tin. He reached Zurich on 6 August and informed Lady Cripps via the British Consul that he wished to see Sir Stafford. He then retrieved the letter signed by Attlee from Max Brown – who had slept with it under his pillow – and took it to the Chancellor at his clinic. Sir Stafford, Wilson later recalled, was 'a bit upset by it' initially.[83] Wilson stayed to tea to bring Sir Stafford up to date on all the factors, including the relentless pressure from the United States, that were compelling the Government to devalue. Two weeks later Sir Stafford flew home to confer at Chequers with the Prime Minister. The final decision to devalue was taken by the full Cabinet on 29 August 1949, but only disclosed on 18 September.

The Government put Wilson in to follow Winston Churchill in the two-day debate which succeeded the devaluation announcement. He criticized Churchill for an electioneering speech, then proceeded to attack the Tories and Churchill for having exploited the Lancashire textile workers and the miners. Churchill retorted; 'I knew Lancashire long before the Right Honourable Gentleman', without letting on that he also knew that Wilson's father had been his sub-agent in Northwest Manchester. Wilson then went on to the serious part of his speech. Britain had to reduce further its abnormal dependence on dollar sources of supply, which now would become more expensive. It must also help other Commonwealth countries to do the same. Britain had already increased the proportion of dollar imports paid for by its exports from the prewar twenty-seven per cent to thirty-six per cent in 1948. But the rate of exports from the UK to the USA and Canada had begun slipping back. 'We need a vast increase in our dollar exports if we are to achieve the stability and the independence of external aid' desired. The new exchange rates would make British exports more competitive. Engineering exports could be increased tenfold and consumer goods threefold, he was sure. 'The tragedy of our situation is that, in spite of our increased dollar exports, we no longer have either investments or sterling area dollar earnings to bridge the gap.' To give more incentive to industry, the Government would now retain only the essential controls. Price controls would be retained because 'we cannot allow the present situation to be exploited by profiteers who seek to lower the people's standard of living by unjustifiable increases in prices.' 'Certain basic controls essential to the maintenance of full employment, to the proper location of industry, to the maintenance of our economy on an even keel – those controls will remain a permanent instrument of our national policy.... What we want to get rid of as quickly as possible ... are those controls which are a hangover from the wartime administration, which restrict the handling or sale or manufacture of goods to specified firms engaged in their manufacture at some date in the past.' He would not decontrol in order to hand back a monopoly to any prewar group of companies.[84]

Just after the die had been cast on devaluation, Wilson shaved off the moustache he had grown to look older. He told his local newspaper that he felt he now looked old enough at thirty-three.[85] But he still astonished people in Washington by his appearance. When Eric Johnston introduced him to Cecil B. DeMille, the latter expressed his surprise. Wilson retorted that Pitt had been Prime Minister at twenty-one, and he was already thirty-three and had not made it yet. In fact he may well have felt that his chance was receding, at least via the Treasury route on which he had placed his hopes. Fred (later Lord) Lee, who was subsequently to be a close associate of Wilson's, was then PPS to Sir Stafford. He asked him who he thought would be his successor as Chancellor. 'Hugh, I suppose,' was Sir Stafford's reply. 'Do you think that Bevan would accept the promotion of Gaitskell to No. 3 in the hierarchy?' asked Lee, without getting an answer.

At that stage nobody worried about whether Wilson would be disappointed if Gaitskell, who was ten years his senior, leap-frogged over him in the Labour hierarchy. Certainly they did not see him in the same camp as Aneurin Bevan. He continued with his 'bonfire of controls', which he had launched on the eve of the 1948 Guy Fawkes day and continued until he had abolished the need for some 200,000 permits and licences. This was far from popular with the 'Keep Left' groups of left-wing Labour MPs who were later to form the kernel of the 'Bevanite' movement. In a memorandum written for this group by Dr Thomas (later Lord) Balogh, who was to become Wilson's intimate advisor from 1952 on, the group was alerted against 'increasing pressure ... being exercised on the Cabinet from within and without the administration to consent to further dismantling of the machinery of control'.[86]

## RIGHT FOR NEW CONSTITUENCY

Wilson confirmed himself as a moderate, if anything slightly to the right of centre of the Labour Party, when he fought his new constituency of Huyton in the February 1950 general election. He had decided on the need to move out of Ormskirk as early as October 1948, when it became clear that it would become much more rural and Conservative as a result of losing two industrial areas under that year's boundary redrawing. He was offered a seat in the Birmingham area but he preferred to stay in the Merseyside area where he had been involved for years in various projects to fight the area's built-in heavy unemployment. He was offered Huyton, on Liverpool's fringe. It would be fairly safe initially because its boundary was redrawn to include part of Widnes. It would become even safer as the new housing estates in Kirkby increased numbers of Labour-voting Roman Catholics from the Liverpool docks. Wilson, although a Congregationalist, got on well with the Catholic hierarchy in the Liverpool area because he went out of his way to help them solve their problems of building enough Catholic schools for their growing flock.

During the campaign Wilson had a joke which he kept repeating. He ran into fog driving the seventy miles between Runcorn and Northwich. 'If it had not been for my well-known habit of keeping to the Left, I would have been in the ditch before now. I think that there is a lesson in that for the country.' In fact his campaign was very moderate. 'There is no problem facing the country which cannot be solved by increased production,' he said repeatedly.[87]

With a constituency four-fifths Catholic he was willing to play an anti-Russian line, thus ridding himself of the 'soft on Russia' reputation some Tories were attributing to him. When someone at Gladstone Docks asked about people riding about in 'luxurious cars', Wilson said he had never seen such luxurious cars as in Moscow. He had been at a dinner there where, after eating for two hours, his host said there were ten more courses. When Wilson asked whether workers could get such meals, his host insisted they could if they could afford it. 'With potatoes at fifteen shillings a pound, and caviare between £5 and £6 a pound and with workers' wages lower than ours, I told him that there did not seem much chance of the Russian workers getting much caviare.'

He had a lively meeting at Rhyl on 14 February because of Tory hecklers. When he joked about the Tory manifesto, 'The Right Road for Britain', a heckler shouted: 'That's better than the right road to Moscow,' clearly referring to Wilson's Russian negotiations. 'I have been on the road to Moscow three times,' Wilson admitted, 'to get trade agreements for Britain with the Soviet Union. Anyone who knows anything about Communism knows that the best bulwark against Communism in this country is social democracy. Why does that expert at the back think that the Communists have been fighting the Labour Government? It is because the Communists know that it is in the diseased spots of uncontrolled capitalism that Communism can breed and spread.' He repeated this theme a few days later.[88]

Overconfidence in the safety of the new Huyton constituency almost ended his political career, at least temporarily, with that election. He was asked to do a whistle-stop tour of marginal seats in the Northwest and North Wales. Then the position at Huyton was re-evaluated by Sydney Gordon, a schoolmaster and local Labour activist: 'When I got down to the facts I realized that in spite of the Labour background of the original Widnes division [on which Huyton was based] the inclusion with Huyton, which was then distinctly middle-class, of Prescot and Knowsley, where there were Tory leanings, made Harold Wilson's own constituency decidedly marginal. So I advised him to stay home and do some hard work.'[89]

It was not very easy to use him effectively in the constituency because, according to his agent then, Arthur Waite, Wilson was still very stiff and very much the civil-servant-turned-politician. He did not then have the knack of mixing with ordinary people in the workingmen's clubs, of making small talk while having a pint. This surprised Waite, who was a Huddersfield man like himself and had gone to the same schools at the same time. In the end Harold and his supporters were shaken when they won by only 834 votes against a Liberal and a Communist as well as a Conservative, Geraint Morgan, who was later to be an opponent in the Commons. It was clear that Labour support would grow as Labour supporters from Liverpool moved into the Liverpool-built council houses in Kirkby and Huyton. But it had been a near thing.

## THE TRANSFORMATION

Within a single year, from the beginning of the new Parliament in March 1950 until a year later, Harold Wilson underwent a remarkable change. He was transformed from the moderate, slightly right-of-centre, loyal young technocrat still hoping for preferment from Prime Minister Clement Attlee to a left-of-centre rebel waiting to resign with left-winger Aneurin Bevan. From the MP who had campaigned for re-election in February 1950 as a critic of the Russians and of Communism, he seemed to many of his colleagues to have changed into a critic mainly of the Americans.

What basically imposed this change was the outbreak of the Korean War on 25 June 1950, when North Korean troops, let off the leash by Marshal Joseph Stalin, crossed the 38th parallel to attack the South Koreans in the mistaken belief that the US would not defend South Korea. When the Americans did go to the support of the South Koreans they insisted that their allies not only support them but also accept their tempo and swallow the disadvantages of precipitate American decisions.

To show unquestioning loyalty to the American alliance imposed special problems on the Labour Government, whose slower economic recovery from its war battering had already imposed devaluation in 1949. The belt-tightening that followed in its wake was already beginning to produce positive economic results in the first half of 1950 when the war-induced runaway inflation of crucial raw materials again subjected the British economy to new strains.

It was the differing reaction of the various elements in the Labour leadership to the special tensions of 1950–51 which produced the famous rebellion of April 1951, which in turn suddenly made an able but little-known Cabinet Minister into a famous rebel. It was not, to be fair, Harold Wilson's own rebellion. This has been dramatized for history in the tag of 'Nye's little dog' affixed to Wilson by Dalton and others on the opposite side of the argument. Had not the tempestuous and volatile Welshman, Aneurin Bevan, finally decided to rebel, Wilson would not have rebelled on his own. Therefore, had not the acting Prime Minister, Herbert Morrison (Attlee was ill), and Hugh Gaitskell been insistent on a showdown with Bevan, Wilson's subsequent history might have been very different. But, equally clearly, Wilson refused to allow Bevan to resign on his own.

Looking back, Wilson believes he first threw in with Bevan in March 1950 in the second crisis over Bevan's resistance to putting a ceiling on the growth of his 'baby', the National Health Service he had fathered. The first had come in the economic cuts imposed in the autumn of 1949 in the wake of devaluation. Bevan insisted on a *free* Health Service which was anathema to the Treasury, who saw not only its mounting cost but a ceilingless commitment. In 1949 Bevan reluctantly accepted a power to impose a one-shilling charge on prescriptions, which, he chortled, he would never impose. So long as his friend Sir Stafford Cripps was Chancellor, Bevan thought he could get away with it.[90]

But even Sir Stafford, under pressure from his Number 2, Hugh Gaitskell, grew tougher, as anti-Bevan Cabinet Ministers like Herbert Morrison complained: 'Nye is getting away with murder.'[91] The first real confrontation, Wilson recalls, took place in March 1950. 'Gaitskell never believed in a free Health Service and was trying to prove that he could be an "Iron Chancellor".' At Buscot Park, the home of the left-wing Lord Faringdon, Wilson heard Bevan declare that he would resign if charges were imposed on the Health Service. So Wilson went to see Cripps to plead that no sacrilegious hands be put on Bevan's 'Ark of the Covenant'. Then he went back to Nye to plead that he compromise with Sir Stafford, who was ill and under a lot of pressure. Bevan and Cripps met and Bevan agreed, in exchange for abandoning prescription charges, that he subject NHS costs to a weekly scrutiny by a Cabinet Committee presided over by the Prime Minister. It was on that Committee that Bevan made his first close contact with Gaitskell. The flamboyant working-class Welshman and the uptight middle-class Englishman took an immediate dislike to one another.[92]

The hostility between the two men could also be experienced at the regular Thursday dinners presided over by Sir Stafford Cripps for Ministers, especially those associated with the economic departments. Rows between Bevan and Gaitskell flared up continually. Wilson recalls that curbing the NHS 'became a mission or obsession' with Gaitskell. John Strachey, who had been close to Bevan in the 1930s but was now closer to Cripps and Gaitskell, recalled that Bevan would give Gaitskell a tongue-lashing while Gaitskell would contradict him coldly and factually. 'I tried to explain to Bevan that the quiet, rather slight man who sat opposite him had "a will like a dividing spear". I might have saved my breath for all the effect I had on Bevan,' recalled Strachey. 'Why,' Strachey asked Bevan, 'are you going out of your way to make a rift between yourself and one of the really considerable men of the government?' 'Considerable?' retorted Bevan. 'But he's nothing, nothing, nothing!'[93] This was not Wilson's judgment. He had been worsted by Gaitskell in the devaluation argument and already suspected he was Cripps's designated successor.

Typically, Bevan finally exploded in June 1950 and stopped going to Sir Stafford's weekly dinners after he had been 'needled' by Gaitskell at a Cabinet Committee meeting on the NHS and had indulged in 'an outburst of resentment', as he wrote to Sir Stafford. 'I have made it clear to you, the Prime Minister and Gaitskell,' he wrote to his old friend Sir Stafford, 'that I consider the imposition of charges on any part of the Health Service raises issues of such seriousness and fundamental importance that I could never agree to it.'[94] But these behind-the-scenes clashes would never have moved to the front of the stage without the curtain having been raised by the Korean war which began that month.

The Korean War had no immediate divisive impact. When President Truman astonished Stalin by going to the aid of the reeling South Koreans, the support of the British Cabinet was immediate and unqualified. No word of dissent was raised. Wilson himself broke his holiday in Cornwall to speak at Truro on 24 August 1950 in support of Britain's commitment to the US–UN side in Korea. He told listeners that they could see collective security at work as never before in Korea and the Government were unanimous that they could not shrink from anything needed to protect world peace, even if it were politically unpopular.[95] On 18 September 1950 Wilson told the Commons, to the evident satisfaction of Winston Churchill, that two vertical borers ordered by the Polish Communist Government would be seized for use in Britain's own rearmament programme. Doubts about the possible escalation of the Korean conflict were limited in the Parliamentary Labour Party to the handful in the 'Keep Left' Group, who feared what would happen if the US got into a conflict with Communist China. Barbara Castle was deputed to see Harold Wilson and Ian Mikardo to see Aneurin Bevan.[96] But there was no indication that either resisted the Government's decision to accept, under US prodding, a £3,600m rearmament programme to be spread over three years. Both doubted that such a large programme could be inserted into a peacetime economy without dislocation. Bevan got into an argument with the Cabinet Secretary Sir Norman Brook (later Lord Normanbrook), because he wanted his 'opposition' recorded.

Marginal differences suddenly seemed more important, for two reasons. First, Hugh Gaitskell succeeded Sir Stafford Cripps in October 1950. In fact, Sir Stafford, who was a dying man, had 'temporarily' retired from his post as Chancellor in July 1950, when Gaitskell had become acting Chancellor. The latter had acquitted himself so well that Wilson accepted that it was 'inevitable' that he would become Cripps's formal successor. In contrast, Bevan exploded when Gaitskell was formally named in October 1950. He objected to the promotion of someone who was not only a grim opponent but had no power base in the Labour movement. He wrote to the Prime Minister to express his 'consternation and astonishment' at Gaitskell's appointment and had a 'tremendous row' with Attlee when he registered his complaint in person.

Next, the gulf between Bevan and Gaitskell suddenly deepened into an abyss as the role of the Americans in Korea changed. Truman's commitment of unprepared US forces to Korea had been supported by the Attlee Government because, like South Korea or Japan, it saw US willingness to defend its allies as Britain's main guarantee of defence against possible Communist aggression. So long as the MacArthur forces were on the defensive, there was no problem. But once the Americans recovered and counter-attacked, doubts began to grow about the danger of the war expanding. Once General MacArthur's forces crossed the 38th parallel dividing South from North Korea and began to approach Korea's border with China, Labour doubts multiplied as fears of involving China in the war escalated. Britain had already recognized Mao Tse-tung's new Communist regime in Peking while the US still backed Chiang Kai-shek. In November the Chinese entered the Korean war.

This development drove a wedge between the enthusiastic pro-Americans, spearheaded by Gaitskell, and the Chinese sympathizers led by Bevan. Gaitskell's prewar anti-fascism had convinced him that only the tightest links with the US could save Europe from the new menace of Communism. He was willing to follow the Americans in their belief that the Chinese Communists were mere satellites of the Russians and that, unless their aggression was halted, Russia might hurl 175 divisions at Western Europe. Bevan rejected the idea that the Chinese Communists were identical with the Russians. Moreover, he was sure the war-battered Russians were in no condition to launch military attacks against a West backed by Americans who had emerged from the war richer and more powerful, with a considerable lead in nuclear weaponry. In this attitude Bevan had a certain amount of support from Hugh Dalton and some sympathy from Harold Wilson.

Like many others, Harold Wilson became very much concerned in December 1950 when it looked as though the activities of General MacArthur and his backers might result in an all-out war with China, including the possible use of atomic bombs by the USA. This was desired neither by President Truman nor by his Chief of Staff, General Omar Bradley, who considered any war on the mainland as 'the wrong war, at the wrong time, in the wrong place, against the wrong enemy'. But at the moment it looked as though General MacArthur, as the US Viceroy, was dictating policy. The pro-Chinese in the Cabinet were worried. 'Nye and I spoke,' Dalton recorded in his unpublished diary. 'He said he had told Clem he ought to fly out to [the] US to see Truman ... I said I didn't like this [situation].'[97] Dalton wrote to Attlee supporting Bevan's advice. Attlee flew to Washington to discover that he and Truman saw things similarly and were both critical of MacArthur.

Wilson's own support for Bevan's position derived much less from foreign sympathies than from domestic difficulties. His job was to speed the recovery of Britain's economy, enabling it to export more and import less. The Korean war and profligate American consumption of the world's raw materials to fuel it were increasingly getting in his way. 'During the past week,' he told a Cotton Board conference at Harrogate on 20 October 1950, 'we have received a rude shock over our supplies of raw cotton from the United States during this year. This ... will present us with real problems in the next twelve months.'[98] By December 1950 raw material stockpiles were twenty-five percent below the previous June.

This sort of shortage became more menacing when the new Chancellor, Hugh Gaitskell, returned from Washington with the news that the assumption that the US would provide funds totalling £550m to help finance Britain's £3,600m rearmament programme was now invalid. Instead of providing the funds originally promised, the US was trying to get Britain to increase further its three-year programme. Bevan argued that there was little chance of Soviet aggression before 1955 at the earliest. Therefore it was more likely to help Communism if the West European NATO allies either overstrained their economies or became over-dependent on US help.

Wilson became increasingly worried about the impact of the Korean war on Britain's exports. 'The main burden of defence will undoubtedly fall on the metal and engineering industries,' he warned the Export Merchants Group. 'The serious shortage of certain raw materials as a result of increased world demand arising from rearmament, as well as stockpiling, is bringing to the fore once again problems of a kind with which we were only too familiar in wartime and the immediate postwar period.'[99]

It was in this context that the Americans asked that Britain's rearmament programme be stepped up again to something like £6,000m in three years, a demand later scaled down to £4,700m. 'We have got to rearm, and rearm swiftly,' responded Gaitskell.[100] 'In December [1950], under American pressure,' Wilson later recalled, 'the UK stepped up its programme to £4,700m over three years. Nye and I fought this in Cabinet, saying amongst other things that it was incapable of realization, as physical resources were not there to meet it, quite apart from the grave raw materials crisis which was developing as a result of US stockpiling.... The defence programme ultimately went through with the two of us opposing it, but succeeding in getting into the PM's statement the qualifying clause about the possibility of review if, through raw material shortage or other reasons, it became impossible to carry it out ... Simultaneously there was a running battle in Cabinet about the branding of China as [an] aggressor [in Korea], in which the protagonists were H[ugh] G[aitskell] and Nye.'[101]

Wilson urged on Bevan in February 1951 that they should resign together on the issue of over-rapid rearmament in a period of grave raw material shortages. Under conditions which were developing, he thought, the Labour Government would lose the next general election which could not be long delayed since it had only a six-seat majority. Labour might be out of office for a Parliament or two. But in the interim, as the previous Margate conference had shown, Labour activists were moving Left. If they resigned and took the issue to the Labour movement, they could return as Prime Minister and Chancellor of a Labour Government in four or eight years. But Bevan demurred, saying that the pace of rearmament and the shortage of raw materials would not arouse the support of their Labour movement.

The China issue came to a climax behind the scenes with Bevan holding the fort against US pressure to back its demand that China be named the 'aggressor' in Korea before the UN. Six MPs in the 'Keep Left' movement wrote a letter to the Prime Minister on 23 January 1951 claiming: 'It is impossible to exaggerate the strength of feeling which exists in the constituencies about the proposal to brand China as an aggressor and to operate sanctions against her. We have never seen anything so strong since 1945.... R.H.S. Crossman, Barbara Castle, Ian Mikardo, W. T. Williams, Marcus Lipton, Michael Foot.'[102] But Gaitskell, by getting Foreign Office support in the absence through illness of Bevin, succeeded in committing the Cabinet to backing the US in a slightly modified 'branding' resolution which passed the UN

General Assembly on 30 January. 'It was all a battle for power,' said Gaitskell later, 'he knew it and so did I.'[103]

Attlee, trying to head off another collision on the Health Service with the next Budget, persuaded a reluctant Bevan to become Minister of Labour, a post which he took in January 1951. Colleagues like Herbert Morrison, who thought that Attlee should force Bevan to toe the line or sack him, received their answer in Bevan's speech in the debate on rearmament on 15 February 1951. In this he outlined brilliantly – winning the admiring support of Winston Churchill – how to sustain the Anglo-American alliance while curbing American adventurism and crudities. It was ludicrous to treat the Russians as all-powerful bogeymen and take it for granted that the Third World War was inevitable; the Russians could not take on the Atlantic community while their economic strength in things like steel production lagged so far behind the West. What was wanted for mankind was 'another breathing space'. Increased arms production must come at a pace that Britain could sustain and not be 'accompanied by a campaign of hatred and witch-hunting', as had occurred in the States.[104]

But Bevan himself was to get very little breathing space. Instead of being able to devote himself to his new job as Minister of Labour, he and Wilson were involved in the behind-the-scenes struggle in which international politics overlaid domestic politics, and the clashes in both were sharpened by the confrontation of personalities. In the absence of Attlee in St Mary's Hospital for an ulcer operation, Bevan's long-standing enemy Herbert Morrison was acting Prime Minister. Hugh Gaitskell was determined to make Bevan finally swallow the nasty medicine of prescription charges. This was not the only difference around the Cabinet table. Thus the US was pressing for the rearmament of the Federal Republic of Germany, a move opposed by the formidable combination of Ernest Bevin, Hugh Dalton and Aneurin Bevan. But prescription charges were the key issue for Bevan, over which he had long said he would resign rather than accept. On 22 March both Bevan and Gaitskell announced that they would resign if they did not get their way. This was at the crucial Cabinet meeting to discuss imposing £13m in charges for false teeth and spectacles in the Budget to be announced on 10 April. Morrison announced that Attlee supported these charges. Gaitskell announced that Bevin, also absent ill, backed them too. James Griffiths, a Welsh ex-miner like Bevan, wanted the subject put off. Wilson was Bevan's only supporter. Bevan demanded to know why the Cabinet insisted on a confrontation on the subject since the charges would only bring in £13m in a Budget totalling £4,000m. Why not take the £13m off the armaments Budget, since the raw materials shortage would prevent the whole of the sum being spent anyhow?[105] Ten days later, addressing a rowdy meeting of Bermondsey dockers, Bevan cut off his own possibility of retreat. 'I will never be a member of a Government which makes charges on the National Health Service for a patient,' he told an interrupter.[106] Some colleagues, like Dalton, thought Bevan was bluffing. 'Nye means business,' Wilson assured Dalton, 'he can't climb down after committing himself in public like that. What's more, if Nye does resign, he'll take over the leadership of the Left throughout the country.'[107] Wilson had not missed noticing that at the previous Labour annual conference in Margate in October 1950 not only had Bevan topped the vote for the National Executive but other left-wingers had strengthened their positions.

It was a case of the inevitable collision between the irresistible force and the immovable object. Dalton, convinced by Wilson that Bevan would resign if Gaitskell brought in charges, went to see Gaitskell. Gaitskell was determined. 'He said he would not always be blackmailed and give way. If we did not stand up to him, Nye would do to our party what Lloyd George had done to the Liberals. It would, he thought, do us good in the country to make a stand on this. Nye's influence was much exaggerated.'[108]

Dalton was surprised by the extent to which Gaitskell seemed to be preoccupied with showing himself as a tough leader to the electorate at large. 'I thought that H[ugh] G[aitskell] thought too little of the party and too much of the general mood of the electorate,' Dalton confided to his diary. This came after Dalton had mentioned to Gaitskell that, in addition to Bevan and Wilson, John Strachey, the ex-Leftist now a wavering moderate War Secretary, thought of resigning. Gaitskell replied: 'We will be well rid of the three of them!' When Dalton tried his hopeless mediation on Bevan two days later he found Bevan's animosity towards Gaitskell bottomless. Gaitskell, Bevan gritted, had behaved like a second Snowden in his efforts to please the Treasury. He was wildly pro-American and therefore had accepted an impossible rearmament programme at their behest. Gaitskell was trying to precipitate his resignation.[109]

Gaitskell confirmed this in the Cabinet wrangle next day, 9 April 1951, on the eve of the Budget. During the discussion which lasted much of the day Gaitskell added provocatively that, even if he could spare the £13m to be earned by spectacles and teeth charges, he would rather spend them on better old-age pensions. Bevan still delayed his resignation, as if waiting for some angel of political peace to save him. He and Wilson went to see Attlee at St Mary's, Paddington, that night. According to Wilson's recollection, Attlee promised to speak to Gaitskell, to ask him 'to be more reasonable'. But that same night Attlee, after listening to Gaitskell, seemed to support his getting rid of Bevan.[110]

Gaitskell made his Budget speech as planned, as a slight concession leaving out only the date when the charges would be introduced. That night Bevan and Wilson went back to the Prime Minister. He urged Bevan to speak to the next morning's meeting of the Parliamentary Labour Party to plead for forbearance and postponement of the crisis. Just before Bevan spoke to the meeting the news was flashed from Washington that President Truman had sacked General MacArthur. Bevan told the PLP that, in response to many appeals, including one from Attlee, he would not resign but would await events. He urged other parties to the debate to show a concern for party unity equal to his own. What he meant was that the actual legislation bringing in the spectacle and teeth charges should be delayed. Most of Bevan's many advisers, except from his constituency, were against his resigning. 'I gather that all went off well at the party meeting,' Attlee wrote to Bevan on 18 April, several days after Ernest Bevin had died. 'The death of Ernie has rather overshadowed these differences, and I hope that everyone will forget them. I think that it is particularly essential that we should present a united front to the enemy.' This was a reference to their talks about the possibility of a general election in two months' time. 'The next few weeks will be very tricky with the USA going haywire over MacArthur. Hope to be back at work by the end of next week.'[111]

But the day before, the Cabinet had decided to bring in the Health Charges Bill forthwith, a decision confirmed two days later, on 19 April. On that occasion Bevan announced he would not be voting for it. Leading Ministers went to see Attlee, who then wrote more brusquely to Bevan on 20 April. 'I shall be glad to know today that you are prepared to carry out loyally the decisions of the Government,' Attlee demanded. He may have been stiffened by the publication in *Tribune*, edited by Bevan's wife, Jennie Lee, and his acolyte, Michael Foot, a biting editorial entitled 'A Dangerous Budget' which showed every evidence of having been written by Bevan. It attacked Gaitskell as another Philip Snowden, widely regarded as having been a traitor to Labour when he joined the MacDonald Government of 1931. 'We have had to wait 20 years for a Labour Chancellor to win such warm approval from Conservative quarters.'[112]

That Friday night, 20 April 1951, Bevan telephoned Wilson who was speaking in East Anglia. 'I am resigning,' he told him, 'they've introduced the Bill.' Bevan wrote out his resignation letter on Sunday 22 April and went on talking with his colleagues that evening and next day. On Monday morning, 23 April, Harold Wilson and John Freeman arrived for their chat. Freeman, a tall, handsome and very smooth-talking young man, had been very far on the Left when he arrived in the House in 1945, 'almost Trotskyist' in the view of

Tom Driberg. But he had been such a highly competent Parliamentary Secretary for Supply that Dalton, the old talent-spotter, was pushing him for a 'No.1' spot as Cabinet Minister even when Freeman was talking of resigning with Bevan and Wilson.

Wilson had already made up his mind to resign, although this was not widely known. The previous day, on Sunday, he had been golfing with Ted (later Lord) Castle, the journalist husband of Barbara Castle. Ted said about Nye's decision to resign: 'At least he has the consolation of being able to address adoring audiences of 2,000 all over the country.' 'Would it surprise you to hear that I intend to resign as well?' asked Wilson. After expressing his surprise and congratulations, Ted added: 'Although you are highly regarded as a departmental Minister, you can hardly be said to arouse enthusiasm as a political speaker – unless you change.' 'I intend to!' snapped back Wilson.

Bevan tried to discourage Wilson and Freeman from resigning when they turned up at his Cliveden Place flat that Monday morning. A single resignation might be the best way to make the point without hurting the party, which would be facing an early general election.

Any chance of dissuading Freeman from resigning had disappeared as a result of efforts by the Government to buy his loyalty. Dalton saw him twice to urge him not to resign and thus bar the way to sure promotion. Labour's Chief Whip, William Whiteley, an obedient Morrison man, had offered him the post of Financial Secretary to the Treasury if he stayed. When he stalked out this was interpreted as a demand for more. He was offered Harold's job if he stayed in the Government after Harold resigned.[113]

Harold rejected the idea that they should not resign with Bevan. 'Look,' he told Nye, 'ninety-eight per cent of the blow has already come from your resignation. John and I are only the small remaining balance.' He was anxious, however, not to worsen his good personal relationship with Attlee. Instead of sending him a letter, which would inevitably seem cold and would elicit a cold letter in response, he went to see Attlee again in hospital to explain himself in person.

His hope of going without publishing his letter to Attlee was achieved. But Bevan's Commons resignation speech was so bitter, so unsuitable, and so badly received, even by his sympathizers, that Wilson had to make his own. Bevan was a brilliant orator, but like many brilliant orators he did not work best from a script. On his best occasions he was inspired by a combination of his own ideas and the reaction of his audience. On this occasion his key audience of Labour MPs did not want him to resign and did not want him to illustrate publicly the split in the party. Because of this hostility he felt it necessary to justify himself, and self-justification turned into a bitter attack on Gaitskell. 'I want to make that quite clear to the House of Commons; the figures for expenditure on arms were already known to the Chancellor of the Exchequer to be unrealizable ... I begged over and over again that we should not put figures in the Budget on account of defence expenditure which could not be realized', partly because of the scramble for raw materials and the 'lurchings of the American economy' which worsened matters. This raw material shortage would intensify the serious under-employment in British industry. Factually he made much sense, if only his audience had known the full facts. But emotionally he could only be comprehended by those who were familiar with his previous eighteen months' battle with Gaitskell. Otherwise it seemed venomous to attack Gaitskell's Budget thus: 'It was a remarkable Budget. It united the City, satisfied the Opposition and disunited the Labour Party – all this because we have allowed ourselves to be dragged too far behind the wheels of American diplomacy.' 'Take economic planning away from the Treasury, they know nothing about it ... It has been perfectly obvious on several occasions that there are too many economists advising the Treasury, and now we have the added misfortune of having an economist in the Chancellor of the Exchequer himself.'

Bevan then proceeded to lose the rest of his audience by trying to justify his resignation about charges which only amounted to £13m out of a total Budget of £4,000m. This was no 'triviality' because a similar 'triviality' – an attack on seasonal workers – had 'started an avalanche in 1931'. 'If [Gaitskell] finds it necessary to mutilate, or begin to mutilate, the Health Service for £13m out of £4,000m, what will he do next year? Or are you next year going to take your stand on the upper denture? The lower half apparently does not matter, but the top half is sacrosanct. Is that right?'[114] There was no cheer to greet him after a forty-five-minute speech by the Commons' greatest orator. He walked out in an atmosphere of hostility, accompanied only by his wife. Emrys Hughes, the Welsh pacifist, alone shook his hands while other Labour MPs glowered or shook their heads sadly.

It was against this background that Wilson decided he had to make his own speech the next day. The House was again packed to see a politician, whom most had misjudged as an ambitious climber, explain the unexpected. It was a splendidly conceived more-in-sorrow-than-in-anger speech which delighted his sympathizers while giving little handhold for complaint to his opponents. While declaring his loyalty to Bevan he made it clear he felt Gaitskell and Morrison had only been able to carry out their plan because of Attlee's absence: 'I particularly wish to say how upset I am personally that this crisis should have arisen in the absence of the Prime Minister. ... I should have thought that there was no need for urgency in pressing on with this legislation and the whole matter could be left until [Attlee] returned ... But this was not thought possible.' He supported Bevan's stand on teeth and spectacles as opposition to 'the first cutting-in to our social services, which we have built up over these past years, and which represent a system in which all of us rightly take great pride. It is a minor cut, I agree, but I cannot believe it to be necessary. £13m out of a Budget of £4,000m is well within the margin of error of any possible series of Estimates.' Here was an economist catching out another economist instead of attacking the whole tribe. He emphasized in particular, of course, the economic reasons for his resignation: the fact that the Defence budget was excessive because Britain was not getting sufficient raw materials to maintain the economy, the essential export trade and the rearmament programme as well. 'Believing as I do that the principle of collective Cabinet responsibility requires from each Minister a full and whole-hearted acceptance of the measures decided upon by the Cabinet, and of the policies underlying them, I felt it was not right either to my colleagues in the Cabinet or to myself that I should remain a member of the Government.'[115] He attracted warm support from his colleagues when he pledged himself to support the party and the Labour Government in the difficult days ahead. But although his reception was much warmer than that of Bevan the day before there was a certain coolness as he walked out with his wife, Mary, who had come to hear his speech. Winston Churchill, to whom she had once been introduced, bowed to her silently as she glanced in his direction.

That night Harold returned home about 3 a.m. to find she had been having a sleepless night. He told her he had received some friendly comments on his speech and some angry predictions that his career was now in ruins. 'And now I have an important personal message for you. Brendan Bracken came up to me in the Smoke Room and said Winston had asked him to deliver a message: to ask Harold Wilson to tell his wife that it was a big step for a young man to give up the fruits of office; he knew because he had done it himself. But she mustn't worry, because if he felt he was doing the right thing, that was all that mattered, and in any case her husband wouldn't have to face the same degree of obloquy that he himself had suffered when he was out of sympathy with his own party before the war. Brendan told me that the old man asked him to get this message to you, and said to be sure you should know how much he felt for you.' Mary burst into tears and asked Harold to be sure to thank Churchill for his kind words.

Wilson sought out Churchill in the House next day to tell him how much his wife had appreciated his comforting message. 'It moved her very much,' he said. Winston Churchill, always an emotional man, could be seen to have moist eyes. Later Wilson joked to a friend: 'Until forty-eight hours ago I had a full-time job. Now it seems my only job is to act as a messenger between my wife and Churchill, each of whom is moved to tears by a message from the other!'[116]

# V. Zigzagging from 'A Party within a Party'

'I am trying to run a Bolshevik Revolution with a Csarist Cabinet!'

Harold Wilson, 1963

'He is an amphibian: sometimes on Mr Bevan's water; then on Gaitskell's land. He may end up in the mud.'

Lord Beaverbrook

It is one of the supreme ironies of Harold Wilson's career that he should have ended his period as Prime Minister in 1976 by elevating entrepreneurs to the peerage and making knights of property magnates and Tory tycoons. It was ironical because his springboard to political power thirteen years earlier was his identification with the Left in the early 1950s.

To the world outside Labour's divided Cabinet in April 1951 there was no serious hint that Wilson, who was considered a rather right-wing technocrat as President of the Board of Trade, was thinking of becoming a rebel identified with Aneurin Bevan, the left-wing bogeyman of *Daily Express* and *Daily Mail* readers. Wilson's resignation was, of course, welcomed by the Left and Centre-Left; it made it that much more difficult to tag the main resignation – that of Aneurin Bevan – as simply an explosion of the Welsh left-winger's short-fused temperament.

Although the colleagues he left behind in the Cabinet treated him as an anti-American left-winger, none of them really considered his resignation to have been caused by left-wing beliefs. Hugh Gaitskell and his Financial Secretary, Douglas Jay, were convinced that Wilson, even more than Bevan, was acting out of pique that Gaitskell had in 1950 secured the job as Chancellor of the Exchequer that both had coveted. The Prime Minister, Clement Attlee, was also affronted by what he thought to be the deviousness of Wilson's tactics, particularly in view of the many opportunities he had given the talented young politician. 'Although I have had many disagreements with him, I shall miss Nye,' Attlee told a Cabinet colleague. 'But I won't miss Harold because I no longer trust him.'

As in most such judgments by opponents in a sharp argument over how to handle a world crisis Wilson's Cabinet critics were only half-right. There was no doubt that he disagreed fundamentally with the willingness of the pro-American wing of the Cabinet, led by Gaitskell, to subordinate the pace of rearmament to the dictates of Washington, even at the risk of ruining the British economy. As a shrewd political tactician Wilson saw that the Labour Government which carried out Washington's wishes would go down to certain defeat at the next general election as a result of inflation, rising prices and curbed wages arising from a semi-war economy.

Wilson foresaw a brief span of Tory rule, to be followed by a Labour Government from which those who, like Gaitskell, had been overly pro-American would be winnowed out of the leadership. The leadership, he anticipated, would fall to those like Aneurin Bevan and himself who had rejected over-identification with American rearmament plans.

Wilson gave the first intimation of his genius as a political tactician by the enthusiasm with which he threw himself into his new role as an agitational left-wing rebel politician. This required a change of political personality almost as fundamental as a change of sex. The man who had been an uptight and boringly donnish Establishment spokesman suddenly set about learning how to be a David operating against the Establishment Goliath with a sharp tongue as his main slingshot.

## HIS NEW 'CABINET' COLLEAGUES

Partly because everything was speeded up by the April 1951 resignations Wilson's need to change personalities had all sorts of manifestations. Suddenly he had given up not only the top job in the biggest Department but also his office, his official limousine and his retinue of personal civil servants. Instead of the ritualistic meeting of the Cabinet he now had only meetings of the 'Keep Left' Group to attend.

He was able to appreciate the contrast very vividly because, within two days of his resignation speech he himself – together with Aneurin Bevan, the latter's wife, Jennie Lee, and John Freeman – attended the first meeting of the expanded 'Keep Left' Group. This meeting, designed to arouse support for the triple resignation, convened on 26 April 1951. The other MPs present were: Richard Acland, Barbara Castle, R. H. S. Crossman, Harold Davies, Hugh Delargy, Tom Driberg, Michael Foot, Will Griffiths, Leslie Hale, Kim Mackay and Ian Mikardo. Ian Mikardo was elected Chairman of the meeting.

The 'Keep Left' Group had been launched in November 1946 as a rebellion led by Crossman and Foot against Ernest Bevin, then the domineering Foreign Secretary. Bevin was strongly anti-Communist and pro-American, and equally strongly anti-Zionist and pro-Arab. Crossman, in particular, was pro-Zionist, and both he and Foot wanted Labour Britain to play a mediating role between capitalist America and the Communist USSR, rather than to line up uncritically with the Americans on everything except Palestine. The Crossman-Foot rebellion was launched in November 1946 as an amendment to the foreign affairs section of the programme for that Parliamentary session. They immediately attracted attacks as 'long-haired intellectuals' from Bevin's loyal supporter, George Brown. Other Labour MPs referred to them as 'Communist lickspittles'. Crossman explained that he feared that the US had 'dangerous tendencies' and he was opposed to the sort of tight alliance called for by Winston Churchill in his Fulton speech.

Those who rebelled against Bevin in 1946 under the slogan of 'Keep Left' – after the traffic injunction – kept up an informal organization of a dozen or so MPs plus two or three economic advisers. They tended to meet every week or so in the House of Commons when the House was in session. At the end of 1950, when the Bevan-Wilson-Freeman rebellion was beginning to take shape, Crossman was the Chairman of the Group. Other MPs who were members included: Richard Acland, Fenner Brockway, Barbara Castle, Harold Davies, Michael Foot, James Johnson, Leslie Hale, Tom Horabin, Marcus Lipton, Ian Mikardo, George Wigg and W. Tom Williams. Their economic advisers were Thomas Balogh, Dudley Seers and David Worswick, a former student of Wilson's.[1]

Early in 1951 Bevan and to a lesser extent Wilson began to discuss their positions with leading members of the 'Keep Left' Group, without necessarily agreeing on tactics. Thus, although they agreed in their opposition to over-rapid rearmament, Dick Crossman and others were opposed to the April resignations of Bevan, Wilson and Freeman on tactical grounds. Nevertheless they welcomed the rebels to their Group meeting on 26 April 1951, without letting anyone know they were there. (In fact, although Michael Foot was himself a member of the 'Keep Left' Group, he virtually omits its activities from his biography of Aneurin Bevan.)

From the beginning this Group acted like a factional caucus, concerting its attitudes, activities and publications. Thus, at that first meeting they discussed what their four members of the National Executive Committee of the Labour Party should do about the NEC's statement the previous day backing the Attlee Cabinet and opposing the rebels. Should Bevan, Castle, Driberg and Mikardo resign? Or should they just send a statement of protest? It was decided to send a joint letter of protest to Labour's General Secretary Morgan Phillips.

The enlarged group decided to try to recruit additional MPs for the Group from those thought to be sympathetic. Wilson volunteered to recruit Cecil Poole. Barbara Castle said she would ask Desmond Donnelly, then a young left-wing journalist and MP who enjoyed drinking and talking to Nye; this was not a very good idea for the Group because Donnelly subsequently began 'leaking' its secrets to the Labour Whips and Hugh Dalton. The Group's members could not decide whether to give it a new name or whether to give it publicity. So the question was postponed to the following week.[2]

From the beginning the Group decided to support each other in speeches in their constituencies. This was important for Harold Wilson, who had won Huyton by only 834 votes in February 1950. The Group had several assets as far as Wilson was concerned, who was not then the political speaker he later became. In Aneurin Bevan it had the best orator in the Labour movement, one who could draw enormous crowds. It also had established political 'Brains Trusts' which had developed considerable popularity. Wilson booked such a 'Brains Trust' for Huyton and volunteered to speak at one at Scarborough at the time of the annual Labour conference.[3]

Harold's fears for his constituency were considerably allayed on 5 May 1951, when he made his first visit to Huyton after his resignation ten days before. 'This is the heartiest reception we have given a member or candidate during my thirty years' connection with the party,' said its Vice-Chairman, A. B. Hankinson. Cheer after cheer came from the crowded room in Progress Hall, Page Moss. 'It is a right and proper practice of our constitution that if a member of the Cabinet differs from his colleagues on a major issue of principle or Government policy and cannot accept the majority view, it is his duty to resign,' said Wilson. The local party carried a resolution calling on the Government 'at the earliest possible moment to redress the balance between rearmament expenditure and the social services' and later burst into 'For he's a jolly good fellow'. He denied he was taking a £10,000 job in the film industry but told his officers he would be working for a Labour-sympathizing timber importer, Montague Meyer.[4] Harold's agent, Arthur Waite, found that local Huyton activists were delighted to find he was not the careerist they feared and that he had, somewhat unexpectedly, lined up with 'the people' (and Nye Bevan) against the Labour Establishment.[5] The day after Wilson's warm reception in Huyton, Bevan led a tremendous procession of 50,000 through the streets of Glasgow to celebrate May Day.

'These resignations will be a source of strength to the party,' Wilson insisted at Knowsley on 16 May, 'and throughout the country members are once again re-examining the basis of their socialist faith and working within the party to get final decisions on some of those issues which might have divided us.' He indicated that his version of the Socialist faith was more realistic by pointing to the ICI works on the East Lancashire Road which had been expected to give work to hundreds but which was standing idle for lack of raw copper which was being hoarded in the stockpiles of the US military. Wilson's vision was supported by Mrs Bessie Braddock, that embodiment of the militant Liverpool housewife in Parliament.[6]

Wilson was correct about the lively public examination of the socialist path ahead. The argument over the tightness of the American alliance, the speed of rearmament, the extent of social sacrifice, which had torn the Labour Cabinet apart, was now taking place in the public print. The resignations of Bevan and Wilson had destroyed the Cabinet's veil of secrecy over its arguments, and when they deployed their arguments in public both their opponents and their supporters knew that, until a few weeks before, they had been privy to all the Cabinet secrets. Therefore they could not be put down by the 'Ah! but if you only knew what we know' type of argument.

Virtually the whole daily press Establishment was committed to the American alliance, with the derisory exception of the Communist *Daily Worker* whose commitment to the Russian side when Stalin was still raging put it beyond the pale, and whose political coverage was very primitive. On Sundays, although Crossman had access to the *Sunday Pictorial* (later the *Sunday Mirror*) and several of the Bevanites had access to Hugh Massingham of the *Observer*, only the Cooperative Sunday paper, *Reynolds News*, was sympathetic. In his column there, Tom Driberg predicted: 'In a few months' time the resignation of these three Ministers may be seen as an act of self-sacrificing patriotism' – as a result of the attention they had directed to the problem of raw materials shortages.[7]

The only place in which their case could be sympathetically deployed was in the socialist weeklies. Crossman was Kingsley Martin's second-in-command on the *New Statesman*. Aneurin Bevan, Jennie Lee and Michael Foot dominated *Tribune*. As a result Crossman was able to deploy in the *New Statesman*'s editorials the arguments worked out in the 'Keep Left' Group's private meetings. He could also call on several members of the Group to write letters to the *Statesman* either to propound their views or to rebut those put forward by their Gaitskellite opponents.

In this way Wilson was deployed against Anthony Crosland, Hugh Gaitskell's protégé, as the 'Keep Left' economists Thomas Balogh and Dudley Seers were deployed against Denis Healey, until recently the intellectual voice of the late Ernest Bevin. Although the tone of the two sets of letters that appeared in print seemed icily polite, so strong was the feeling behind them that for years afterward, boasted Crosland, he did not greet Wilson in the corridors of the Palace of Westminster.

Crosland was probably angered by the way in which Wilson damned

Chancellor Gaitskell with faint praise in a speech in Bedford in July for having brought in dividend limitation, which he claimed did not go nearly far enough. 'Now, in my view, is the time for a dramatic attack on the cost of living, and an announcement by the Government that the cost of living index will not be allowed to rise above its present level for a period of six months by means of subsidies and price controls,' insisted Wilson.[8] In the *New Statesman*, in an unsigned editorial, Crossman stigmatized Gaitskell's move as 'a remarkable confession of failure ... But Mr Gaitskell knows well that, economically, these proposals are both insignificant and irrelevant.'[9] Crosland wrote, asking for the *New Statesman*'s 'own alternative policy. Once you favoured dividend limitation and stiffer price control, but now that Mr Gaitskell has announced them, you describe these proposals as "insignificant and irrelevant".'[10]

Wilson wrote back to say that Gaitskell's action would have been better had it been taken earlier, at the time of the April Budget. 'Had the Chancellor taken a strong line about dividends in April and made a substantial addition to subsidies, that part of the inflation which was City-generated could have been avoided, and we should have escaped the injustice of a situation in which property owners and shareholders were becoming richer while millions of workers and their families were becoming poorer.'[11]

While such point-scoring letters appealed to Labour intellectuals and semi-intellectuals, the Group's main thrust in the months after the resignations was at the hearts and brains of party activists through a pamphlet which finally appeared as 'One Way Only' in July 1951 to a torrent of ridicule and acclaim. It had been decided to produce alternative proposals for Labour policies in the form of a pamphlet on 10 May in a private meeting in the Commons. Michael Foot agreed to publish it as part of a *Tribune* series. Crossman, Michael Foot and Ian Mikardo agreed to write the section relating to the international situation; Bevan, Wilson, Freeman and Balogh agreed to do the part on the domestic situation – initially in chapter headings.[12]

So, if he no longer took Government documents back to his Hampstead Garden Suburb home, these were now replaced by memoranda or drafts. If he did not have to go out on Ministerial visits to give Government speeches he went on 'Keep Left Brains Trusts' or offered continuing testimony that he had been correct to resign. Thus, he spoke to the Progressive Business Men's Forum on 10 May 1951: 'The key lies in the hands of the American authorities, particularly those charged with stockpiling. If they go on piling up supplies, the production programme of the Western world will be wrecked.'[13]

Harold had to go to the many conferences on 'One Way Only',

outside the Group's weekly meeting in the Commons to discuss drafts. He learned that he was not considered a sprightly writer. The drafting of the second half would be done by Ian Mikardo, who had a more colloquial style.[14] Everything was gone into very carefully in these private meetings. On 12 June they decided on the title of the pamphlet. They decided to hold a press conference on 5 July, with four of the journalists in the Group – Driberg, Foot, Crossman and J. P. W. Mallalieu – detailed to handle arrangements.[15] Then, in the 16 June issue they disclosed that they would publish their pamphlet in three weeks' time, announcing it in *Tribune*.

They felt they had to be circumspect in what they did and said because they did not want to give their opponents within the Labour Party any excuse for expelling them, as they had Konni Zilliacus, for example. They wanted, through their carefully deployed arguments in 'One Way Only' and in their speeches, to win the Labour Party over to their viewpoint, from within, not be pushed outside the party. This was one of the reasons why, instead of listing the names of twenty-five Labour MPs who supported the pamphlet, they decided to list only the three resigning Ministers – Bevan, Wilson and Freeman – as signatories to the pamphlet. Had twenty-five MPs signed 'One Way Only' it would have seemed there was a rebel caucus of that size. Having it signed only by the resigning Ministers made the pamphlet seem merely an expansion of their resignation speeches. This is also why they did not rename the 'Keep Left' Group, although they originally considered it, and only expanded it slightly and by invitation. All these precautions seemed worthwhile when 'One Way Only was published on 10 July 1951.

The impact of the pamphlet was demonstrated negatively. Even the allegedly 'news' stories on the pamphlet largely misrepresented its argument, which Sir Winston Churchill was largely to accept as his own eight months later. The *Guardian*'s news story on 9 July came closest to a fair summary, giving at least a key quote: 'When we promised the Americans that we should spend the £3,600 millions, the promise was given on the understanding that they in turn would contribute £550 million worth of dollars towards the total. When we raised the stakes to £4,700 millions we did so knowing that this understanding was not going to be carried out. Thus the real rise in the programme was over fifty per cent.' Editorially it was attacked in the *Guardian* as containing 'some very fine rhetoric but some extremely muddled thinking. If this is really what Mr Bevan and Mr Harold Wilson believe the country is to be congratulated on having lost their services.'[16] The *Financial Times* thought that 'as a contribution to either economic or political thought the "Bevan" pamphlet is hardly worth notice.'[17] War Secretary John Strachey said that there were arguments in 'One Way Only' with which he did not agree, but had his audience ever seen a pamphlet greeted with such hysteria?[18]

History, however, was confirming the pamphleteers and disproving the hostile editorial-writers. A week after the pamphlet appeared, the *News-Chronicle* accurately reported: 'The Cabinet is extremely worried about the recent worsening of Britain's trading position ... World prices of raw materials and foodstuffs have soared since rearmament started ... The Government believes that the new problems are not due primarily to our own rearmament programme but to the world rise in prices resulting from everyone's rearmament.'[19]

By August it became apparent that car production was dropping as a result of the shortage of steel and other materials.[20] Wilson rammed home the lesson in a letter to the welcoming *New Statesman*: 'The overloading of the system due to the present scale of rearmament has held back exports both by lengthening deliveries and because raw material shortages have restricted the output of important export industries ... That the estimates of the overseas balance have worsened in only three months by £300m surely justifies your statement that the Budget financial policy is dead. It equally justifies the view of the Chancellor's critics, that the hope of realizing the arms programme, and maintaining a balance in our overseas payments, was an illusion from the start.'[21]

By September, Chancellor Hugh Gaitskell was in Washington pleading for help in providing steel and coal-mining machinery and for a delay in Britain's obligation to repay its dollar loans. On 9 September he announced that the US would provide 800,000 tons of steel. Next day the British Government turned against the Peking Government it had recognized and voted to bar it from the International Bank.

Meanwhile Harold Wilson and his colleagues were deeply involved in a different type of mutual aid. Very early in the 'Keep Left' Group discussions they had decided that those of the rebels, like Harold Wilson, with marginal seats would be in considerable danger from being caught in any crossfire. They would have to contend not only with their Conservative and other opponents but also with the coolness of leading party and trade-union figures. Therefore they would have to help one another very much more to make up for it. Those like Wilson with very small majorities should be given priority.[22] A map was drawn up to show the location of the constituencies, with the majorities indicated; Wilson's was the third lowest, after Mackay (527) and Donnelly (729).[23] Aneurin Bevan turned up in Huyton on 22 July to speak as Harold Wilson's guest. Bevan criticized America's immaturity in foreign affairs in its opposition to the Chinese revolution. 'We believe the Chinese people should work out their destiny in their own way ... We are not prepared ... to enter into an alliance which might consolidate Franco in Spain.'[24] Not a word was reported of what Wilson said on that occasion. Normally only the local newspapers, the *Liverpool Daily Post* and the *Liverpool Echo*, reported what Wilson had to say, whether on Merseyside or elsewhere in the country.

Despite this exclusion from the national press, Wilson felt he was making sufficient headway through his exposure in the *New Statesman*, *Reynolds News* and *Tribune* to stand for Labour's National Executive in the constituency section. This was elected on the basis of the votes of constituency activists, who tended to be on the Left of the party. Wilson decided to stand for the National Executive against the advice of some of his colleagues in the Group. When it was announced at the Group's 24 July meeting that nine left-wingers were standing for the National Executive, there was some dismay. It was particularly worrysome at the 'top' end – Bevan, Castle, Driberg, Mikardo and Wilson – who were thought to have a chance. There was fear of splitting the vote too much. Mrs Barbara Castle was already on the National Executive in the Women's Section, for whose election the support of the larger unions was necessary. Since it had been made clear to Mrs Castle that the right-wing union leaders were furious with her for backing Bevan and Wilson she had decided to contest in the constituency section. Wilson's candidacy was thought to imperil her success. 'Several members of the "Bevanite" Group appear to have remonstrated with him, urging him not to stand for NEC. He was not as popular in the movement as Mrs Castle, and might do himself harm. He might also split the anti-leadership vote. But he showed his determination.'[25]

## ATTLEE'S COUP

Suddenly Attlee sprang a surprise on all his colleagues, particularly on the Right, by announcing on 19 September that there would be an election on 25 October. This caught Foreign Secretary Herbert Morrison on the hop in Canada; he had been in favour of delaying the election into 1952. Attlee had spoken in a desultory manner of an October election, which had the support of Bevan, who preferred to have Tories in power doing Tory things unless the Labour leadership could be altered.

Attlee never disclosed the real reason for his sudden decision to go to the country, although he indicated that he was afraid that the King, George VI, might not be in the country if the election were delayed. In fact it was discovered by the King's doctors on 16 September that he had a cancer of the lung which would require the removal of the left lung. On 18 September Attlee was told by the King of the impending operation, having previously urged him to have an early election. Attlee, who had a very deep affection for the King, replied: 'I have come to the conclusion that the right course would be to have a dissolution of Parliament in the first week of October.' When the dissolution ceremony was held in Buckingham Palace on 5 October 1951, His Majesty was so weak that he could hardly be heard by his Privy Councillors to say 'Approved' and had to be helped to sign the document.

Attlee was not only fond of the King, he was also attempting to restore Labour unity. By announcing, before the Labour conference, that a general election would be held after it, he papered more thickly than usual over the growing cracks. In the absence of factious Herbert Morrison, others, including Aneurin Bevan, Hugh Dalton, Morgan Phillips and Sam Watson, were able to agree a unifying election manifesto. Some rearmament was accepted, without specifying a precise figure.

On the surface the 1951 Scarborough conference *was* unifying. Bevan warmed the conference with: 'We must avoid at all costs a repetition here of what has happened to continental socialist movements. We must never carry doctrinaire differences to the point of schism; that is why our movement is based primarily on the industrial masses.'[26]

However, the very success of the Bevanites in the voting for the constituency seats on the National Executive guaranteed the arousal of the praetorian guard of the Right, the right-wing leaders of the mass trade unions, then led by Arthur Deakin, Ernest Bevin's equally square-built chief of the transport workers union. Left-wing constituency activists were thrilled when it was announced that Aneurin Bevan had again come first in the voting, with his vote increased by 9,000. In second place, in her first try in the constituency section, came the fiery red-head, Barbara Castle. Two other members of the 'Keep Left' Group, Tom Driberg and Ian Mikardo, increased their votes by 58,000 and 194,000 respectively to keep their seats on the Executive. Harold Wilson, curiously disguised by Transport House ballot-printers as 'J. H. Wilson,' managed to win 396,000 votes, making him second runner-up after veteran Emanuel Shinwell.

The rise of the Left meant a corresponding fall on the Right. Barbara Castle's victory in the constituency section knocked off Defence Secretary Emanuel Shinwell after eleven years on the NEC. He packed his bags and left Scarborough in high dudgeon. Herbert Morrison slipped from third to fifth place and Dalton and Jim Griffiths saw their votes drop.

Such results did not appeal to the more authoritarian right-wing trade-union leaders. Arthur Deakin, the irascible T & GWU General Secretary, gathered them in his hotel room and secured pledges from Tom Williamson, General Secretary of the General and Municipal Workers Union, and Sir William Lawther, General Secretary of the

National Union of Mineworkers. They decided to stop the Bevanites, not only because they seemed to be making headway on the National Executive but because they had the temerity to criticize trade-union leaders. 'Going Our Way' had followed after 'One Way Only'. Sir Will Lawther was the first of the union leaders to show in public their hostile intentions toward the rebels. 'Trade unionists willingly accept the decisions of the majority of their members, and those who deliberately seek to wreck majority decisions, in our view, must get out.'[27]

## THE REAL ELECTION

However close he had come to a seat on the National Executive, Harold Wilson was anxious not to be runner-up at the declaration of the poll for Huyton. He ran scared in October 1951. Huyton was a seat eighty per cent of whose voters were Roman Catholics at a time when the Catholic Church was very anti-Communist throughout the world. The Roman Catholic Bishop of Leeds, John Heenan, had denounced the 'crypto-Communists' in the Labour Party, widely taken to refer to the Bevanites. Wilson's opponent in Huyton, a sand merchant and Tory county councillor called Francis Neep, used similar tactics. Neep said a vote for Wilson was a stab in the back for Attlee and a pat on the back for the extreme left-winger, Aneurin Bevan. Bevan he made into an anti-rearmament pro-Communist bogeyman by quoting 1937 and 1939 statements: 'Our party should oppose the Government arms plan root and branch' and 'I am not frightened of an alliance with the Communists'.[28]

Wilson countered this by protesting his loyalty to Attlee and his detestation of Communism. In a speech at Prescot Wilson said he was a member of the Parliamentary Christian Socialist Group. 'I would not make quite so much of this, only that Mr Neep is trying any kind of poisonous slime to try to discredit me with people whose approach to politics comes from the religious side.'[29] To make sure Neep's effort had no impact, Wilson played his Roman Catholic card to the full extent. He knew how much he had helped local Catholics expand their schools. At the suggestion of a local priest he approached the Catholic Archbishop of Liverpool. The latter urged him to write to the Bishop of Leeds who would, he was sure, deny that he had meant Wilson when referring to 'crypto-Communists' and who would compliment him on his good work for Roman Catholic schools. Not only did Roman Catholic priests speak up for him to their congregations but they pointed out to Wilson's agent, Arthur Waite, which Catholic homes specially-prepared leaflets could be distributed to. Wilson was helped by the fact that Leslie Hale – whom he later raised to Lord Hale – had persuaded the Home Secretary to write into the 1951 election manifesto a promise to increase aid for Catholic Schools. Hale, an agnostic, had the second largest concentration of Catholics in England – after Scotland, Liverpool – in his Oldham constituency. His local priests had convinced him that state aid for Catholic schools had been based on the assumption of postwar deflation as had happened after the First World War, instead of – as had actually happened – postwar inflationary circumstances.[30]

As a further demonstration that he was no godless 'crypto-Communist' Harold Wilson also wheeled Mary Wilson into play. He featured on his election manifesto these words from her: 'He is a good man. He is conscientious and sincere; and as you all know, and as many have had material proof, he is deeply concerned for the welfare of the people of the Huyton division.' She went to Huyton to be seen on his platforms, not a usual performance for Mary Wilson.

The most powerful platform in that campaign was the one fielded at Liverpool stadium on 7 October when Aneurin Bevan turned up to support Wilson, as promised at the Group. Bevan made a powerful speech on how to improve foreign Powers by treating them better: 'Are we going to repeat in China the same folly in 1951 that we committed against Russia in 1918?' Wilson spoke on the sore subject of Merseyside unemployment, on which he had been active for six years. Mrs Bessie Braddock took up the 'Whose Finger on the Trigger?' theme of the *Daily Mirror*, warning that Britain would be endangered by a third World War if the Conservatives were returned to power.[31]

In the end, the combination of Catholic and Bevanite appeals saw Wilson back into the House of Commons again with a majority of 1,193 in a straight fight with his Conservative opponent. Although Wilson had increased his majority and Labour had slightly increased its vote it nevertheless lost its majority. Next day Clement Attlee handed his seals of office in to the dying Monarch, and Winston Churchill was again Prime Minister by a majority of seventeen over all the other parties.

The biggest victory for Wilson and Bevan was to come soon, after Winston Churchill had had a chance to study the much-debated subject of the pace of rearmament. In his first major speech on Defence as Prime Minister, on 6 December 1951, Winston Churchill conceded that Aneurin Bevan and Harold Wilson had been correct in their assessment of the impossibility of carrying out the £4,700m rearmament programme in three years. 'We shall not, however, succeed in spending the £1,250m [scheduled to be spent] this year and some of the late Government's programme must necessarily roll forward into a future year. The point was, I believe, made by [Aneurin Bevan] after his resignation.' When Bevan seized on this and tried to get Churchill to expand on it, Churchill retorted: 'I am not really wishing to embark on a debate with the Right Honourable gentleman. I was giving him an honourable mention in despatches for having been right by accident.'[32] Churchill had a motive in giving Bevan and Wilson a leg up. He was hoping to see the growing conflict between the Bevanites and the Right grow into a full-scale civil war in Labour ranks. 'The arms programme was not carried out, being cut in half in terms of the annual burden by Churchill two months after assuming office in December 1951,' chortled Wilson in a memorandum written later.[33]

## WILSON CHAIRS THE NEW MILITANTS

Although Labour had narrowly lost the October 1951 general election, the Bevanites, as they now were increasingly called, felt good. At the end of the campaign the tone of the Labour counter-attack had been almost Bevanite, and more Labour supporters appeared to be returning to the fold. What the polls had predicted would be a runaway victory for the Tories turned out to be a very narrow Tory victory, with Labour actually chalking up more votes over the country. Bevanite candidates did marginally better than non-Bevanite Labour candidates.

Within the Group there was a sharp argument over whether it should remain a 'small, hand-picked and self-appointed ... private enclave ... black-balling its potential friends on this score or on that like a snob West End club and turning them, if not into enemies, at least into critics.' These words were used in a memorandum from a member, Benn Levy. He favoured turning the Group into an open forum of 100 on the Left of the Parliamentary Labour Party. Levy urged that Group members should approach their colleagues outside and say: 'Listen, duckie, Keep Left has been during the last five or six years a small, haphazard Group, self-appointed on no particular principle, as always happens in these cases. We kept it small for the practical reason that it is always hard for a large group to function. However, we would like you to join forces with us, as we suspect you to be socialistically inclined!'[34]

This memorandum was discussed at the Group's meeting on 30 October 1951. 'Fenner Brockway and Jennie Lee emphasized the importance of not remaining a small, exclusive group,' recorded Crossman in his diary, 'and a long discussion took place on how to enlarge the Group and make it open to all who want [to join], without at the same time losing its cohesion.' At this meeting, which took place at the Crossman home at 9 Vincent Square, the question of whether to continue as rebels was considered in the context of whether Bevan should allow his name to be considered in the imminent election to Labour's 'Shadow Cabinet'. The right-wing ex-Ministers wanted him to stand, as did Crossman and John Freeman. 'But he himself had made up his mind. What was the good of resigning in order to be free to speak if he at once surrenders that freedom by joining the [Parliamentary] Committee (or "Shadow Cabinet")?' wrote Crossman.[35]

This discussion was continued at the next meeting on 6 November. It was decided there that the two aims of cohesiveness and non-exclusiveness could be achieved by adopting two propositions: '(1) the Group should continue as at present, expanding slowly by ones and twos; and (2) from time to time meetings should be held on specific subjects and with speakers to which all members of the Parliamentary Party should be invited. The first of these would be held at 5 p.m. on Tuesday 13 November, when Tom Balogh would speak on the economic situation.'[36] Not all the Group's members were as anxious to keep its proceedings private. Three weeks later, Hugh Dalton's private diary disclosed that Desmond Donnelly, a Group member, was telling him and the Chief Whip what was happening at Group meetings.[37]

At the same meeting Ian Mikardo, who had been serving as Chairman since the previous April, urged that the Group should have a fresh Chairman. It was agreed that he should be selected before the Christmas recess. On 4 December 'it was unanimously agreed to invite Harold Wilson to take this post.'[38] After a long report a fortnight later Crossman described how he, as the founder of the Group, then viewed its new Chairman: 'Harold Wilson was as neat and competent as ever, and whenever an idea is put forward, remembers without fail an occasion on which he did it or set up a committee on it at the Board of Trade. His complacency must be unique, but he has a good mind, is an excellent member of a group and is likeable into the bargain.'[39]

Wilson was moving ahead as a politician. On 4 November he had addressed a private political conference of the Amalgamated Engineers in the Sheffield area. He had warned them that 'this reversion to government by crony and jobs for the boys is not going to provide the administration we need.'[40] After this the Sheffield Engineers asked whether the Bevanites could provide them with more speakers for the political education campaign they were planning. Wilson raised this at the next meeting of the Group.[41] After a week's thought the Group decided Wilson should approach Bevan to organize a public meeting in Sheffield, but that any such public meeting should be cleared with the Amalgamated Engineers nationally and with the Sheffield City Labour Party. Bevan agreed.

Although the Group was anxious to expand its influence and its membership it proceeded cautiously, examining each new MP suggested for suitability. Thus, on 13 November 1951 it was agreed that Tony Wedgwood Benn should be approached to join by Fenner Brockway and Walter Monslow, a former locomotive driver, by Ian Mikardo. But it was decided to defer further consideration of Sir Leslie Plummer and

Dr Santos Jeger, and to discuss Kenneth Younger at the next meeting.
At the group's 27 November meeting it was decided to drop the idea of
inviting Kenneth Younger, who had at one point thought of resigning
with Bevan, Wilson and Freeman before they were ready to resign. This
invitation to Younger may very well have been dropped bec. use there
had been some sort of personal misunderstanding between Younger and
short-fused Jennie Lee over an imagined slight. But invitations to
join the Group did go out to Cledwyn Hughes (via fellow Welshman
Tudor Watkins) and Cyril Bence (via Archie Manuel).

This caution and circumspection was shown in various ways. Thus,
Fenner Brockway urged the Group to establish links with comparable
left-wing socialist groups in France. 'It was agreed that it was desirable
that individual members of the Group should have contacts with
European socialists, but that it was preferable not to make this a Group
activity.' That would pre-empt National Executive powers and thereby
make the Group liable to accusations of being 'a party within a party'.

It was decided that members of the Group should join each of the
specialist groups organized by the Parliamentary Labour Party, to
ensure that the Bevanite position was made known – except for the
Groups on Arts and Amenities and on Public Information. Harold
Wilson, together with Harold Davies, Marcus Lipton, Ian Mikardo and
Stephen Swingler, would join the Finance and Economic Group. By
then Wilson had assumed the position of the Group's own 'Shadow
Chancellor'.

This was made clear when the Group met on 14–15 December 1951
at Buscot Park, the stately home of Lord Faringdon, the left-wing
Fabian who was one of their supporters. It was agreed that Wilson
would open with a paper on the new Budget that the Conservative
Chancellor, R. A. Butler, was likely to present, and how it would differ
from that which might be presented by Hugh Gaitskell. His paper
would be followed by one on Anglo-American relations by Crossman.
Bevan would lead the summing-up discussion at the end of the second
day.

They did not know what they were in for until Wilson opened his
3,500-word speech on Saturday morning. He reported to the Buscot
Conference with the seriousness and competence he would have shown
in a Cabinet Committee. He had economic analyses, quotations from the
Journal of the Institute of Export, etcetera. Not only did he indicate
what he thought Butler and Gaitskell would do, but also what the Tories
would have done had Churchill named a more right-wing Chancellor
such as Oliver Lyttelton. Although overlong, like so many Wilson
speeches, it had some excellent insights. 'We are, in fact, in a cleft stick,'
he made clear. 'When raw material prices are high . . . the Sterling Area

has no dollar problem, but the UK has a very serious overall payments problem ... When, on the other hand, raw material prices are low, our balance of payments with the Southern dominions improves, but the Sterling Area as a whole has a crisis in its payments with North America.' He said this could be slightly ameliorated by trading more with Eastern Europe. 'But any conceivable increase in East-West trade, even if the limitations on our strategic shipments are removed, will not solve the problem.' What was needed, he felt, was the long uphill struggle to get more dollar-saving imports from within the Commonwealth, particularly Africa.

Wilson had some fun at Gaitskell's expense, commenting that 'the problem of the Chancellor next April ... is made far worse as a result of the deficiencies of his predecessor.' A Gaitskell Budget 'would be not very dissimilar to the Butler Budget, though its presentation would be different and for twenty-four hours would leave the impression on some people that it was a Socialist budget. Failure to take action last spring [when he and Bevan had resigned] has made the problem almost insoluble,' Wilson admitted. 'That is why we can no longer propose the methods advocated in "One Way Only" (increase of food subsidies, introduction of clothing subsidies, etc.). The wage inflation we sought then to prevent is now well under way. Essential steps are, of course, a reduction in our own arms programme and vigorous efforts to reduce the Atlantic arms programme while at the same time getting a fuller share for Europe of the material available.' He showed himself to be much more left-wing than when he had indulged in a 'bonfire of controls', now proposing: 'The Budget would have to be part of a crisis build-up to deal with the cost of living problem and to justify the case for sweeping changes in taxation, not excluding a capital levy and increase of death duties. The proceeds of these would be devoted to a strong effort to hold the cost of living by subsidies and a price-freeze with further steps to follow aimed at reducing the cost of living by transport and fuel subsidies.' He also suggested non-Budget actions such as 'extended nationalization, increased controls over industry, control of the investment funds of insurance companies'.[42]

After observing Wilson's detailed, technocratic and 'competent' approach to the Budget, and Nye Bevan's soaring and wide-ranging introduction to the final session at Buscot next day, Dick Crossman wrote in his diary that 'Nye Bevan and Harold Wilson ... have virtually nothing in common.' They were lumped together by their joint challenge both to the new Churchill-led Government and to the Attlee–Morrison–Gaitskell official leadership of the Labour Opposition.

Wilson's approach, when writing or speaking to Labour audiences, was to pretend that the postwar Churchill Government was no different from that of the prewar Tories. Writing in *Reynolds News* on 22 December 1951 he said that the Tories were using the crisis as an alibi for slashing the social services and for introducing class measures, as they had in 1931. The crisis had been brought on by British and world rearmament, 'as some of us warned would happen'. But Hugh Gaitskell was just as self-satisfied. Writing in the *Leeds Weekly Citizen* he said that 1951 production would increase by four per cent, as against the previous seven per cent, 'no doubt primarily due to raw material shortages, as we foresaw'.[43] When the Tory Government brought in a steel allocation system for February to cope with a shortage of 1.5m tons, most Labour activists concluded the Bevanites had been more nearly right. Reinforced by such events, a new hard-hitting Wilson began to emerge. 'Within the next few months we shall probably see the biggest increase in the cost of people's food since the Irish potato famine over a century ago,' he predicted to constituents at Knowsley.[44]

Harold and Nye were so convinced that things had moved their way that on 21 January 1952 they discussed giving up a Bevanite pamphlet on which they were working and rejoining the Labour Front Bench. The Group had set up a subcommittee of four – Bevan, Wilson, Crossman and Mikardo – to outline a third pamphlet which Nye and Harold thought might prove too provocative at a time when Labour unity might emerge. They were agreed on this but Dick Crossman was opposed because he feared the danger of the US getting into war with China. He feared that the strongly pro-American leadership of the Labour Party was already too compromised with Washington under conditions where American policy in Asia seemed too provocative. They were discussing this against a background of Winston Churchill's recent visit to Washington, where he had addressed the US Congress and attempted to harmonize Anglo-American policy in war-troubled East Asia. The crucial question was what would happen if the Chinese broke the truce in Korea, particularly by air. Churchill agreed that if the Chinese attacked on the ground, the US/UN forces would limit their operations – both on the ground and in the air – to Korea. But if Communist air attacks "jeopardized" US/UN forces they could retaliate by bombing Chinese bases near the Korean frontier, mainly those in Manchuria. Churchill secured from President Truman the promise that Britain would be consulted before Chinese bases were bombed.

The first meeting of the Bevanite Group under the chairmanship of Harold Wilson took place against a background of widening fears that Britain might be dragged into a war with Communist China as a result of closer ties with the United States. Wilson himself only partly shared this fear. In a speech at Leamington on 10 January he had said that he did not think that either the American people or Truman's administration – which included some of his former students at Oxford – wanted war. That was why the pamphlet 'One Way Only' had drawn attention to the danger of US atom-bomb bases in Britain being used without British concurrence – a danger which Winston Churchill now acknowledged.[45] But fear of war with China was widespread enough for Labour's National Executive to convene a special meeting with Trades Union Congress leaders on the subject at the end of January.

The Bevanite Group did not convene at the Commons, which was closed for the Christmas recess. With Mary's veto on politicians crossing her threshold in mind, Harold Wilson could not offer his Suburb home as a meeting place. So the Group met at the flat of Barbara and Ted Castle, at Cholmeley Lodge, Highgate Hill, as difficult to reach as Hampstead Garden Suburb. Harold Wilson turned out to be 'quiet and unassuming' as the new Chairman, 'only intervening to make relevant points', recalls Lord Hale.

The implications of Churchill's trip to Washington were considered, and Bevan and Crossman were put up to speak if the question was discussed at the Parliamentary Labour Party meeting the following Tuesday. The Group also discussed the synopsis of the third pamphlet which Bevan, Wilson, Crossman and Mikardo were working on. It was decided that it 'was not possible or desirable, at this stage, to produce a pamphlet' – although Mikardo still wanted to go ahead with it – 'and that the matter should be considered again in a few weeks' time.'[46]

The next weeks were to be momentous, headline-producing weeks, with Wilson getting the small type sizes. On the front of the *News Chronicle* of 29 January 1952 ran the headline: 'LABOUR THREATENS FIGHT TO SAVE UTILITY SCHEME'. Gaitskell had opposed the argument of the Tory President of the Board of Trade, Peter (later Lord) Thorneycroft, that the utility scheme might be changed because of unemployment in the textile industry. The utility scheme, which ensured standardized, low-priced but quality-controlled goods, had been introduced to satisfy the postwar hunger for goods without profiteering. Wilson chimed in that Thorneycroft's references had been 'ominous' and that any attempt to damage the scheme – 'one of the best protections that our housewives have got' – would be fought not only by Labour but by housewives throughout the country.[47]

The two factions in the Labour Party soon diverged on the best method to oppose the Churchill Government. When the Government called for a cutback in expenditure to cope with the fall in gold and dollar reserves Attlee wanted to recognize the urgency of the crisis. Bevan insisted that, but for the rearmament programme, there would be little crisis to cope with. Therefore the Labour Opposition should demand a cutback in defence expenditure to avoid cuts in the social services. Bevan's speech had a powerful effect on the Parliamentary Labour Party, which generally accepted his argument that to admit the urgency of the crisis was to give the Government a blank cheque. As a result, on 31 January 1952 Attlee moved an amendment which attacked the Government's social services cuts and Health Service charges. Bevan made a rumbustious speech, cheered by his supporters, which ridiculed the Government, among other things, for alleging that Britain was menaced by 400 to 500 submarines while running down its stocks of raw materials to save money. In this he was echoing what Wilson had said in a more restrained way, without cheers, the day before. 'Harold could not inspire the passionate affection that Nye could,' recalled Lord Hale. 'Nye was brilliant where Wilson was highly competent. The two most attractive brains in politics were Winston and Nye, with Nye being the reverse side of the Winston coin.' Within four hours of the announcement of the Tory National Health Services Bill authorizing charges on the NHS, Bevan issued a statement attacking it, on his own responsibility. If it passed into law, he warned, 'the free Health Service is dead'. This statement was interpreted by his critics as asserting his claim to lead Labour.

At a meeting of the Bevanite Group on 5 February it was agreed that one of their number should try to get into the two-day debate on Churchill's American visit in December on each of the two days. It could not have been imagined just how Churchill would play into their hands when the debate took place after a three-week delay caused by the King's death and the succession of Queen Elizabeth II.

Herbert Morrison, as Labour's foreign affairs spokesman, tried to attack Churchill's speech to the US Congress as having been too belligerent, while claiming credit for his support for the US in Korea as following in Labour's footsteps. Churchill turned the tables to devastating effect. He disclosed that in May 1951 – a month after the Bevan–Wilson–Freeman resignations – the Attlee Cabinet had agreed that, in the event of heavy air attacks from Chinese bases, Britain would associate itself with US/UN attacks on these Chinese bases near the Korean border. Bevan, with equal tactical brilliance, leapt to attack Churchill for his impropriety in disclosing secrets of the previous Government, underlining that Churchill was giving the game away instead of playing the usual bipartisan politics in foreign affairs. As a result of this disclosure Morrison and Labour's right-wing were further weakened and the Bevanites strengthened – as Churchill wished.[48] The right-wing of Labour was thus identified with the USA just as John Foster Dulles, with typical verbal extravagance, threatened that the USA would 'not stand idly by while any part of the world remained under the rule of either Communist or Fascist dictatorship'.[49]

It was under these conditions that the Conservatives published their Defence Estimates, promising an increase of £500m in the coming year's arms expenditures. Since the expenditure was a slightly scaled-down version of what had been proposed by Labour the previous year – and had helped produce the Bevanite resignations – the Labour Front Bench's room for manoeuvre was limited. They used the old Opposition tactic of approving the proposals but expressing a lack of confidence in the new Minister's ability to carry them out. This aroused some mirth, since it suggested that the previous Defence Secretary, Emanuel Shinwell, was more efficient in this field than Viscount Alexander of Tunis. The Bevanites – Harold Wilson, Dick Crossman and Stephen Swingler – had devised their own 'reasoned amendment' which Attlee had agreed to submit to Labour's 'Shadow Cabinet'. This refused the burden planned by the Government on the ground that it would impose 'on the British people an unfair share of what should be a common burden of the democratic nations' and would endanger 'the economic stability and independence of the United Kingdom'.[50] It was written largely by Wilson and Crossman. But the 'Shadow Cabinet' refused to accept this Bevanite view, since it would have meant admitting they had been wrong the year before.

## THE '57 VARIETIES' REVOLT

Wilson warned the Parliamentary Labour Party on 4 March 1952 that the country would face economic bankruptcy if the Government's arms programme were pushed through. He was supported by Bevan, after whom Dick Crossman put forward the amendment they had devised in place of that favoured by the Front Bench. It was defeated, after appeals by Attlee and Shinwell. When it was suggested that as many as forty Labour MPs would be unable to support the amendment favoured by Attlee and his front-bench colleagues, every MP was sent a letter signed by Attlee, Herbert Morrison and William Whiteley, the Chief Whip, urging them to back the Labour amendment supporting the Government's rearmament policy while doubting the Tory ability to execute it and abstaining on the Conservatives' own motion. In the event an astonishing total of fifty-seven Labour MPs defied their leadership and voted against the Government's White Paper instead of abstaining as directed. The fifty-seven included the resigning Ministers, all the members of the 'Keep Left' Group and another score, mainly pacifists, who had never joined.

The fury of the orthodox leadership and, even more, of the right-wing trade-union leaders led by Arthur Deakin made it clear that strict discipline was on the point of being imposed unless the rebels recanted. Bevan himself was defiant, speaking to constituents at Rhymney: 'If we are asked to recant, I shall say, "No, we won't." If they ask us to promise not to do it again, I will say, "No, we can't." If you think what you did was right, you cannot promise not to do what you think right again!' He attacked the press for over-personalizing the issue. 'There are much more important things happening in the world than the careers of one or two individuals. If I disappeared tomorrow the same issues would be there.'[51]

Wilson's approach seemed more moderate. Speaking at Wigan the same night, he stressed 'the supreme importance of the unity of this party of ours' and 'the realization that in this great party there must be and always will be discussions on policy. I appeal to you not to play the Tory game and say that discussions on policy are bids for party leadership.' He said that if there were a ballot for the Labour Party Leader the next day, 'my vote would go to Clem Attlee.'[52] When newspapers overemphasized his support for Attlee, he complained. 'But don't think that Mr Wilson is Mr Facing-Both-Ways,' the *Evening Standard* warned its readers next day. 'Oh, no. Like others of his party, he blames the newspapers for giving this impression. Mr Wilson is upset because only the point about his devotion to Mr Attlee was reported. So today I gave him another opportunity. I asked Mr Wilson whether, like Mr Bevan, he would declare he did not mean to recant from the Bevanite position. Mr Wilson replied: "After last night, I have no confidence that if I made a statement it would be correctly reported."'[53]

In fact, the newspapers were correct about Nye Bevan having been carried away by the warmth of his own oratory and his constituents' adoration. When the Group met the next evening Dick Crossman reported in his diary that the atmosphere 'was a little strained, and Nye was very careful to concentrate discussion on what should be the line tomorrow [at the critical Parliamentary Labour Party meeting]. There was no direct reference to his statement in his constituency on Sunday night, but Barbara Castle and Harold Wilson made it clear that they wanted caution; and so did the Group, when it asked for John Freeman to speak first, and when it suggested that I should also speak. Indeed, the suggestion that Nye should speak came rather late. I think he was very quick to observe this.'[54]

Wilson and others in the Group anxious to avoid playing into the hands of their strongest critics turned out to be correct next day, when almost all the Labour MPs crowded into the Grand Committee Room of Westminster Hall. Attlee put to the meeting a three-point plan to chastise the fifty-seven rebels. Under his resolution the fifty-seven who voted against the Tory defence plans would have been criticized, the disciplinary Standing Orders which had been in suspense since 1945 would have been reimposed, and every Labour MP would have had to sign an acceptance of these Standing Orders. Those who backed this plan anticipated that all but Bevan and half-a-dozen of his closest supporters would sign their acceptance, leaving them fairly isolated and open to expulsion. It was one of the iron rules of Parliamentary Labour politics that only rebellions of less than ten were punishable.

A group of middle-of-the-road ex-Ministers – George Strauss, John Strachey and Kenneth Younger – put forward a much softer amendment in order to avoid expulsion and retain party unity. This simply ignored the rebellion of the fifty-seven and supported the imposition of 'such Standing Orders as will make it obligatory on all members to carry out decisions of the Parliamentary Party, taking into account the traditional conscience clause'. This amendment received support from an unexpected source, Tom O'Brien of the cinema technicians' union, who was sensitive to the Bevanite ferment working among union militants. Attacking the Attlee proposal he said that if the party wanted to destroy itself it should move into nearby Westminster Hall, where previous trials and executions had taken place. Alongside the plaques for Charles I and William Wallace could be placed another: 'On this spot the Labour Party committed suicide, aided and abetted by Clement Attlee and Aneurin Bevan.' Attlee was asked to withdraw his motion on behalf of the moderate amendment but curtly refused. When the vote came a surprisingly numerous 162 voted for the moderate amendment and only seventy-three against. 'Among those whom I saw vote for extreme measures,' Crossman dictated to his diary, 'were Tony Crosland, Douglas Jay, Patrick Gordon Walker, Woodrow Wyatt, Roy Jenkins, as well as the whole ['Shadow Cabinet' or] Parliamentary Committee. We certainly felt it was a triumph and celebrated it in the Smoking Room with Tom O'Brien. The fact is that, without Bevin to advise him, Attlee has completely misjudged the attitude of the unions, which realistically assess the strength of Bevanism in the rank-and-file. Attlee's support was almost exclusively middle-class in the meeting.'[55] That afternoon Wilson and Crossman listened to Butler read his Budget speech from the upstairs gallery of the Commons, prior to a Group meeting at 5.30. This discussed the Budget as well as the impending imposition of Standing Orders. In the latter case it decided to do nothing in view of the victory of moderation.

Battle resumed in the Parliamentary Labour Party on 19 March 1952. It was the meeting convened to impose strict Standing Orders. One of the leading speakers in favour of this was Charles Pannell, a right-wing loyalist ex-engineer, who attacked the Group as a 'party within a party' which was 'organized, secret, with their own whips on'. In fact someone in the Group was clever enough to move to revoke the 1945 suspension of Standing Orders. This was carried, which Crossman thought 'a very smart trick', because it meant that a Labour MP could be suspended only for persistent disobedience of party decisions.[56]

## TO GROUP OR NOT TO GROUP

Charlie Pannell's open attack on their secret Group made it clear to all that their discretion had been to no avail in the face of an active tale-bearer in the shape of Desmond Donnelly. There were all sorts of ideas about what to do next. Geoffrey Bing thought they might think about suspending the Group before it was suspended for them, but this imminent crisis only sharpened the argument which had been going on for some time about how best it could function.

Although collectively described as 'Bevanites', with an ideology called 'Bevanism', there was little coherence within the Group even about what it should do. Crossman wanted a coherent ideology. Mikardo wanted a tight structure as well. Bevan, who was an ideas man and a vivid talker and fabulous orator, wanted neither. 'Aneurin Bevan can never be persuaded to have any consistent and coherent strategy ... we have not even got the beginnings of a coherent constructive policy,' complained Crossman in his diary. 'So far from being a great strategist and organizer of cabals,' continued Crossman, 'Nye is an individualist, who, however, is an extraordinarily pleasant member of a group. But the last thing he does is to lead it. He dominates its discussion simply because he is fertile in ideas. But leadership and organization are things he instinctively shrinks from.'[57]

The Group had a special meeting on 10 April to discuss its future, almost exactly a year after the Bevanite resignation. 'Nye, who had not been attending Group meetings for two or three weeks ... indicated that he thought the Group should cease to be exclusive, and a long discussion followed on how to retain cohesion and leadership for Bevanism and yet to avoid the obloquy of being a secret cabal inside the Parliamentary Party. Nye has never liked the cliquiness of a closely-knit group, such as Ian Mikardo delights in organizing. Moreover, as he always resents any idea of seriously thinking out policy, he instinctively rejects the raison d'être of the Group, which is precisely to think out policy. On the other hand, he wants support ... The final conclusion was that we should propose to a full meeting [of the Parliamentary Labour Party] after the [Easter] recess that in our view we should let it be known that anybody who is likeminded with us will be welcome [to our meetings] at 1.30 each Tuesday.'[58]

As Chairman of this meeting Wilson was not able to make his own view clear. He agreed with Bevan in not wanting the Group to be so aggressively sectarian as to make the re-uniting of the party more difficult. He too wanted Bevan's emergence as leader, and his own as principal economist and Chancellor-designate. He was unlike Bevan in seeing the usefulness of the Group as working out alternative tactics with which Labour could fight the Tories more effectively and thus win over the support of more Labour MPs. He was also unlike Bevan in that he was willing to work hard on the nitty-gritty of Labour politics – the drawing-up of Bevanite amendments instead of Attleeite amendments, the composing of Bevanite resolutions for the Labour conference such as the one he was asked to prepare on defence: 'This conference (1) *reaffirms* its belief that it is necessary to build up and maintain armed forces adequate for national and Commonwealth defence and for fulfilling international obligations; (2) *repudiates*, however, the Tory theory that armed strength should be given overriding priority. (3) It therefore *urges* the National Executive to issue a full statement on Labour's defence policy, making it clear that the size of the arms programme should be limited by four conditions, namely (a) it should not impose on the British people an unfair share of what should be the common burden of collective security; (b) it should not endanger the solvency and independence of the UK; (c) it should not jeopardize the speedy development of the plans for the backward areas which are democracy's most effective long-term defence; and (d) it should not involve cuts in the fabric of the Welfare State which weaken the defence of democracy, which it is intended to strengthen.' This draft resolution is interesting in that in one place, after fulfilling international obligations, the subsequent passage – 'in particular, for providing our full contribution to the Atlantic Defence Community' – is cut out.[59]

Although Wilson was fully stretched in this sort of drafting, at which he was very clever, there was no enthusiasm at that time for using him in big mass meetings. He had not yet developed the style he was to develop over the next three or four years. So he swallowed a number of disappointments, one of which was observed by Dick Crossman, who was conscious of Wilson's sense of insecurity. 'We were in the Smoking Room with Harold Wilson, Ian Mikardo and others, and Nye was complaining to me that his throat and chest were bad and that he was doubtful if he could get to Wallsend this weekend, where he is to address a monster demonstration, with all the tickets already sold. Then he turned to me and said, "Can you take my place?" ... When Nye made the suggestion I saw Harold Wilson looking rather bleak.'[60]

Things began to get difficult for the Group. Apart from public attacks from outside by the press and by right-wing trade-union leaders like Deakin, there were niggling obstructions within the Palace of Westminster: obstacles were put in the way of notices of meetings being pinned on the notice board. So it was decided that the Group would meet every Tuesday at 1.30 p.m. in Room 8 until further notice. The

Group began to pull in its horns. Thus it was agreed not to hold a 'Brains Trust' meeting at Morecambe at the time of Labour's annual conference. There was, however, agreement that they should attempt a 'considerable widening of the Group by individual approaches'.[61]

The 22 April meeting – a year after the Bevan–Wilson–Freeman resignations – considered a memorandum possibly prepared by Geoffrey Bing. In this it was pointed out that the Group had previously decided it would be nice to blur the edges between them and their sympathizers, but had never found a practical way of doing so. The situation had changed over the past year. The Group had grown in size and influence. It was no longer necessary to explain its position. Therefore it could be thrown open to 'like-minded people', but it would not be possible to throw it open to all, because this would attract 'obstructionists' who would come to sabotage rather than contribute. If the Group were thrown open it would be impossible to organize 'Brains Trusts' at such open meetings or plan specific actions at PLP meetings. It would no longer be possible to have minutes or secretaries; notices would have to be sent to everybody who had attended one or more of the last three meetings.[62]

Although a high-powered group in political terms it was hardly well financed. At the end of its first year its accounts showed that it had spent almost £29 in all: £7 8s 4d for stamps, £6 15s 11d for stencils, £4 16s 6d for duplicating paper, etc. Of the thirty members, twenty-nine had paid up their £1 levy to cover these expenses: 'one member (he knows who it is) owes us £1. We ought now to have another levy: we suggest ten shillings per member.' The accounts were signed by the two secretaries, Jo Richardson (later an MP) and Rose Cohen.[63]

When possible new recruits for an expanded Group were discussed on 29 April, Wilson suggested bringing back Lord Silkin, who had been dropped for non-attendance. Harold Lever was suggested by Will Griffiths, Elwyn-Jones by Cledwyn Hughes, and some fifteen others in all. Then an attempt was made to divide these recruits into 'highly commended', 'commended' and 'others suggested'. A. Wedgwood Benn was only 'commended', while A. J. Irvine was moved up to 'highly commended'.[64]

The Group got a shot in the arm because of the emergence on the political agenda of German rearmament, a rallying cry for the broad Left of the Labour Party and a dividing force on its Right. It had been a rumbling argument since the Americans had first raised it with a reluctant Ernest Bevin in September 1950 in the first weeks of rearmament in the wake of the Communist attack on South Korea. The West Germans represented the main untapped reservoir of military manpower in Western Europe, no matter how reluctant their former

Second World War opponents may have been to rearm them. The American military planners, preoccupied with the 'Chinese menace' in East Asia and self-convinced that the Soviet tanks would roll into Europe in 1955, insisted that West German ground troops would be needed.

The Group moved with zest on this issue, since many of its members – if not Wilson himself – had come into the Labour movement in the period of the Popular Front against fascism. Despite this, Dick Crossman wrote a notably cautious draft resolution for the forthcoming annual Labour conference. This recalled 'the conditions laid down by Mr Attlee as Prime Minister in February 1951: (i) that the rearmament of the members of NATO must take precedence over German rearmament; (ii) that German rearmament must not bring with it a revival of German militarism; and (iii) that it must receive the consent of the German people.' Without these three conditions West Germany's immediate acceptance into the European Defence Community would be a violation. The 'whole issue of German rearmament shall be postponed and . . . a renewed effort should be made to reach a negotiated settlement with the Soviet Union.'[65]

This was well calculated because Bevan was able to get support from his opponent, Hugh Dalton, at the Foreign Affairs Group of Labour MPs. At the next meeting of the National Executive Attlee also supported his February 1951 position adopted by the Group. The National Executive decided to support delays in German rearmament until further discussions with the Russians and fresh elections in West Germany. When the PLP decided against opposing the Government in the May discussion on German rearmament, the Group put down an Early Day Motion signed by Bevan, Wilson, Freeman and twenty-seven others calling for a delay in German rearmament until fresh German elections and a conference with the Russians had been held. The Bevanite journal *Tribune* attacked Attlee for weakening in his opposition to early German rearmament. By 30 May fifty-seven Labour MPs had signed the Motion calling for a delay in German rearmament.

It was at this period that Wilson developed a new interest. The publisher Victor Gollancz wrote a letter to the *Guardian* about the need to eradicate poverty in the under-developed world and asked people who shared his views to send him a card. He received 4,000 cards and some contributions. He then set up a high-powered committee. Two of its members, Leslie Hale and Sir Richard Acland, both Bevanites, went to see Wilson to ask him to join. He did, and wrote for them a 30,000-word pamphlet in six weeks while sitting outside the Committee rooms of two Bills on steel and transport denationalization. 'We had twenty days of committee,' he later recalled. He went to see William Clark, the

*Observer* journalist, about a title, and then thought of one himself, 'War on Want'. It was published in mid-June 1952, and the subject remained an interest of his for many years.

Wilson was an indefatigable worker. When the Group met on 17 June to discuss a paper by economist Dudley Seers on the impact of rearmament on the economy, Dick Crossman recorded: 'We had a good meeting of the Group today, with a lot of new members ... taking a very full part in the discussion. As usual on these occasions it was found that Harold Wilson had nearly completed a tremendous work on the subject and he is preparing a summary of his proposals for presentation in a fortnight's time. After the meeting I had a word with him and Michael [Foot], and the obvious tactic seems to be that a *Tribune* pamphlet by Wilson on a Plan for the Crisis should be launched in August, which would provide both a Group policy and useful advertising for him for the elections to the National Executive at Party Conference. I discussed whether Michael and/or I should stand, and clearly Harold Wilson was very relieved when I said that, if either of us did, the result would most probably be not to get six Bevanites on, but to knock one off.'[66] Crossman had discussed the same subject with Nye Bevan several weeks before, on 29 April. Bevan 'in one of his cautious moods' was also against Crossman and Foot standing because he seemed 'unwilling to have a whole Bevanite slate run'.

Wilson was beginning to feel that he would win his seat on the National Executive because the pro-American Attlee–Morrison–Gaitskell leadership had a habit of lagging badly behind events and then acting in an aggressively defensive way towards its critics. Typical of this was the uproar over the US/UN bombing of the Chinese/Korean power stations on the Yalu. On 24 June Bevan and Sydney Silverman raised the question of the bombing. A debate was arranged for the next day, in which Attlee was sufficiently critical to satisfy all party factions. He promised to censure the Government the next week. When the critical motion was published it was so weak that even Churchill did not consider it a censure motion since it asked only for better consultations. So on 30 June the Group formulated its own Early Day Motion criticizing the Government sharply. The same sort of battles went on over German rearmament and the pace of British rearmament, with the official leadership on the defensive.

The party leadership refused all offers from the Group to patch up differences, possibly because the Bevanites were still winning adherents. A number of Group members were willing to dissolve the Group provided there was still some looser forum – the term 'Labour Forum' was proposed – in which Bevanite ideas could be discussed openly. Ellis Smith discussed the possibility of sending out notices for it on the

'Whip', the weekly notice which went out to all Labour MPs, but Carol Johnson, Secretary of the Parliamentary Labour Party, was 'uncooperative', Smith reported to the Group.[67]

Even before that, Dick Crossman had discussed the problem during his period out of active politics as a result of his own illness and the death of his second wife through a brain haemorrhage. 'While I was in hospital I discussed informally with Eddie Shackleton, Patrick Gordon Walker, Dalton and Aneurin, what the reaction would be if, say, Aneurin, Harold Wilson, John Freeman and I stood for the Parliamentary Committee next October on the clear understanding that, if we were elected, the Group would be disbanded.'[68] This seemed to be taken by the Group's critics as an offer of surrender, an attitude, particularly on Gaitskell's part, which so irritated Crossman that he exploded at the 24 July meeting of the Parliamentary Labour Party: 'Gaitskell made a defence which so irritated me that I forfeited in two minutes all the party's sorrow at my bereavement by a polite reminder to Mr Gaitskell that he and Mr Jay had been wrong on every issue for eighteen months and that the poor boobs like ourselves had happened to be right; and couldn't he, for once, suggest a cut in armaments before Mr Churchill and Lord Swinton, rather than tagging along afterwards?'[69]

Wilson's approach was quite different. He felt that Gaitskell was increasingly discredited and therefore could not play the role in the next Labour Government he had played in the last. 'At the Monday *New Statesman* lunch we had Harold Wilson, who fascinated me,' Dick Crossman recorded. 'When we got down to the questions I have just been discussing [about future relations between Left and Right], he said that Nye had completely the right idea. What he was going to do after we had won the next election was to go to Attlee and demand that the Treasury should be deprived of control of economic planning. John [Freeman] and I protested that this meant absolutely nothing. With the best will in the world how could Attlee reply to that demand. Then we gradually began to realize what Mr Wilson was really getting at was that Mr Gaitskell, who could hardly be refused the Chancellorship, should be subordinated to the new Minister of Economic Planning, Mr Harold Wilson.'[70] Crossman was sceptical about the realism of the desire shared by Wilson and Bevan to downgrade Gaitskell substantially.

Suddenly the solution for the survival of the Group was discovered, and was announced at the 1 August meeting. It was a relaxed meeting because, at the PLP meeting which had preceded it, Nye Bevan had been mellow. Instead of calling Christopher Mayhew a 'pimp', as he had George Brown the week before, he had merely laughed at him and got the party laughing with him. At the Group meeting Michael Foot, its

Editor, disclosed that *Tribune* would be published weekly instead of fortnightly, in tabloid form. This opened up the prospect that the Group could become *Tribune*'s Parliamentary support group, thus avoiding difficulties. 'If, as we have all agreed, three of four of us are to stand for the Parliamentary Committee, it will really be impossible for the Bevanite Group to go on as at present,' Crossman recorded. 'Four members of the Parliamentary Committee could not possibly report back to the Group outside without violating the principle of collective responsibility. However, we might perhaps change the character of the Group into an organization concerned with *Tribune* affairs generally, and stop it being a strict [caucus] group in its present form. During the last ten days I have been discussing this idea with Aneurin and Harold Wilson. Harold Wilson is in complete agreement. One is never sure about Aneurin, but he has always been concerned with constitutional proprieties, and when he was in the Cabinet he kept no contact whatever with us in the 'Keep Left' Group, or with anyone else. Moreover, it would be a definite advantage if the Brains Trusts could now be overtly called "Tribune Brains Trusts", so that the collections could be used for *Tribune* and we could get away from the word "Bevanite".'[71]

When the August recess came, the Wilsons went off with Hugh Delargy and his wife for a tour of France. Hugh had been partly educated in France when he still thought himself destined for the priesthood. Manchester-born of Irish origins, Hugh was good company, and was already a drinking companion of Nye Bevan in the Smoking Room of the Commons. Wilson had left behind him the manuscript of his pamphlet 'In Place of Dollars' to be published the next month on the eve of the Morecambe conference. It was a call for less dependence on the mercurial American economy, which had been imposing strains on a vulnerable Britain through over-rapid rearmament. Alternatives to dollar raw materials should be developed in the Commonwealth. American efforts to curb East–West trade unnecessarily should be resisted. The burden of the rearmament programme should be eased and the economy regenerated by 'a degree of socialism and planning far greater than anything we have so far known in Britain'.[72] The *Daily Express* found it 'an anti-American blueprint for a Bevanite Britain'.[73]

## CONFLICT AT MORECAMBE

The weather was blustery and wet at Morecambe on the Lancashire coast at the end of September, but it seemed increasingly sunny to Harold Wilson. Reports had been growing that the Bevanites would do well and that it was likely he would win a place on the National Executive, perhaps at the expense of Hugh Dalton. He anticipated this with some glee, since he had not forgotten or forgiven Dalton's jibe.

The conference hall was packed on the morning of 30 September to hear the results of the previous day's ballot for seats on the National Executive – particularly for the seven seats in the constituency section. When the vote was read out the first hint came when Bevan remained top of the poll, having picked up a further 100,000 votes. Barbara Castle, Tom Driberg and Ian Mikardo were all on, with their votes well up on the previous year. Even before Mikardo's vote, as sixth man, Wilson's vote of 632,000 was read out to loud cheers, putting him on as fifth man. After Mikardo came Dick Crossman as seventh man. The Bevanites had swept six of the seven places in the constituency section, leaving only the broadly popular Welsh ex-miner Jim Griffiths. Hugh Dalton and Herbert Morrison had both been knocked off the Executive after decades of service to the Labour movement. *The Times* reporter described this as a 'resounding success' for the Bevanites and 'a heavy blow at the more orthodox leadership of the party'.[74] Wilson told a friend; 'Nye's little dog has turned round and bitten Dalton where it hurts!'[75]

While this turmoil was happening Clem Attlee doodled on imperturbably on the platform. He then made his speech ignoring the shift of power. But this was not typical. A leading trade-union official rushed out of the conference after the vote, shouting: 'After this there'll be no more bloody money for this bloody party!' So furious was he that he spat out his false teeth.[76] Sir Will Lawther made a more public show of his feeling as the miners' leader by saying he was 'very much disturbed at the attempts being made – and I say this deliberately – to drive a wedge between the trade union movement and the rest of the movement.' He then went on to suggest that the Bevanites were as traitorous as the MacDonaldites: 'In that dark period of 1931 it was the intellectuals that funked the issue.... That is why we want you to realize that if there is any attempt made along those lines, we will fight to the death, if needs be.' When interrupted by a heckler he shouted: 'Shut your gob!', and went on. That afternoon, George Brown, a loyal supporter of Arthur Deakin, began by saying: 'It seems to me this Conference is rapidly going mad.' The following morning, his union chief, Arthur Deakin, as the 'fraternal' delegate of the Trades Union Congress, shook a heavy fist under Bevanite noses. He congratulated defeated Herbert Morrison for his 'magnificent contribution' and then warned Conference that those who paid the piper should call the tune. 'What I have said is that we are entitled, having regard to the contribution we make, not merely in money but in loyalty to the Movement, to criticize and to reply to criticism... Those people within the party who have set up a caucus, using differences of opinion which no longer have any real significance, are using a subterfuge... What most people are thinking is that there is a great struggle for leadership going on ... We are going to have a straight and clean fight within our Movement... Organization has been set up, well, organization will be set up to counteract that.... Let them get rid of their Whips, dismiss their business managers and conform to the party constitution. Let them cease the vicious attacks they had launched upon those with whom they disagree, abandon their vituperation and the carping criticism which appears regularly in *Tribune*.'[77]

Perhaps it was lucky that Mary Wilson, with her distaste for political brawls, was not there to see and hear the threats and attacks on the occasion of her husband's victory. But she missed as well the Bevanites' victory celebration with their supporters on the Wednesday night, 1 October, in the Winter Gardens Ballroom under the auspices of *Tribune*. Except for another example of Crossman's ability to be misunderstood, it was a meeting in which delegates showed their enthusiasm at having used the Bevanites to defeat the orthodox leaders on Labour's platform. The speakers were a mixed bag. Harold Wilson gave what was really a Parliamentary oration; J. P. W. Mallalieu told football stories about Huddersfield; Jennie Lee appealed for money in her arch and treacly way. But Bevan made one of his most powerful speeches, both lifting his listeners out of their seats with inspiration and opening their eyes with insights. 'One can say what one likes about Bevanism being a policy,' recorded Crossman, 'but it's clear that without Nye absolutely nothing whatsoever could have been achieved, and that, with him, about a fifth will be achieved of what one would like to be achieving, since he so hates policy.'[78]

Having made their advance, the Bevanites were anxious to extend the olive branch, partly because they wanted to lead a united Labour Party into more effective action against the Conservatives. Crossman had tried to say this at conference, provoking some jeering, and Bevan made it much clearer at the *Tribune* meeting: 'I say to my friends, Arthur Deakin and Will Lawther: it is all right, boys, we are the same kind of chaps. I say sincerely I would rather be attacked in the blunt language with which I am familiar than be surrounded by smoothies. We have always been a rough party. Some delegates imagine we have been witnessing a pretty rough house this week. Not a bit. I recall that Stafford Cripps once organized a rebel conference and I was one of the speakers. The rebellion was about more seats for the constituency parties. When I heard Arthur Deakin being indignant at the Labour Party Conference now, it is nothing to what Ernest Bevin said about us then. We have to keep our sense of proportion about these things ... In public life for every kiss you get two slaps, and the decisions of democratic votes are not declarations of individual worth. Those who are defeated are not defeated because they are not respected. We respect them all. We respect those who this week after many years of service receive what may appear to be a rebuff.'[79]

## THE GAITSKELL ATTACK

It suddenly became clear that orthodox and right-wing Labour leaders would not take the Bevanite advance lying down when Hugh Gaitskell launched his famous attack at Stalybridge on 5 October, just after the Conference. 'A most disturbing feature of the Conference', he insisted, 'was the number of resolutions and speeches which were Communist-inspired, based not even on the *Tribune* so much as the *Daily Worker* ... I was told by some observers that about one-sixth of the constituency party delegates appear to be Communist or Communist-inspired ... It is time to end the attempt at mob rule by a group of frustrated journalists and restore the authority and leadership of the solid, sensible majority of the movement.'[80] Gaitskell's facts were disputed, even by those on his side of the anti-Bevanite camp. What was not disputed was that he was putting himself forward as the political spearhead for the right-wing counter-attack in place of Herbert Morrison who was tired and ageing and not hungering for battle.

The Bevanites' opponents wanted not only the dissolution of the Group but also the muzzling of *Tribune*, as Gaitskell suggested in a *Spectator* article and private conversations with Hugh Dalton.[81] Dick Crossman was astonished at the fierceness of Gaitskell's feelings. Bevan thought it would result in Attlee remaining Leader much longer to avoid having a hard right-winger as his successor. When Attlee seemed to join Gaitskell on 11 October, describing as 'intolerable' the continuance of the Bevanite Group as a 'party within the party', Bevan decided it was necessary to dissolve the Group. He started writing an article for *Tribune* dissolving the Group even before conferring with Wilson, Crossman, Mikardo and Foot at his home on the evening of 13 October 1952.

Wilson sided with Bevan but played a rather neutral role in over three hours of argument. Bevan proposed that some of the Group should stand for the Parliamentary Committee but that the Group should be thrown open for everyone's attendance to show that stories about it had been wildly exaggerated. Mikardo asked why, after a great victory at Morecambe, the Group should suddenly capitulate. Why not wait until the Parliamentary Labour Party decided on abolishing groups and abide by the decision? Bevan grew angry with Mikardo and Crossman: 'To continue the Group now is to perpetuate schism,' he flared. 'If you were to continue the Group in these conditions and I were the Leader, I would have you expelled. The Group is intolerable.' Crossman asked: 'Then why hasn't it been intolerable for the last six months?' 'Well, of course it's been intolerable,' Bevan replied, '[but] we've got away with it. That's the point of Morecambe. We're in a strong enough position not to need protection, and if we go on with it we shall alienate the people in the Parliamentary party we are trying to win, and we shall lose the support of nearly half the constituencies within twelve months because they will be able to pillory us as a sectarian conspiracy.'[82] It was agreed to throw open the Group meetings, and Crossman and Bevan wrote articles proposing this for the *New Statesman* and *Tribune*.

These articles were already in type when the Group met on Wednesday, 15 October, to discuss what to do. Because the articles would appear, regardless of what rank-and-file members of the Group decided, Crossman saw this as a 'delicate operation' because 'the Group was committed to the policy which it was called to decide on. Harold Wilson and Nye operated with considerable skill, although they took a fantastic risk in never revealing any of this to the Group and counting on it coming to the right decision.... Personally, I had a distinctly uncomfortable feeling about diddling forty colleagues in this way, and said so to Harold Wilson on the way out. He was baffled, which shows what good politicians he and Nye are.'[83] After the meeting they issued a statement that Bevan, Wilson and Freeman would offer themselves for election to the Parliamentary Committee or 'Shadow Cabinet' and that Group meetings would be thrown open to all Labour MPs. In fact, when this happened on 21 October only four outsiders turned up: Emrys Hughes, a left-wing pacifist, Norman Smith, who was cranky on Social Credit, Lord Strabolgi, and John McKay of Wallsend. None of their main critics bothered.

Attlee, under considerable pressure for having stayed too aloof, took off his kid gloves in the PLP meeting of 23 October. The Tories were doing badly, he insisted, and only Labour disunity would lose it the next election. There would have been unity had it not been for the Bevanite Group. 'You can argue a lot about Groups, but they're like the elephant. I may not be able to define one, but I know one when I see one ... what I disapprove of is an omnicompetent group like the ILP used to be. This Group has, in fact, operated under separate leadership, and the writings of a number of socialist journalists have been in support of an organized group. The proposal to throw the Group open to other members of the party is not good enough, since it would only create a rival party meeting.'

In his reply Bevan did not dispute policy differences. Arguments which had gone on had been intensified by the Korean war. This attack was coming only because rebels had secured increased support at Morecambe. His Group was no different from the XYZ luncheon club attended by Hugh Dalton, Hugh Gaitskell and Douglas Jay – except that it could not afford such expensive lunches. He would love to see an end to personal attacks – he would be the main beneficiary as the principal target of the *Daily Herald* and other papers. The best thing to do, he urged, was to hand the resolution banning all Groups over to the new 'Shadow Cabinet' about to be elected. But this was rejected by the PLP by a vote of 188 for the ban on groups; fifty-five voted against, with about a dozen abstentions. The Group, in its meeting five days later, agreed to dissolve and to have Bevan, Wilson and Freeman stand for the 'Shadow Cabinet' and Nye contest the Deputy Leadership against Herbert Morrison.

Although the Group dissolved formally, it soon reassembled informally – at Dick Crossman's house at 9 Vincent Square, some fifteen minutes' walk from the House of Commons. An informal meeting on 30 October attracted fully twenty-four of the thirty-two Group members, anxious to chew over once again whether the leaders of the rebellion should allow themselves to be hamstrung by joining the Front Bench. Nye had changed his mind, again. 'What was the good of resigning [from the Government the year before] to be free to speak if he at once surrenders that freedom by joining the [Parliamentary] Committee?' Bevan asked. Nothing was decided that week[84] and another meeting was held the next week at which Bevan, Wilson and Freeman were put up for election to the Parliamentary Committee.

After the nominations were in, the rules for election were changed. On the first round, Attlee announced, only those who had a clear majority of the votes cast – each Labour MP cast twelve votes – would be declared elected. In the second round, the unelected among the top eighteen would have to stand again, whether they liked it or not. On the first ballot Bevan ran twelfth with 108 votes, Wilson sixteenth with ninety-one votes, but neither had the 134 votes needed to be elected. Bevan tried to withdraw from the second ballot, but under Attlee's rule he could not. On the second ballot, Bevan scraped in with 137 votes as the twelfth member of the 'Shadow Cabinet'. Wilson was fifteenth, or third runner-up, with 116 votes. *Tribune* denounced this as 'Morecambe in reverse' because Bevan, who was top of the pops so far as constituency activists were concerned, was bottom so far as predominantly moderate Labour MPs were concerned.

There was no doubt that this result was 'engineered', as Hugh Dalton confessed later to Dick Crossman over dinner on 25 November; he told of how 'when he was sitting on the Front Bench, he had been shown the piece of paper with the list of candidates to be backed by all right-minded – or perhaps Right-minded – persons.'[85] The intention, of course, was to 'cage' Bevan again. But the disbanding of the Group and Bevan's reappearance on Labour's Front Bench did have the effect of reducing tension within Labour's ranks, as Crossman cheerfully confessed.[86]

## WILSON'S NEW ROLE

By this point Wilson was well into his new role as a member of the National Executive. At his very first meeting, on 28 October, he archly baited Gaitskell (who was not a member) by asking whether the charge of Communist infiltration, launched by the ex-Chancellor, should be investigated. He was supported by Sam Watson – who sided with Gaitskell. But General Secretary Morgan Phillips said the charge was completely unfounded.[87]

It was lucky for Harold Wilson that he had a new focus for his thrusting energies on the NEC because the Bevanite upsurge as such had come to a peak in the Commons. On 11 November the vote for the Deputy Leadership was announced with Herbert Morrison winning by 194 votes to eighty-two votes for Aneurin Bevan. This was judged by the *Evening Standard*'s political correspondent as exceeding 'the most optimistic estimates of the Bevanites', since the Right outnumbered the Left in the Parliamentary party by about three to one in those days. Therefore there was no great future for Wilson in a factionally divided Parliamentary party as a pure Bevanite.

He was still deeply involved with Bevan, Crossman and the Group's economic adviser Dr Thomas Balogh and others in their discussions on how to further their viewpoint in the Labour Party. Thus, they met on 25 November for dinner to discuss the stand the six Bevanites should take at the next day's NEC meeting. At first they discussed how badly the Group had disintegrated since it had been formally disbanded. It was decided to appoint six 'scoutmasters' to contact six or seven other Bevanite MPs. These six would work with the six Bevanites on the NEC. After Christmas, it was planned, there would be weekly lunches of this inner group at Crossman's house every Tuesday. This would be broken to the Group at a Christmas party at Nye's house, followed by a beginning-of-term party at Vincent Square towards the end of January.[88]

Bevan, Wilson and Balogh then went on to discuss what industries to nationalize. It was agreed that the Bevanites on the NEC should press for heavy chemicals, heavy engineering, aircraft production and rented land. This was not as far-fetched as might have been expected within the Labour Party, as Crossman discovered a few days later when Douglas Jay attended the Monday luncheon of the *New Statesman*. Jay had prepared a plan for developing the economy over the next ten years as part of a Fabian lecture. He had come to the conclusion that it was necessary to increase engineering production by forty per cent. Asked what he thought of Wilson's plan for widespread nationalization – which he had made public in a speech two days before – Jay said that he agreed with Wilson, to Crossman's surprise.

On 12 December the Bevanites on the NEC again dined at the Crossmans on the eve of the two-day conference of the NEC at Brown's Hotel. One of the key subjects was to be a five-year-plan to make Britain viable, proposed by Jim Griffiths. Having been briefed by Wilson and Balogh, Bevan made the point that, to increase, say, engineering by forty per cent it would be impossible to rely on privately owned plants. 'Harold Wilson was extremely persuasive throughout this in his highly competent way,' recorded Dick Crossman, 'and every now and then, when we were nearing agreement on some tentative conclusion, Ian Mikardo would biff in to say something so Bevanite that the agreement disappeared.'[89]

The chance of Wilson reaching agreement with his non-Bevanite colleagues was made difficult by the combination of abrasiveness and touchiness on both sides of the divide. After the New Year's Honours list had included a knighthood for Lincoln Evans, leader of the steelworkers' union, *Tribune* 'needled' him with a story demanding to know why he was accepting a knighthood from Churchill, whose government was denationalizing steel. The thin-skinned trade-union leaders were so irritated by this that the General Council of the TUC actually sent a formal complaint to the Labour Party's NEC, which was meeting at the same time at the end of January. Bevan ridiculed this, pointing out that Deakin, Lawther, Williamson and other union leaders had attacked him much more fiercely and he had never complained. Harry Douglas, also of the steelmen's union, insisted 'the next logical thing to do is to examine the *Tribune* Brains Trusts and see if they are a party within a party'. Dr Edith Summerskill shrilled that the NEC had been too soft, and stronger measures were now needed: 'I mean expelling those who are suspected of fellow-travelling,' she spat out, impaling Ian Mikardo with her angry eyes. The NEC decided by seven to five[90] to rebuke *Tribune*. Three weeks later, the NEC's Organization Sub-committee spent over three hours discussing the Brains Trusts, finally passing a resolution urging their banning. It was not until 26 February, a month after the row had started, that Attlee calmed it down, pointing out that the Parliamentary party was not concerned with the Brains Trusts, and that an independent socialist weekly had to be able to collect money by public meetings.

The clashes between the Bevanites and their opponents was often much ado about almost nothing. Early in February 1953 Balogh produced a paper which made it clear that expenditure on military equipment was *below* the £3,600m programme to which Bevan and

Wilson had agreed before baulking at the burden of the £4,700m programme. On top of this there was now surplus capacity and unemployment. Therefore the Group decided it would be 'totally irresponsible' to oppose that year's Defence estimates, for fear of hastening a depression.[91]

This was no news to Wilson. On 12 December 1952, in an article in *Tribune* called 'Death of an Arms Programme', he pointed out that Churchill had signalled on 4 December that the £4,700m programme was now to be spread over five instead of three years. 'The £4,700m arms programme is dead,' he chortled. 'All that is left is Bevan.' Churchill, in effect, had removed the basis of the Bevan–Wilson battle with Gaitskell.

Wilson's own economic views could hardly be distinguished from those of Jay or other Gaitskellite economists. Cross-examined by Crossman, Wilson admitted in February 1953 that he had not the faintest idea of what Labour should do about the 'appalling situation' – as Crossman described it – in both the nationalized industries and the private sector. 'The fact is,' recorded Crossman not for the first time, 'that Nye and Harold are not interested in rethinking policy at all.' Before this discussion Balogh had been pressing Crossman to get Wilson and other experts to work out a policy for the two sectors. Crossman was persistent. He pressed the subject again at a Bevanite lunch on 3 March. 'Harold Wilson said he frankly did not know what to do about the private sector and was disappointed to hear that some [National Executive] report on the nationalized industries was not good.'

Against this background it was not surprising that when the economists from the rival factions gathered on 27 March to discuss Labour's election plans there was not as wide a gap as expected. 'Actually, what should have been a fiscal survey degenerated, not unfavourably for us, into a discussion of our proposals, with Hugh Gaitskell strongly pressing us to include in our education programme the abolition of fee-paying in public schools, although, as I pointed out, this would cost the Exchequer £5m a year,' Crossman recorded. 'I found it rather interesting debating with Hugh and seeing how Harold and Tommy [Balogh] behave in Committees. Both were, quite properly, I think, deferential to Hugh in accepting the statement he made on the economic background. The meeting drifted on for hours and hours, with Alice Bacon wreathed in smiles when Harold Wilson observed that the education part of the programme seemed to be one of the best things we should have to offer.'[92]

## THE END OF ISOLATION

Although the two warring wings had already converged earlier, their new friendlier relationship became visible for all to see in the Commons on 16 April 1953, when a joint attack was launched on the Budget of the Conservative Chancellor, R. A. Butler. The Liberal Leader, Clement Davies, said the Tory Chancellor had 'done what I did not think would happen for some time. He has united the socialist party. Mr Bevan, Mr Wilson and Mr Gaitskell not only sit cheek by jowl on their Front Bench – they actually enjoy one another's jokes. No member of the socialist party has so far brought about such an extraordinary result.' Reginald Maudling baited Gaitskell for having come so close to becoming a Bevanite, by jibing: 'I have admired the skill with which you have threaded your way through the socialist party by swinging from olive branch to olive branch.' Wilson described Butler's proposals as a 'rich man's Budget' in passing, but concentrated on the difficulties of selling British equipment to the US – mentioning the cancellation of electrical equipment for a US dam – and the need to ship faster to Canada.[93] In *Tribune* he warned that the cutback on war production in the US might mean a slump in British exports there. He emphasized the need to develop the underdeveloped countries.

Crossman feared that the end of the civil war in the Labour Party might mean serious setbacks for those who had been tagged 'Bevanites'. After seeing the cartoons of Gaitskell with Bevan and Wilson he wrote. 'My view of the prospects of the Bevanites is very dim ... I can't see how we are going to win all our six seats [on the NEC] at Margate [at the annual conference election] next October, but I suppose one shouldn't be upset if the Group gradually liquidates itself.'[94]

Crossman was dead wrong. The Group's gradual withdrawal from self-isolating sectarianism suited the temper of Labour activists. All six of the Bevanites won their seats on the NEC in the constituency section. All of them enlarged their vote, with Wilson increasing his more than the rest, soaring from 632,000 to 934,000, while the more militant Ian Mikardo increased his vote by only 7,000, falling back to last place. 'It is Mr Harold Wilson's meteoric rise to third place which disturbs some of the pioneer Bevanites,' claimed Trevor Evans, the industrial editor of the *Daily Express*. 'Some of his immediate colleagues would prefer a less spectacular ascent for the young and sometimes independent-minded Mr Wilson.'[95] Gaitskell was the first runner-up that year. Morrison regained his seat on the National Executive as Deputy Leader.

That year Wilson seemed to be moving out of the fairly narrow rut he had occupied for almost two years as a left-wing rebel reduced to the back-benches. In February 1953 he began a long research project for the United Textile Factory Workers Association, which resulted four years later in 'A Plan for Cotton', for which he refused payment. He was able to earn extra money as foreign trade consultant for Montague Meyer, who paid him about £1,500 a year plus office, car, secretary and travel expenses. In 1952 they sent him to the States. In May 1953 he made his first trip to the Soviet Union on the firm's behalf, seeing the Soviet Foreign Minister Molotov whilst there. The talk was arranged by his old friend, Mikoyan. He was not one to hide his achievement as a back-bencher who was able to have an hour's interview with the inaccessible Soviet Foreign Minister, and he released the information to the news agencies. The British Ambassador, as is normal in such occasions, attended the talks with him, to report its gist to the Foreign Office. Wilson then flew on to Budapest to talk about the resumption of Anglo–Hungarian trade. He confirmed that there would be no re-sumption of that trade until the Hungarians released Edgar Sanders, an imprisoned British businessman. Wilson was flattering when he re-turned. The USSR, by concentrating on modernizing its industry, had carried through in thirty years an industrial revolution which had taken others 200 years.

The Wilsons began to live better in 1953, thanks to his Montague Meyer job. They had been to the Scilly Isles in 1951 at the suggestion of Ernest Kay and his wife, and they returned there in 1952; in 1953 they began planning to build a cottage there. That same year they moved next door from 10 to 12 Southway in the Suburb, to a £7,000 four-bedroom house; instead of selling the old house they rented it to a family with five children. Mary now had the help of a Swiss *au pair* girl. This inclined her even less to attend political meetings at the Commons, except for ceremonial occasions such as the June 1953 Coronation. This the Wilsons attended with Marjorie Kay and their *au pair*.

Harold's life at home was much more like that of an ordinary suburban executive rather than a politician because he still could not take his political friends home. Mary tried to justify her ban: 'I don't think a woman married to a politician should be a *political* wife,' she said.[96] What she meant as well was: 'I don't think my husband should bring his politics home.'

## MOVING AHEAD

The Parliamentary year 1953–54 proved a crucial one for Wilson. It indicated that the overshadowing chief of the Bevanites was standing still while he was inching forward. Intellectually Bevan could soar far above the head of Wilson, spinning theories and sparking off insights, which Wilson could never equal, but he lacked Wilson's ability for slogging hard work and the patient application of self-advancing tactics. Thus, although it was Wilson who had much more experience of the Soviet Union it was Bevan who saw the new possibilities which opened up with the death of Stalin in 1953. It was also Bevan's impatience with those like John Foster Dulles and the timid leaders of British Labour who could not share his vision that caused him to explode and blow himself off the Front Bench.

Because he was the leader of their Group the Bevanites gloried in his assets while suppressing their criticisms of his dilettantism, self-indulgence and mercurial changes of position – as recorded in Crossman's diary. Where all the Bevanites could agree was on the need to explore whether the passing of Stalin might represent some change in Soviet thinking before taking what might be an irrevocable decision on the rearming of Western Germany. German rearmament had been proposed by Washington as early as September 1950 in the immediate wake of the Korean war, but Labour had delayed making a decision on it because the subject was deeply and emotionally divisive. Not only was the whole of the Left arrayed against it; the Right was also deeply split. Ernest Bevin had opposed it. Hugh Dalton warned that 'German rearmament might prove to be an irrevocable step on the road to hell on earth'.[97] Herbert Morrison, the former Foreign Secretary, was the leading Labour protagonist of German rearmament. Clement Attlee was ambiguous.

The argument therefore overhung the new elections for Labour's Front Bench when the Commons resumed sitting in the autumn of 1953. Bevan again stood against Morrison for the Deputy Leadership. 'This time I voted gloomily for Morrison,' recorded Hugh Dalton, 'because Bevan had been so impossible a colleague in the Shadow Cabinet, and so rude, so often, to Gaitskell and other friends of mine.'[98] Bevan again trailed Morrison, this time by seventy-six votes to 181, in much the same relative position.

In the Shadow Cabinet election Bevan did better than the year before, moving up to ninth place from twelfth. Wilson also improved his showing, running thirteenth, or first runner-up to the twelve-man Shadow Cabinet. This result drew a tart comment from J. P. W. ('Curly') Mallalieu, MP, a columnist in *Tribune*. He wrote an article on 13 November 1953 in which he quoted a constituent asking: 'What goes on? How come that at the annual conference the constituency parties voted virtually the straight Bevanite ticket, while the constituency parties' representatives in Parliament put Bevan three places from the bottom of the Shadow Cabinet and excluded all his associates? ... It looks as though some of these chaps say one thing in public in the country and another thing behind closed doors in the party meetings.'

Bevan's opponents, many of whom *did* pretend to be militant when talking to constituency activists, were furious. Bevan was in a minority of one in a Shadow Cabinet demanding Mallalieu's head and insisting that he be charged for breaking the rule against personal attacks. When Mallalieu was seen he insisted he had been discussing policy, not attacking personalities. When this was raised on 25 November there was talk of withdrawing the Whip, i.e. expelling Mallalieu from the Parliamentary party. Bevan warned against 'the danger of discipline'. Gaitskell spoke of 'the dangers of indiscipline'. Then Bevan glared and retorted: 'You're too young in the Movement to know what you're talking about!' He then pointed out that *Tribune* was the only paper speaking for his viewpoint, which is why the rest wanted to suppress it. 'In my dispute in the party *all* the press, Tory, Liberal and the despicable *Daily Herald* are on one side. But you want unanimity, you want totalitarianism.' Jim Callaghan jibed: 'You're trying to find another excuse to resign from this committee.'[99]

In fact, of course, this was not really an argument over free speech, nor were the anti-Bevanites in any way totalitarians. It was a struggle for power to lead the Labour Movement. This was made clear by Roy Jenkins to Dick Crossman, who bemoaned the good old days when he and Ernest Bevin could bash each other over Palestine without either trying to curb the other's freedom of speech. Jenkins said: 'Well, they – I mean we – feel that every speech, every action must now be considered as part of the power fight within the party. That's why we hate Bevanism. Before it began, one could have free speech. Now one can't afford to ... We on the Right feel that every force of demagogy and every emotion is against us. In the constituency parties, which are now Opposition-minded, the Bevanites have it all their own way.' Jenkins explained why a right-wing win was so important. 'The electorate is extremely conservative-minded and we can never win except with the kind of attitude represented by the right-wing leadership.'[100]

Turbulence within the Shadow Cabinet and within the Parliamentary Labour Party and the Labour Movement as a whole intensified as pressures mounted for a decision to rearm Western Germany. The October 1953 annual Labour conference at Margate had put off the decision by attaching conditions, including further talks with the Soviet Union. These took place in February 1954 against the background of John Foster Dulles's threat of an 'agonizing reappraisal' of US defence policies if the interminable argument over rearming Germany in the European Defence Community was not concluded.

Morrison and Gaitskell insisted that the Russians had proved themselves irreconcilable and that now the party's support for German rearmament within the EDC could no longer be withheld. In the absence of Dalton in hospital, it was pushed through the Shadow Cabinet over the objections of Bevan, Chuter Ede and Jim Callaghan, with Shinwell abstaining. At a fully-attended meeting of the PLP on 23 February the Shadow Cabinet's motion was moved by Herbert Morrison and carried by only nine votes. Then Harold Wilson moved a further amendment that no German rearmament should take place before another effort at East–West negotiations. He vigorously assailed the view that the Berlin conference had explored every possibility of German unity. He wanted to wait until April's Geneva conference. This was defeated by only two votes, 111 to 109, with peers being allowed to vote. A motion supporting German rearmament was carried less narrowly at the NEC, with Wilson again actively against. When Jim Griffiths said that he was not happy about voting for German rearmament Wilson intervened to ask why, if he was so unhappy, he had voted against postponing a decision. However, it was made clear that the final decision would have to go back to the next annual conference.

Wilson also played an important role in the Commons debate on the Berlin conference on 25 February, lifting it 'out of the simple context of German rearmament', according to next day's *Times*. 'He is convinced (and it should be remembered that he recently visited Moscow) that there has been a change in the Russian outlook and that there is a desire for peaceful co-existence with the West. For that reason he advocates a comprehensive effort to ease world tension rather than attempts to solve specific problems ... Mr Eden spent half an hour answering the Labour minority critics and particularly Mr Wilson.' Wilson's approach had been very practical: 'Suppose there is a rising in Eastern Germany. Is there not the greatest danger that Western Germany, incorporated through EDC in NATO, will press very strongly to go to the relief of that rising and go to their help without waiting for the rest of NATO? Does that not mean the immediate danger of World War Three?'[101]

Bevan saw as the basic danger the attempt by John Foster Dulles, President Eisenhower's new Secretary of State, to impose his leadership on what Dulles called 'the Free World'. 'Peace diplomacy must displace war diplomacy,' insisted Bevan. 'For example, when Mr Foster Dulles declares that the aim of the "Free World" is the defeat of Communism, he is using the language of the hydrogen bomb ... When he demands that Chinese Communists should cease to be Communist before they are allowed into the United Nations, he is employing the diplomacy of totalitarianism. Its natural child is the hydrogen bomb. It means total submission or total destruction.'[102]

Bevan himself exploded like a grenade when, after Dulles's visit to London in April 1954, Attlee did not seem to understand what had been agreed with Sir Anthony Eden. Sir Anthony had accepted Dulles' Asian Treaty Organization, or SEATO, to contain the Communists. When Attlee replied to Eden's announcement by mildly asking whether everyone would be able to join, Bevan thought he had missed the whole dangerous point. Clambering over the knees of his Front Bench colleagues, he fumed that this would be 'deeply resented' as 'a surrender to American pressure' and Britain would be assisting in 'imposing European colonial rule upon certain people in that area', thus estranging local Commonwealth members – meaning his friend Nehru of India. Next day, when he was rebuked at the Shadow Cabinet, he followed it up by announcing at the Parliamentary Labour Party meeting that he had resigned from the Shadow Cabinet. In a statement he said he was 'deeply shocked' by Attlee's response to an action which would threaten the Indochina settlement about to be negotiated at Geneva and which would amount 'to the diplomatic and military encirclement of China'.[103]

However right Bevan may have been – as all the Bevanites felt – his tactics were as much at question with them as among his delighted detractors. Did he *have* to upstage Attlee so brutally in public? Did he *have* to resign from the Shadow Cabinet instead of apologizing while explaining why he felt so strongly? Could he not have consulted with *some* of the people he was supposed to lead? These thoughts raced through Wilson's mind with particular force that Easter recess, not only because he was much more tactically minded than Bevan but also because he was the runner-up, the thirteenth man in the election for the Shadow Cabinet. If someone died or resigned it was his decision whether to take his place.

Wilson very soon thought the unthinkable. He felt it had been wrong of Nye to throw away the only beach-head the Bevanites had in the Shadow Cabinet in a fit of pique, no matter how correct Bevan's analysis. If he refused to take the seat vacated it would be taken as a declaration of war on the anti-Bevanites on a subject – Southern Asia – about which few people in the Labour Movement had convictions.

On meeting his Bevanite colleagues for lunch after that Easter recess Wilson discovered that his taking Nye's seat on the Shadow Cabinet was still considered unthinkable by all except Dick Crossman, who agreed with him and had discussed it with him. Crossman then approached Bevan to try to persuade him that Wilson *should* replace him. Bevan was furious. Not only did he feel that it was something akin to treachery to replace a man who had resigned on the principles in which Wilson also believed, but that it would wreck Harold's own political career. Bevan thought this was a time to attack the orthodox leadership, who were split on rearming Germany, not to appease them. Finally Crossman persuaded him to see Wilson. Wilson went with Crossman to the home of Bevan and Jennie Lee in Cliveden Place. Wilson proposed that he would proclaim his support for Bevan's views but take his place. Bevan opposed this, but he knew he could not stop Wilson. The discussion was to proceed next day at the normal Tuesday lunch at Crossman's home in Vincent Square. It was not certain that Bevan would attend. John

Freeman sent him a letter urging: 'I hope you will come to lunch at Dick's tomorrow. I don't mind what you say when you get there; but if you don't come, I fear it will mean that the inner circle of your following may be broken up – perhaps irreparably. This would be a great pity for the party, and I think for yourself. Dick's folly and Harold's ambition have created a disastrous situation. Tomorrow we have to discuss – as comrades – how we can make the best of it. Such a discussion would be futile without you. JOHN FREEMAN.'

Bevan did attend the lunch, which stretched on throughout the afternoon as the argument raged. He never agreed to Wilson's plan to join the Shadow Cabinet in his place, but they did agree to differ fairly amicably.[104] Wilson then consulted Attlee to read to him the letter he was planning to send the Secretary of the PLP, Carol Johnson: 'I am in entire agreement, as the party knows, with Aneurin Bevan on the policy issues involved – on the dangers not only of Mr Dulles's policy in Southeast Asia, but also of German rearmament. Obviously, therefore, it is extremely difficult for me to accept co-option to the vacancy caused by his resignation. Nevertheless, what matters in the last resort is the unity and strength of the party. I have given a great deal of anxious thought to this question in the last ten days and have not lacked advice. My conclusion is that, in the party's interests, it is impossible for me to refuse co-option. In view of the number of statements which have appeared in the press and the speculation as to my position, I feel this letter should be published.'[105] Attlee, having listened, simply said 'Quite!' A number of Bevanites thought Wilson's decision was a 'betrayal' of Nye. A. J. Irvine, the Labour MP for Edge Hill, Liverpool, attacked Wilson that weekend for letting the other Bevanites down. The *New Statesman* said that he had had the choice of sitting with Bevan on the back benches as a demonstration of left-wing unity or making a 'gesture of conciliation' to the leadership. 'No one can envy him the torment of a decision which he clearly found so difficult.'[106]

The superiority of Wilson's *tactical* judgment over that of Bevan was demonstrated very shortly, in June 1954, when Arthur Greenwood died, leaving vacant the Treasurership of the Labour Party. This was a post elected by the annual conference. Because of the dominating size of union block votes it is in effect decided by the big unions, notably the four largest – the Transport, the Municipal and General, the Engineers and the Miners. In 1953 these right-wing-led unions had tried to replace Greenwood, who was amiable, aged and ineffective through drink, by a more active right-winger in the shape of Herbert Morrison. But he had infuriated them when he had withdrawn at the last minute because his victory over 'good old Arthur' was not guaranteed, getting on the NEC instead as Deputy Leader. Now, they made it clear, Gaitskell, who had only just failed to get on the NEC through the constituencies in 1953, would be their nominee for Treasurer. Bevan decided that he would fight what everyone knew was the inevitable. He decided to go ahead even though he learned within days that he would not be backed by his own union, the National Union of Mineworkers, by whom he had been sponsored since 1929. He ran into Sam Watson, the Durham miners' leader, and asked whether he could count on the miners' backing. 'I had to tell him that the NUM had already decided that its nominee for the succession was Hugh Gaitskell,' Watson later recorded. 'How can you support a public schoolboy from Winchester against a man born in the back streets of Tredegar?', Bevan demanded angrily,[107] forgetting how many times he had attacked the miners' leaders as unrepresentative. Although he knew he could not win Bevan insisted on giving up the sure seat on the NEC he could continue to win – by contesting the constituency section – in favour of a hopeless contest against Hugh Gaitskell for Treasurer.

In the five months between the time Wilson replaced Bevan on the Shadow Cabinet and the moment when he replaced him as top man in the constituency section in the ballot at Scarborough he was very much on the move. Early in June he was in Geneva, where he had private business talks. He met Chou En-lai, then the Chinese Foreign Minister, who was helping to negotiate the end of French control of Indochina. A fortnight later he was in Moscow for the fifth time. Once again he saw Russia's trade chief, Mikoyan, who enabled Wilson to become the first British politician to meet Stalin's temporary successor, Georgi Malenkov. He was touristically active while there, taking photographs – for which he was briefly detained by an overzealous policeman – and being photographed. He concluded, as he told readers of two articles in *Reynolds News*, that standards of living were rising rapidly in the Soviet Union, although they were still behind those in Britain. He found they had improved markedly in Moscow and Leningrad over what he had seen the previous year. He was accompanied not by his wife but by his then secretary, Mrs Elise Cannon, a tall, dark girl who was photographed with him when he visited the ancient monastery of Zagorsk.

By the time the Scarborough conference began he was seen as a rising star. 'The mild manner hides limitless application and ambition,' judged the *Observer*. 'He is always on the job. A speech here, a little research work for a trade union there – nothing is too much trouble. ... Recently he has managed to give the impression that he is moderate and sensible – a person who might reconcile the left and right wings of the party.'[108]

Lord Beaverbrook was not as admiring. He described Wilson thus: 'He is an amphibian. Sometimes on Mr Bevan's water; then on

Gaitskell's land. He may end up in the mud.'[109] A number of observers, however, saw Wilson as the vanguard of 'Bevanism without Bevan'.

## NEW PARLIAMENTARY SESSION

History imitated hyperbole that autumn. Having come top of the poll for the constituency section in Bevan's absence – with 1,043,000 votes – Wilson then came twelfth in the ballot for twelve seats on Labour's Shadow Cabinet when the new Parliamentary session began.

Wilson came on to the Front Bench in his own right in the wake of the narrow defeat of the Centre-Left on the crucial subject of German rearmament. The defeat had taken place at the October 1954 Labour Conference, by a vote of 3,270,000 to 3,022,000, accompanied by arm-twisting by right-wing trade-union leaders, who managed to 'persuade' the Woodworkers' leader to vote against the decision of his own conference. There were tasteless points of drama, as when Desmond Donnelly, Bevan's drinking companion in private and leaker of Bevanite secrets, turned to point an accusing finger at him at a time arranged with the TV producers. Bevan himself also suffered a predictable blow when he was defeated in the contest for Treasurer by Gaitskell by 4,338,000 votes to 2,032,000. Those votes were almost the last gestures of a passing generation of clumsy right-wing loyalist trade-union leaders. Within two years the leadership of the Transport and General Workers Union was to come under the hand of Frank Cousins. But for Wilson to appear to be deserting Bevan at that stage left a bad taste in some mouths.

Wilson and Crossman discussed this often at the time, feeling their isolation from their pro-Bevan comrades in the Group. Crossman came to the conclusion, to which Wilson assented, that there was a fundamental difference of approach within the Group. The Wilson–Crossman interest in the Group was basically operational and sought to use the 1951 rebellion and the group itself as a way of moving the top Labour leadership to the Left. Its supporters did not think that Bevan himself could ever become the accepted leader of a united Labour party. Therefore they were always building bridges towards the Centre and Right of the party. That did not appeal either to the sectarians or to the Bevan-worshippers in the Group; nor did it appeal to those outside the Group who resented their serving as respectable 'front men' for it. It did, however, make an impact on Hugh Gaitskell, Attlee's successor as designated by the Centre–Right. On the day after he was elected Treasurer in October 1954 he told George Gale of the *Daily Express* off-the-record: 'The only Bevanites I would have in a Government' – that is in a Cabinet – 'would be Dick Crossman, Harold Wilson and Barbara Castle.'[110]

The final drama of the German rearmament debate within the Labour Party approached in November 1954. The Conservative Government wanted Parliamentary support for the Paris Agreement just concluded, so as to clear the way for German rearmament. Initially the Shadow Cabinet – over the opposition of Dalton, Wilson and Callaghan – decided to support the Government. Then opposition mounted in the Labour Party. Crossman booked a room on the Committee corridor of the Commons in his own name to talk to members of the Group about their tactics, but then decided it would be dangerous to turn up for fear of being accused of organizing a 'party within a party' and being expelled. So the room was taken over by Leslie Hale, a member of the Group and also of Sydney Silverman's Victory for Socialism, a rather sectarian body mainly made up of ex-ILP pacifists. They decided that they would vote against the Paris Agreement at whatever cost. The Labour Shadow Cabinet, fearing that a large minority of Labour MPs would vote with this small group if they insisted on voting for the Government, sent out a three-line Whip calling on all Labour MPs to abstain, hoping thus to maintain party unity. In the event, after a two-day debate six left-wing Labour MPs led by Sydney Silverman and Emrys Hughes voted against the Government and one right-wing Labour MP, John McGovern, voted for the Government. Bevan, Wilson and virtually all the Group members abstained with supporters of German rearmament like Herbert Morrison. Crossman made a powerful speech attacking German rearmament but explained he was not voting against it to avoid being expelled from the Labour Party. The Group did, in fact, avoid the fate dished out to the seven rebels. The expulsion had a humorous note when John McGovern, who had voted with the Tories, pointed an accusing finger at Morrison and others and said: 'It was I who had the courage of your convictions and now you are expelling me for it!'[111]

It was a period in which it was difficult to air strong convictions while simultaneously holding an official position. A ridiculous controversy erupted when *Tribune* attacked Transport Workers' leader Arthur Deakin for calling a rebellious 'Blue Union' of dockers 'Communist-inspired'. Deakin immediately demanded the expulsion of the three MPs who ran *Tribune*, Michael Foot, J. P. W. Mallalieu and Jennie Lee. Bevan warned Attlee that if these three were expelled he would have to be expelled too. Wilson thought this an unnecessary expansion of the conflict. 'Bevanism cannot do without Bevan,' said Wilson, 'but it could do without *Tribune*.'[112]

Unfortunately for his more moderate admirers Bevan could not help putting his neck within the noose which Arthur Deakin and his cohorts wanted to pull tight. There was nothing extreme about Bevan's *policies*.

He wanted high-level talks to avoid or slow down a nuclear arms race that might become out of control and so bring hard-liners into power in the leadership of the super-Powers, particularly the Soviet Union and, to a lesser extent, the United States. It was an aim shared by Sir Winston Churchill. But Bevan's compulsive desire to give a lead with his *ideas* was always confused by his critics with a desire to grab the leadership itself. In fact, when he cuffed Attlee, Morrison or others it was overwhelmingly because, as a brilliant teacher, he was impatient with slow learners.

Defence arguments at this period were particularly complicated. Tension was rising over Quemoy and Matsu, where it seemed possible that the US, in support of its Kuomintang allies in Formosa, might get involved in a war with the Chinese Communists. Given the disparity between US and Chinese manpower, it was feared that this might involve the American use of the H-bomb as well as sucking in Britain through the SEATO alliance. The British Government was on the point of announcing that, despite the successful beginning of the process of recruiting West German military manpower, it was planning to manu-facture H-bombs itself.

Intellectually daring, Bevan wanted the whole process of German rearmament and British H-bomb manufacture stopped while another effort was made to reopen talks with the new Soviet leadership. When he approached Attlee on this subject in January 1955 he was suspected of trying to reverse the vote endorsing German rearmament. When he tried to get the Parliamentary Labour Party to agree to high-level talks he was defeated by ninety-three votes to seventy because it was thought he was trying to outflank Attlee. He then put his motion on the Order Paper, securing the signatures of 110 Labour MPs. Just as Bevan published in *Tribune* an article accusing the Labour leadership of backsliding on its previous policy, the Government announced that Britain too was to manufacture the bomb. Then, although Bevan's Motion had been signed by such loyal Attlee supporters as Michael Stewart, John Strachey and others, Attlee secured the support of the PLP, by 132 votes to seventy-two, for a formal rebuke of Bevan for proceeding with his Motion, while Wilson naturally voted against the rebuke.

This minor humilliation did not make Bevan less sensitive on the issue of H-bombs and the arms race, although his position was much more complex than many of his followers. In addition to a number of old-style pacifists on the Left of the Labour Party, there was a new breed of nuclear pacifists, initially spearheaded by Tom Driberg and Sir Richard Acland, who later spawned the Campaign for Nuclear Disarmament. In contrast, Dick Crossman, egged on by George Wigg, became the chief protagonist of the theory that nuclear weapons would enable Britain to cut back sharply on the over-heavy burden of conscription and conventional armament. In the arguments which raged over lunch every Tuesday at Crossman's Vincent Square home Bevan refused to distinguish between H-bombs and A-bombs or to make a complete distinction between nuclear bombing and saturation bombing with conventional bombs. Bevan, like Wilson, had been a member of the Attlee Cabinet which had authorized the development of Britain's own A-bomb. He was not a sentimentalist on defence but closer to Crossman as an advocate of *realpolitik*. Although he did not sign the key article in the *New Statesman* of 26 February 1955, it was suggested in Bevanite circles at the time that he dictated the final paragraph of the article signed by Crossman and George Wigg. The article argued that if Britain wanted to remain influential and stay in NATO, it would automatically be an H-bomb target whether or not it had the H-bomb itself. The best role for Britain, the authors insisted, was to have the H-bomb and remain in NATO as a check on the instability of the Americans and the Germans. It recognized Britain's 'painful dilemma. If, in a general war, we have recourse to nuclear weapons, we shall commit national suicide. But if we forswear them, the Red Army, whenever it wanted to, could reach the Atlantic seaboard.' Wilson who never enjoyed theoretical arguments or showed a talent for military theorizing, seldom contributed to this debate.

What disturbed him, however, were the tactics which Bevan used in the debate on defence which lasted for two days on 1 and 2 March 1955. Bevan objected to the Labour amendment which accepted that 'it is necessary, as a deterrent to aggression, to rely on the threat of using thermo-nuclear weapons'. Bevan tried to find out from Sir Winston Churchill – without success – whether Britain would use its A-bombs and H-bombs even if attacked by Soviet tanks. He could not resist posing the same question to his own Front Bench, not once but twice. 'We have either to agree with our enemy or commit suicide,' Bevan warned both Front Benches and then asked Attlee not to 'align the Labour movement behind that [Tory] recklessness' of relying on a nuclear deterrent. He warned that 'if we cannot have the lead from *them*, let us give the lead ourselves'. Twice Attlee refused to distinguish his position from that of the Churchill Government. Therefore, when the vote on Labour's amendment was called at 10 p.m. that Wednesday night, Bevan and sixty-two other Labour MPs abstained from supporting the official Labour amendment. But these did *not* include leading Bevanites like Harold Wilson, Dick Crossman, John Freeman and a few others. There was talk of a 'split within a split'. But Harold Wilson and others were anxious neither to split the party wide open when the Tories were deciding when to call an election nor to offer their heads on a plate to Arthur Deakin and his supporters.[113]

Wilson had been keeping his head down on this divisive and explosive subject, preferring to concentrate on subjects which united the Labour Party. Both in the Commons and in the press that was sympathetic to him he was active in attacking the Conservative government for not doing enough to fight monopolies, which kept prices up. Thus, in the *Sunday Pictorial* of 16 January 1955, he told of a Stockport trader who had been 'hauled before a private tribunal in London, put on trial and given a sentence' for having sold two motor-cycle tyres below their fixed price. He expanded on this story when he opened the Labour attack on the Government's 'slow progress' in breaking monopolies which fixed prices. When Tory MP Reader Harris interrupted him to defend price-fixers in the tyre trade, Wilson referred to him as 'the Torquemada of the tyre trade' and attacked 'the contemptible position' in which he found himself. He was developing the sharper Commons debating style which increasingly made him a hero to Labour back-benchers. The fact that the debate was wound up on the Labour side by Hugh Gaitskell illustrated the closer collaboration between the two men.[114]

Wilson was also active in strengthening his trade-union and regional links. He had been very active the previous year in fighting the 'black pact' which allowed textile imports from Japan, and it was natural that he should serve on the delegation from the Lancashire and Cheshire group of Labour MPs to the Legislation Committee of the United Textile Workers Union which met in Manchester at the end of February 1955. There, as a former President of the Board of Trade, he put forward a plan for enabling the cotton industry to overcome its difficulties. It called for all cotton yarn and cloth imports to be purchased in bulk by a Government-created Cotton Goods Import Commission which would be instructed to discriminate between those goods that were fairly competitive and those based on unfair com-petition, particularly on dumping or subsidies.

## TRYING TO SAVE BEVAN

Wilson still had to stand up and be counted among MPs trying to prevent Bevan being expelled by those who insisted that his H-bomb rebellion had 'humiliated' Attlee. The prime mover in the effort to expel Bevan was Arthur Deakin, who operated chiefly through George Brown, who in turn was sponsored by his own union. 'We must clear up once and for all this question of leadership of the party,' said Brown at Belper; 'we have seen the policy and Mr Attlee's leadership of it publicly repudiated in the most humiliating and damaging way by a man who seems determined never to accept a majority decision unless he makes it himself.'[115] More important, Deakin operated in support of Hugh Gaitskell, whom he had backed for the post of Treasurer and whom he and other trade-union right-wingers were offering more money in exchange for more votes at Labour Party conferences. Deakin was not 'corrupting' Gaitskell, who was quite fanatical on the subject. 'Bevanism is and only is a conspiracy to seize the leadership for Aneurin Bevan,' he told Dick Crossman at a secret meeting. 'It is a conspiracy because it has three essentials of conspiracy: a leader in Bevan, an organization run by Mikardo, and a newspaper run by Foot . . . It's got to be cleaned up. There are extraordinary parallels between Nye and Adolf Hitler. They are demagogues of exactly the same sort.'[116]

On 7 March 1955 the Shadow Cabinet met to consider Bevan's expulsion. 'I'm against expulsion,' said Attlee, opening the discussion with that muttered sentence. Morrison, Edith Summerskill, Hugh Dalton and Alfred Robens all supported the move, as did Gaitskell, who said he had been persuaded by Morrison. Callaghan urged something less than the withdrawal of the Whip. When it came to the point four voted against expulsion – Wilson, Jim Griffiths and two others – and nine in favour – Herbert Morrison, William Whiteley, Edith Summerskill, Sir Frank Soskice and five others. At the end Attlee muttered: 'I'm against drastic action.'[117]

Wilson supported the effort of Dick Crossman and others to take the steam out of the situation by getting Bevan to issue a statement from his sickbed: 'What I have said or done is not a challenge to the personal authority of Mr Attlee as Leader of the party.'[118] Since Gaitskell and others in the majority on the Shadow Cabinet made it a matter of principle to press on with the move, Attlee had no choice but to follow suit, although he snapped at Gaitskell on one occasion: 'You wanted to expel him, I didn't. I was against it from the first, but you insisted, and now look at the mess we're in.'[119] Bevan himself did not make it easier for Attlee to mediate when the Parliamentary Labour Party met on 16 March 1955 to consider his expulsion. Bevan pointed out that, unlike Brown, who had tried to have Attlee replaced in 1947, he had never plotted against Labour's Leader. He charged that Gaitskell had lied in saying he had attacked Labour's lead on the H-bomb, insisting that what he had been attacking was Churchill's position. He insisted that his whole loyalty was to the Labour movement. The motion to withdraw the Whip from Bevan was carried by 141 to 112, with Wilson voting in the minority. It was not a very convincing majority.

All over the country attempts were made to start a 'backfire' to prevent Bevan's expulsion. On 19 March a meeting of the Northwest region of the Labour Party was scheduled. Will Griffiths, MP, telephoned Stan Orme, not then an MP but a delegate to the meeting, to urge him to move an emergency resolution. If it were refused by the chairman, a Deakin appointee, they should attempt to remove him. Orme got together a group of left-wingers. Harold Wilson, one of the two MPs on the Executive of the region, approached Orme and said that if the chairman were removed he would be willing to take his place. Orme tried to move the pro-Bevan emergency resolution. It was refused. An attempt made to remove the chairman was narrowly defeated, with Wilson voting in favour. Afterwards the pro-Bevan left-wingers had a talk with Wilson about Nye's chances.

The decision now moved to the National Executive, of which Wilson was also a member. Arthur Deakin, knowing Attlee was averse to a final decision, warned him in public to 'give a very, very clear lead' and to put 'into reserve ... people who won't play ... in the team'.[120] Wilson sharply opposed this in a statement to constituency officers which he released: 'Speaking for myself, I would say, surely enough harm has been done to the party in the past few weeks without wantonly indulging in action which would have disastrous consequences for the party throughout the country ... Over the past year, too often policies have been forced through by the narrowest of majorities and the resultant decisions made binding on reluctant and large minorities.'[121] 'In this crisis in the party we need loyalty, yes, but we need more than that. We need a spirit of true comradeship, based on a real desire to see one another's point of view and to achieve the widest possible area of agreement.'[122] On the eve of the National Executive meeting there were tortured discussions among Bevanites about their tactics. The question was raised as to whether they should threaten to resign collectively from the NEC if Bevan were expelled, although it was known that this would delight Arthur Deakin. Barbara Castle was on the point of threatening resignation publicly but was dissuaded. Press cynics did not expect Harold Wilson to indulge in suicidal gestures. 'Supposing Mr Bevan does go,' speculated 'Cross-Bencher' in the *Sunday Express*, '...you can be perfectly certain that brisk little Mr Harold Wilson will simply inquire what comes next on the agenda.'[123]

There were divisions among Bevan's opponents as well. Arthur Deakin's lieutenant and successor, 'Jock' Tiffin, was not anxious to expel Bevan, and Deakin had to threaten to withdraw his support from him in the impending election for his successor. Deakin also threatened Hugh Gaitskell that if Labour did not expel Bevan his union and others would reconsider their promise to increase contributions. On the eve of the National Executive meeting Bevan met Attlee to inform him that he had been told that if he were expelled by the NEC for something he had done as an MP, this might be construed as a breach of Parliamentary privilege, since an outside body was trying to coerce him.

Attlee proposed to the NEC that Bevan be asked for a statement and then be interviewed on it by a sub-committee. After this was accepted by fourteen votes to thirteen, with Wilson voting in the majority, Bevan prepared a statement which he had Attlee vet. Then, with a general election in the offing as a result of Sir Winston's resignation, the sub-committee accepted Bevan's statement, being helped by the fact that the preponderantly anti-Bevan press was shut by a strike for three weeks. When the NEC were considering the sub-committee's report on Bevan's expulsion, Wilson tried to modify a motion condemning Bevan and warning him that the NEC would 'take drastic action against future violations of party discipline'. Though Wilson failed to moderate it, by twenty votes against six, Bevan was still in the party, thanks mainly to the outpouring of support from constituency activists who had deluged Attlee and others with letters and resolutions. On the day the Bevan expulsion was avoided, 30 March 1955, Attlee had a cordial meeting with Bevan and Crossman in which he said that he would have to include Hugh Gaitskell in any future Cabinet, but he would try to avoid having him as his successor.

Although Crossman was in closer contact with Bevan at this time than Wilson was, this did not stop him from being critical both in public and in private. The fact that the other Bevanites had helped prevent Bevan's expulsion did not mean that they approved of the bouts of oratorical self-indulgence which made Bevan and themselves vulnerable. Both because he was a topical journalist and because he had a compulsion to write the truth as he saw it, Crossman had to take a lot of stick from Bevan when he criticized him publicly. Thus, in his *Sunday Pictorial* column of 6 March 1955, Crossman wrote: 'Once again, at a critical moment, Aneurin Bevan has shown himself the finest orator in the Labour Party – and his own worst enemy.' The speech for which he had nearly been expelled was 'one of the best of his career', partly because it 'forced the Prime Minister to his feet to reveal that President Eisenhower had in fact vetoed high-level talks' with the Russians. But Crossman could not see why Bevan had to threaten to abstain unless Attlee cleared up the Labour ambiguity. By abstaining Bevan had lumped himself with pacifists or nuclear pacifists, which Bevan was not. 'I say to him,' wrote Crossman: ' "Don't be provoked, Nye! Remember your enemies are praying for a chance to get you on a charge of indiscipline. Don't let them! The Labour Party cannot afford to lose you – and you can afford to lose the Labour Party even less." '

Bevan was furious. 'In moments of crisis when the knives are out, equivocation is tantamount to treachery,' he told Crossman. After thinking it out Crossman wrote a fascinating letter to Nye, explaining their differences: 'As you have often remarked, I am an intellectual, which means that, though I have warm personal feelings, my loyalty is primarily to ideas and to chasing ideas in argument, which is the only way I can think. That is why I was so angry with you when I thought you had been *intellectually* equivocal with regard to the H-bomb. You, on the other hand, are far less sensitive to intellectual equivocation, but much more sensitive to anything you regard as equivocation in *action*. . . . What I think you sometimes forget is that, on the four critical occasions when we have discussed either strategy or tactics in the last twelve months, I have been in disagreement with you and said so – first when you retired from the Parliamentary Committee, then when you decided to stand for the Treasurership [against Gaitskell], then your *Tribune* speech at Margate' – in which Bevan attacked Gaitskell or, perhaps, Wilson as a 'desiccated calculating machine' – 'and finally this last December muddle. I believe your strategic aim is fantastically over-ambitious; my own is limited to trying to restore a proper balance between Right and Left in the party by strengthening the Left. In so far as my "piddling little aim", as you would no doubt call it, coincides with yours, we work happily together. But when your actions obviously militate against what I am trying to do, we disagree, and it's silly for either to charge the other with treachery and disloyalty.'[124]

Because of his affection for Nye, Crossman left out the additional factor: Bevan's ability to get intoxicated with his own oratory and lash out much more harshly than perhaps he had intended. Wilson, of course, was not nearly as much a man of ideas as Crossman, and not irritated to that extent with Bevan's inconsistencies. What infuriated him even more than Crossman was the poverty of Bevan's tactics which were hidden by the richness of his strategy. Bevan knew that Wilson was critical. He himself often referred privately to Wilson as 'all head and no heart'.

The May 1955 general election called to endorse the Tories' new Prime Minister, Sir Anthony Eden, simply served to endorse the fact that Labour had been too busy fighting among themselves to battle effectively against the Tories. In the new Parliament the Tory Majority rose to fifty-eight overall from the seventeen they had had after the 1951 general election. For Harold Wilson the main consolation was that his own seat, Huyton, was safer, with a 2,558 majority over a Welsh barrister, Geraint Morgan, largely caused by the addition of 5,000 new working-class voters to the list, mainly on a Liverpool housing estate at Kirkby.

One of the difficulties for Labour was that its team had become too elderly, with seventy-two-year-old Clement Attlee having as his second-in-command sixty-seven-year-old Herbert Morrison. Seven others in the outgoing Shadow Cabinet were also over sixty-five. The mass-circulation, pro-Labour tabloid, the *Daily Mirror*, launched its 'Make Way for Youth' campaign, with which Attlee did not wholly disagree. He hesitated to go because he did not want Morrison, a confirmed and sectarian right-winger, to inherit. He also had some doubts about Hugh Gaitskell.

Despite this Attlee warned the 6 June meeting of the outgoing Shadow Cabinet that it had until October to make dispositions for his departure. When Attlee began to make the same announcement to the 9 June meeting of the Parliamentary Labour Party, Bevan interrupted him unexpectedly to say: 'Clem, I implore you, do not fix a time limit!' He then explained that a time limit would only encourage intrigues within the party. He did not have to add that Attlee, as the central balance-wheel of the party, had saved him from expulsion; nor that the only possible successors to Attlee were Morrison and Gaitskell, since the Parliamentary party was two-thirds right-of-centre. Bevan did add: 'I have no ambition so far as the Leadership or Deputy Leadership of this party is concerned.'

This represented a victory for Crossman, Wilson and others, who had been arguing with Bevan for days not to stand again against Herbert Morrison for the Deputy Leadership. These contests, they had argued, had too much of a factional flavour and only hurt him in the eyes of uncommitted Labour MPs. Bevan had argued for a time that he had to offer himself as a standard-bearer of the Left around whom left-wing MPs could rally, but, typically, he had belatedly accepted the argument against which he had previously fought.

With Bevan a subsiding volcano, Wilson was able to make two important moves forward. On 21 June he was named Chairman of a dreary-sounding committee established by a sub-committee of the National Executive to examine party organization. The total Labour vote had dropped by 1,500,000 from its 1951 high. Why? To what extent was this due to an organization far inferior to that of the Conservatives as established by Lord Woolton in the years after the Tories' 1945 setback? Wilson was put in charge of a committee to investigate Labour organization and to report back.

His more public advance came in the June 1955 elections to the Labour Shadow Cabinet. Instead of coming twelfth, as he had the previous year, he came fifth, with 147 votes as against 120 the previous year. Bevan, who had not stood for the Shadow Cabinet the previous year, now came seventh with 118 votes. Crossman ran twentieth with only sixty-two votes. Henry Fairlie, a very shrewd political correspondent then writing for the *Spectator* had judged Wilson thus: 'He is a man who, because of his personal characteristics, is disliked and therefore underestimated by many political observers. But he has more political shrewdness than most of his Left- and Right-wing colleagues. I have frequently argued ... that the future of the Labour Party lies with the man who can create a genuine Left which is not Bevanite. I have frequently suggested that Mr Wilson is fitted and willing to play this role. I still think that he should be watched' (10 June 1955). After the election of Wilson in fifth place ahead of Bevan at seventh, Fairlie called attention to 'the relative positions of Mr Harold Wilson and Mr Aneurin Bevan', concluding that this 'adds some support to my contention over the past few months that Mr Wilson is slowly but surely reaching the position where he will be able to take over the leadership of the Left-wing of the Labour Party, and as such become a far more serious challenger for the Leadership of the party than Mr Bevan.'[125]

# VI. A Man with Two 'Wives' on a Triangular Landmine

'That Lady Falkender's influence with Harold Wilson was powerful – indeed, all-pervasive – is undeniable, however much it may be denied. No one who worked in his office, in Downing Street or in Opposition, for more than a few minutes could be unaware of it. Every typist and every civil servant knew of it and could testify to it. Many of them went in dread of her; the fact of her power was like a baleful cloud hung permanently over their heads. . .'. Any future historian's appraisal of Harold Wilson's role as Prime Minister and Leader of the Opposition will be incomplete unless he comprehends the full extent of her sway.'

Joe Haines, on Marcia Williams' role as 'office wife'[1]

'I made Harold Wilson and I could break him!'

Baroness Falkender[2]

'I was like a rather unwilling recruit to a group of professional soldiers when I first went to No. 10. Lady Falkender's help and advice were invaluable to me in all the work I tried to do there. Of course there were tears and tensions – particularly at election times.'

Lady Mary Wilson[3]

In the twenty years prior to his resignation as Prime Minister, and while at the peak of his political prowess, Harold Wilson lived atop a 'landmine' of tremendously destructive potential. Its explosive force derived from his triangular relationship with two women, one repelled, the other fascinated by politics. His danger lay in the fact that, had any considerable area of this relationship been exposed to public view earlier, his effort to reach Number 10 would have been blown to bits or his tenure as Prime Minister terminated much earlier. What if Joe Haines had blabbed in 1970 instead of in 1977?

The fact that his wife, Mary, would not even allow his fellow political intimates into their Hampstead Garden Suburb home in the 1950s was a serious disadvantage to Harold Wilson. He covered it publicly by pretending that most of his friends preferred meeting him in the Palace of Westminster. In fact, of course, his closest political intimate, Dr Thomas Balogh, lived ten minutes away down the Finchley Road in Hampstead. Balogh and others did not complain at the time because criticizing the Wilsons would help the Gaitskell or George Brown factions.

Although rumour-mongers got busy in the Palace of Westminster soon after Harold Wilson acquired a pretty if toothy blonde political secretary in October 1956 even these rumours were very slow to reach the outside world. If his friends soon began to complain about the too-strong hold that Marcia had over him they kept their complaints largely within the fold. It only became a political weapon against him when in 1960 he dared to challenge Hugh Gaitskell for the Leadership of the Labour Party. On that occasion some of the less scrupulous people supporting Gaitskell launched a whispering campaign which could only be squashed by a semi-public tea-party in which Harold and Mary were joined by Marcia and her presumed husband. A similar whispering campaign was launched in pubs all over the country in June 1964, presumably in the Conservative interest.

Marcia Williams satisfied for Harold Wilson the need of such a deeply insecure and enormously ambitious man for a woman obsessively devoted to realizing his ambitions. Because his wife, Mary, despised his political ambitions as a rejection of her deep longing for the security of being an Oxbridge don's wife, he accorded Marcia the privileges of being the 'office wife'. Marcia could therefore come late to official functions, could keep him waiting at airports, nag him in front of strangers, use his chauffeur, his doctor, his lawyer, crowd his office with her relatives, and 'borrow' his helicopter.

One of his Cabinet colleagues who worked most closely with Wilson was astonished at the extent to which the forceful and outspoken Marcia arrogated to herself the rights of the nagging 'office wife'. 'You cannot go on TV with your fingernails in that condition!' she said on one occasion. She would write outspokenly critical comments on the side of draft speeches, like 'This is just like you!' On another occasion she shrilled at the Prime Minister: 'You can't just drop people after you've used them!' Although this Cabinet Minister thought Marcia intensely political – even more political than Wilson himself – he thought her brother a political 'illiterate'. He could not understand how Marcia could have persuaded Harold to take on Tony Field as his office manager.

Although Wilson was not at all nepotistic on behalf of his own family, the nepotism exercised on behalf of the Field family seemed endless. In November 1975, when still Prime Minister, Wilson asked civil servants to prepare a letter recommending Tony Field to the Crown Prince of Saudi Arabia, where Field and new business partners were seeking contracts. When it was pointed out that such a letter would mean the British Ambassador travelling hundreds of miles to present it to the effective ruler of the country, Wilson was not deterred.

Since James Callaghan, then Foreign Secretary, was about to go off to Saudi Arabia, Wilson foisted on him the chore of endorsing and encouraging the career of Marcia's brother, which had suffered severe setbacks due to publicity about his 'land reclamation'.

What is most significant about this curious relationship was Wilson's willingness to risk the most precious thing he had – his career – on Marcia's behalf. Incredibly, three of his election campaigns were imperilled by the woman most dedicated to his success. His most successful, that of 1966, was endangered when she stormed off, taking the office keys and bringing the Wilson campaign to a temporary halt. It was on that occasion that Mary Wilson, for the first time in the hearing of others, demanded that he fire Marcia Williams as he had often promised her he would do but never had. If any of this had got out at the time it is doubtful whether he could have achieved the Labour majority of 100 he did chalk up.

Wilson's success in 1966 apparently encouraged him to continue to 'live dangerously' by keeping on Marcia Williams as his political secretary and siding with her in virtually every dispute. Thus, although she was not a civil servant and thus not entitled to see secret and confidential papers, he had pressed his Principal Private Secretary, Derek Mitchell, to allow her to do so. In a letter to the Prime Minister Mitchell wrote: 'You said that you would like Marcia to see in future all the Cabinet and Cabinet Committee papers which you now see ... As a result of this I would like to suggest that Marcia should see Secret and Confidential papers dealing with domestic subjects only ... She would of course see the minutes of meetings at which the papers were discussed and this would extend to Cabinet conclusions.' Wilson frequently denied that Marcia had access: 'She did not see any secret documents, or other classified documents,' he said in an ITN interview on 15 February 1977, only a week before the *Sun* published the above 1965 document, which had been hoarded by George Caunt, a longstanding opponent of Marcia's.[5] Lord Wigg was of the opinion that although Marcia and Harold had fought the civil service for her *right* to see secret papers, once this was conceded she did not actually see them.

During the 1970 and February 1974 general elections the Labour high command had to live in the presence of a landmine which any pro-Conservative newspaper could have exploded by the simple announcement: 'The Prime Minister's confidential and political secretary has had two children, in 1968 and 1969, after her divorce from her husband in 1961.' Such a statement could have resulted in people misattributing the paternity of Marcia's children to Harold Wilson. Again, the last days of the February 1974 campaign and the weeks after it were dominated by accusations about a land reclamation involving Marcia's brother, Tony Field, who had carried on his activities while office manager to Wilson in Marcia's absence at home. Some of his deals had been discussed in Wilson's office, enabling the forger and confidence trickster, Ronald Milhench, to secure his stationery.

Harold Wilson was far from being the first British politician to allow his professional helpmate to exploit such influence. As he knew from the head of his Policy Advisory Office, Dr Bernard Donoughue, co-author of the authoritative life of Herbert Morrison, Morrison's first wife had let hardly any of his political colleagues set foot in their house and rarely attended political functions. Morrison had had as his 'permanent tiger at the gate' of his office Ethel Donald, who was heard occasionally to berate him loudly and sometimes crudely. In fact, Morrison's premarital girl friend, Rose Rosenberg, had played the same role to Ramsay MacDonald.

What has distinguished Marcia Williams from her predecessors as political secretaries to political leaders is that she had emerged from the grey anonymity which normally obscures such 'office wives'. Her immensely hard work and super-loyal defence of his political career have been obscured by the harsh light of often-hostile publicity. In curious contrast the hostility of Gladys Mary Wilson to her husband's political career has been either ignored or else she has been depicted in soft tones as the 'good little woman' in Harold's background, keeping the home fires burning.

Caught in the crossfire between the two of them, Harold Wilson has been true and loyal to both. When close political colleagues, knowing her distaste for politics, have asked whether Mary Wilson disliked the life, he would insist she had been delighted. R. H. S. Crossman provides a brilliant example of this typical Wilson reaction when in March 1966 he asked about an unruly meeting in Birmingham, when something had been thrown at Mrs Wilson which scratched her neck. 'I said that Mary must hate it. "Oh no," he said. "She liked the meeting last night a great deal." As I was going downstairs I ran into Mary and said, "I hear you really enjoyed last night after all?" "Enjoyed it!" she said, with agony on her face. "Who told you that? That man?" Her relationship with Harold is fascinating,' went on thrice-married Crossman. 'I am sure they are deeply together but they are now pretty separate in their togetherness. It is one of those marriages which holds despite itself because each side has evolved a self-containedness within the marriage.'[6]

## SUBURBAN PAIR ON A TENNIS COURT

Harold and Gladys Mary Baldwin met first on a tennis court on 4 July 1934, in the Wirral. He had nearly finished his final school exams and was restless after having crammed Christopher Marlowe's *Dr Faustus*. A stroll took him past a tennis court, where he envied the carefree young people of his own age, who did not feel compelled to swot for exams. An exceptionally pretty and graceful young girl of his own age caught his eye. By the end of the week he had joined the club and introduced himself to Mary, who recognized the rather untidy young eighteen-year-old who had been staring at her some days before. Within three weeks he decided he wanted to marry her.

Harold was neither a 'womanizer' nor a 'fast worker' where girls were concerned. Admittedly he had played Henry VIII in a play put on at Royds Hall, his Huddersfield school, but this was hardly his role as a schoolboy, as contemporaries confirm. Harold Ainley said that 'Willy was willing to carry notes for others but did not chase girls himself before he left Royds Hall at fifteen. He was privately sweet on one girl – to whom he confessed it only after becoming Prime Minister, but he was so shy that the closest he dared approach her was to walk home her best friend.'

Gladys Mary Baldwin, then a shorthand typist at the Port Sunlight offices of Lever Brothers, was shy and lonely in her own way. She was the daughter of very puritanical and religious parents. Her mother had run a loom in Lancashire. Her father had also started that way. 'At twelve he was working half-time in the mill – Dugdale's mill, Padiham, near Burnley – and studying in his spare time. He always wanted to be a Congregational Minister. Doing it that way, he didn't become a minister until he was twenty-nine. His health was never very good, and it was because of the way he'd starved himself as a student while he was in lodgings training to be a minister. He used to live on stewed apple, or rhubarb – anything to keep going. My mother worked at the mill until he got his first post, and she left to marry him and go to his first ministry. He was a great reader. He was always quoting poets as well as the Bible in the pulpit. Especially Wordsworth', Mary Wilson remembered.

She had been a lonely child because, since her parents moved around every three years, they had packed her off to a very strict school for the daughters of ministers: Milton Mount College, near Crawley in Sussex. 'It used to be a country house, and the owners had to sell it,' she recalled, 'and it became a boarding school. You were allowed to read novels three afternoons a week. You drew them from the library, and then you returned them at the end of the afternoon. Apart from that, if you were a compulsive reader, which I was, you had to read and read your set books. Palgrave's *Golden Treasury* was the only one I could go on reading.' She resented this curb on her romanticism. 'I was a rebel at school . . . I founded a club called "The Rebels".'[7] But she kept her rebellions largely bottled up. She agreed to take a short-hand and typing course and was on her first job at Port Sunlight at eighteen when she met her future husband. Supporting herself at eighteen she felt much more mature than the schoolboy Harold, who was expecting to go to Oxford.

They had things in common apart from their age. Both their families were Liberals and Congregationalists. They could attend services in the same church in the Wirral, and he could walk her home to her digs. This worried her landlady somewhat and she wrote to Gladys Mary's father, who was preaching in Penrith. Gladys Mary was flattered by Harold's attentions but did not take them too seriously at first. She found him considerate and placid. When she met his parents, she understood more. The Wilsons were much more self-contained and undemonstrative than her own parents, although they came from a similar background in Lancashire.

Although they had already agreed they were 'going steady' there were long separations once he started at Oxford a few months later in October 1934. His parents promised to visit him once a term, bringing Mary with them, and she promised to write to him twice a week. Writing was no difficulty for her. When she had been ill at school she had acquired the habit of reading and writing poetry. 'I have been writing since I was a little girl,' she later confessed. 'It helps me relax.' Since she suffered from asthma, relaxation was important.[8]

They behaved like affectionate young friends rather than lovers. They went to the theatre in London together occasionally, several times to Noel Coward's *Bitter Sweet*, from which she particularly liked 'I'll See You Again'. Harold's friends at University had their doubts about Gladys Mary when she came down with his parents on their once-a-term visit and then, finally, for the ceremony in which he got his First-Class Honours in the summer of 1937. Although he had been turned down for his first two applications as Lecturer at St Andrew's and Christ Church, he had won the Webb-Medley Senior Research Scholarship, then worth £300 a year. He looked set for a don's career. Some of his friends thought she might hold him back because she had so few of the middle-class talents needed to advance an ambitious young man. She tended to agree. When she attended her first sherry parties at the university, she found herself doubly tongue-tied. Partly it was her religious background, in which temperance was so important. Partly it was, as she later explained it, because 'I am an introvert. . . . I admit that with the best will in the world I don't find it easy to talk to strangers.'[9]

However, the prospect of a quiet, secure life in Oxford pleased her. 'I thought he was going to be a University teacher. He used to talk sometimes about going into politics, later on, when he was about thirty, but I didn't take much notice – thirty seemed ages away, anyway. . . . I had been brought up near Cambridge and I knew Cambridge well – my brother was at Cambridge . . . and when Harold told me he wanted to teach at Oxford I thought it was wonderful. My idea of heaven. I can tell you, there's nothing I would have liked so much as being a don's wife . . . very old buildings and very young people. There is everything anyone could want, music, theatre, congenial friends, all in a beautiful setting, and within a fourpenny bus ride. It symbolized so much for me.'[10]

This symbolism was carried forward into their wedding on Monday, 1 January 1940, the first day of the week, the month, the year and the decade. Curiously, everyone was expected to dress in academic gowns, which was a lot cheaper, although inappropriate, say, for Harold's father. The organist played the academic march 'Gaudeamus Igitur' instead of 'Here Comes the Bride'. The ceremony was held at the Nonconformists' Mansfield College, with its Principal, Dr Nathaniel Micklem, conducting the ceremony with the assistance of the bride's father, Reverend Daniel Baldwin. Mary herself refused to say 'I obey'. With Harold's agreement they substituted 'love, honour and cherish' because she felt this was 'more affectionate' and because she wanted 'all women to be treated as equals'. After the ceremony they had a stand-up buffet and fruit cup, but not only no champagne but no confetti either. There were about fifty guests, mainly young dons from the University, but not Sir William Beveridge, Harold's boss at University College, although he sent them two red Venetian glass bowls. Both Harold and Mary were hoping for a substantial gift from Harold's wealthy Uncle Harry. 'We were hoping for money,' Mary Wilson later recalled. 'We hadn't a home so money was most useful. The present turned out to be two still-life paintings, neither of which I would ever have chosen.' The weather was also anticlimactic. While the reception was at its height the driver of the hired car which was to drive them to Minster Lovell arrived with an ultimatum. 'Unless we started to leave that minute,' Mrs Wilson recalled, 'he said he wouldn't be able to take us. Apart from snow, it was getting foggier and he wanted to get back to Oxford that night.' So they had to leave the reception to get changed. 'I was rather shattered when I looked at the car as they drove off,' recalled Freda Baldwin, later Mary's sister-in-law. 'All I could see was the back of the car stacked with books.'

However odd his friends found Harold's behaviour, they thought the couple were both lucky and brave to get married. They had, in fact, been planning to marry when the war upset their plans. Mary had given up her job at Port Sunlight to spend some time with her mother learning house-running skills. They had planned to marry in the spring of 1940, but instead of staying with her parents she decided to go to Oxford to be close to Harold who might, after all, be called up and shipped overseas.

So she took a room over a café in the old part of Oxford and a job with the Potato Marketing Board.

The disadvantages of university life were made evident even before the honeymoon in the Cotswolds was over, when a telegram from Sir William Beveridge, Master of University College and Harold's boss, arrived to insist that he return to his statistics. So the honeymoon ended after a week, and Mary's life as a don's wife in Oxford lasted only a few weeks more. After he secured a job with the Ministry of Supply in London they had rooms first in Earl's Court, then Pimlico, then a rented flat in Twickenham. When the bomber raids came Mary went to Cornwall to stay with his parents. She then secured a room in the house of a chemistry don at Jesus College, Oxford. Since Harold's new department, the Cabinet Secretariat, had an Oxford hideout ready, he was allowed to work there for long weekends. However, Mary decided to rejoin him in London and they took a rented flat in Richmond.

Although she was in London with Harold he worked such long hours that she was alone very much of the time, despite her work as an air-raid warden in Richmond. She found it particularly nerve-wracking to be on her own after the arrival of their first child, Robin, born in December 1943. She tried to occupy her mind with reading or puzzles, but the threat of bombs, particularly the buzz-bombs, was unnerving. She felt she had to be on the alert to climb protectively over her child's cot. On alternate nights he had to sleep in the Ministry.

Finally she evacuated to Duxford, in Cambridgeshire, where her family had now settled. Harold visited them as often as the three-hour journey by slow train would allow. His working in London, with her in isolation in the country, was the reverse of what she had hoped for. 'I have always claimed that he married me under false pretences,' she later half-joked.[11]

She was somewhat dismayed when she learned in the winter of 1943–4 that he was thinking of a political career at the war's end instead of returning to Oxford. Naturally she was not as bitter as he when he tripped up and allowed his constituency to adopt him formally in October 1944, forcing him to resign from the civil service. It ended up with his securing a job of sorts, as Domestic Bursar, at University College. Now she was back at her beloved Oxford, on Staircase Eleven, Back Quad, University College. She took little Robin to play in the Fellows' Garden. She had to hang up her washing out of sight 'at the back'.

At first she did not worry too much about his adoption for Ormskirk for the looming general election. She had been reassured that it was likely to be won by the Conservatives. She went along to one or two meetings, to find that she did not like the rough-and-tumble of politics.

'At the beginning I was terribly upset by it,' she later recalled. 'In 1945, when I went to my very first meeting, it was quiet and orderly and I said to Harold, wasn't it nice and quiet. He didn't think it was nice. It was too quiet and dull. The next meeting was terrible, I thought. A lot of shouting and anger and at the end of it I found I was actually trembling. But he was delighted. That was a lesson to me. I stopped minding. Why should I mind if he didn't?'[12] At the end of the campaign there was a three-week delay so that the Services' vote could be counted with the others. When it came to the count she did not accompany Harold to Ormskirk. His father went instead. When the count put him in with a majority of 7,000 votes it delighted him and dismayed her.

## VOTING WITH HER BACKSIDE

Mary Wilson demonstrated her dismay by remaining in Oxford for two and a half years longer than she need have. Since his appointment at University College lasted until December 1945 – because of the shortage of economists – they were entitled to quarters there. Their rented flat in Richmond was being occupied by his parents; his father had a post in the Ministry of Supply at the time.

Had she put top priority on being with her husband presumably she and Robin had first call on the Richmond flat, but they decided, because Mary preferred Oxford so, that he would become a 'weekend husband'. He would do his work as an MP and Minister during the week in London, living there with his parents in the Richmond flat. At the weekends he would be in Oxford, teaching on Saturday and Sunday and spending the rest of his time with his family. Even this plan was undercut very soon after his election, when the Prime Minister called him on his first weekend back in Oxford after the swearing-in to offer him his first job as junior Minister at Works.

Quite understandably Mary treated every advance for her bright and ambitious husband as a setback for herself. She had looked forward to a quiet life in Oxford with her husband and child. Instead she was left alone with her child, seeing her husband on an occasional weekend. So she could not really share with him his hopes of promotion. She made it clear that she regretted his becoming a Minister because it absorbed so much of his time. Even when he could join his family he brought too much work home and had too little time for his family.

Harold Wilson was anxious to be reunited with his family – in the London area. In 1946 he met Ernest Kay and his wife, Marjorie, who lived in Hampstead Garden Suburb. Mrs Kay later recalled the dinner: 'He was helpful, easy to talk to and interested to know about my family and myself. But, equally keen, too, to talk about his wife Mary and his son, Robin, and concerned about finding a home for his family so that he could have them as soon as possible with him in London, instead of miles away in Oxford.'[13]

At the end of that year this separation was stretched further. In October 1946 the Prime Minister sent the young Minister to Washington to lead the British negotiation on the Food and Agriculture Organization. On his first absence he was away almost three months until Christmas. During that absence, she later told close friends, she met another man. In her *Selected Poems* published twenty-four years later, she wrote:

'How like a man to choose a crowded train
To say that we must never meet again!
Or was it masculine cunning
So that I could not make a scene? ...

'We had to shout to make our voices heard
But still I understood each telling word –
"We can't go on like this,
I thought you understood;
You must see it's no good."

'... And still you stood there, silent and unbending.
God! What an ending!'[14]

'"Mary," you said, and "Mary!" once again;
You grasped my cold, cold hands within your own
Too tightly, but I did not feel the pain,
I could not think or speak – my heart was stone.'[15]

'I think the charm of poetry,' Mrs Wilson later wrote, 'lies in the fact that it can capture an emotion, or describe a scene or happening without any preliminaries or stage-setting.'[16] With some irony she dedicated her volume of poems to her husband. But she did not describe her feelings when he returned that Christmas 1946 and she told him her news. She told intimates that she was furious that *he* was *not* furious. She said he simply made it clear that he would fight to keep her, and that he wanted appearances maintained. She was livid that his placid temperament could be unruffled in such a circumstance, and that he could think of his political career first, and the fact that the Attlees, particularly Mrs Attlee, saw the Wilsons as the ideal young political couple.

What Harold did do was to take Mary back to Washington with him. Little Robin, then three, was left behind in the care of his paternal grandparents in Richmond. Harold and Mary had three or four weeks together in Washington, returning on the *Queen Elizabeth* at the end of January 1947 to a Britain in the gloom of the great 'freeze'. Giles, born in 1948, was the product of the warm reconciliation which followed their Washington trip.

'I've never worried much about so-called sin in personal relationships,' Mary Wilson said later. 'What I mean is that I don't care for religious attitudes and ideas of morality which seem to depend on intolerance of one kind or another. Especially intolerance of personal weaknesses, in matters of sex, for instance. I'm much more intolerant about people ill-treating each other.'[17]

Mary intensified her public complaints about not seeing enough of her husband, using the opportunities of his promotions. When he was put in charge of a Cabinet Committee to guide the new export drive when still a thirty-one-year-old Secretary for Overseas Trade, she complained to the *Daily Mirror* reporter asking her reaction: 'That means I shall see less of him than ever. He works a sixteen-hour day already. I saw him for two weekends only during the summer.'[18] When, two weeks later, he was promoted to the Cabinet as President of the Board of Trade, he made it clear to reporters that one of his priorities was to find somewhere for his family to live together in London. She echoed his call: 'We are looking for somewhere to live in London. At present I live in a flat at Oxford with Robin, and Harold stays with his parents during the week to be near his office. He is supposed to visit us at weekends, but out of the last fifteen, he's had two free ones.'[19]

This led them to buy their first house, at over the odds, in Hampstead Garden Suburb. He bought for £5,100 a three-bedroom leasehold house from Sir Gurney Braithwaite, a Conservative MP. Although he had just been promoted to President of the Board of Trade at £5,000 a year he did not have enough money for the deposit. His father loaned him the needed £800.[20]

From his point of view, preserving the marriage rather than playing the heavy husband was well justified. Clement Attlee and his wife Violet liked Mary Wilson very much. Attlee described her as 'the best wife in the party'.[21] The Prime Minister found her an entertaining companion at luncheon at Number 10. 'When I came here to lunch with Clem Attlee and Vi back in the 'forties,' she said after she moved into the Prime Minister's residence, 'I told him that I liked all the wrong people in history. I find characters like Oliver Cromwell and John Knox far too austere. Gladstone I can't *stand*. Harold admires Gladstone, but I find his character unattractive. I told Clem I liked people like Bonnie Prince Charlie and Charles II, Mary Queen of Scots and Disraeli. I like the ones who are a bit – flamboyant, raffish, if you like ... He said, "Oliver Cromwell had his points." '[22] Her uninhibited romanticism made her the firm friend of the Attlees, particularly the Prime Minister's conservative-minded wife. After their second child, Giles Daniel John, was born on 6 May 1948, he was christened in the Crypt of the House of Commons on 23 September 1948, with Mrs Attlee present.

Mary Wilson was able to enjoy herself with the Attlees because she liked being with them. Marjorie Kay, by now a close friend in Hampstead Garden Suburb, described her then as 'small and slim. Her blue eyes, fair hair and fine skin made a first impression of extreme femininity. . . . As we talked and exchanged ideas, I discovered that Mary had a quick sense of humour, mischievous yet compassionate, a complete lack of all pretension and a set of values which were able to resist any kind of seduction from the path which she felt . . . was the only one to follow. It was quite surprising to find so much strength of will existing beneath an outward appearance of feminine charm . . . A high regard for politeness made her a good listener to well-meant advice, but she was equally polite in disregarding it.'[23]

Of course, both Harold and Mary did have a good bit of the 'aren't-we-lucky-to-be-among-the-high-and-mighty' attitude one might expect from someone from their modest background. Harold would tend to tell his newspaperman neighbour, Ernest Kay, then a correspondent for the *Express and Star* in Wolverhampton: 'Do you know what the King told me yesterday?' Mary was less preening. 'You know,' she would tell Marjorie Kay, 'the Queen always asks about Robin and Giles and she never forgets their birthdays.'[24]

Harold and Mary could never agree on priorities. He put his career as the main one, deploring as he did the limitations on his home life. She, having been deprived of home life as a child, put top priority on home life. ' "Home" was a word which meant more to her than it does to most women,' confirmed Marjorie Kay, 'probably because she had moved all over England too often as the daughter of a Congregational minister. . . . She hated always to leave her small boys – hate is not really the proper word, detested is more like it – as much as she detested her husband's absences.'[25]

Mary never stopped trying to get him to give up politics for the academic serenity she craved. 'When he comes home after a bad day, I say why don't you go back to Oxford,' she confided. 'I lie awake worrying, but he can go straight to sleep.' He sometimes retaliated by excluding her from the work he thought important. 'When he was President of the Board of Trade,' Mary recalled, 'and I asked him what they were going to tax, he just replied, ". . . inquisitive women for a start!" '[26]

Mary Wilson was not always reassured on those few occasions on which she did accompany her husband – as to the opening of the West Cumberland exhibition in August 1948, an area which she knew from her father preaching there. When Harold and Mary and thirteen other people stepped on a platform made of scaffolding it sank about three feet to the floor without any warning.

Occasionally their excursions were more pleasant. In April 1949 Mary was able to motor with him to Annecy, a charming little lakeside town in the Savoy area of France. This was Harold's first real holiday in the almost two years he had been President of the Board of Trade. But even this had elements of a busman's holiday about it. As we have seen, there was a trade conference going on in Annecy, some of whose sessions he attended as an observer. Nevertheless she was able to stroll through Annecy's cool white arcades which made it a favourite of holidaying French families.

These tensions were unknown to Harold Wilson's political colleagues because he kept quiet about them in Westminster and because his colleagues did not set foot in his home: not even Patrick Gordon Walker, the former don and Labour candidate in Oxford, whose family were close neighbours of the Wilsons in Hampstead Garden Suburb. In sixteen years the Gordon Walkers only set foot in the Wilson house once. This was partly because Mary, a shy and private person, was not easy to befriend. 'It was not easy to get to know her,' confirmed Marjorie Kay, 'but once friendship was established, I found that the really close ones she makes stay with her for always.'[27]

These tensions within the Wilson family were not disclosed even to fairly close friends like the Kays, who were their neighbours in the Suburb and fairly close friends in the 1950–55 period. To outsiders they preserved the façade of the happy young couple. This was aided by Harold's always referring to Mary as 'Pie' – short for 'Sweety Pie'.

Harold and Mary temporarily moved closer together when he faced his first big crisis over whether to resign with Aneurin Bevan. Mary first realized that he was troubled because, for the first time in their married life, he had difficulty sleeping soundly. When he explained in outline what was troubling him she was very sympathetic. She had been more fundamentalist, more pacifist and more Leftist than he and sympathetic to Bevan. If Harold felt so strongly that he would consider giving up the position as President of the Board of Trade he so prized, she knew he was responding to deeply-held feelings.

Mary Wilson knew that there would be a heavy cost to pay for Harold's adherence to principle. He would drop from the £5,000 then earned by a President of the Board of Trade to the £1,000 earned by back-bench MPs. They still had some £4,000 to pay on their mortgage. In addition she and her brother, a lecturer, were helping to support their widowed mother. Harold's parents, too, were nearing retirement age.

For Mary, however, there was a different consideration as well. As a back-bencher Harold might not have to suffer the tremendous Ministerial demands on his time, the constant flow of red boxes that kept even his weekends occupied. He might become more of a husband

and father. So she backed him wholeheartedly in his plan to resign. She went with him to the House of Commons to hear him make his speech justifying his resignation on Tuesday 24 April 1951. She was both proud and sad about his able speech, which was fairly well received in the Commons, but she was disturbed by some of the angry glances as they walked out together. She then left him behind in the Commons to go back to the Suburb to cook tea for the boys. After she put Robin and Giles to bed she later went to bed herself, but found it difficult to sleep. It was easier after Harold came back about 3 a.m. and gave her Winston Churchill's message that she should not worry too much so long as Harold was doing the right thing as he saw it.

In all ways but one, Harold's resignation with Bevan turned out to be a disappointment for Mary. The sudden drop in their family income was not as bad as expected. Of the many offers which came in for Harold's services he felt able to accept £1,500 a year as a consultant to Montague Meyer, the Labour-supporting timber merchant, whose firm also provided a car, a secretary, Mrs Elise Cannon, and an office for Harold.

She was horrified by the level of political vituperation which came flooding in. She had never been able to enjoy political heckling at political meetings. Nor had she thought 'fair' the attacks on Harold and his colleagues by Conservative newspapers, out to make party points. Now all that was put in the shade by the concentrated attack on the 'Bevanites' as they were tagged. They were all lumped together, even by previously friendly newspapers like the *Daily Herald*, the *Daily Mirror*, the *News-Chronicle* and the *Guardian*, as though the resignations proved them ambitious, scheming friends of the Communist Powers and opponents of the United States. Former colleagues were among the worst. Hugh Dalton's oft-quoted reference to Harold as 'Nye's little dog' was one that hurt Harold and Mary particularly, since he had often seemed friendly and sympathetic. Sir Hartley (later Lord) Shawcross, Harold's successor at the Board of Trade, dismissed Harold as one of those 'highbrows educated beyond their capacity'. Such attacks made Mary turn her back even more squarely on politics and politicians.

Any hope that she had that she would see more of her husband disappeared as he became a left-wing 'groupie' and politician instead of a slightly right-of-centre Minister. Within two days of his resignation speech Harold Wilson, together with Aneurin Bevan, John Freeman and Nye's wife, Jennie Lee, were attending, on 26 April 1951, the first meeting of the expanded 'Keep Left' Group.

Because of her aversion for the rough-and-tumble of political life Mary Wilson missed most of the excitement of 1951–55, the most tempestuous period in recent Labour history. The only time that she allowed herself to be drawn into her husband's political life was in his efforts to rebut the allegations of his Tory opponent in October 1951 that he was an extreme left-winger. Mary's endorsement that he was a good family man and her presence with him on platforms in the Huyton area were thought to be reassuring. So she obediently went along.

Mary Wilson was missing not only from the stormy annual party conferences at various seaside resorts but also from the exciting Bevanite meetings in the London area. She was absent too from the social life which accompanied the faction-ridden political life of the time. Since the Bevanites considered themselves to be a band of endangered brothers who had to concert their strategy they carried their planning over into their evenings and weekends as well as their luncheons. Meetings were most often held at Crossman's Vincent Square home and on at least one occasion at the Highgate flat of Barbara Castle and her husband, Ted – but never in Hampstead Garden Suburb at the Wilsons. She seemed curiously reluctant to meet Aneurin Bevan socially, and she and Harold never turned up for the annual Christmas drinks at Ann and Stephen Swingler's, fifteen minutes from the Wilson home, in Belsize Park. 'I would not have known what she looked like,' recalled Ann Swingler. 'And when the call came in 1964 for Stephen to go to the Wilson home to take a job in his Government, he had difficulty finding it because he had never been there before.' The Swinglers were the most social of the left-wing Labour MPs and virtually all the Bevanite MPs and their wives and children – and their press sympathizers – turned up at these Christmas affairs. At the time the failure of the Wilsons to turn up tended to be blamed on Harold, who was considered rather cold and calculating, in contrast to the warmth of Nye Bevan.

For Harold Wilson himself it meant a split existence. On the one hand he had the stimulation and excitement of his political life but little emotional support in it, partly because he lacked the assured warmth that evoked genuine camaraderie. On the other hand he had the quiet middle-class suburban life of the Wilson home, where he could play the father and husband but where his main preoccupation and occupation, politics, was frowned on.

Imperceptibly everything changed in June 1955 in the wake of Eden's success in the May 1955 general election. On top of his Parliamentary post as Trade spokesman Wilson received a key party assignment on the National Executive. He was put in charge of an NEC committee to investigate the efficiency of the Labour Party machine which had just performed so inadequately against the better-organized and better-financed Tories. Serving with him on the committee were three right-wingers: union leader Jack Cooper, Arthur Skeffington MP, Herbert

Morrison's ally in the Cooperative movement, and Peggy Herbison MP, representing the women's section of the NEC.

What came to be tagged Wilson's 'penny-farthing bicycle' investigation inevitably reflected on the management of Transport House by Morgan Phillips, the Welsh ex-miner who was Labour's General Secretary. Policies in the May 1955 general election had been left in his hands and those of Jim Griffiths, who happened to be chairman of the Policy Sub-committee of the NEC; there was no consultation whatsoever with Attlee or Morrison or the party Chairman, Edith Summerskill. Wilson felt not only that Transport House had been inefficient but that Morgan Phillips had been unnecessarily hostile to those Labour candidates who did not support the Attlee–Morrison–Gaitskell line.

## ENTER MARCIA WILLIAMS

Unexpectedly Wilson began to receive anonymous letters from within Morgan Phillips's inner office which confirmed how badly the election campaign had been conducted. These, she later confessed to Wilson, had come from Marcia Williams, a tall and toothy blonde graduate who had joined Phillips's staff just before the election. Then aged twenty-three, she had been born the daughter of a local builder in the Northamptonshire village of Long Buckby. Starting in a village school this very intelligent young lady had progressed to the Northampton High School for Girls. After winning an Honours degree in History at Queen Mary College, London University, and attending a secretarial school she had applied for a job as Morgan Phillips's secretary. Her socialist enthusiasm initially made up for the poor pay at Transport House.

Wilson benefited from the public speculation over the findings of his committee. On the eve of the Margate conference, where he was standing for re-election, the NEC decided that the Wilson report should be made public in time for a debate in secret. In a 'leak' to Margaret Stewart of the *News-Chronicle* it was disclosed that his committee had found the party organization was still in the 'penny-farthing stage' in an era of jet propulsion. So rusty was it that it was surprising not that so many seats had been lost but that so many had been retained. To overcome this more agents would be put into marginal seats, which would get extra help, and the NEC would exercise tighter control over the party machine. When the report was published on 5 October Wilson was generous in denying that there had been any effort by Transport House to gag the Committee. 'The first person I ever heard suggest that this report be got ready for publication was Morgan Phillips himself two months ago,' Wilson insisted. 'At that stage I myself had doubts. We

thought at that stage of producing a confidential report for the Executive
and a separate handout for the press. But day by day we felt more and
more that this document would be appropriate for publication.'[28]

Wilson won his second victory that summer when he was again top of
the poll in the constituency section in the annual conference election at
Margate of a new National Executive, with 1,066,000 votes – up 23,000
votes; he was trailed by Barbara Castle, Anthony Greenwood and Dick
Crossman. Aneurin Bevan was massively defeated in his contest for the
Treasurership by Hugh Gaitskell, winning only 1,225,000 votes against
5,475,000. He had lost the support of two Bevanite unions, the NUR and
USDAW. Later that day Wilson outlined his 'penny-farthing' report on
party organization to a secret session of the conference.[29] In that report
Wilson and his colleagues said they 'were deeply shocked at the state of
party organization' in many parts of the country. When Bevan rose to
speak in the discussion that followed he insisted that it was not
organizational weakness that had caused Labour's defeat but the
preoccupation of right-wing trade-union leaders with driving him out of
the movement. Many shouted: 'We want Nye back!'

Wilson sat on the platform of the *Tribune* meeting on Wednesday
night, 12 October, the annual occasion for Bevanite revivalism.
Normally this was the high-point for Bevan's speeches, but this time he
had raised the roof with his attack on right-wing trade-union leaders the
previous afternoon. Wilson did not speak, although Michael Foot did. It
was symptomatic of Wilson's evolving position of being 'with the
Bevanites but not of them'. He did not want to identify himself too
closely with *Tribune*'s bitter attacks on trade-union leaders, but neither
did he want to abandon the support he had gained among constituency
activists as a result of his identification with the Bevanites for four years.
Political observers had begun to make sport of his clever tactics, of his
slow separation from Bevan and his acceptance of the reality that
Gaitskell would almost certainly overtake Morrison in the race for the
succession to Attlee. Mr Wilson, wrote the *Observer*, had been a long-
distance runner at Oxford. 'There the art was to let the more exuberant
boys flash ahead, to hang back in the fourth or fifth place, and then,
relying on one's stamina, to come thrusting through at the last.' At that
point, thought the *Observer*: 'He is lying, one might say, about fourth or
fifth in the race for the party Leadership.... It would be unwise to
assume that he has deserted Mr Bevan and gone over to Mr Gaitskell ...
Mr Wilson, to use another sporting metaphor, has switched from
outside Left to inside Left.'[30]

That was a useful position to be in. When the NEC met to set up its
new Organization Sub-Committee Wilson tied with Alice Bacon, a
right-winger, for the position of Chairman. Miss Bacon was a supporter

of Morgan Phillips. Since the Organization Sub-committee was entrusted with carrying out the forty-one recommendations of the Wilson Report, her nomination was a form of Phillips-inspired sabotage. But three weeks later she withdrew her name, giving him a clear run. He was well-placed in the party leadership as well as the Parliamentary party.

Wilson's friend, Dick Crossman, began to suggest rather delicately that Wilson might be considered as a possible successor to Attlee. Morrison's succession would not 'now be much more than a reward for past services'. 'Gaitskell wants the party to forget the rusty platitudes of the past and to consider whether new conditions create new objectives. The Left believes that the original socialist objectives remain valid, but it is now coming to see that they may be achieved by something other than the old formulas and methods . . . [But] neither Mr Bevan nor those who cheer him have yet translated their principles into a viable statement of policy . . . This is why the Wilson report means something more than an attempt to give Labour a technically efficient machine. For in its frank self-criticism the rank-and-file member sees hope of a leadership which is both politically imaginative and professionally competent. Mr Wilson not only tops the constituency poll; his committee has also been permitted to touch the levers of power. And this, to a frustrated membership, is an important augury of change; once there is a serious attempt to overhaul the party organization, other changes must follow.'[31] But a *New Statesman* editorial could plant ideas, not change political realities.

When it was intimated to Wilson that he ought to stand for the leadership when Attlee called it a day he disclaimed such ambitions, for realistic reasons. Gaitskell clearly had the support of most of both the trade-union loyalists and the middle-class moderates in the two-thirds of the Parliamentary Labour Party that was right of centre and Bevan had the support of most of the third that was left of centre. Wilson was too shrewd not to realize that the trade-union leaders and Hugh Dalton, Gaitskell's main sponsor, had done their work well. Dalton, by withdrawing on grounds of age, had pulled the rug from under Herbert Morrison.

As a tactician Wilson could hardly enthuse about the decision of Bevan suddenly to grasp the outstretched hands of the Morrisonians once Attlee announced on 8 December 1955 that he was retiring as Leader. Because support for Gaitskell had very substantially overtaken that for Morrison, 'Manny' Shinwell, a strong Morrisonian, hit on a clever device. He asked Bevan whether he would agree to stand down, with Gaitskell, to give Morrison a free run. Bevan, knowing he had no chance himself at that time, agreed in the hope that over the next year or two the odds might change. Gaitskell refused to withdraw his name, and the poll showed the following: Gaitskell 157, Bevan seventy, Morrison forty. Gaitskell won the poll by a clear majority on the first round.

On the eve of the announcement of the result Wilson became involved in a rather embarrassing exchange with a cantankerous Tory, Cyril Osborne, who objected to Wilson's fiery attack on the emergency Budget. Osborne complained that 'he jeered at us because he said that there would be [Ministerial] jobs going because of a change of com-position of the Government. I should have thought that he would have been the last person to say anything like that. At least, we have not ratted on a friend when he is in difficulties and changed places to keep a job because the other man is going to come out on top.' Wilson immediately intervened: 'Will the honourable Member justify that remark or withdraw it?' Osborne retorted that Wilson had previously supported Bevan, 'who is now down the sink'. Wilson asked for the protection of the Deputy Speaker, insisting this was 'a most offensive and inaccurate statement' based on nothing but Osborne's 'reading of "Cross-Bencher" in the *Sunday Express*'. The Deputy Speaker finally forced Osborne to withdraw his remarks.[32]

## THE NEW WILSON

The year 1956 was one in which Harold Wilson might safely change gear and direction. By losing decisively to the much younger Gaitskell Bevan put behind him the chance of leading Labour, short of a radical change in the whole character of the Labour movement. In fact, that change began to occur in 1956 when, due to the premature death of Jock Tiffin, the leadership of the Transport Workers fell into the hands of Frank Cousins. This marked the first time a big mass union had been led by a left-winger. Bevan was fairly slow to appreciate that this was the beginning of a major shift in emphasis and continued in his unpredict-able role, first hurling sectarian scorn at his colleagues – as at Manchester in February 1956 – and then collaborating with them, accepting the portfolio of colonial affairs spokesman from Gaitskell. Bevan was still a big man, despite his irascibility, and garnered 111 votes against Jim Griffiths's 141 when he stood for the Deputy Leadership in January 1956. But nobody knew how to tame the Welsh tornado. It was a mark of Gaitskell's respect for Wilson that he made him Labour's 'Shadow Chancellor' – the very post he himself had held under Attlee – when he deployed his team in February 1956. In fact, when Gaitskell announced Wilson's appointment it was seen that his field covered both the Treasury and the Board of Trade, with three men under him: Douglas Jay, Arthur Bottomley and Patrick Gordon Walker. Wilson exploited his launching pad by hurling himself against the new Chancellor, Harold Macmillan, like some magnificent firework. It was during the 20 February 1956 debate on the economic situation that the 'new Wilson' surfaced. His enormously lengthy speech, delivered at high speed, was full of expertise and sardonic humour, to the delight of those who had got used to economics as the 'dismal science'. Next day the *Guardian* described his effort as 'his wittiest and most effective debating speech. No one will make the mistake of under-rating his equipment for the Parliamentary tourney in future.'[33] The *Daily Express* described as 'one of the major developments in the last week ... the re-emergence of Harold Wilson as one of the major figures' in the Labour Party.[34] J. P. W. Mallalieu said that his speech had converted Wilson from 'a doughy debutante into a considerable Parliamentary figure'.[35]

Wilson's satiric wit reached an even higher pitch in reply to the Chancellor's Budget speech. It got cheers from Labour benches and plaudits from the less Tory-partisan press. In fact he went over the top in dismissing Harold Macmillan's introduction of premium bonds as 'a squalid raffle', predicting that the Tories would fight the next election on the slogan 'Honest Charlie always pays' – which brought the House down. But interspersed among the barbed satire were elements of a serious alternative economic strategy. He urged a capital gains tax and warned that tax avoidance was becoming a 'major national industry'.[36] The *Daily Telegraph* commented: 'Rarely has the clown been played to such effect ... He pranced deftly around the Government Front Bench – and the Back Benches as well – tweaking a nose here, flinging a custard pie there. But no quip missed its mark, nor was there a quirk in bad taste. No one in the House enjoyed this galvanic display more than the Lord Privy Seal, Mr Butler, against whom so many of Mr Wilson's thrusts were delivered. It formed a welcome contrast with Mr Gaitskell's performance when he was attacking the former Chancellor last autumn.'[37]

Those two speeches on economics, in February and April 1956, not only established Wilson's reputation as a witty speaker on economics but also established him as a duelling partner of Harold Macmillan, whom he much admired. Wilson enjoyed those clashes. He had 'a great respect for Macmillan in debate. I ... had some tough clashes with him in the Commons, and I've called him all kinds of names. I christened him "Mac the Knife", for example. But he knows that it's all done without personal malice and he slings it back in the same spirit.'[38] 'I loved those debates. It was real rapier stuff and sometimes I ended up flat on my back, sometimes him, and the whole House used to fill up. I felt very affronted when he was taken away from me [in 1957] and made Prime Minister.'[39]

Although Wilson could be outspoken he could also be quiet when necessary. One such occasion occurred in April 1956, when the National Executive gave a dinner for the Soviet Communist leaders, Marshal Bulganin and Nikita Krushchev. From his own trips to the Soviet Union Wilson knew how differently the Russian leaders saw the events leading up to the Second World War. At the dinner a clash of interjections between two extroverts, Krushchev and George Brown, led to considerable tension. This was not helped when contrasting stories about this private dinner were 'leaked' to the press. The Transport House report on the meeting had been made by Morgan Phillips' secretary, Marcia Williams, but 'leaked' by someone else. This dinner was the first occasion on which Harold Wilson and Marcia Williams were together, united also by their joint distaste for George Brown's hostile behaviour towards Krushchev. Wilson, with his heavy personal investment in improving trade relations with the Russians, deplored any unnecessary provocation and was glad about the 'kiss and make up' meeting next day in the Soviet leaders' Claridge's suite.

For a while it looked as though Wilson might be tacking in the wrong direction, despite his continuing successes in Parliamentary debates. One such success was his satirical attack on 20 June 1956 on the sale of British-owned Trinidad Oil to an American firm. His strong pro-Commonwealth feelings and his fear of US economic domination gave his wit an added cutting edge. He contrasted the action of Chancellor Harold Macmillan with Winston Churchill's purchase of shares in Anglo-Iranian or Disraeli's buying of Suez Canal shares. How could the present Conservatives, a group of 'drooping primroses with palsied hands', be compared to those giants? Labour benches lapped it up. After the Chancellor announced a £100m cut a fortnight later Wilson described Macmillan as 'Mac the Knife' in the Conservatives' Three-penny Opera. The *Guardian* warned: 'The one danger Mr Wilson runs is of becoming unbearably brilliant. A party leader whose speeches always crackle with jokes like the pages of *Punch* might end in boring people.'[40] But *Guardian* leader-writers did not speak for those who sat in the Press Gallery of the Commons.

Although Labour MPs were warming to Wilson constituency militants cooled slightly now they saw him joining the Parliamentary Establishment. That year Aneurin Bevan again stood for the Treasurership with his hopes increased by the elevation of Hugh Gaitskell to leader. George Brown was not as appealing a replacement for right-wing trade-union leaders, who were having difficulty in holding their subordinates in line. Instead of the previous year's clobbering for Bevan this contest was proving to be a neck-and-neck race, with all constituency activists' and trade-union militants' eyes on Bevan and Brown, with Charles (later Lord) Pannell coming well up in the rear. When it was announced that Bevan had beaten Brown by 3,029,000 to 2,755,000, a tremendous roar went up in Empress Hall, Blackpool. This final breakthrough for Bevan completely overshadowed the fact that Wilson had lost his place at the top of the poll for constituency representatives on the National Executive, coming third with 877,000 votes. After the announcement Wilson rushed over to congratulate Bevan, secure in the knowledge that he had, quite sensibly, refused an offer to let his own name go forward for the Treasurership. To have split the left-wing vote might have destroyed him.

In contrast, when the new session of Parliament began, Wilson came top of the poll for the 'Shadow Cabinet' in November 1956 instead of fifth as he had done the previous year. Alfred Robens and Aneurin Bevan came second and third. 'His position has never been stronger,' thought the *Evening Standard*, 'and he has now become the most formidable contender for the Premiership of a socialist Government.'[41]

What preoccupied everyone at the time, however, was the Suez adventure on which the ailing Tory Prime Minister, Sir Anthony Eden, had launched his expedition amidst considerable secrecy. Initially there were some fears of Labour divisions. In his first reaction Gaitskell attacked Nasser's seizure of the Suez Canal as akin to the aggression of Hitler, and he seemed rather timid in warning the Tory Government against attacking without UN permission. But he became quite fierce when it was apparent that the Eden Government had launched its military adventure without consulting its US allies and in defiance of their warnings. Aneurin Bevan, grudgingly promoted to foreign affairs spokesman, scored notably in this position for which he was brilliantly suited. Wilson, already as pro-Israeli as Bevan, tended to stay out of details of Suez, keeping to his 'Shadow Chancellor' speciality. But at Marsden, Huddersfield, he attacked the Government as having given every would-be aggressor an immaculate cloak with which to cover the nakedness of their aggression. It had dealt UN collective security a serious blow.[42]

## JOINED BY MARCIA

In October 1956, just as Britain lost an ally, Harold Wilson gained one in Marcia Williams. At the height of the Suez crisis she walked out on Labour Party General Secretary, Morgan Phillips, and became Wilson's political secretary. They had met when he had picked her up at a Hampstead Garden Suburb bus stop, recognizing her as a Labour Party employee. She informed him that she had been his anonymous source within Transport House when he had been investigating the efficiency of the political machinery there. She made it clear that she identified with his view of Labour politics rather than that of Morgan Phillips, then rather more right-wing than he later became.

Wilson welcomed her as an aide because he was reaching a position where he required a devoted assistant totally committed to his cause but with considerable political savoir faire. The Bevanite Group had fragmented in the winter of 1955–56, with himself and Dick Crossman taking almost open dislike to Bevan's quite unpredictable tactics and uncontrollable speeches. So the old warmth of having a dozen or so political cronies with whom tactics and approach could be concerted had evaporated. Wilson still saw a good deal of Crossman and Balogh, but because of the former's journalistic commitments he did not always have him to turn to in Westminster. And certainly he could not talk politics to a sympathetic ear at home. So he came to talk more and more with his twenty-four-year-old secretary, who strongly reflected what activists in the Labour movement outside felt about issues of the day.

There were murmurs from his colleagues, which later grew louder, that he was playing too solitary and too cautious a role, not joining enough with them. For example, he was nowhere to be seen when a handful of Labour MPs started the anti-Suez agitation before the leadership took it up. Nor was he to the forefront during the famous Trafalgar Square 'Law Not War' rally at which Bevan was the featured speaker on 4 November 1956. He seemed determined not to put a foot wrong.

This caution was also suggested by the fact that he declined to sign a letter sent to *Pravda* by five colleagues from the Bevanite Group, complaining about the Soviet newspaper's description of the Hungarian rising as 'counter-revolutionary' and about Soviet intervention in Hungary. Since the group of signatories included Crossman, Barbara Castle, Anthony Benn, Fenner Brockway and George Wigg, they could hardly be described as 'anti-Soviet'. At the same time Wilson was willing to sign a letter to the *New Statesman* asking for support for opponents of apartheid in South Africa.

## LOSING A SPARRING PARTNER

When Harold Macmillan became Prime Minister Harold Wilson was surprised and disappointed at losing his sparring partner. Like most other Labour leaders Wilson had expected R. A. Butler to follow the ailing Sir Anthony Eden as the new Conservative Prime Minister in January 1957. Wilson felt like a darts-player who has had his dart-board taken away. He tried to maintain the momentum in a speech on 12 February 1957, when he said the new Prime Minister had had 'a very expensive education – Eton and Suez'.[43] In private Wilson was always much more admiring of Macmillan. 'You know, John,' he told *Sunday Express* editor John Junor at a private dinner early in 1957, 'the man's a genius. He's holding up the banner of Suez for the party to follow, and he's leading the party away from Suez. That's what I'd like to do with the Labour Party over nationalization.'[44]

One of the areas in which he was being quietly energetic was the National Executive of the Labour Party, where he had been elected to the Ownership of Industry and Control of Industry working parties on 28 November 1956. In March 1957 he was put on a sub-committee with Gaitskell to negotiate with the Cooperative Union a new political relations agreement. The old one had been strained at Wednesbury where John Stonehouse had been elected with the aid of a selection committee 'packed' by Cooperative delegates despatched there by Mrs Stonehouse, his mother, who was a leading Co-op figure.

Wilson won wild plaudits with his attack on the Budget. His speech, judged the *Guardian*, 'raises his already considerable reputation appreciably. He exhibited once again, and brilliantly, his powers of ridicule. At the same time he avoided the splenetic partisanship to which he has been prone. But it was in the solid criticism of the Budget and of the Government's economic policy that he surpassed his earlier efforts.'[45] So telling was his attack on Macmillan that the Prime Minister seemed flustered while R.A.Butler found his discomfiture vastly amusing. Wilson pointed out that Macmillan had promised to cut the Budget by £100m but had actually increased it by £372m over Butler's Budget. Wilson recalled that Macmillan had reached his resolve under the severe gaze of the Treasury portrait of Gladstone. 'Turn Gladstone's face to the wall, Harold,' urged the other Harold. 'Never more mention his name. You have brought disgrace to the Treasury and should bow your head in shame.' Labour and Tory MPs alike howled with laughter.[46] This sort of speech did great things for his prospects – at least in the mind of the *Sunday Times* political correspondent: 'It is Mr Harold Wilson, the Third Man, whose position has been significantly strengthened by recent events. Both in the Parliamentary party and at annual conference he enjoys the support of Right and Left to a degree unequalled by either Mr Gaitskell or Mr Bevan; he has a surer 'feel' for a political situation than the former and a shrewder sense of reality than the latter.'[47] The *Punch* Parliamentary correspondent also wrote lengthily about Wilson's ability to perform 'like a television don', showing 'that the whole of the economy had been knocked haywire by the Suez folly ... But the cracks were therefore mainly at the expense of Mr Macmillan and Mr Butler, and of the two Mr Butler seemed to enjoy them more.'[48]

Exploiting the Tories' discomfiture over the failure of the Suez invasion was one of Wilson's strong suits at the time. He followed this same line when he spoke to a Labour rally at Brighton on 28 April: 'This week will see the pay-off for the lunacies of the last six months, as

Britain will be forced to accept a Suez Canal settlement far less satisfactory than we could have had and were on the point of getting last October.... Mr Macmillan climbed to power on the back of Lord Salisbury because the die-hards thought he was more likely than Mr Butler to follow an imperialist foreign policy. Well, now Lord Salisbury has been ditched and Mr Macmillan has had to accept the realities of the international situation.'[49] By concentrating his attacks on the Tories and Suez, Wilson was able to avoid committing himself either to the pro-American line of his leader, Hugh Gaitskell, or to that of Aneurin Bevan, who was very critical of the American initiatives. Gaitskell was neither fooled nor amused by Wilson's tactics. He described Wilson rather condescendingly as 'very clever and extremely energetic' in an interview with Alan Wood.[50]

This avoidance of full commitment became more important in April 1957 when the argument over nuclear tests split the Labour Party. The previous month Prime Minister Macmillan had agreed at Bermuda with the US President, Dwight Eisenhower, to test the first UK H-bomb at Christmas Island in the Pacific. Labour Leader Hugh Gaitskell and his Defence spokesman, George Brown, were inclined to give their support, since both were strongly pro-American, but they were blocked at a meeting of the Parliamentary Labour Party by a group partly led by Bevan's wife, Jennie Lee, which urged a suspension of tests pending an attempt to achieve international agreement. When Bevan himself returned from India he described the H-bomb tests as 'immoral' and urged Britain to give 'leadership in the opposite direction'.[51]

The caution with which Wilson approached this issue was highlighted in the satirical style of 'Cross-Bencher' in the *Sunday Express*: 'As the night train from Liverpool clatters over the points into Euston this morning, picture a tired traveller in his sleeper sipping British Railways tea. Tired but not depressed. For him the message which the carriage wheels hammer out on the metals is heady and exhilarating. "It could be me. It could be me." The traveller is Mr Harold Wilson, socialist Shadow Chancellor of the Exchequer. And the thought which buoys him up after a long day in his Huyton constituency? That sometime in the next few months he could become Leader of the Party. Consider the hard reasons for this exciting idea. Whatever Mr Wilson may assert in public, privately he knows that the H-bomb rift will mean a rout in the General Election. After all his toil in patching up the party machine, that is a sad outlook. Yet for Mr Wilson the gloom is lit up by one blazing expectation. That an election defeat will mean the end of Mr Hugh Gaitskell as Leader. Who then, would succeed Mr Gaitskell? Could it be Mr Aneurin Bevan? Hardly. It was he who actually stood up before the party conference and insisted that a [Labour] Government must keep the H-bomb. It was he who proclaimed that, as Foreign Secretary, he could not go naked into the council chamber. On this issue Mr Bevan and Mr Gaitskell are as closely linked as two survivors clinging to the same spar after a shipwreck. And even if Nye could wriggle out of his responsibility [Labour] MPs declare that the old fire and fury have gone out of him. Nowadays, they say, he is tired and disinterested. They doubt if he has the gusto to revive a shattered party.

'Any other possible leaders in the Commons? Just two. Mr Alfred Robens and Mr George Brown. And neither of them has any chance at all. Both are irretrievably committed to retaining the H-bomb. In the new mood of the party these two would be even less acceptable than Mr Gaitskell. Which leaves only Mr Wilson. Yet what is Mr Wilson's record on the bomb? It is proof against all criticism. It is blank. He has no record at all. Since the row blew up not a word from him has been reported on the issue. He has stuck to another theme on which few socialists anywhere disagree with him – businessmen's tax-free expenses.'[52]

Wilson stayed in the economics field, which had far fewer land-mines. The publication, in July 1957, of *Industry and Society* looked like opening up some old wounds, but even here he was careful. The document was prepared by Peter Shore, then in the Labour Party Research Department, for the approval of the NEC's Control of Industry sub-committee, on which Wilson served. It was at this point that Shore and Wilson became quite close. The document Shore produced demonstrated how the 500 biggest companies virtually controlled the British economy without their investors having any serious say in their management. The NEC sub-committee decided that, once in office, a Labour Government would take shares in some of these companies. This was a compromise between those on the sub-committee like Gaitskell who wanted to nationalize very few companies and those like Ian Mikardo who wanted to take the lot into public ownership. Harold Wilson, writing in *Forward*, which had been established by Gaitskell's moderate friends as a rival to *Tribune*, was only slightly more militant than Gaitskell about nationalizing companies. He was clearly keeping his head down.

## BANK RATE
Wilson demonstrated his ability to *sound* radical and anti-capitalist in September 1957, when he demanded an inquiry into whether the Bank of England's decision to raise the Bank Rate to seven per cent had been 'leaked' the day before it occurred on 19 September 1957. The *News-*

*Chronicle* wrote of 'heavy sales of Government securities ... late on Wednesday and on Thursday by people who evidently knew that the Bank Rate was to be raised', and called for an inquiry. This was seized upon by Wilson who wrote to Enoch Powell, then Financial Secretary, in the absence of his chief, Chancellor Peter Thorneycroft, in Washington. 'As the Chancellor is away,' wrote Wilson, 'I am writing this letter to you ... to draw to your attention the very disquieting reports ... about a premature leakage of information about the increase of Bank Rate to seven per cent last Thursday. ... I would ask you to draw this letter to the attention of your senior colleague with a view to an inquiry being instituted.' Powell, after consulting the Prime Minister and the Governor of the Band of England – who claimed that the extent of the change had come 'as a complete bombshell' – replied to Wilson that investigation had disclosed no evidence of a leakage. Wilson then provided more information on 2 October. In the meantime the Governor of the Bank of England, Cameron Cobbold, had written to the Prime Minister to inform him that two Directors of the Bank were connected with companies which had sold Government securities. He did not tell him that two companies in which Lord Kindersley was a principal had sold £3,750,000 of Government securities and W. J. Keswick's company had sold gilt-edged to the tune of almost £1m. Wilson told the Brighton conference of the Labour Party that if the Conservative Government had nothing to hide it would have agreed to an inquiry. At that point the Tories were 18.5 per cent behind Labour in the Gallup Poll, the lowest point they had ever reached.

Wilson's demand for an inquiry into a possible City scandal kept him in the public eye without involving him in Labour in-fighting. At Brighton temperatures were running very high over the H-bomb. Just before the conference an anti-bomb meeting in Trafalgar Square had attracted 5,000 people, who were addressed by Barbara Castle, Ian Mikardo and Tony Greenwood. But Bevan had always had a more sophisticated and, he would maintain, realistic approach to international affairs than some of his supporters. He wanted to use Britain's leverage as a nuclear Power to try to persuade the nuclear super-Powers to withdraw from the nuclear arms race. During the debate at Brighton Bevan said that it falsified the issue to present it as a simple argument between those who supported the H-bomb and those who opposed it. He dismissed as an 'emotional spasm' the effort of the composite resolution supporting unilateral nuclear disarmament. It would 'disarm' a British Foreign Secretary in a crisis, send the nations of the world to cluster around the Russians or the Americans and might have 'disastrous consequences throughout the world'. He won the vote by 5,836,000 to 781,000 but lost the support of militants who saw the issue in black-and-white terms. Bevan dismayed his most emotional friends and delighted his long-standing opponents. The people who suffered least were those who shared his more sophisticated vision of the world without being tied too closely to him – those like Crossman and Wilson. The Tribunites were torn apart, with Michael Foot writing editorials attacking his long-time hero and Bevan urging his friends, including Jack Hylton, the impresario, to withdraw their financial support from *Tribune*.

In the incandescent argument over the H-bomb and the resulting split between such old left-wing friends as Aneurin Bevan and Michael Foot, little public attention was paid to the small but gnawing doubt growing among Wilson-admirers on the Labour benches and among some who were not his admirers. The doubt was over the amount of time spent with and authority allocated to Marcia Williams by Wilson.

The irritation of some of his colleagues was intensified by the fact that much of this time Wilson was away from the House of Commons in his office as a consultant to Montague L. Meyer, the timber consultants, at Villiers House on the Strand. The facilities afforded MPs in the Commons were still fairly primitive, and he was still not senior enough, even as a former Minister and front-bench spokesman, to be sure of a room large enough to accommodate him and a secretary in the Palace of Westminster. Therefore, between 1956 and 1959, when Wilson's presence was not required in the Commons on the Front Bench or on some Committee, he and Marcia Williams got through a lot of work together in the more comfortable Montague Meyer office. It was only in 1959, when Wilson became the Chairman of a senior Committee, that they both moved full-time into the commodious office assigned to them in the upper corridor of the House of Commons.

A number of Harold Wilson's colleagues were also slightly irritated by the degree of authority which he increasingly transferred to Marcia, particularly after her first year with him. If they wanted to make an appointment he would almost always say: 'Fix it up with Marcia.' Colleagues resented having to apply to a pretty, fresh-faced young girl who made it clear that they were very lucky to be given time to talk to such an important and rising politician as Harold Wilson.

Because they worked so hard over such long hours both their spouses became irritated. Because the House normally sits until 10 p.m. from Monday through Thursday when in session, and because Marcia was willing to slave for her admired boss so long as he needed her, frequently neither of them would return to their homes in Golders Green and Hampstead Garden Suburb until after midnight.

The degree of Marcia's devotion to Harold helped to end her marriage, although it did not terminate formally for another three

years. In 1957 her husband, Ed, a talented engineer, was offered a
highly-paid job with Boeing in Seattle. It was a time of the 'brain
drain' which siphoned off many of Britain's talented technicians. But,
according to close friends, one of the reasons for Ed's departure was
his feeling of neglect by his wife. He was an attractive man, over six
feet tall and addicted to Italian suits, who liked to think that he was
the centre of his wife's consciousness. However, she was utterly devoted
to her work on behalf of Wilson. Ed liked Harold and enjoyed the
occasions on which he dined with the Williamses at their Golders Green
home. But he did not like being neglected when his wife felt it
necessary to work such long hours for Wilson. Ed Williams was not
surprised when his wife declined to accompany him to Seattle.

Mary Wilson was not always as philosophical about the increasing
closeness between her husband and his young secretary as later
appeared to be the case in public. Behind the scenes she occasionally
urged her husband to get rid of Marcia. When he refused she declined to
appear anywhere – on the few occasions she *did* make public appearances – if Marcia was also to be there. On one occasion, when
Wilson was due to appear in a TV studio, Mrs Williams asked a
colleague in the Parliamentary Labour Party to accompany him to the
studio. 'Why don't you go?' she was asked. 'You will see when you get
there,' she replied. When the colleague arrived at the TV studio Mary
Wilson was waiting.

These behind-the-scenes tensions were known only to a handful of
people who largely kept their mouths sealed. They resembled the quiet
ticking of a time-bomb whose moment for exploding was quite unpredictable. But the tensions, apart from dividing Wilson's political life
from his home life, did not impede his rise.

At Brighton, while Bevan's reputation had sagged in the eyes of his
closest admirers, Wilson's had risen. He had launched a scathing attack
on the Government's economic policy in the first major debate. This
gave the conference the optimistic feeling that a winnable general
election was just around the corner; Wilson was able to suggest the
battle going on behind the walls of the Treasury over how to handle the
mounting crisis. He later presented the National Executive's statement
on the future of public ownership and attempted to clarify just how a
Labour Government would take over those big firms which were 'failing
the nation'. He spoke as a moderate on behalf of a moderate NEC when
he introduced the policy statement 'Industry and Society'' to the
October 1957 conference of the Labour Party. 'It is not a means of back-
door control. . . . When for economic reasons we need to acquire an
industry or firm for economic control, let us be honest about it and say
so, and seek direct power to exercise that control. If our motive in

acquiring shares in any company is to share the capital appreciation that should not of itself be used for control.'[53] Conference approved his report by a majority of four million on a card vote.[54] Wilson remained on the NEC, only 25,000 votes behind the front-runner in the constituency section.

Wilson was again top man on the 'Shadow Cabinet' poll when the Commons reconvened, but he was not satisfied with the stand-off he had been accorded by the Prime Minister in his demand for an investigation into the alleged 'leak' of the increased bank rate. It was Wilson who kept alive the demand for an inquiry. It was only when he referred to the alleged involvement of Oliver (later Lord) Poole and his 'vast City interests' as Lord Cowdray's chief lieutenant that Macmillan gave in. Under pressure from Oliver Poole and the Chancellor, Peter Thorneycroft, the Prime Minister set up the Bank Rate Tribunal under Lord Parker.

A number of biographers have suggested that his insistence on the Bank Rate Tribunal was somehow a great 'error' for Wilson, because the final decision did not go in his favour and he lost the respect of many City Conservatives. This tends to ignore the many interesting aspects of City and Conservative activity uncovered by the Tribunal which were made public property for the first time. These discoveries considerably enhanced Harold Wilson's reputation in Labour eyes. The Tribunal provided fascinating insights into the personal relations among 'top people' in the Bank of England and the City. The classic such one concerned the memorable meeting on a Scottish grouse moor between Nigel Birch, then Economic Secretary (and later Lord Rhyl), and W. J. Keswick, the slope-headed chief of Jardine, Matheson, the famous China Coast traders. Keswick's reluctant agreement to accept the urgings of his Hongkong company to sell sterling securities was quoted as follows: 'Perhaps the time has come to sell ... Again this is anti-British and derogatory to Sterling, but on balance it makes sense.' Although he was able to exploit this quotation from many platforms, technically Wilson was found to have been in the wrong in suggesting that Oliver Poole, then Deputy Chairman of the Conservative Party, had been given information on the Bank Rate increase and 'improperly' passed it on to someone in Conservative Central Office. It transpired that Poole had been told about financial measures *other* than the Bank Rate increase in a briefing given the day before.

Wilson had his back to the wall on 3–4 February 1958 when the Commons debated the report of the Parker Tribunal. The Tory spokesmen, R. A. Butler and Reginald Maudling, had Wilson squarely in their sights, with the Report providing them with plenty of ammunition. Now that Wilson's 'original evidence was proving so feckless', said Butler, Wilson thought it right 'to dredge up every accusation he could think of'. He had, for example, elaborated imputations against Oliver Poole after a Labour MP close to Wilson, Sir Leslie Plummer, had smeared him. 'These insinuations were made under the cover of [Parliamentary] Privilege,' Butler pointed out.

Speaking in the teeth of intense Tory distaste, which produced frequent shouts of 'Withdraw!' to indicate that he should apologize, Wilson stood his ground. He quoted the Conservative Attorney-General Sir Reginald Manningham-Butler (later Lord Dilhorne) as having said that an inquiry was vital once *The Times* had spoken of 'inspired selling'. Then he quoted the Governor's letter, eight days after the increase, which said: 'In the past two days private information has come to me, as Governor of the Bank of England, about transactions by three corporations in which Directors of the Bank, as members of the Boards of these corporation, might be, or held to be, concerned.' He insisted that Labour had only said that there was 'a case for an inquiry'. Tories laughed at him when he claimed that one of his motives was to save people from 'possible victimization'. But Labour MPs listened to him with interest as he clarified how he had discovered, step by step, the briefing of Oliver Poole, despite Government efforts to disguise this. Wilson said he and his colleagues accepted 'unreservedly' the clearing of the names of Keswick and Kindersley, the Bank of England Directors, despite the evidence raised about the sale of government securities by their firms. When Wilson sat down there was a delighted roar from Labour benches to acknowledge the effective fight he had put up.[55] Wilson may have won further Labour regard, but he had 'cast himself as the Enemy No. 1 for the Tories,' thought the *Sunday Times*. 'Long after the issues of the case are forgotten, the Tories will still be after his scalp.'[56] Nor did Bernard Levin admire him.[57]

After his Commons excitement it was almost a quiet holiday for Wilson to travel to China at the end of February. Although he was accorded an interview with Prime Minister Chou En-lai he quite clearly did not hit it off well with his hosts. On his return he described China as 'a ruthlessly run Communist country with all that means'. His interest appeared to be mainly in selling China British goods. He pointed out that almost all the factories he had seen were equipped by the Russians and other East Europeans. 'So far,' he warned, 'trade between Britain and China is little more than a trickle ... If we stand still, it can mean the emergence of a new trade rival as dangerous as Japan or Germany or the Soviet Union. An industrialized nation of 600 million hard-working Chinese can dominate the markets of the world,' he warned. 'But if we look on China as a market for our goods we can plan on the basis of 600 million customers and an almost limitless demand for British engineering products.'[58]

## PLANNING AS CHANCELLOR

Wilson alluded to the need to limit Chinese exports to Britain because he was already thinking partly as a future Chancellor of the Exchequer. After all, the argument about how to handle the economic crisis had been severe enough within the Tory ranks to produce the resignation of Chancellor Thorneycroft and his two lieutenants, Enoch Powell and Nigel Birch. A general election was almost certain some time in 1959, and Labour was ahead in the opinion polls. This probably explains why Wilson's attack on the April 1958 Budget as 'a pathetic little mouse' was described by the *Guardian* as 'less partisan' than usual. 'He was also more serious, curbing for once that facile wit of his.'[59] He was also beginning to think seriously about a wages policy. While complaining publicly about the Government's efforts to prevent wage increases he was privately worried. 'As Chairman of the Labour Party's policy committee on the future control of industry,' wrote the *Sunday Times*, 'Mr Wilson has made substantial progress in drafting the blueprint of socialist economic policy. It sets out the economic controls for a socialist programme, the mechanics for dealing with exports, imports and [the] balance of payments, with great emphasis on the apparatus of controls over investments to help production and development priorities. But unless Mr Wilson can get TUC cooperation on wage restraint, in return for his promise of a price freeze, stability cannot be assured... His Executive colleagues say Mr Wilson has shown much dexterity in avoiding the many burdens doctrinaire planners would load upon Labour's Chancellor. For instance, the party's agricultural policy will show that the subsidy commitments have been limited, though the promise of guaranteed fixed prices for selected commodities only will be included, supported by a new scheme of medium-term credits and an extension of the powers of the Mortgage Corporation.'[60] He was helped considerably in this planning by Tommy Balogh, with whom he met almost every week. Dr Balogh was a strong believer in a wage-control policy.

Partly because of Balogh's preoccupation Wilson showed a very considerable interest in the efforts of the new, left-wing leader of the Transport Workers, Frank Cousins, to achieve better wages for London Transport men. Wilson claimed that the Tories were insisting on a 'showdown' instead of trying to reach a settlement. But some observers thought that he was trying to commit Labour to a 'wages policy'. 'Some leading trade unionists fear that he is. And they bitterly resent the idea.'[61] Such was the influence of his 'economic Svengali', Dr Balogh, but although more intense it was less pervasive than that of his young secretary, Marcia Williams. Labour MPs complained that he preferred talking to her to conferring with them.

His special approach to a wages policy was due in part to his longstanding preoccupation with the cotton industry, an industry with low wages and low industrial militancy. His own 'Plan for Cotton' had been produced in November 1957 after four years of work on behalf of the leading union in the industry. Under his scheme, a 'Cotton Industry Reorganization Commission' with representatives of both sides of industry would draw up a scheme of amalgamation. This could 'enforce a more rapid rate of equipment', with the State taking a controlling interest in key firms. Interestingly enough, some leading employers found this plan 'most attractive and acceptable, if workable', according to a *Daily Telegraph* reporter. One of the reasons for this was Wilson's plan to limit imports of cotton goods from India, unless an agreement could be reached between the two countries. When Wilson debated the cotton industry on 30 June 1958, his 'Plan for Cotton' had been made official Labour Party policy. He received widespread support from his Labour colleagues for his presentation. Many Labour seats in Lancashire and Yorkshire had been made more marginal than usual by the textile crisis and the subsequent loss of jobs and Labour voters.

As the second half of 1958 began Wilson became increasingly cautious out of fear that the Labour victory he thought was impending might be lost by some rash action. Thus, in the July 1958 debate on National Insurance he advised Gaitskell to be careful not to overcommit Labour before seeing the books on taking office. That same year when the British Government occupied Jordan in tandem with the American occupation of the Lebanon, actions intended to stop Nasser taking over the whole Middle East (which phoney intelligence had led the US to expect), Wilson was again cautious. 'The present situation shows the bankruptcy ... above all of the belief that the flames of rising nationalism could be fought by tanks, guns and paratroops,' he warned.[62]

## CAUTION TO THE EXTREMES

Wilson paid the forfeit – at least temporarily – for carrying caution to its extreme when the subject of nuclear disarmament suddenly grabbed the guts of Labour activists in the first half of 1958. Those wanting Britain to disarm unilaterally in the nuclear field had been defeated by Bevan at Brighton in October 1957, but the Christmas Island tests had aroused opinion. The Hampstead-based unilateralists began to pick up supporters. A high-powered group, including Earl Russell, Kingsley Martin, ex-US diplomat George Kennan, J. B. Priestley, Professor (later Lord) Blackett, and Commander Sir Stephen King-Hall – whom Wilson had ousted from Parliament in 1945 – decided to launch the Campaign for Nuclear Disarmament at a Central Hall meeting in February 1958. The meeting, to the surprise of its organizers and the press, turned out to be a tremendous success, overflowing into every other hall available in Westminster. At Easter this largely spontaneous revulsion against nuclear fall-out erupted in the first 'Aldermaston March', initially from London to the Atomic Weapons Research Establishment at Aldermaston. The CND attracted many of the old Bevanite Group – including Michael Foot and Mikardo, but not Bevan, Crossman or Wilson. It certainly attracted most of the Left Labour activists who had enthused about the Bevan–Wilson–Freeman re- signation from the Attlee Cabinet in 1951.

Unilateralism naturally became a point of conflict within the National Executive, as illustrated by its meeting of 6 March with the TUC General Council. Gaitskell's pro-Americanism made him dead-set against considering any curb whatsoever on Britain's use of the nuclear weapon. Bevan wanted, at least, a declaration that Britain would not use nuclear weapons first, if threatened by Soviet conventional forces. Crossman wanted the US to have the NATO monopoly of nuclear weapons, with Britain using wholly conventional weapons. The spokes- man for the new unilateralists was Ian Mikardo. In these arguments Wilson kept his head down, although quite close to Crossman.

This attempt to avoid being tarred by the brush of divisiveness or indiscipline brought Wilson both benefits and disadvantages. In July 1958 he was invited to speak at the Durham Miners' Gala, along with Gaitskell, Alfred Robens and Alice Bacon; these invitations are tra- ditionally extended after a ballot throughout the coalfield. 'Friends of Mr Harold Wilson claim he is lying a handy third on the rails,' pointed out the Political Correspondent of the *Daily Express*. 'But I fear that Mr Wilson, only forty-two, has much longer to wait than he thinks.'[63] This was an effort to suggest that Wilson was risking falling between several stools, admired for his cleverness and hard work by all but fully trusted by few.

The fact that he had lost the trust of many left-wing activists was illustrated in the balloting which took place at the Scarborough conference on 30 September 1958. He dropped from second place the previous year to fourth place. But he remained an influential figure on the NEC, taking his place on the Chairman's Committee set up on 22 October 1958 to concentrate on the looming general election.

His strength lay mainly in his powerful parliamentary oratory, as in his speech on 3 November on the Queen's Speech. He was in rollicking form, with Labour colleagues cheering each new witticism. His main attack was on the Government for taking off the lid in anticipation of an election after having deflated too long. No one now could talk about former Chancellor Thorneycroft, who had wanted to tighten deflation still further. 'They have turned Peter's face to the wall.' He accused the

Prime Minister of 'narcissism'. Mr Macmillan, he went on, 'has inherited the streak of charlatanry in Disraeli without his vision, and the streak of self-righteousness in Gladstone without his dedication to principle.'[64] The Chancellor, Heathcoat (later Lord) Amory, dismissed Wilson as a 'comedian'. But 191 votes put Wilson at No. 2 in the election for the Shadow Cabinet, outstripped only by Bevan with 206.

The ever-malicious 'Cross-Bencher' in the *Sunday Express* described Wilson at the time as 'as placid as a cat full of double Devon cream' because 'whoever loses the general election, Mr Wilson reckons he is bound to win. If the socialists triumph at the polls Mr Wilson will, of course, become Chancellor of the Exchequer. That would make him the youngest Chancellor since Austen Chamberlain in 1903. As the man who reorganized the socialist election machine he would have immense authority in the party. But if the socialists lose, just consider how comfortably Mr Wilson is placed. The rest of the fellows in the Shadow Cabinet have a most urgent personal need for a job in the Government.... Their lives would be utterly transformed. But for Harold his £5,750 a year as Chancellor would make no difference. His MP's pay of £1,750 a year is already mightily buttressed by his salary as economic adviser to the £6,500,000 Montague L. Meyer timber firm. The privilege of an official black Humber car is no attraction either. Like most big business executives he enjoys that perquisite too. At present he drives round in a shiny beige and blue Ford Zodiac. Registered in the name of Montague L. Meyer Ltd.

'Politically, look at the advantages which another period in opposition would bring to forty-two-year-old Mr Wilson. There are many who believe it would eliminate Mr Hugh Gaitskell as party leader, on the grounds that he could not conceivably survive after three Tory election wins in a row. While for the ageing Mr Aneurin Bevan it would hasten the day of his retirement to his farm in the Chilterns.... As he is acceptable to both Right and Left wings, no one could possibly challenge Mr Wilson's succession to the Leadership. And even after a further ten years in opposition he would be only the same age as Mr Gaitskell is today. True, Mr Wilson tells his friends that a spell at the Treasury is indispensable experience for a Prime Minister. But he knows it to be an experience full of risks. One economic crisis might ruin his prospects for ever. Who would blame Mr Wilson if, secretly, he is willing to skip that perilous apprenticeship?'[65] Naturally Wilson resented this *Sunday Express* exaggeration of his income from Montague L. Meyer and the suggestion that his income was therefore bigger than any other member of the Shadow Cabinet. But he could hardly object to its emphasis on the inevitability of his final victory.

The emphasis on his business experience did not harm him in the economic Establishment to whom he was trying to appeal as a future Chancellor. He wrote regularly to the *Economist*, *The Times* and the *Guardian*. Thus, in September 1958 he wrote warning that the Government had missed the opportunity for 'rapid expansion and a big increase in industrial investment in both the public and private sectors'.[66] In December he wrote to the *Economist* complaining of the 'high cost of industrial stagnation' and the need for 'controlled and purposive ... expansion'.[67] He told the American Chamber of Commerce that the Government should have relaxed industrial investment allowances.

His picture of the directions in which trade should expand was still directed quite strongly towards the Commonwealth and Eastern Europe. Thus, after the US had cancelled a low bid by English Electric, he wrote in the *Sunday Express*: 'Trading with the Americans is like trying to play a game of football with a team which insists on boarding up its goal-mouth before the kick-off.'[68] For Mr Wilson protectionism was fair if it kept enough Indian goods off the British market to protect British wage-earners but not if it kept too many British generators off the American market to protect American wage-earners.

He was still hostile to the European Economic Community. In the Commons he praised the 'patience, good humour and indefatigable hard work' of Reginald Maudling, who was trying to keep the European Free Trade Association (EFTA) going in competition with the EEC. In an interview he emphasized the danger that the EEC was coming 'more and more under cartel domination' and insisted that it was 'impossible to say whether the European Common Market ... will survive the internal stresses and strains to which it is bound to be subject in its early years, particularly if there is an intensification of trade depression and unemployment in the countries concerned.'[69]

## BUDGET ANTICIPATION
Since the Conservatives had cut taxes before their victory in the 1955 general election Wilson expected them to reduce taxation by £350m in the April 1959 Budget. He under-estimated by £250m, but managed to exploit his opportunities to poke wicked fun at them in the Budget debate on 8 April. He welcomed the Tories' adoption of investment allowances for industry: 'It is something we have urged for four years. Now you see mass conversion. There has been nothing like it since an Emperor of China baptised a whole army with a hosepipe.' This joke was a steal from Aneurin Bevan, who more accurately ascribed this mass baptism to a Chinese General, the famous 'Christian General'.

Wilson complained about the way in which the Tories had cut taxes. 'If the country is more prosperous, for whatever reasons, it is the

Government's duty . . . to make provision first for the underprivileged and not for the better off,' he insisted. He complained that £200m was returned to income-tax payers, particularly the highest ones. The Chancellor, he complained, was playing 'Robin Hood in reverse', 'robbing the poor to give to the rich'. He pretended to know that it was the Prime Minister, Harold Macmillan, who inspired the twopence off a pint of beer. 'It is all part of his condescending "Masters and Men" approach,' Wilson contended. Macmillan had calculated that 'the masters' would get hundreds off their tax a year and had said: ' "Let's give the men twopence off a pint".'[70]

Wilson was fast developing a talent for verbal radicalism which made him a great attraction at Labour functions all over the country. He told the Scottish TUC at Dunoon that unemployment was rising in their area because Tory decisions were taken on Scottish grouse moors and in City bankers' parlours. 'We have always known – as the country has now come to see – that Tory freedom works only when you have factories, machines, and above all workers, standing idle.'[71] He went on to attack Macmillan in Glasgow a week later after the Prime Minister had attacked Labour for its 1951 slogan 'Whose Finger on the Trigger?' designed to depict Churchill as a war-monger. 'Is he forgetting Suez, when his finger was on the trigger?' demanded Wilson. 'You remember that the Marquis of Salisbury made him Prime Minister, but he was only made Prime Minister because the lunatic fringe of the Tory Party – the Suez Group – thought he was one of them. He had been, of course. He was the leader of the Suez Group in the Cabinet and he was more than any other man responsible for that act of lunacy, but when the invasion began he got cold feet. As his Suez record showed, it was first in, first out, but he still boasts that the Suez operation was right and honourable and still refuses our demand for an inquiry. The Government could not survive for one day after what would come out of an impartial inquiry.' Wilson bemoaned the fact that Macmillan had paid a 'lightning visit' to the Rangers v Celtic football match in Glasgow, shaking hands with the players, getting all the publicity and then leaving without bothering to see the match. 'That is him all over,' complained Wilson, 'anything for publicity but no follow-through. We had the same thing a month or two ago on his visit to Moscow – plenty of publicity around his white fur hat. We were told he had taken a wonderful new initiative for peace.' Wilson admitted that Labour would not possess the Tories' modern capacity for 'gimmicks' or the 'super-streamlined organization, their vast expenditure on public relations, or even their private industrial empire' in the next general election.[72]

Understandably he was preoccupied with what he considered to be the uneven contest impending between the 'penny-farthing' electoral machine of Labour's that he had made an effort to improve organizationally and the better-financed, more efficient Tory machine. In June 1959 he demanded an end to company contributions to parties, insisting that the Chancellor act immediately. 'Let me make it clear that if he fails to do so we shall put the matter beyond all doubt. Another step we shall take which will help to raise standards of public decency in both industry and politics is to introduce legislation requiring all political parties to do as Labour does and publish their accounts in detail.'[73]

Harold Wilson earned the title of 'the Danny Kaye of the Commons' from Tory MP Geoffrey Stevens when he performed one of his most brilliant 'knockabout turns', as Stevens described it. The *Guardian* described Wilson's depiction of the Tories' 'Windfall State' as 'a brilliant sketch in the pre-election Impressionist school'. 'He flogged the takeover men – without, he had to confess, losing much sleep over the troubles of Old Etonian brewery owners.'[74]

## THE ELECTION CRUNCH

For Wilson and the rest of the Labour leaders these Parliamentary jousts were merely skirmishes preparatory to the general election contest, which took place in October 1959. The critiques of Tory Budgets and presentations of alternative approaches to the economy were first drafts of the 1959 election manifesto. For Wilson the build-up was particularly serious. His weekly meetings with Dr Balogh were not to provide gags for his 'knockabout turns' in the Commons but to prepare him to take over the Treasury. He had hoped to gain the post of Chancellor in 1950, when Gaitskell succeeded Cripps. Now he hoped to get the post from Gaitskell's hands. He had outlined his approach in a number of speeches in previous months; he wanted 'a steady and high rate of investment' in industry with employers helping to achieve 'more stable prices by accepting lower profit margins'.

Wilson also felt he had made his contribution to improving the efficiency of the Labour machine by his 1956 'penny farthing' report. The party machine had improved 'beyond recognition', he insisted at a Birmingham press conference on the eve of the campaign. He was sure Labour had enough supporters in marginal constituencies to turn the tables.

During the campaign he hardly spent any time in his own constituency, which had ceased to be marginal with the addition of a further 17,335 voters after the 1955 election, mostly in Kirkby from Liverpool's overspill. His reputation was solid as a friend of Catholic schools and as the creator of the Huyton Industrial Estate when he was President of the Board of Trade, with factories lined up on Wilson Road (named after him).

Wilson himself made a party political broadcast on 25 September which emphasized Labour's campaign for inquiries into takeover bids. The most important aspect of that programme lay in the answers he gave to Woodrow Wyatt. Wilson said, as agreed beforehand by Labour's campaign committee, that Labour's plans for making Britain a better place were going to be paid for not out of increased taxation but out of increased production. 'We are going to resume the steady increase of industrial production that we had in the years before the war. That of itself will provide over £3 or £4,000 million more of real resources. Over the period of the Labour Government it will bring more revenue into the Exchequer automatically without increasing taxation, and that will more than pay for all the commitments that we have entered into.' He also insisted on the need to get rid of purchase tax on many household essentials. Macmillan accused Wilson and Gaitskell of 'perpetuating the biggest Budget leak in all history'. R. A. Butler described their tactics as 'a bribe a day keeps the Tories away'. Wilson spoke in northwestern marginal seats like Nelson and Colne and Stockport, attacking the Tories for 'years of standing aside, watching the industry bleed to death' and now 'playing out the last act of the cotton tragedy'. In his election address to his own Huyton constituency he said: 'I do not believe the problems of this confused and disordered world can be solved by outmoded notions of gunboat diplomacy and imperialism. In place of the philosophies that gave us Suez, Cyprus, the Hola massacres and the tragedy of Nyasaland, a Labour Government will bring to the conduct of world affairs an approach based on partnership, tolerance and a genuine belief in the brotherhood and dignity of man, irrespective of class, colour or creed.'[75] He wrote articles on Labour's plans to reshape the economy which were syndicated to various newspapers.

The disappointment of Labour leaders when they lost by 100 seats at the final count after appearing to have been in the lead halfway through the campaign was boundless. 'Looking back, this defeat was unavoidable,' wrote Roy Jenkins later. 'No radical leader could have carried the country in its 1959 mood. . . But the inevitability was not so obvious at the time. The whole Labour Party began to cast about for the causes of the setback.'[76] Jenkins admits that Gaitskell 'was subsequently critical of himself for one major mistake' – the pledge, midway through the campaign, that Labour would not increase taxes to pay for its expanded programme; this, it was mainly believed, lost Labour much of its credibility among marginal voters.

## WILSON AS A SCAPEGOAT
At the time Jenkins and other moderates around Gaitskell sought scapegoats to the Left of Gaitskell, beginning with Wilson. The strategy

and tactics were devised at Gaitskell's home in Frognal Gardens, Hampstead, on Sunday, 11 October 1959, three days after the electoral defeat and a day after Gaitskell had secured Bevan's agreement to stand for the Deputy Leadership in succession to Jim Griffiths. Having the ageing and ill Bevan as Deputy Leader was important for Gaitskell and those who gathered at his Hampstead home, because it deprived the Left of a human totem around which to rally against the 'revisionism' of the Gaitskellites.

At the strategy meeting at Gaitskell's home his supporters – Roy Jenkins, Douglas Jay, Woodrow Wyatt, Patrick Gordon Walker and Anthony Crosland – discussed a wholesale transformation of the Labour Party. They decided that the election had been lost because Labour seemed too much a working-class party devoted to socialism. This conclusion was reached despite the fact that the 1959 Manifesto, *Britain Belongs to You*, was very moderate, pledging only the renationalization of the steel industry and road haulage and municipal ownership of privately-rented property.

Although there were many disagreements among the Gaitskellites gathered at their leader's home, the basic decision was made to refashion the Labour Party as a British version of the US Democratic Party, to be led almost wholly by committed supporters of Gaitskell, with the exception of the left-wing totem figure of Aneurin Bevan. All mention of the party's commitment to public ownership would be expunged, including Clause IV in its constitution – until then only known to card-carrying members of the party. Douglas Jay even wanted the party's name to be changed, to avoid resistance from potential voters who might consider themselves as having risen above the working class.

Wilson, like others outside the Gaitskell cabal, learned about the Frognal Gardens meeting piecemeal as various participants voiced their version of the Gaitskellites' new consensus. His irritation with their analysis turned into fury when he discovered that they not only wanted to reshape the Labour Party but also to dump him as its economic spokesman in the Commons. It soon became clear that the main charge against him would be that he had voiced the pledge not to increase income tax. 'Let them bring it out into the open,' Wilson told one confidant; 'we'll soon see who supported and who opposed the stupid pledge!'

Wilson's indignation became public in his speech to the Cambridge University Labour Club on 23 October, a dozen days after the Frognal Gardens conclave. 'There is a lot of talk about the image of the Labour Party,' he said. 'I cannot think it would be improved if we were to win, and indeed deserve, a reputation for cynicism and opportunism by throwing over essential and fundamental parts of our creed for electoral purposes.'[77]

Wilson knew that the Gaitskellites were after his job because, after offering the Deputy Leadership to Aneurin Bevan on 13 October, Gaitskell stopped off at Crossman's Vincent Square home. Gaitskell asked Crossman to suggest to Wilson that he 'stand down' as Shadow Chancellor and 'give someone else a chance'. The bait held out to Crossman was that he might become top man in Transport House. Gaitskell felt that Wilson had given Labour too Left an image by his activities on the Bank Rate tribunal in particular.

This infuriated Wilson as soon as Crossman informed him. He stormed into Gaitskell's room in the House of Commons to challenge him: 'If you want to put this up to the Parliamentary Labour Party – as to whether I should lead on economics or Douglas Jay – I'm willing to abide by the vote!' Gaitskell declined the challenge because he knew that the Left and the trade unionists would vote solidly against Jay, who had by this time come out in favour of dropping the word 'Labour' from the party's name. Wilson's strength in the PLP was demonstrated in the subsequent voting when he came out top man, having come second the previous year.

Wilson's political strength in the Parliamentary Labour Party was again demonstrated on 10 December when the Economic Group met to elect officers for the new session. Wilson, as spokesman, was re-elected Chairman unopposed. But, although Gaitskellites Douglas Jay and Roy Jenkins tried to become Joint Vice-Chairmen, they secured less than forty votes. The victors were: Alfred Robens, Fred Lee and Douglas Houghton with forty-nine, forty-eight and forty-five votes respectively. Douglas Jay's defeat was noteworthy because he had been Vice-Chairman the previous year before he proposed dropping the word 'Labour' from the name of the party.

Wilson then went on to the offensive. In the discussion within the Shadow Cabinet he opposed Gaitskell, who wanted to maintain discipline through Standing Orders. Wilson, strongly supported by the new Deputy Leader, Aneurin Bevan, crusaded for the suspension of Standing Orders, which had been imposed in the bad days of 1952. When Gaitskell refused initially to have the subject discussed Wilson threatened to have him voted out of the chair of the Shadow Cabinet, knowing he had seven of the twelve votes present on his side. Gaitskell finally agreed to discuss the subject. Standing Orders were suspended and replaced by a code of conduct.

As the Gaitskellites moved Right and against nationalization, Wilson moved Left. 'If we lost votes,' he told a home-town audience, 'it was partly because our policy was misrepresented and because it was the subject of an expensive advertising campaign, but mainly because we ourselves failed to speak of the successes of nationalization. I hope that we are not going to be defeatist about the records of publicly-owned industry. If we had not nationalized coal in 1947, this country would have been on its knees by this time as an industrial power.'[78]

Warfare between Wilson and Gaitskell carried over to Blackpool at the end of November, where a foreshortened annual conference was held, having been delayed by the election. Wilson did not hide his glee at the tactical clumsiness with which Gaitskell allowed his rather inept right-wing speech to be sandwiched between the more skilful left-wing speeches of Barbara Castle and Aneurin Bevan. Afterwards Bevan told Wilson that he had avoided putting the boot in so far as Gaitskell was concerned because he thought he had time to smother him.

'After Gaitskell's speech, Bevan told me that Gaitskell would have to go and that either he or I would be Leader, probably me,' Wilson later told a confidant. Bevan had decided before the election that if Labour lost it would be necessary to get rid of Gaitskell, whom he considered a 'Jonah' so far as the Labour Party was concerned. Gaitskell's whole interest, Bevan felt, was in making capitalism work more efficiently and humanely. Bevan realized that getting rid of capitalism would not be easy because of the predominantly right-wing character of the Parliamentary Labour Party. He also knew that his own challenge to Gaitskell was hindered by the fact that he was ageing and ailing. This was why he turned to Wilson as a possible executor of his determination. Gaitskell became aware of Wilson's renewed determination to oppose him. 'That man will only become Leader of the Labour Party over my dead body,' he told Gaitskellites, with great prescience.[79]

The battle between the two sides of the party, the Gaitskellites and the anti-Gaitskellites, widened. Harold Wilson appeared with Woodrow Wyatt – who had urged a Labour–Liberal electoral pact – on the same TV show to discuss it. 'This was one of the rare occasions on which I had spoken to him for many years,' Wyatt later recalled. 'He informed me that it was only because the Labour Party was so tolerant that it had not expelled me for making this dreadful idea public.'[80]

Wilson's fury with Gaitskell threatened to get him into trouble. At Blackpool he had told Cousins that Gaitskell had not informed the National Executive in advance that he intended to cut from the party constitution Clause IV declaring the party's aim to be socialism defined as public ownership of the means of production, distribution and exchange. 'Hugh has passed the point of no return,' Wilson had chortled. Unfortunately for him, the *Daily Mail* got hold of part of the story. 'Mr Harold Wilson is leading a new anti-Gaitskell movement among ex-Bevanites and left-wing MPs. It creates the biggest split in the party for years.'[81] It mentioned 'secret talks' and that he had recruited Dick Crossman for his anti-Gaitskell intrigue. Next day

Wilson took the unusual course of making a personal statement to the Parliamentary Labour Party when it met in private. He attacked the *Daily Mail* report: 'I have held no secret meetings either in London or in Blackpool.... Since my views and opinions have been challenged, let me again stress ... my view that the [Blackpool] conference showed its overriding desire, demand even, that all of us must do everything in our power to maintain the unity of the party in the difficult days that lie ahead. Reference has been made in the article to my recruiting my friend and NEC colleague Dick Crossman as an ally in these alleged operations. No doubt the *Daily Mail* correspondent observed that I went off the platform with him during Sunday morning's session for the five minutes necessary to discuss the new situation which had arisen about the election of the Chairman and Vice-Chairman.'[82] Ian Mikardo's defeat meant they had to decide who would be Vice-Chairman. They decided on Crossman.

To make himself more available and less vulnerable Wilson surprised many by announcing his intention to drop his Montague Meyer consultancy and to take on the onerous task of Chairman of the Public Accounts Committee. This post was usually held by an 'elder states-man', not a Front Bench occupant. 'I can recall no precedent for the work being done by a Shadow Chancellor,' wrote 'Peterborough' in the *Daily Telegraph*. 'One compensation will fall to him which in the present state of House of Commons accommodation is not to be sniffed at. The Chairman of the Public Accounts Committee gets a room of his own.'[83]

This accommodation enabled Wilson to move Marcia Williams out of Montague Meyer into the Commons and made him less vulnerable on two scores. First, his public renunciation of a full-time consultancy diminished his vulnerability to gossip paragraphs. 'His earnings as economic adviser to the Montague L. Meyer timber firm are enough to make him independent,' had conceded 'Cross-Bencher' in the *Sunday Express* ten days before. 'Just one little hardship has overtaken him. Last year he drove round in a car belonging to the Meyer concern. But before he hotted up his attacks on businessmen's perks there was a change. The car he now uses is registered in his own name.'[84]

At the annual meeting of Montague L. Meyer in November 1959 a shareholder had asked Deputy Chairman John M. Meyer why Wilson was employed. 'He is useful to the company in a general advisory capacity. He has a great deal of financial experience which is of great use to the company,' Meyer replied. It was made public at the end of December that Wilson was giving up the appointment to devote more time to research and writing.[85]

It might be thought a big sacrifice for a man to give up £2–3,000 a year in fees and expenses just to avoid the odd gossip paragraph and whispers on the Parliamentary grapevine, particularly now that his sons had entered fee-paying University College School and there were dependent relatives on both sides to help support on an inadequate Parliamentary salary. In fact his formal renunciation of the Montague L. Meyer contract was not quite so dramatic as it seemed. He continued to serve as a part-time adviser for Meyer, interceding for them with the Remploy organization. He also did work for Marchon, in which Frank (later Lord) Schon was the leading figure. And he helped boost the fortunes of Joseph ('Gannex') Kagan.

The second advantage of the new accommodation was that, by having Marcia Williams in the Commons throughout the day, Wilson managed to diminish the snide comments of colleagues who had either resented his relative inaccessibility or had been irritated by her control over his appointments. She did not entirely enjoy being isolated all on her own in the Upper Corridor, even if it was in a commodious, wood-panelled room superior to the cheek-by-jowl crowding suffered by other MPs' secretaries.

Curiously enough, the efforts of the Gaitskellites to oust Wilson as economic spokesman only served to consolidate his position as Labour's 'Third Man' in journalistic headlines, after Leader Gaitskell and Deputy Leader Bevan. 'IT'S THE THIRD MAN WHO NIPS IN TO WIN!' predicted Douglas Clark in the *Daily Express*. 'Will Mr Wilson be the next Leader of the Labour Party? On present indications there is every prospect that he will be. He has been known to murmur behind his hand: "I'm lying third on the rails – and nicely placed." ... Mr Wilson is accumulating influence and authority almost effortlessly.... He is in no particular hurry. He is young and can wait ... He must not try to run away with the party; he must let it come to him.'[86]

Wilson had tried to play the prescribed central role in his *Sunday Times* article on 'Labour After Blackpool' the day before. He had tried to play down the serious rift the Gaitskellite swing to the Right had precipitated. 'The difference with the Labour Party is that ... we have to prolong and intensify the agonies by arguing everything out in the full light of day, and parading our differences for the gratification of the Press and our opponents,' wrote Wilson after pointing out the Suez and Thorneycroft-resignation difficulties of the Tories in 1956–7 and 1958. 'I would say that the sooner we get over our introspective mood and lose our inferiority complex the more likely we are to produce a dynamic and challenging policy.'[87]

## ON GAITSKELL'S TRAIL
Just after Christmas, as New Year 1960 dawned, Wilson took off for an

18-day lecture tour of American universities in New York, Chicago, Minnesota and Regina, Canada. 'I shall be visiting some of the same places as Mr Gaitskell but not at the same time,' he said.[88] Just as well. Having tried hard to accommodate himself to Gaitskell for the three or four years prior to the October 1959 general election he was now at daggers drawn. It was just as well that Gaitskell did not accompany Wilson on his American trip, because Wilson used it to travel to Seattle with Marcia. Marcia's husband, Ed, had asked for a divorce because he wanted to marry a young woman he had met in Seattle. Marcia resisted this request. Both Marcia and Harold feared this would damage his political career. When they reached Seattle Ed Williams was flattered that so important a politician should have thought so highly of Marcia to plead her case. But their pleas fell on deaf ears. Ed Williams was insistent on being free to marry again. So they asked him to be as discreet as possible about the divorce proceedings when he proceeded with them later that year.

Wilson knew that the grave abdominal operation Aneurin Bevan had had at the end of December 1959 was for cancer and that he was not likely to live out 1960. Therefore, in the ghoulish world in which politicians calculate, he knew that a place would open up to the Left of the party's Centre in opposition to the Right-moving Hugh Gaitskell. He knew that he had the tacit support of the dying Aneurin Bevan. At a meeting of the *Tribune* Board just before he went into hospital, Bevan had told Michael Foot and others: 'We are living in the presence of a conspiracy.'[89] By this he meant the conspiracy of Gaitskell and others to transform the Labour Party into a social-democratic party without working-class influence or socialist targets. Lacking Bevan's working-class background or quasi-Marxist orientation, Wilson knew that Gaitskell was going against the whole spirit of the Labour movement. Moreover, he felt threatened personally. For Gaitskell and the Gaitskellites even his *verbal* attacks on the City were too radical.

Their attempted 'purge' was not directed against Wilson alone. Dick Crossman, who had made a major contribution to campaign publicity, was suddenly dropped as the highly-paid columnist on the *Daily Mirror*, which became increasingly Gaitskellite after the election. Although neither a fullblown Leftist or a Marxist, Crossman was a danger to Gaitskell and a support to Wilson in the battles opening up on the National Executive. Crossman was the first to understand that the Gaitskellites were trying to jettison socialism in favour of social reform and to offer Labour as a businesslike rather than a radical alternative to the Tories. So long as Britain's society remained relatively affluent, he felt, the electorate would prefer capitalists to run a successful capitalist system. Therefore Labour's function was to work on the understanding that capitalism could not cure its own basic ills and should prepare for the deep-rooted changes which would be needed. His ideas, set out in a pamphlet, 'Labour in the Affluent Society', published in June 1960, had been discussed with Wilson in frequent strategy meetings at Crossman's house.

The attempted Gaitskellite 'purge' of the Left and Centre-Left and the effort to dilute Labour's mild socialism with Gaitskellite 're-visionism' made Wilson join up with a group of factional fighters willing to push him. His links with Crossman and Balogh were strengthened, and the intelligence provided by Peter Shore, head of Transport House's Research Department, became more useful.

Although the battle took an ideological form – about the type of economy, society and defensive alliances Britain should have – the position Wilson adopted relied little on ideology. He became anti-Gaitskellite partly because – as a tactical 'pro' – he despised their tactics. He was shrewd enough to realize that, however hurtful it was to him personally to be unwanted by the Gaitskellites, they were hurting themselves more. Since getting rid of him was part of their swing to the right they were rejecting a whole portion of the Labour and radical tradition in British politics. But the real strength of his anti-Gaitskellism came less from an ideological gulf than from personal-social antagonism. Gaitskell and most of his friends were either Southern middle-class or, like Roy Jenkins, aspiring to the middle class. They made it clear that they considered Wilson a slippery Northern lower-middle-class type who was 'too big for his boots'. Some, like Wyatt, had not talked to Wilson for years. Not only did they not like him but they were now pushing to deprive him of his post as economic spokesman. Under these circumstances the fact that Dick Crossman, Tommy Balogh, Peter Shore and Marcia Williams rallied loyally to his defence and to the repelling of the Gaitskellite 'boarders' was important to him.

The strength of his position became apparent when Parliament reconvened after the Christmas recess. Bevan was away on his final illness. 'Cross-Bencher' in the *Sunday Express* mischievously pointed out that Gaitskell was not appointing an acting Deputy Leader in Bevan's absence because, on 'seniority, the third man in the hierarchy, Mr Harold Wilson, might have been expected to step up. Easy to see, though, how disquieting that would be for the Labour Leader. He knows that, when the final clash comes on his anti-nationalization policy, the only man who could possibly challenge him for the Leadership would be Mr Wilson. Why then give his rival such a splendid chance to enlarge his prestige.'[90]

In order to make himself less vulnerable Wilson emphasized the battle *for* unity in the Labour movement and the fight *against* the Tories in Parliament. This made it appear that his Gaitskellite critics were, in effect, playing the Tory game. 'I have taken the line up to now,' he told the Parliamentary Press Gallery on 10 February 1960, 'that though I have pretty strong views on this question [of altering the all-out-nationalization clause in Labour's constitution], I should reserve the expression of those views to the National Executive, where it is essential for us to work for the maintenance of party unity and the reconciliation of differences. I should like to have continued in that way, despite the jibes about my silence, accusations about sitting on the fence until I see which way the cat jumps, and other mixed metaphors.'

Wilson pointed out, very shrewdly, that it was not the unknown Clause Four that had lost Labour the election but the moderate plan to invest in private companies: 'It was this proposal, not Clause Four, which launched a thousand loudspeaker vans and sent them to works gates saying: "The socialists will nationalize this firm, you'll be out of a job, and what about your HP commitments then?" It is worth pointing out that we have had Clause Four in every election, win or lose. We are told this is the first time we've lost heavily because of our association with nationalization, yet our election manifesto – for the first time – used the phrase, "we have no further plans for nationalization."'

'In my view,' he emphasized, 'we must settle the argument on policy first, and then, and only then, decide what, if any, additions are necessary to Clause Four. Let us unite on policy, not divide on theology.' And then he could not resist a side-swipe at Gaitskell, who had asked at the November 1959 Blackpool conference whether socialists had to nationalize 'every shop'. 'I have not met anyone who even in the long term, a century from now, intends to nationalize every shop and garage. They are not doing that even in China.'[91] In fact, they began doing it fairly soon in China.

## CAMPAIGN FOR TREASURER

By then Wilson had worked out his strategy: he would pick up the job which Bevan was already destined to drop, even if he did recover. 'Mr Wilson knows precisely what he wants,' confidently reported 'Cross-Bencher' in the *Sunday Express*, to which Wilson contributed quite regularly, 'the job of Treasurer. The present Treasurer, Mr Aneurin Bevan, after his promotion to Deputy Leader [in November 1959], must surrender the job in October [1960] whether he is completely fit or not. And, apart from Mr Wilson, only one other candidate is in sight, Mr George Brown.'

'Why is he not trying to oust the man who has staked his future on amending ... Clause [Four], Mr Gaitskell himself? The answer is that shrewd political instinct runs deep in Mr Wilson.... For Mr Wilson's instinct has given him this warning: That, though lots of people like Mr Wilson's policies, few of them consistently like Mr Wilson . . . and would be prepared to make him Leader only if circumstances absolutely forced them.'[92]

Wilson's attack continued on two fronts. In the Commons he attacked Conservatives with at least verbal radicalism. On 24 February he criticized them for giving money to private firms without insisting on a Government Director. After Prime Minister Harold Macmillan had been elected Chancellor of Oxford, Wilson welcomed him back with a Latin translation of the alleged Macmillan slogan: 'You never had it so good.' Cracked the *Guardian*: 'Only he knows how to be generous and churlish in the same breath.'

He waged discreet war against the Gaitskellites in a style which, he hoped, would guarantee him the support of the Centre and Left as well as many traditional trade unionists. At Hendon on 21 February he attacked 'faint-hearted colleagues flushed with defeat'. But he was rebuffed on 29 February when he tried to get the NEC to abandon its Gaitskell-sponsored review of Clause Four. Nothing daunted, he tried to demonstrate how clever he was at improving the efficiency of nationalized corporations. He put forward a plan in the *New Statesman* for the Government to take responsibility for railway lines, just as it did for roads, charging British Rail an operating rent. This would remove a burden from BR while enabling the State to exploit the valuable sites of railway terminals in big cities.[93]

Gaitskell suddenly and belatedly got clever, in an almost Wilsonian way. Beginning in mid-February he called for the retention of Clause Four so long as a new declaration of aims was placed alongside it. At the 13 March meeting of the NEC a 12-point draft submitted by Gaitskell was adopted with the opposition of only the T & GWU representative, Harry Nicholas. The draft said that there should be common ownership of 'the commanding heights of the economy'. This phrase was a Wilsonian metaphor designed to satisfy the Left without committing the Right. Taking 'the commanding heights', he immediately explained, did not involve 'a sweeping programme of expropriation and nationalization of industry'. The draft also affirmed that 'both public and private enterprise have a place in the economy' and that any 'further extension of common ownership should be decided from time to time' in line with Labour's objectives.[94] It was a compromise from which all factions could claim victory, from *Tribune* to the Gaitskellite *Forward*. What Gaitskell could have had from the outset without a divisive fight he achieved only after dividing the party and alienating Centre-Left elements like Crossman and Wilson. Wilson thought Gaitskell's bridge-building had come too late. When

Labour lost marginal Brighouse and Spenborough he thought it a black eye for Gaitskell. 'He believes that the slump in the party's poll is a vote of censure on Mr Gaitskell's leadership,' wrote 'Cross-Bencher', who dined regularly with Wilson. 'Surely, he argues, the rank and file must eventually insist that this Jonah should be heaved overboard.'[95]

Whatever Wilson told intimates in private, his public performances continued to be rollicking, if predictable, fun. On Budget Day he congratulated Chancellor Heathcoat Amory for belatedly taking up suggestions he had long before made. 'You could not see the Tory faces behind you when you were speaking yesterday,' he told the Tory Chancellor. 'They looked rather like a collection of St Bernards who had lost their brandy.' 'For Mr Wilson, the Budget debate has become an annual display of wit,' snapped the *Daily Telegraph*. 'This may delight his supporters. But it is not politics.'[96] It may not have been Tory politics, but it *was* Labour politics.

Wilson was deploying his parliamentary skills to fight off the growing challenge of George Brown for the post of Treasurer, soon to be released from the dying hand of Aneurin Bevan. 'We should all be watching Mr Brown with more than usual attention these days,' the *Observer* had warned in mid-March. 'He has been playing his cards with great skill ... Extravagant and even Arabian fantasies may be passing through his mind: for instance, he might become Deputy Leader if Mr Bevan no longer wants it.'[97]

Underestimating the Brown challenge initially, Wilson was, within a month, trying to avoid a showdown he feared he would lose. He supported the idea that both he and Brown should step down for the previous Deputy Leader, Jim Griffiths, much as Bevan had once tried to avoid defeat by Gaitskell. 'As nomination [for the post of Treasurer] has not yet been asked for, it is clearly not the time for anyone to talk about making arrangements with another person to stand down,' snorted Brown disdainfully.[98]

Although Wilson was a clever calculator, he was also being calculated against. Thus Gaitskell named him to wind up the 27 April debate on the abandonment of the 'Blue Streak' missile, although Wilson was the economic and not the defence spokesman. Gaitskell's intention was to compromise Wilson and appease the Left. Wilson was his usual witty-disparaging self. 'Today [the Defence] Minister says that Skybolt [the air-to-ground] missile is the thing. Every new Minister comes along with a goose and says it is a swan. And in the end it is a dead duck.'[99]

This sort of sophisticated humour went down well with some in the Commons, but it was more difficult for Wilson to 'sell' it to the earnest and single-minded 'Ban the Bomb' nuclear disarmers. This was brought home to him when he made a 35-minute speech at the end of the May Day parade in London. Several times he was unable to make himself heard above hecklers. 'You cannot talk about the brotherhood of man in a world dominated by the nuclear arms race,' he said to cheers. He added that Summit talks should not take place in a world dominated by the world suicide club, 'where one false step, one unidentifiable mark on the Fylingdales [radar] screen could plunge the world into nuclear destruction.' Cries came from the crowd: 'Who first made it?' but Wilson went on: 'We shall also bitterly oppose any proposals to bring Western Germany in as nuclear partners making strategic missiles. Our suspicions and anxieties were in no way alleviated by German overtures [made by Dr Adenauer] to Franco Spain.' When he attacked the Tory ex-Defence Secretary, Duncan Sandys, as a 'highly expensive and discredited Minister', shouts mounted: 'What about the Bomb?' Finally he was driven to retort: 'We did more in the House of Commons last week [in attacking the Conservative defence policy] than all of you with all your shouting ever will!'[100]

Wilson's plans to fight for the Treasurership were suddenly destroyed by another nuclear disarmer, Frank Cousins, the General Secretary of the Transport union. Cousins had his own candidate for the party Treasurership in his lieutenant, Harry Nicholas. Moreover, he had assured his success through the normal deals with right-wing trade-union leaders to help one of their nominees get on the NEC. Wilson did not want to fight Cousins's man, although he would have had to fight George Brown.

Wilson was particularly desirous of becoming Deputy Leader should Bevan be unable to return to active duty. But, he thought, this did not seem a decision he would have to make until the autumn of 1960. He wanted to become Deputy Leader on the assumption that this would make him heir presumptive to Gaitskell, ten years his senior. 'If a successor has to be sought for Mr Gaitskell,' thought the political correspondent of the *Daily Telegraph*, Harry Boyne, 'the party will look a good deal nearer the throne. Mr Wilson, who has been seizing every opportunity offered by parliamentary routine to don Mr Bevan's mantle, stands out as the most prominent candidate. The party admires and revels in his nimble wit: the combination of "cheekie chappie" and economic pundit can be most endearing. Unfortunately for Wilson, wit and brilliance are not enough. The party does not yet quite trust him. It fancies it can see the outline of a dagger up his sleeve.'[101]

Despite these doubts about his reliability Wilson felt he could depend on the political ineptitude of Gaitskell. Thus, in the meeting between Labour Party and trade-union leaders on 1 June 1960 to decide on a new defence policy in the wake of Britain's forced abandonment of 'Skybolt', Gaitskell seemed to go out of his way to bait Frank Cousins, who leaned towards nuclear pacifism. When Gaitskell got on his high horse and told Frank Cousins that *he* was the Leader of the Labour Party and that he was not prepared to be dictated to by anyone, the meeting almost broke up in disorder.

But Wilson too had his failings. 'The worst thing about the future,' a left-wing Labour MP told me at this time, 'is that the most likely successor to Gaitskell, Harold Wilson, has many of the same vices as Gaitskell. He is just as solitary, taking advice only from his secretary [Marcia Williams], not realizing that his "image" is created not only by his speeches in the House or in the Parliamentary Party meetings but also in informal meetings with his colleagues. But he never stops to chat with the boys at the bar, or in the Tea Room. Nor does he keep contact with his colleagues in the Shadow Cabinet.'

Without consulting his colleagues, except for Crossman, Wilson managed to get up to some quite clever tricks. Thus, in the debate on the NEC on 22 June 1960, a resolution pledging loyalty to Hugh Gaitskell was proposed, largely to put the Centre–Left and Left on the spot. Wilson appended to it a reaffirmation of belief in majority decisions – anticipating the possibility that the forthcoming Scarborough conference would support unilateral nuclear disarmament. Gaitskell, seeing the trap, opposed Wilson's amendment, saying that the Parliamentary Labour Party had to pursue its own course regardless of Conference decisions.

## THE DEATH OF NYE

Then, on 6 July 1960, Aneurin Bevan died in his sleep at his Ashridge Farm after a half-year's absence battling against cancer. His death removed from the Left a giant who could irritate his friends but always arouse their admiration by his powerful oratory, deep insights and remorseless pursuit of what he saw as essential truths. Wilson and Bevan had been allies but never close friends. Bevan had a quasi-Marxist background which led him to look at the world in big, theoretical terms rather than to operate by the clever-clever political tactics which seemed to obsess Wilson. When Bevan had been told that Wilson's son Robin was to become a mathematician he had made the famous remark: 'Just like his father, all bloody facts and no bloody vision!' From the grave Bevan might have applied to Wilson the tag of 'desiccated calculating machine' had he been able to know that on 7 July 1960, the day after Bevan's death, Wilson informed the National Union of Mineworkers that he would not stand for the Treasurership and would support Harry Nicholas for the post. This cleared the way for his fight to succeed Bevan as Deputy Leader.

With Bevan's death Wilson could see himself as the standard-bearer of the Left, failing anyone else to the Left of Centre having his credentials and seniority. That is why his identification with Labour's annual conference intensified as the fateful Scarborough meeting approached. Gaitskell's strength was in the Parliamentary Labour Party, which was two-thirds Right of Centre. Labour activists were much stronger among constituency delegates, which explained why most of the seven constituency delegates elected to the NEC were Left of Centre. Now the domination of the annual conference by right-wing trade-union leaders manipulating their block votes was breaking up. The first break had come when Frank Cousins took control of the Transport and General Workers Union in 1956 and gradually shifted Britain's biggest union from the Right towards the Left.

This shift was a key factor in the argument raging over whether Labour should withdraw Britain from the nuclear arms race as an independent Power. The nuclear pacifists had been clobbered by huge majorities previously – by 5,611,000 to 890,000 in 1958. In his general support for NATO and the American defensive shield which protected Britain, Wilson did not differ basically from Gaitskell, although he did not wholly share Gaitskell's adoration of the United States. What he objected to about Gaitskell's handling of the defence issue was that Gaitskell was so much more sensitive to Establishment thinking – including the US Defence Establishment in the Pentagon – than he was to the peaceful desires of Labour activists. 'I supported Gaitskell's policy right through to 1960,' Wilson later told a confidant. 'I had to oppose him because of his attitude towards the party.'

The difference between the two men was quite simple. Gaitskell tended to decide what the best defensive system was for Britain after consulting rather orthodox Establishment sources. He then expected to be able to persuade the Labour Party to accept his firmly-held conclusions. Wilson tended to estimate the balance of thinking within the Labour Party and then decide how best to sell them a realistic defence policy, or one that they would swallow.

It was easier for Wilson to work with George Brown, whose flexibility was helped by the leftward drift of his own union, the T&GWU. The cancellation of the 'Blue Streak' missile by the Macmillan Government in early 1960 created a new situation, as unanimously recognized by the Shadow Cabinet. 'The argument for maintaining the independent British deterrent for political reasons is one thing when you have it,' Brown told the Commons in the Defence debate of 27 April 1960. 'The argument for going back into the business when you are out of it is an entirely different thing . . . Even I cannot be expected to go on supporting a policy which has no chance of ever existing.' Wilson agreed: 'What we have seen today ... is the end of the independent nuclear deterrent.'[102] When Gaitskell returned to the country he seemed to be reproaching Wilson in particular. 'Nothing said by Labour's official spokesmen could possibly mean they wanted Britain to disarm unilaterally, give up NATO and become neutralist. They did not say we should give up our existing nuclear weapons. They were concerned solely with the future – what our position would be in five years' time.'[103]

In the run-up to the Scarborough conference, Wilson later claimed, he addressed more constituency parties in defence of the agreed NEC policy on defence than anyone except Gaitskell. 'I felt, however, that we should stress more positively the two salient points in our policy: on the one hand our loyal membership of NATO, and on the other our decision that, while the West must have modern weapons as long as Russia had, Britain's role in the alliance should – once Blue Streak had failed – be a non-nuclear one. If we had stressed these points, and concentrated more of our guns on the Conservatives – after all it was their policy which had broken down – we would have remained united, we would have carried Conference with us, and we would have had a viable and effective defence policy.'[104]

Wilson continued to show assurance in battling against the Tories in the Commons. When the Chancellor again raised Bank Rate in July Wilson led off with a slashing attack on this 'tired and discredited witch-doctor' who had once again given his ritual incantation. But he was full of hesitations and calculations as to how actively to fight the Gaitskellites at the looming Scarborough confrontation. At least one Gaitskell lieutenant, Woodrow Wyatt, was so anti-Wilson that he proposed that there should be no election for Deputy Leader but that Gaitskell should appoint his Deputy. 'That is the only way to see the Leader gets as his chief assistant a man he can trust and on whose judgment he can rely. In other words, somebody who will be working in harmony with the Leader and not jockeying for position and moulding his speeches to get maximum support at an annual election.' It was not only Wilson's opponents in the Labour Party who had these hesitations. Barbara Castle, who was to the Left of Wilson and was very anxious that he fight for the Deputy Leadership to defeat right-winger George Brown, expressed doubts to colleagues about his contrived calculations.

Wilson and Crossman thought it necessary to manoeuvre to try to isolate the Gaitskellites so that, if there were a split after the Scarborough Conference, it would be the Gaitskellites splitting off, if possible, leaving the Centre and Left in control. They saw the impor-tance of this strategy increased when the strength of the unilateralist feeling showed up at the TUC's annual conference a month before the

Scarborough conference of Labour. At the subsequent NEC meeting on 21 September, Crossman submitted a Wilson-supported 900-word resolution urging the NEC to take note of the *wording* of the Transport workers' resolution and not to consider it hostile to Labour's policy. But Gaitskell rejected it out of hand, and his friends in the press, the *Daily Mirror* and *Daily Herald*, began a strenuous anti-Cousins campaign.

Wilson allayed any remaining doubts with his speech at the traditional Sunday night pre-Conference rally. His whole speech – especially his homily on the need for Leaders to obey conference decisions – was a gauntlet thrown down to Gaitskell. During the conference he tried to sound as radical as possible without committing himself overmuch. 'There is, in my view, an unanswerable case for the public ownership or nationalization of the defence industries,' he said bravely. 'If you do not do that there is no way of protecting you as taxpayers from hundreds of millions more going down the drain.'

Wilson changed his style somewhat when he spoke to Conference on Tuesday morning, replying to the debate on 'Labour in the Sixties', a document prepared by Morgan Phillips, the party's former General Secretary, who was ill. Wilson was in good heart because he had just been re-elected to the NEC in third place after Barbara Castle and Anthony Greenwood but ahead of Tom Driberg, Dick Crossman, James Callaghan (the only non-left-winger) and Ian Mikardo. The debate had gone quite well. Even the introductory speaker, right-winger Ray Gunter, had emphasized that 'never in history have socialist principles been more relevant than they are in the '60s' and 'I did not join this party to become a left-wing Liberal.'[105] People in Gaitskell's immediate entourage had seemed divisive. Woodrow Wyatt had described the meeting as 'the most depressing Conference we have ever been at' and attacked 'silly talk among people who should know better about getting rid' of Gaitskell 'as though we were a primitive tribe and the ritual sacrifice of our Leader would somehow make the harvest come'.[106] Anthony Crosland had criticized the NEC for 'rejecting every single proposal for modernizing the party' and complained that it gave the country 'increasingly the impression of disliking the larger public corporation, but not offering anything in its place. . . . Almost everybody here would agree that nationalization is not the same as socialism.' He had been answered by a Liverpool shop steward named Eric Heffer who said that Crosland's proposals, as spelled out in *Encounter*, would make Labour as little socialist as the German Social Democratic Party. 'If he wants to leave and join the Liberals that is his affair . . .'[107]

Wilson began by identifying himself with tributes to the ailing Morgan Phillips and, as usual, defended himself by attacking the press. 'Five years ago at the time of the so-called "Wilson Report", the press, in their usual manner, had a lot of headlines about rows between Morgan and me. Morgan and I worked closely and harmoniously in the whole of the organization work of the party,' he said with understandable exaggeration. He left out any explanation of why his Committee had neither requested information from, nor shown an advance copy of the 'Wilson Report' to the then General Secretary. The burden of his reply emphasized two points. First, the Tories favoured the affluent in the 'Affluent Society': 'The Chancellor of the Exchequer can knock £5 million off the tax on port but cannot find an equal amount for removing individual prescription charges for old-age pensioners and the chronic sick.' But the main burden of his speech was a try-out for his 1963 speech on the scientific revolution. 'It is a terrible reflection on us that in 1945 four out of five scientists voted Labour, whereas I do not think last October one out of five voted Labour.... Our problem first is more scientists, better scientific education and facilities ... Our problem too is better deployment of scientists: not only are too many highly qualified scientists and technologists employed on defence ... we have far too many in this mass advertising society who are wasting their time trying to produce new gimmicks or meaningless additives to give advertising barkers something to shout about.... Let us use the National Research and Development Corporation, the invention of Stafford Cripps, which I had the honour of piloting through the House. Perhaps it is not generally known that the computer industry of this country was founded on the Manchester University electronic brain developed under a contract from the NRDC.... This is our message for the '60s – a socialist-inspired scientific and technological revolution releasing energy on an enormous scale deployed not for the destruction of mankind but for enriching mankind beyond our wildest dreams.'[108]

Wilson's speech was outshone the next day by the powerful speech of Hugh Gaitskell as he promised to 'fight, fight and fight again' to return the Labour Party from its temporary and marginal move into unilateralism. It was a keen debate involving many major Labour figures: Sam Watson, Frank Cousins, Ian Mikardo, George Brown, Philip Noel-Baker, Michael Foot, Denis Healey and Hugh Gaitskell. When two union-backed unilateralist motions were carried there was a mighty cheer in the hall which represented the delight of some that not only had a blow for peace been struck but also a blow against the Establishment, including the Labour Establishment. After a decade of battle this was the first major occasion on which constituency activists, supported by Left-moving unions, had beaten the platform.

When the exciting vote was over Wilson seemed less than enthusiastic. When I asked him how he thought the Parliamentary Labour Party would now divide when it elected its Leader and Deputy Leader, he insisted that, in a rapidly changing situation, it would be both foolish and wrong to try to predict what the line-up and atmosphere would be. Perhaps he realized how little room the confrontation between the Gaitskellites and the unilateralists left for peace-seeking multilateral disarmers like himself.

Although it was years before the Gaitskellites forgave Wilson for challenging their hero for the Leadership in October 1960, in fact he had to be carried almost kicking and screaming into the fray. Wilson felt strongly that Gaitskell had been wrongly inflexible before Conference in refusing to concede that it was the basic policy-making body when Labour was out of office; instead of accepting that, for many, the vote for semi-unilateralism was a sentimental gesture for peace and a revulsion against 'the Bomb', Gaitskell had unnecessarily insisted on tagging all unilateralists as 'neutralists' wanting to opt out of NATO, when all they needed was a soothing form of words.

For Wilson, however, it was an enormous step from merely being critical of Gaitskell among his cronies to opposing Gaitskell for Leader – knowing the PLP was at least two-thirds Right of Centre and therefore heavily loaded towards Gaitskell. But everywhere Wilson went he came under pressure to stand against Gaitskell for Leader. At Transport House, Peter Shore, then head of the Research Department there, felt Gaitskell had lost the confidence of Labour activists which Wilson could regain. A deputation led by Jennie Lee, Bevan's widow, tried to persuade him to stand. Wilson said he would think about it, but he had actually decided not to fight Gaitskell but to fight for the Deputy Leadership instead.

What nobody except Marcia realized was that Wilson had an additional cloud hanging over his head. Marcia's husband, Ed, was on the point of beginning the suit for divorce in King County, Seattle, State of Washington. Marcia had been busy and upset with pleadings and the negotiations on property settlement. Knowing that virtually the whole of the press were backing Gaitskell against the unilateral disarmers, Harold and Marcia knew what use the divorce action would be put to by Fleet Street if they got wind of it when Wilson was daring to challenge the hero of the hour, Hugh Gaitskell.

It took a whole series of pressures, both personal and political, to persuade Wilson to fight Gaitskell. By his hesitations which lasted more than a fortnight he convinced fifteen to twenty Labour MPs, mainly in the Centre, that he lacked moral courage and combativeness. One of the events which helped persuade him was Gaitskell's attempt, at the Shadow Cabinet meeting of 19 October, to agree a resolution to be presented to the PLP on 26 October supporting multilateral against unilateral disarmament. Wilson, Crossman and Fred Lee opposed this on the grounds that it was prejudging the issue before the elections to the new Shadow Cabinet in a fortnight or so and before its talks with the TUC and the NEC. George Brown also opposed Gaitskell on the grounds that it was bad tactics, designed to embarrass multilateralist MPs in the eyes of their activist unilateralist constituents.

Wilson was also under other pressures. Anthony Greenwood, a soft leftwing Labour politician who had turned unilateralist, resigned from the Shadow Cabinet saying he refused to serve under Gaitskell so long as the latter continued to defy the decision of Labour's annual Conference. A day or two later he proclaimed that he would stand against Gaitskell in the Leadership election unless someone 'broader' in appeal – meaning Wilson – would stand.

Everywhere Wilson went he was badgered by those trying to inject backbone. At a dinner in Hampstead Garden Suburb given by professionals in the Labour Party he was urged again. 'No,' he replied, 'I wouldn't stand a chance. What I want is the Deputy Leadership. With Hugh as Leader and me as Deputy the party will steer an even course. He can never get away with this "fight, fight, fight again" nonsense, of course, and when I am No. 2 I'll see to it that he doesn't.' They argued until after midnight, with Mary Wilson among the seven who were unanimously against him. Wilson again insisted it would be suicidal to oppose Gaitskell. 'But, surely,' chipped in one guest, 'if you *don't* fight Gaitskell now everybody will believe that you support his policy through thick and thin and that wouldn't be at all good for you.' 'And,' chipped in another, 'if you leave the field clear for Tony Greenwood, *he* will emerge as the alternative Leader; but if you fight Gaitskell openly and fearlessly you will get not only a bigger vote than Greenwood could hope for, but *you* would be seen as the alternative Leader.'

Finally Wilson conceded. 'You know,' he said after a long pause, 'I think you're right. If anybody is to fight Hugh it should be me. I'll consider it very seriously – very seriously indeed. And I'm pretty sure now that I'll do it.' He then added with a frown: 'Of course, you know that this will cost me the Deputy Leadership.'[109] Next night Wilson underwent the same pressures at the Highgate flat of Barbara Castle and her husband Ted. Most of the guests were old friends from the Bevanite Group. To explain his hesitation, Wilson said that he had no really basic quarrel with Gaitskell over defence: it was mainly a difference of political approach. He underlined the irony that he had much less in common with the other guests on the subject of defence, since they were far less enthusiastic for NATO and far more enthusiastic for unilateralism than he. But, unlike the snooty Gaitskellites, they had always treated him well personally. About the same time Wilson was also the recipient of a furious telephone call from the *New Statesman* editor,

John Freeman, who had resigned with him from the Government in 1951.

Wilson then informed the Lobby (the political correspondents at Westminster) of his decision to fight Gaitskell. 'It is being said that if Hugh Gaitskell is returned unopposed as Leader of the party, this will be taken as a mandate from his Parliamentary colleagues to ignore the National Executive Committee, and to plunge the movement into still worse conflict. I cannot allow this approach to go unchallenged.'[110] Next day, 21 October, he announced at Blaenau Ffestiniog, in the slate-quarrying area of North Wales, that he would stand against Gaitskell on the issue of 'unity versus civil war' in the party. 'I believe it is essential, also, to restore confidence by stating categorically that we are against the British H-bomb, and not allow the suspicion to remain that we are only waiting for the development of some new American rocket to justify a proposal that Britain should once again become a nuclear Power.'[111]

On that weekend of 22–23 October 1960 there was a crucial meeting of Wilson's chief supporters and strategists, including Dick Crossman, George Wigg, Tony Greenwood, Walter Padley and Stephen Swingler. Over and over again the point was made that the showdown would come on 26 October when there would be a meeting of the NEC in the morning and of the Shadow Cabinet that same evening. It was decided that Gaitskell ought to be put 'on the spot' at the NEC by being asked whether he accepted the supremacy of Conference decisions for the NEC. Again, Wilson and his supporters on the NEC were warned at least ten times not to support or sign any multilateralist declaration before the election of a new Shadow Cabinet.

Both these warnings were ignored on the day. At the NEC Gaitskell was *not* put 'on the spot' by Crossman or Wilson. At the urging of Lena Jeger, in particular, a motion was voted calling for consultation between the Shadow Cabinet, the TUC and the NEC. Even worse, at the Shadow Cabinet both Wilson and Crossman fell into a Gaitskellite trap and supported a resolution committing them to the multilateralist approach. Wilson admitted he was outmanoeuvred. Crossman gave a long and involved explanation ending up with: 'Oh, well, it's a dying Committee anyway and I won't be on the new one!'

Wilson looked silly later that evening at the meeting of the PLP when Gaitskell announced, with heavy underscoring, that *every* MP on the Shadow Cabinet had supported the resolution. Gaitskell's cronies, who had obviously been in on the trap, grinned with satisfaction. Wilson's supporters, who had warned him repeatedly against precisely this sort of trick, looked at each other with dismay. Wilson's faltering explanation did not convince anyone that he was a man of real moral courage. Gaitskell's friends were sure he would defeat Wilson by 140 to seventy, and even Wilson's friends cut his maximum vote down from 110 to ninety.

The anti-Gaitskellites were even less inclined to be patient with Fred Lee, who had been chosen to contest the post of Deputy Leader. He had already irritated them with his ambivalent speech to the crucial delegation of the AEU – his own union – at Scarborough. Then he remained in Northern Ireland when he should have been canvassing for support, as George Brown and James Callaghan were doing very effectively. When he did start canvassing he tried to get the best of both worlds by not committing himself against Gaitskell and in favour of Wilson. In fact he only came out for Wilson after half-a-dozen left-wing Labour MPs had sent him telegrams saying that unless he did so they would canvass against him. Even when he did belatedly commit himself, a dozen or so Leftists said they would not support him.

Wilson, with the help of Crossman, made a comeback with an effective anti-Gaitskell attack in the normally inhospitable columns of the *Daily Herald*: 'Many who support [Gaitskell] say: "The party cannot be saved; the split is there; now let us hive off any who will not toe Mr Gaitskell's line." I reject this view ... Many of my colleagues feel that they are being stampeded into unilateralism. Many feel there is a fundamentalist difference which makes unity impossible. But the existence of the pacifist Left has not prevented unity in the past. ... I am not a unilateralist and never have been one. ...' He supported 'multilateral disarmament, collective security and membership of NATO. But any restatement of our defence policy must at the same time reflect the aspirations of the movement.'

This sure-fail contest was an ordeal for Wilson. 'The only time I couldn't sleep was when I opposed Hugh Gaitskell for the Leadership,' he later recalled. 'I didn't want to, but I felt I had to.'[112] 'It was the most difficult and upsetting decision I have ever had to take in my political life. In office or in Opposition I have never been one to lose sleep over any problem. When I was faced with this one I lay awake night after night.'[113] What daunted him was not the assurance that he would be defeated as the Left and Centre–Left candidate for the Leadership, with Fred Lee as their candidate for the Deputy Leadership. The composition of the Parliamentary Labour Party guaranteed that he would be defeated by at least two-to-one, although Gaitskellites like Jack (later Lord) Diamond thought the odds would be much longer. Wilson feared that Gaitskellite anger might cause him to lose his seat on the Shadow Cabinet and his post as Economic Spokesman, which Douglas Jay and Anthony Crosland had coveted the previous November.

Wilson had the backing of the two women most important in his life.

Mary Wilson was herself a unilateralist because of her detestation of nuclear weapons. This feeling led her to write a poem entitled 'After the Bomb Has Fallen', which described 'the last sad cry, when the earth was burnt-out cinder'.[114] Marcia Williams was also more militant than Wilson because she stood to the Left of his rather Centre position. But, as the Wilson–Gaitskell contest hotted up, some of Gaitskell's campaign managers began spreading stories about the closeness of Harold and Marcia. To counter this, Wilson's own campaign managers arranged for a well-publicized tea for the foursome in the Harcourt Room of the House of Commons where all MPs could see Harold and Mary Wilson having tea with Marcia Williams and her male companion, who was presumed to be her husband and was probably her brother Tony. In a few days' time, on 1 November to be precise, her husband was to sue her for divorce in Seattle.

Before the voting, due to be announced on 3 November, Wilson made a speech on the economic aspects of the Queen's Speech, in which the Government's plans for the new session are traditionally announced. 'The Tories gibe that we have two defence policies,' he said. 'But they haven't got one at all – and it has cost the country nearly £15,000 million to find it out.' When the vote was announced, Wilson was found to have chalked up eighty-one votes and Gaitskell 166. By securing almost a third of the votes Wilson had consolidated behind him the Left and Centre–Left.

Wilson was then plunged into a new crisis in the contest for the Shadow Cabinet. He had two problems. First, the right-wing majority had two-thirds of the votes. Since everyone had to vote for a slate of twelve candidates there was a good chance this two-thirds would give Wilson a black eye by refusing to vote for him, although he had come top of the poll the previous year.

The other problem was that when Tony Greenwood had stepped down to give him a free run against Gaitskell for the Leadership he had exacted from Wilson the promise that he would not contest the Shadow Cabinet elections but would stand aside from the Parliamentary leadership so long as it was in defiance of Conference decisions. Wilson found it impossible to stand by this promise. He felt the bottom of the world would drop out if he could not attack the Tories from the Front Bench as Labour's spokesman. Therefore he begged Greenwood to release him from his promise. Greenwood reluctantly gave in.

On 8 November Wilson held a meeting with those who had supported him and Lee in the contest against the Gaitskellites. The 'hard' anti-Gaitskellites warned Wilson and Lee that they would become 'caged tigers' if they stood. Moreover, even if they wanted to vote for Wilson and Lee, under the 'slate' system where they had to cast twelve votes it

would be difficult for them to vote without also supporting others who
backed Gaitskell against Conference decisions. Wilson made it clear he
would stand. To make it easier for the Left to support him he persuaded
a number of 'soft' anti-Gaitskellites like Joyce Butler, John Rankin and
Victor Yates to stand as well. The tactic worked successfully, partly
because the Gaitskellites thought he was safer in harness than on the
back benches, though the 'hard Gaitskellites' like Woodrow Wyatt
agreed with the *Economist* that at the Scarborough Conference 'it is the
bright-eyed men – the Wilsons, Greenwoods, Castles and all – who
have emerged as the real villains.' The *Economist* had described
Wilson's conference speech as full of 'backstabbing thrusts at Mr
Gaitskell'.[115]

For the next months Wilson felt very much like a thin slice of ham
between thick pieces of bread. The Gaitskellites were on the offensive.
Crossman was dropped as pensions spokesman because of his 'persistent
and public advocacy' of views differing from Gaitskell's on defence.
Despite this, Wilson and Fred Lee, together with USDAW President
Walter Padley and Dick Crossman, tried to work out various ways of
uniting the two main factions in the Labour Party. Early in 1961 the
NEC set up a Committee of Twelve to draft a new policy on defence.
Wilson proposed a six-point plan to the 24 January 1961 meeting of the
NEC, TUC and PLP: permanent rejection of the independent nuclear
deterrent, continued membership in a reformed NATO, no nuclear
arms for NATO but their retention by the USA so long as they were
possessed by the USSR, no foreign nuclear bases in Britain, no German
troops in Britain, no nuclear arms for Germany. Three major drafts
were submitted: one by Gaitskell and Healey which was wholly committed to the NATO alliance, one by Frank Cousins which was anti-
nuclear but which rejected 'unqualified repudiation' of NATO, and one
by Crossman and Padley which was supported by Wilson: 'A repudiation of NATO and an attempt to commit the next Labour
Government to withdraw from it would not be a contribution to world
peace. Our job is not to get out of NATO but to reform it.'[116] At the 22
February 1961 meeting of the NEC Wilson voted for the Crossman-
Padley compromise, which was defeated by fifteen votes to thirteen. He
voted against the Gaitskell–Healey statement, which was approved and
finally emerged, slightly modifed, as the new Labour defence policy.
But this left him and Fred Lee isolated within the Shadow Cabinet.
Nevertheless Gaitskell let him keep his job.

As a result Wilson managed to continue his able attacks on the Tories.
He was credited with a 'brilliant and polished' attack on Government
economic policy in the 7 February debate; in this he called for a four-
year expansion plan. On 8 February he attacked what he called the

'excess profits' of the drug industry, demanding that fuller discosure of costs be insisted upon by the Minister of Health.

## OVERTAKEN BY CROSSMAN

During this period Wilson was overtaken by Crossman as the open critic and alternative to Hugh Gaitskell. 'A few months ago he was dismissed by most of his colleagues as a butterfly theorist – waywardly flitting from idea to idea,' wrote Douglas Brown in the *Daily Mail*. 'Today he represents the strong and developing urge for unity, and he has the capacity to translate this emotion into practical and theoretical terms.'[117] There were several reasons for Crossman soaring ahead of Wilson. First, he was Chairman of the Labour Party for 1960–61 and therefore bore the responsibility for speaking for the party in the country. Second, as one who had long been interested in foreign affairs and defence, he actively worked with George Wigg and others on realistic formulae to unite the peace-minded Centre of the Labour Party with the unilateralist Left; this mostly meant opting for a purely conventional role for Britain, leaving the nuclear role in the NATO alliance to the Americans alone. Third, Crossman did not mind risking his political career because he had alternatives in journalism and therefore could readily seem braver than Wilson.

At the end of 1960 and the beginning of 1961 Crossman confronted Gaitskell on the subject of opting out of a nuclear strategy for Britain. He, Shinwell and Wigg could support Parliamentary Motions urging the Government to 'call a halt to the perilous support of its nuclear strategy' along with the unilateralist Left whilst Wilson stood aside as a Front Bench spokesman for Gaitskell. In mid-December 1960 Crossman criticized Gaitskell for his 'intransigence' in putting down a Labour Motion on defence which would 'divide the Parliamentary Labour Party on old lines'.

In fact, almost seventy Labour MPs abstained from supporting Gaitskell's defence policies. This so undermined his position as Leader that a meeting of the PLP on 14 December 1960, called nominally to discipline left-winger Konni Zilliacus for allegedly personal attacks on Gaitskell, ended up with Gaitskell back-pedalling and praising Zilliacus. When Crossman was attacked for his criticisms of Gaitskell by an obscure loyalist, Ernest Popplewell, he replied by clarifying his role as Chairman and thus custodian of Conference decisions and by detailing the history of Gaitskell's divisiveness in the year since the 1959 general election. Crossman left the PLP meeting the hero of the anti-Gaitskell Centre and Left. Wilson could not share in it because he had loyally supported Gaitskell's Motion as a Front Bench spokesman.

From January 1961, when the new Kennedy regime took over in

Washington, Crossman drafted more and more of the Centre–Left compromises presented to Labour's NEC. At a meeting of the NEC on 22 February 1961 there were three draft defence statements: the Gaitskellite one drafted by Denis Healey, the unilateralist one presented by Frank Cousins and Tom Driberg, and the 'conventionalist' one presented by Crossman. Crossman's was defeated by fifteen to thirteen, with Wilson supporting it, and the Cousins–Driberg draft by eighteen to seven, with Wilson voting against it. Wilson also voted against the Healey draft, which was accepted. Crossman criticized Gaitskell for insisting that 'in view of NATO's weakness on the ground, we must at present retain the right to launch these weapons of annihilation even against Russian conventional attack.'[118] Gaitskell had insisted on Britain's right to use nuclear weapons first in a private meeting of the PLP on 23 February 1961. Wilson played a very quiet and passive role as a Crossman sympathizer. At a Fabian meeting in March Crossman derided Wilson's importance as an alternative so long as he stood isolated from everyone but Fred Lee.

Crossman again played up Wilson's lack of political courage by placing himself at the head of seventy-eight MPs who demanded that Michael Foot and four other rebels be brought back into the PLP after they had been suspended for voting against the Service estimates in mid-March 1961. Wilson chimed in on 17 March 1961, describing as 'plain daft' a proposal to expel the five from the PLP.

Crossman himself thought Wilson's timidity was due basically to his lower-middle-class lack of self-confidence. For the first time Crossman secured access to the Wilson home in Hampstead Garden Suburb after entertaining the Wilsons at his wife's farm at Banbury and driving them back home. There was some embarrassment after Mrs Wilson invited him in for coffee and then offered him Nescafé instead. Afterwards Crossman described, with malicious glee, the rows of pottery ducks on the wall as a symbol of pure suburbanism.

By June 1961, however, the NEC was working much more harmoniously, with Crossman, Gaitskell, Brown and Wilson conferring together for the first time since the October 1959 general election. They were planning a programme for the next general election, and Wilson proposed a Four-Year Plan along the lines he had already indicated in the columns of the *New Statesman*.[119] One of the developments which helped unite three of them was that the Tories were swinging into their pro-Common Market propaganda and, although not yet revealed publicly, Gaitskell was on the same anti-Market wavelength as Crossman and Wilson.

In June 1961 Wilson paid another visit to Moscow, where he was able to see his old negotiating opponent, Deputy Prime Minister Mikoyan, on behalf of some of the companies for which he was serving as a consultant.

## THE GAITSKELL 'PLOT' TO DUMP WILSON

The atmosphere cooled for Wilson as Gaitskell's 'plot' against him worked out. Ever since his defeat at Scarborough in 1960 Gaitskell had thrown everything into reversing the decision of Labour's annual Conference in support of unilateralism. For Gaitskell there were no neutrals in this fight; failure to support him was considered outright opposition. In the course of his battle to win support for a nuclear-armed Britain in an American-led NATO he struggled to win over trade-union leaders and politicians. This battle was spearheaded by the CDS, or Campaign for Democratic Socialism, led by William Rodgers and financed by Jack Diamond and Harry Walston, among others. By the time the 1961 Conference began at Blackpool at the end of September Gaitskell was guaranteed an overwhelming victory.

This strengthening of Gaitskell's hand meant a weakening of Wilson's position in the latter's eyes particularly because, Wilson felt, Gaitskell had won over James Callaghan and George Brown – both of whom had opposed his 'confrontation' tactics with the unilateralists – by offering them promotion. This affected Wilson because Gaitskell had offered Callaghan Wilson's job as 'Shadow Chancellor', although Wilson had continued to perform brilliantly in this field and Callaghan was completely without specialist knowledge in economics. Gaitskell's plan was 'leaked' to the newspapers on Sunday 8 October 1961 just after the conference. Wilson urged Gaitskell to name Patrick Gordon Walker instead, but without avail.

Wilson felt he had to take the post of 'Shadow Foreign Secretary' because he lacked either the desire or the charisma of Aneurin Bevan to push himself forward as Deputy Leader by mobilizing constituency activists. He was no unilateralist so, unlike Michael Foot, for instance, he could not reach agreement with the activists on that score. What is more, even his style of radical-sounding oratory, which was much appreciated in the Commons, was being punctured by the New Left, which was gaining influence among constituency activists. Thus, after his wind-up speech on the discussion on 'Socialism in the Sixties', his performance was described as 'hollow', though almost 'too effective'. His speech, it was said, was in 'a somewhat shallow but traditional mode': he had mimed Galbraith in contrasting private affluence with public squalor, rapidly citing twenty British examples. He had presented 'a moral rejection of the Tory version of affluent society' but basically accepted an efficient and productive mixed economy rather than full-blown socialism in the eyes of Leftists.[120]

It was relatively easy for Wilson to make the verbal transition to foreign affairs. Unlike Bevan, Wilson did not have any strong unconventional commitments to Marshal Tito and Pandit Nehru. Admittedly he was pro-Russian on trade, but this tendency was outweighed by the strength of his pro-American feelings on defence. Wilson's support for more aid to the underdeveloped or third world was not a divisive issue. Therefore he saw his main object as being to discomfort the Tories and to unify as broad a band as possible of Labour supporters.

The easiest aspect of his stint as Labour 'Shadow Foreign Secretary' was opposing Edward Heath, who had been installed as Lord Privy Seal and No. 2 in the Foreign Office with the task of negotiating Britain's way into the Common Market. Just three months before Wilson became Labour's foreign affairs spokesman, Macmillan had secured his Cabinet's backing for an effort to enter the EEC as a way of overcoming the new British economic crisis. At that stage Wilson was as opposed to entering the EEC, both intellectually and emotionally, as Heath was in favour. He saw the EEC as an inward-looking organization run by a Bonn–Paris 'axis' increasingly dominated by two crusty old men, Dr Adenauer and President de Gaulle. He could enjoy himself at the expense of Heath's rebuffs at the hands of those leading the Common Market, although initially he was somewhat cautious because he did not know Gaitskell's own inclinations.

Possibly because he realized that most of Gaitskell's friends were pro-EEC and because he was still uncertain about the leader's attitude, Wilson started quite cautiously. On 28 November 1961 he prodded the Prime Minister on why he had refused to let the Canadian Government have a copy of the speech Edward Heath had made to members of the EEC on Britain's desire to enter.

He was very strongly pro-American on the Congo. On 6 December 1961 he complained that the British Government was not giving its 'clear and unequivocal support' to the UN operation there, unlike the United States Government. He seemed to be completely uncritical about US aims in Africa. Eight days later he attacked Heath fiercely because the Government had called for a ceasefire in the secessionist state of Katanga, while the US was supporting the UN forces' efforts to maintain Congo unity. He accused Heath of favouring the Katanga secessionist leader Moise Tshombe at the instigation of Sir Roy Welensky, of the Central African Federation. He attacked the Macmillan Government for their 'abject surrender' to the Suez Group in refusing to supply British bombs to the UN forces in the Congo. He demanded the removal of white mercenaries from Katanga to prevent Communist-backed mercenaries being sent to the other side.[121]

In his first wide-ranging speech on foreign affairs, during the 20

December 1961 debate on the Queen's Speech, Wilson showed himself basically pro-American but sensitive to Soviet feelings as well. Thus, while supporting the 'inalienable democratic right on the part of the West Berliners to choose their system of Government', he also urged that the West should make it 'clear, by word and by deed, that we are prepared to renounce the use of Western Berlin as an advance battle headquarters and centre of provocation in the cold war. The price we pay, in terms of suspicion and ill-will, for insisting on keeping West Berlin for Radio Free Europe and similar organizations, and as a centre for spies and provocateurs, is out of all proportion to any value that may be thought to derive from these activities.' He pointed out that the Russians were fearful of the Germans, having lost 17 million in dead during the Second World War.[122]

He enjoyed his first visit to Washington as 'Shadow Foreign Secretary' in January 1962. He found three of his former students at Oxford were now key officials in the Washington administration, but he was somewhat discomfited to discover that George Ball, then Under-Secretary for State in Kennedy's State Department, was insistent that Britain had to be in the EEC to make it a success. Ball, he found, was not amused by his anti-EEC remarks.

When he took a delegation of forty-two Labour MPs to Berlin in June 1962 he seemed almost over-anxious to demonstrate his loyalty to the NATO alliance as interpreted by orthodox Americans and pro-Americans. He was photographed on the Berlin Wall and quoted on the subject of its offence to freedom. 'We have said that there must be two non-negotiable conditions: First, freedom for the people of West Berlin to live under a system of society of their own choosing, and secondly guarantees of access going beyond mere paper agreements.' Although an expert on trade with Eastern Europe he showed no indication that he understood the *economic* argument of the East Germans: that the Wall was a method for preventing East Germans from getting their training in the East and exploiting the superior job opportunities in the West. It was only after he was back that he suggested that, as part of a 'package deal' guaranteeing West Berlin, 'we should be prepared to show flexibility especially, for example, by showing willingness to accept Germany's Eastern Frontier with Poland and Czechoslovakia. We should also show flexibility in the matter of some measure of recognition of the East German administration as a purely factual arrangement pending, and without prejudice to, the ultimate reunification of Germany on a basis of free elections.'[123] Since anyone but an idiot knew the Russians would not be agreeable to losing East Germany through free elections, this could only be Wilson's way of removing the possible 'taint' of having been linked with the anti-Gaitskell 'unilateralists'.

He also showed a strong desire for respectability in the debate on
Laos in May 1962, when the effort to keep that country neutral was
crumbling. In his questioning of Heath he showed none of the
knowledgeable irreverence of Philip Noel-Baker, the aged Nobel Prize-
winner, who asked that the CIA stop supplying military equipment to
the right-wing government of Laos. Wilson more even-handedly
attacked the 'Communist Pathet Lao' and 'the forces of the right-wing
element in Laos'. When he returned to questions a week later Wilson
was again outflanked on the Left by Noel-Baker,[124] who had become a
'unilateralist' radical in his old age and made Wilson seem like someone
seeking the Foreign Office seal of approval.

Wilson was delighted to be handed an open general licence to attack
the Common Market at the Brighton Conference of the Labour Party
over which he presided. This was at the end of his year as Chairman,
which was far from being as exciting as the previous year when
Crossman had been in the chair. Crossman had not been on hand to egg
him on because in January 1962 he had collapsed with a burst ulcer
which brought him close to death. For the rest of that year his activity
was largely limited to writing book reviews.

Wilson was as surprised as Gaitskell's close friends by their Leader's
explosively anti-Market speech at Brighton; they had thought him, at
worst, neutral on the Market. Most of Gaitskell's close friends and
associates, with the exception of Douglas Jay, had declared themselves
strongly pro-EEC. The Campaign for Democratic Socialism, or CDS,
which had been so invaluable in pushing back the challenge of the
CND, was also strongly pro-Market. Therefore Gaitskell's fiery and
deeply emotional anti-Market position aligned him with the Left and
others, including Wilson, who saw the EEC as a Catholic-capitalist
conspiracy.

Winding up that Conference Wilson claimed that Labour was now
more united than at any time for the previous decade as a result of
Gaitskell's great speech. There was a nice by-play that same morning
when Harold's father, then aged eighty, was called on to second the
customary vote of thanks to the Chairman. 'I pay a respectful tribute
to the seconder of the Motion for his Maiden speech at a party
Conference,' Harold Wilson replied, 'and that is not the only thing I
have to thank my father for.'[125]

## FIGHTING GEORGE
Gaitskell's public espousal of the anti-Market case helped encourage
Wilson to challenge George Brown for the Deputy Leadership. The fact
that Gaitskell and he were on the same side and Brown was on the other,
pro-Market side was one reason why Wilson could expect wide support.

There was also a private reason for Wilson's hopefulness. He had helped expose the fact that Brown had been on the *Daily Mirror* payroll for several years without disclosing it. This had come about during the July 1962 argument in the Shadow Cabinet over what posture a new Labour Government would adopt over commercial TV, whose introduction Labour had opposed. Christopher Mayhew, Labour's broadcasting spokesman, had prepared a plan under which a reformed Independent Television Authority would buy programmes from contractors but handle advertising itself. Gaitskell agreed to this, but Brown persuaded Gaitskell that it should be discussed by the Shadow Cabinet. There Mayhew narrowly lost, with Brown voting against him. 'I think you were very badly treated,' Wilson told Mayhew as they walked away. 'You know, I agree with your plan. I don't mind being beaten. But why don't people declare their interests? I presume you know that George is on Cecil King's payroll.'

Mayhew immediately wrote to Brown saying that he did not believe the allegation but wanted Brown to deny it. Gaitskell then called in Mayhew and said: 'What terrible things have you been saying about George?' When Mayhew explained that he had only asked Brown to deny he was on the payroll of the *Mirror*, which had TV interests, Gaitskell interjected: 'I can't believe it!' To which Mayhew replied: 'Did George deny it?' 'Well, not in so many words,' Gaitskell admitted. Mayhew then went to Brown, who finally admitted it. 'You will tell the PLP, of course,' Mayhew then said. 'Like hell I will!' 'If you don't,' Mayhew warned, 'I will!' Brown then hastened to inform, first of all the Trade Union Group, of which he was Chairman and which provided his main Parliamentary base. Wilson naturally thought this disclosure, which subsequently appeared in the press, would weaken Brown's popularity among Labour MPs.

Wilson also thought there would be a cumulative reaction to a number of incidents in which an overtired Brown had launched unjustified attacks on MPs and members of the PLP staff. One such incident the previous Christmas had caused much comment. Wilson, at Marcia's suggestion, had given a small Christmas party in his room for members of the PLP staff. Brown, hearing about this and fearing that Wilson was trying to undermine his position as Deputy Leader, gave his own party. After he had become a bit 'merry', Brown proclaimed: 'I know there is a spy amongst you, reporting details of my activities to the Communists!' Later it turned out that a secretary he had selected for himself had a Communist boyfriend. Brown had also lost popularity in the spring of 1962 by trying to expel from the Labour Party Earl Russell, the patron saint of the 'unilateralists', nominally for being behind in his subscription. But so, it turned out, was Gaitskell!

Wilson encountered a solid wall of press opposition, from the *Daily Mail* in particular. Part of this was pure misrepresentation, claiming that Brown had declared his interest before opposing Mayhew's proposal on reforming commercial TV, which was patently untrue. Wilson and his supporters were sure from the splutterings of some members of the Trade Union Group that Brown's belated disclosure had alienated some of his closest friends, but when the vote was counted for Deputy Leader about a score of such complaining Labour MPs preferred the erring but warm-hearted Brown to the hard-working but aloof Wilson. The vote was 133 for Brown and 103 for Wilson. Some of the Labour MPs appear to have voted for Brown because his dismal performance three days before put them in a forgiving mood; they felt he had been punished enough for the time being.

A fairly accurate expanation for Wilson's defeat had been given by James Margach in the *Sunday Times* just before the vote was taken: 'Harold Wilson, they say, is undependable; he has been too much a weather-cock, reacting to pressures and shifts of sectional opinion; variously a Bevanite, then veering to the Centre though retaining strong sympathies with the Left; a professional who is over-trained in the techniques of politics; clever, but, alas, often too clever. If he became Deputy Leader the party would be top-heavy with double dons and double Firsts, a duality in intellectualism and professional politico-economics.'[126] Anthony Howard, in the *New Statesman*, had predicted accurately that Gaitskell would decide how far above 100 votes either candidate would rise.[127] Wilson took his defeat without a murmur in public. On the night of 8 November 1962, just after his defeat had been announced, he made one of his wittiest and sharpest attacks on the Government.

It was, however, the performance of a great entertainer, with the greasepaint hiding the tears and pains of defeat. If he could not win against an erratic opponent like George Brown, who had alienated so many of his own side, what future was there for him? If, as he suspected, Gaitskell had intervened to save Brown from defeat, what point was there in maintaining publicly his loyal posture? The only consolation Wilson had was that if Brown had lost it was widely predicted that he would be finished – whereas, although he himself had lost, he still had a future. 'Mr Wilson, who is forty-six, had much to win and nothing to lose in the contest,' wrote *The Times*'s Political Correspondent. 'His status in the Labour movement inside and outside Westminster is always assured not only by his exceptional abilities.'[128]

Wilson again came third, with 151 votes, in the balloting for the Parliamentary Committee or Shadow Cabinet. He was down by twenty-four votes from the previous year. James Callaghan came first that year, with 164, and Sir Frank Soskice (later Lord Stowe Hill) came second with 160. Fred Lee scraped on in twelfth position, but Dick Crossman did not make it. Wilson had been the top man in the balloting at the Brighton Conference with 735,000 votes, Callaghan being an also-ran with 444,000. Wilson had moved up from third man the previous year.

Wilson talked over with Balogh and Crossman the reasons for his unexpected defeat. They agreed that the crucial element had been the doubts about his loyalty to Gaitskell, which had been exploited on Brown's behalf by Gaitskell himself. What they did not and could not know was that, within ten weeks, Gaitskell himself would be suddenly removed from the scene.

Before Gaitskell himself fell into his terminal illness at the end of December there was every indication that he would be the next Prime Minister of Britain, probably in less than a year. Support for the Macmillan Government was collapsing. Despite his 'July Massacre' earlier in 1962 – largely to secure a Chancellor more reflationist than Selwyn Lloyd – the economy was still lagging. Then, in December at Nassau, Macmillan was unable to persuade President Kennedy to retain the 'Skybolt' missile needed to keep Britain's bombers useful in a nuclear period. The combination of these two setbacks was reflected in opinion polls which put Labour 9 per cent ahead. By 5 January 1963 the *Economist* was writing of Labour as 'The Alternative Government'.

When this article appeared Wilson was about to take off on a private trip to lecture at US universities. There had been some hesitation about his filling these long-established commitments. Uncertainty about Gaitskell's health had developed in the wake of the latter's return from Paris on 4 December 1962 after a luncheon of the Anglo-American Press Association where he had insisted that Britain could enter the EEC on five conditions, one of them being protection for the Commonwealth. Although Gaitskell had complained of rheumatic pain he had worked until 14 December, when he had entered the trade unionists' Manor Hospital near his Hampstead home. He was diagnosed as suffering from virus pneumonia.

There was general relief on 23 December 1962 when Gaitskell was discharged from hospital and pronounced fit to accept an invitation from Krushchev to visit Moscow. There was dismay among Labour leaders at the news of Gaitskell's relapse that same evening. The Soviet Ambassador was summoned to Frognal Gardens to learn, in the presence of Gaitskell's physician, Sir John Nicolson, that the trip was off. The Queen's Physician, Dr Bodley Scott, soon confirmed that the virus infection associated with pneumonia persisted. But there were some complications. On 4 January 1963 he was moved by ambulance to the Middlesex Hospital, which had superior facilities. Anxiety deepened as it became clear that the illness was serious enough to keep him out of action for several months.

Since those were sure to be vital the Labour Chief Whip, Herbert Bowden (later Lord Aylestone), called a secret meeting of the Deputy Leader, George Brown, the Foreign Affairs spokesman, Harold Wilson, Shadow Chancellor James Callaghan and Patrick Gordon Walker. When this was disclosed first in the *Daily Mirror* and then described next day in Dick Crossman's *Guardian* column as a 'Regency' council, the Chief Whip denied it unconvincingly.[129] By publicizing the meeting Crossman wanted to emphasize that the party was not being left in the hands of Brown as the heir-apparent.

Although Gaitskell's health still looked bad it was decided that it would be ghoulish for Wilson to give up his scheduled US trip. His critics would say that he could not wait to step into a dead man's shoes. So, on 13 January 1963, Wilson flew from London airport to Chicago for his first lecture. Marcia Williams remained behind in his wood-panelled room on the Upper Committee Corridor to keep him informed of events.

It was in St Louis on the morning of Wednesday, 16 January, that Wilson received the first of several crucial telephone calls from Marcia Williams. George Brown had suddenly cancelled a tour of northwestern areas of high unemployment to fly back to London in an RAF plane requested of the Prime Minister. He turned up at the Middlesex Hospital where Hugh Gaitskell was described as 'battling for his life'. Wilson knew that, not being Gaitskell's loyal Deputy, he had not the same right to fly back uninvited. He told Marcia to ask Chief Whip Bert Bowden to telephone him next day. When Bowden called he said that Wilson could only add to the gathering tension by flying back when Gaitskell was sinking.

Wilson flew on to New York for lunch with U Thant, UN Secretary General. On returning to his hotel that afternoon he learned that Gaitskell had died minutes before on that Friday, 18 January. By then he had already conversed twice with Mrs Williams, at 3 a.m. and 8 a.m. New York time. He had learned previously that left-wing Labour MPs had met to discuss what would happen if Gaitskell died. An American-born political correspondent had informed Marcia Williams that many of these left-wing MPs were temporarily at least swinging towards George Brown as Gaitskell's successor. Their fear was that Wilson, so embittered by his bad treatment at the hands of the Gaitskellites, might precipitate a 'civil war' in Labour's ranks if he became Leader. 'All right, I'm coming back then,' Wilson told Marcia. 'I'll be at London airport tomorrow.'[130]

On the flight back he had plenty of time to think about his tactics. He had paid a generous tribute to Gaitskell in New York. He would have to maintain this attitude despite their differences, and he would have to avoid seeming ambitious to succeed him. As he alighted from the plane on Saturday, 19 January, pressmen immediately asked about his chances. 'I don't think we can begin to think about that when the Leader has died only a few hours ago,' he said tactfully. 'The policies of Hugh Gaitskell will stand. There will be no split in the party.'[131]

After the press had gone Wilson lunched with his wife, Mary, his son, Giles, and Marcia Williams, who had driven the family car out to the airport. 'I suppose this means you're going to stand for the Leadership?' Marcia asked him as they drove back from London airport. 'Yes, I expect so,' he replied. His weariness with the prospect may have been put on for Mary's sake. That same evening after dinner he drove to the home of Dr Balogh in Well Walk, Hampstead, for a strategy meeting with his closest advisers – Balogh and Crossman.

Crossman, Balogh and Wilson had two problems to worry about. The first concerned their natural supporters: the Left, Left–Centre, Centre–Left and others who had voted for Wilson in 1960 and 1962 but were now hesitating. Too many of these, particularly those who had been with Wilson on relaxed social occasions, had become conscious of his thin skin and the many scars caused by the slights, snubs and rude remarks of Gaitskellites. Wilson's total recall of these humiliations had led many to conclude that his emergence as Leader might open the door to civil war. Because of that some even preferred George Brown, despite his emotionalism and worship of the Pentagon. Something had to be done to reassure these would-be faithful.

The other problem was to avoid provoking excuses for a 'stop Wilson' campaign by his varied opponents on the Right of the Parliamentary Labour Party. If they could do this the various would-be heirs to Gaitskell on the other side of the party would be sure to squabble. Central to all this was the mercurial quality of George Brown, who could be rude to his friends and make them squirm with his extrovert exuberance. The snobs among the Gaitskellites were sure to wonder whether they could afford to have a Leader who was not a University graduate.

To exploit these possibilities Crossman urged that they must allow their opponents to make the mistakes. Wilson himself must remain out of the contest. There must be no aggressive canvassing on his behalf. First of all there must be a counting of heads; once the doubtfuls were known they could be approached discreetly.[132]

'When the others left,' Crossman later recalled, Wilson 'stayed behind and I could not resist asking him a question that was lurking at the back of my mind. "Harold," I said, "what real difference would it make to the party if we succeed in making you Leader?" To my surprise, the reply came without the slightest hesitation. "If I get the job, I believe the party will be able to liberate the frustrated energies of thousands of young scientists, technologists and specialists, who feel there is no room at the top for them under the present anti-scientific old-boy network in industry and Whitehall." "I know that most of them voted for us in 1945," [I] said, "but by 1959 four-fifths of them had become anti-working class and anti-Labour." "Well, the only way to win them back is to make Labour the party of science. At present we are treating science as a gimmick. That is why the first-rate team of scientists which have been working with us for years are so disgruntled. At our next conference we have got to make them feel we take them seriously. Then there will be scores of them ready to be mobilized if we give the word."[133]

The accuracy of Crossman's analysis was demonstrated two nights later in Anthony Crosland's flat in The Boltons, Kensington. He had invited all the leaders of the anti-unilateralist Gaitskellites: Jennifer Jenkins, who represented her husband, Roy, who was in the USA; Dennis Howell, the chief organizer of the Campaign for Democratic Socialism; Bill Rogers, its Secretary and organizing genius, and Dick Taverne, its Treasurer; Jack Diamond, the wealthy accountant who had helped finance CDS; Desmond Donnelly, the ex-Bevanite turned right-winger; Reginald Prentice; Fred Hayday, Chairman of the TUC's General Council; and John (later Lord) Harris, the Labour Party's Director of Publicity and admirer of Roy Jenkins.

The purpose of the meeting, which was to choose the best successor on whom all Gaitskellites could converge, soon proved to be beyond them. They knew too well the virtues and vices of George Brown to think him their perfect candidate. He was a brilliant orator, very popular with working people and a man who had won a warm spot in many hearts, but he was impulsive, mercurial and egotistical, capable of being rude not only to his friends but to important people like Krushchev. His tendency to be domineering, in the style of Ernest Bevin and Arthur Deakin, had already been demonstrated since, as Chairman of the NEC's Organization Sub-committee, he had tried to expel Earl Russell from the Labour Party. Anthony Crosland, backed by the Jenkinsite, John Harris, felt that James Callaghan had a better chance to stop Wilson if everyone united behind him.

Those with doubts about George Brown were soon to have them justified. Brown returned that same Monday from the North believing he was the agreed heir to the Gaitskell throne. His first blow came when the dry right-wing intellectual, Patrick Gordon Walker, told him that day that he might find it his duty to stand for the Leadership. A dazed Brown, understandably astonished, thanked him for his frankness. Then Brown called in Jim Callaghan to ask him for a pledge of his support. Mistakenly he unveiled Gordon Walker's astonishing confession. This naturally emboldened Callaghan to say he must 'reserve his own position' as he had been urged to stand (by Denis Healey and Douglas Jay). Having been hit hard by his friends Brown had the rug pulled from under him by Harold Wilson.

That same evening, after the eve-of-reassembly meeting of Labour's Shadow Cabinet, Wilson approached Brown in a corridor just off the Commons chamber and suggested an informal pact. There should be no personal attacks during the campaign. Whoever won would back the other and serve under him as Deputy Leader. Brown was delighted with this olive branch, thinking it virtually Wilson's concession of defeat. Wilson then 'leaked' the story to the *Daily Telegraph* and *Daily Mail*. 'WILSON AND BROWN BURY THE HATCHET' and 'LABOUR RIVALS IN UNITY PACT' read the headlines. Brown, fearful that he was being portrayed as a man willing to accept the No. 2 post, promptly denied the story in his constituency paper, the *Derby Evening Telegraph*. This, of course, doubled the value of Wilson's ploy. It had been a signal, mainly to those on his own side who were fearful of a civil war, that there would be none if he could avoid it. Now Brown had allowed himself to appear as the opponent of party unity. To finish the operation off, Wilson informed Harry Nicholas, the Labour Party Treasurer, at the 23 January meeting of the NEC that he had been wrong to 'leak' the pact. 'Harold Wilson thinks he owes you an apology' read the note Nicholas pushed across to Brown when the latter arrived a bit late at the meeting. 'Thinks?' scribbled Brown, 'he bloody well does' and pushed it back. Wilson then came over to Brown, beckoned him into a corner and apologized handsomely.[134] Brown was impressed. But he had been used to re-establish unity in the Wilson ranks while the other camp kept splitting.

Two more meetings of the Gaitskellites were held in Jack Diamond's flat in Greycoat Place, Westminster, with John Strachey in the chair, but no agreement could be reached for all to support the same candidate against Wilson. On 24 January, having told Brown the previous day that the proffered position of Deputy Leader did not interest him, Callaghan threw his hat in the ring. Even before this Wilson was fairly sure both that this squabbling among his opponents could not be healed quickly.

Brown had been deeply aggrieved by Callaghan's suggestion that in the end he would be better able to beat Wilson than Brown. This led him to 'lean' on those whom he considered natural supporters, including Reg Prentice, who was also a T & GWU-sponsored MP. When Brown demanded that he proclaim his support for him Prentice promptly decided to vote for Callaghan and let it be known to the press.

On Wilson's side there was consolidation. The five 'rebel' MPs who had lost the Labour Whip two years before over the H-bomb – Michael Foot, Sydney Silverman, S. O. Davies, Emrys Hughes and William Baxter – applied for readmission to the Labour fold.

There was a crucial Gallup Poll in the midst of the election campaign. It showed that, if a general election were held immediately, Harold Wilson would have a lead of fourteen points over Harold Macmillan, but that George Brown would only have eleven. It showed too that Wilson had more appeal to Tory and Liberal voters, but that Brown had more support than Wilson among Labour supporters – by forty-two per cent to thirty-six per cent, with Callaghan trailing with eight per cent. 'Harold Wilson is the only man to measure up to the task,' insisted Tory journalist Peregrine Worsthorne. 'Wilson has few friends; still fewer feel confidence in him. But his deviousness in personal relations, so difficult for colleagues to forgive, is a fault that all Prime Ministers are forced by circumstances to cultivate eventually.[135]

As if to illustrate this quality Wilson pretended that Dick Crossman was only a 'self-appointed' campaign manager and that it was accidental that George Wigg was carefully counting heads with the help of his old friends from the North Staffordshire WEA, left-wing MPs Stephen Swingler and Harold Davies. George Wigg, a former professional soldier, had the barrack lawyer's well-developed nose for personal intelligence. None of these active Wilson supporters were officially named. Nor did Wilson publish a list of sponsors – as Brown did – on the basis that there had been an agreement to ban any public canvassing.

Harold Wilson's allegedly too-close relations with Marcia Williams never surfaced during the race for the Leadership, no more than George Brown's alleged bibulous habits. Ex-miner William (later Lord) Blyton nevertheless urged that Mary Wilson attend more frequently in the Commons. She was conspicuous on Harold's arm at the memorial ceremony for Hugh Gaitskell at St Margaret's, Westminster. She also began putting in an appearance again in the gallery of the Commons, listening to debates.

The probability that Wilson was home and dry was all but confirmed on Thursday night, 31 January, when it was announced that three nominations had been received: Brown, Wilson and Callaghan. Callaghan's standing, although he knew by then that he had no chance, was enough to split the anti-Wilson camp. Had others stood – Sir Frank Soskice or Patrick Gordon Walker – this might have stretched the voting out long enough for the anti-Wilsonians on the Right to regroup. It did not help Wilson when on Friday, 1 February, the day the ballots went out, the *Guardian* came out for Callaghan, although Wilson had 'better qualifications than perhaps any Prime Minister ... since Bonar

Law' to lead 'the country out of an economic wilderness'. They preferred Callaghan because he was a man of the Centre, more reliable and more widely acceptable in Labour ranks.

Dick Crossman, the wartime psychological warfare specialist, turned up that same morning in the *Guardian* with the disclosure that Gaitskell, in 'one of his last acts before he fell ill', had appointed 'a very high-powered committee under Harold Wilson's chairmanship' to investigate West European economic relations once de Gaulle and Adenauer were out of the way. Crossman claimed that Gaitskell had believed 'new opportunities would arise' in the future to 'create a really outward-looking European Community which Britain could gladly join'. This disclosure was clearly intended to win over those wavering pro-Europeans alienated by Brown but fearful of Wilson's anti-EEC prejudices. However, there were no direct approaches; Wilson offered to pay a pound to anyone who could prove he had solicited a vote.[136]

Wilson was, in fact, covering the whole of the political spectrum in the run-up to the leadership election. In the *Sunday Express* he was attacking the possibility of the Germans having a 'finger on the nuclear trigger'.[137] In the Commons on 24 January, in the wake of Heath's failure in the EEC negotiations, he proposed the negotiation of an 'Atlantic partnership' embracing the USA, the EEC, EFTA and the Commonwealth. In the Commons on 31 January he called for an end to Britain's 'vain nuclear posturing'. 'The Labour Party is completely opposed, utterly and unequivocally, now and in all circumstances, to any suggestion that Germany, West or East, directly or indirectly, should ever have a finger on the nuclear trigger.'[138]

Wilson was in even better form on 7 February, the day the results of the first ballot were announced. He called for an inquiry into the whole tangled tale of the Congo, including Tshombe's relationship with Sir Roy Welensky and the role of the Katangese propaganda organization. 'We know perfectly well who is behind all this propaganda: a former official of the Conservative Central Office who is making big money representing in this country not only Union Minière and Katanga Concessions but the Spanish and Portuguese Governments and the whole record of Portuguese aggression in Angola and Mozambique ... It would be a revealing commentary not only on what goes on in darkest Africa but on the seamier side of our political life in this country.'[139]

Wilson was helped by sniping in the camps of his opponents to the very last day. On Monday, 4 February, Brown said to Callaghan, sitting next to him on the Front Bench: 'You must have a pretty good conceit of yourself to think that you can be Leader of the Labour Party – why are you doing it?' Callaghan replied: 'Because a lot of people think I'd make a better job of it than you.'[140]

Finally, on the evening of 7 February, Harold Wilson stood on the threshold of power, with only eight votes separating him from the Leadership and, with it, the keys to 10 Downing Street. Wilson sat impassively puffing his pipe as he heard the almost inaudible announcement at 6 p.m. that he had beaten Brown by 115 votes to eighty-eight, with Callaghan coming third with forty-four. This meant that Callaghan would be knocked out and the other two would go to a second round because a clear majority was required. The two leading contenders had heard five minutes before that they would go to a second round. Callaghan was glad to have done so well. Wilson knew he needed only one in five of Callaghan's votes to be across the line. A friend sprinted out to telephone Mary Wilson, but her phone was out of order and she was kept in suspense for an hour. So Marcia learned first.

The decision was, indeed, virtually in the bag. On Thursday night George Wigg had begun a canvas of the forty-four who had voted for Callaghan, to determine their second choice. Wilson needed eight of their votes. Before the House rose Wigg discovered a round dozen who had decided to switch to Wilson. He was able to deliver this message to Dick Crossman's house where something of a celebration dinner was going on. Mary had been waiting there for Harold in the event of his winning an outright victory on the first round. She knew that she would have to come out of purdah if Harold became Leader. It was an emotional evening. After Wigg had brought the good news Harold Wilson raised his glass and proposed a toast to Nye Bevan's memory. None of them had been as close to Nye as, say, Michael Foot, but Harold Wilson was underlining the fact that his victory represented a defeat for the Labour Establishment that Bevan had so long fought.

The Wilson camp wondered for a moment whether Brown would go on fighting fiercely when, in a speech in Wilson's home town of Huddersfield, he pointed out that he and Harold had differed in their 'attitudes on vital issues'.[141] This was interpreted as a way of frightening off Wilson's moderate supporters by raising again the issue of 'unilateralism', but Brown then decided not to follow it up after being warned off by Labour moderates.

For his sins Brown was in the chair as acting Leader when the second ballot was declared in Committee Room 14 on 14 February. The resultant victory for Wilson was decisive: 144 for him to Brown's 103. Of the Callaghan votes, Wilson appeared to have picked up twenty-nine while Brown had gained fifteen. It was a hard blow for Brown, but he managed to congratulate Wilson. However, he would withdraw, he said, to think about things for a while; so far as serving under Wilson as his Deputy, 'I will have to consider my own position.'

Wilson, rising to an ovation, insisted that he wanted Brown to continue as Deputy, as he was sure the whole party would. The party needed Brown's dynamic qualities. Indeed, Wilson went on, the three-man contest had so enhanced the party's strength that he had thought that perhaps the party would be better run as a 'troika', as the Russians put it. But Brown, who felt the triangular contest had scuppered him, was not amused.

When Harold Wilson went on to a press conference at Transport House he was suddenly humble at the prospect of being the next Prime Minister. 'You will understand that, at a time like this, even somebody not normally at a loss for words finds it a little difficult to find words to express himself.' He was publicly generous, even over-generous, to George Brown, to whom he gave 'a good deal of the credit' for keeping the party together in the election campaign. He put himself forward as a non-factional Leader. 'I regard myself as being elected not by 144 votes but by the party – the whole party.' Yes, he planned to visit Washington – which was on his schedule when Gaitskell died. Yes, he planned to take up Gaitskell's invitation to Moscow. The general election? 'We are confident that if the election is held next month we shall have a resounding majority.'[142]

The danger of an early election dominated much of Wilson's planning and tactics over the next months. Because Harold Macmillan could call an election if there was any hint of Labour disunity – as Eden had done in May 1955 – Wilson had to ensure that none appeared. In order to avoid ruffling any feathers and avoiding any doctrinal battles Wilson felt he was virtually committed to taking over the personalities and policies that Gaitskell had endorsed as Leader.

Wilson knew, of course, that the main motive power behind his election was the backing of the Left, Left–Centre and Centre–Left. He spent the night of his victory at a celebration at the Pimlico home of Ben Parkin, left-wing MP for Paddington. They had to wait a long time until Gannex-clad Wilson arrived at 10.30 after the press conference and radio and TV interviews. Parkin, an intense but whimsical man, proposed a toast to the new Leader, who allowed himself the luxury of a few tears. When an erratic left-winger, William Warbey, asked Wilson how he could contemplate working with George Brown, Wilson assured him: 'He will have to go in the end, but it will have to be at a time of our making, when it suits us. And when we do drop him, you won't even hear a splash!'

## PLAYING HIMSELF IN
Wilson knew that indulging any such inclinations would have to wait until after a general election which could come at any time. To win that election he had to be seen to be the attractive and competent head of an

able and united team. It was therefore important to cement George Brown in place as Deputy, where he could serve as a symbol of Labour's unity.

Initially it proved tricky to neutralize him; he had flown off to Scotland with his wife, using assumed names to avoid detection. His address was known only to a handful of people, including Desmond Donnelly and Harry (later Lord) Walston. But he had left behind with Chief Whip Herbert Bowden a letter written before his final defeat. This explained that he wanted to continue as Deputy Leader under Wilson provided he could be foreign affairs spokesman as well. When Bowden showed him the letter, Wilson replied: 'It wouldn't possibly do. Think of what the Tories would make of it.'

Instead Wilson offered the post of foreign affairs spokesman to the reliable right-winger, Patrick Gordon Walker, who had thought of himself as a possible Leader. This appointment had several advantages: it would reassure the Americans, make it clear that Wilson was not dependent on the Left – who complained about Gordon Walker's appointment – and make it impossible for Brown to complain. Wilson named Denis Healey to take over Gordon Walker's previous job as defence spokesman, and Charles Pannell became spokesman on Works. All of these had been active Gaitskellites and none had supported his candidacy. The only promotion of a supporter went to Dick Crossman, who became spokesman on science.

Press publicity was still focussed on the absence of Brown, and Wilson had to handle this first. He told Brown's secretary that for the good of the party she should ring George and ask him to ring back. Brown, disturbed by reports in the press that the foreign affairs job had gone to Gordon Walker, telephoned Desmond Donnelly to find out why the letter he had left with the Chief Whip had not been publicized. Donnelly thereupon released the letter to the *Evening Standard*. This apparent ultimatum helped cook Brown's goose.

The delayed Wilson–Brown meeting was finally held on Thursday, 21 February, a week after Wilson won the Leadership. Brown had flown back to London to be met at London airport by a chauffeur-driven car belonging to the David Brown Corporation, for which Donnelly worked as a consultant. Brown capitulated and accepted the post of spokesman on home affairs in addition to being Deputy Leader. The two men, together with Herbert Bowden, then announced the new Shadow Cabinet. That night on TV Brown was candid about his rebuff as foreign affairs spokesman, saying: 'If I was in the driver's seat, I'd have had it my way. As he's in the driver's seat, he has it his – and maybe he's right too.'[143]

Having settled his largely Gaitskellite team Wilson worked hard at creating a new 'image'. The 'image' he sought to create was one of a forceful, purposeful Labour team that would liberate the productive capacities of the British people. His problem was to create a slightly more dynamic, less 'Establishment' image than that left by Gaitskell without disturbing the agreed programme on what might be the eve of a general election. He showed greater hostility to Bonn and Dr Adenauer, alleging they were trading with the East Germans while inhibiting British trade; he favoured accepting the reality of East Germany without supporting its diplomatic recognition. He spoke at a Trafalgar Square rally of the Anti-Apartheid Movement, demanding an immediate ban on arms exports to South Africa, which he described as a 'bloody traffic in the weapons of oppression'. He sought to depict the Macmillan Government as composed of class-ridden fuddy-duddies. Speaking in Cardiff the night after he named his new team, he said: 'Spare a little sympathy for Mr Macmillan. Last night, when the list of Shadow Cabinet appointments came out, there he was in Admiralty House with Mr Macleod, looking for all the world like Steptoe and Son, if in more elegant surroundings, puzzling over the list. You can just see Mr Macmillan scratching his head. "What?" he says. "Hasn't the man got any relatives?" It would never occur to him that you appoint people on suitability for the job, not on their family or school connections. For Mr Macmillan's record in family appointments reveals a degree of nepotism that would have brought a blush to the cheeks of a Borgia pope. What would the press say if a Labour Prime Minister appointed a whole team of nephews and in-laws to his Government? I have in fact a nephew, just one. He is a sixth-former at Cardiff High School. He would, in fact, make a far better Cabinet Minister than the Duke of Devonshire, Mr Macmillan's nephew. But, in view of the nation's need for scientists, I propose to leave him where he is.'[144]

This bit of knockabout was designed to plant several ideas, some of which Wilson had attempted to plant before: first, that the Tories were a tightly-knit group of Old Etonians who favoured their own, including their relatives, regardless of talent or lack of it; second, that Labour was the party of opportunity for ordinary bright people, the sort who went to Cardiff High School instead of Eton: third, that Wilson, coming from an ordinary background, could liberate the talented of all sorts.

In his image creation Wilson tried hard to break out of the middle-to-upper-middle-class image of the Gaitskell era. Since Mary would not let him invite his inner circle home to Hampstead Garden Suburb he could not have the precise equivalent of Gaitskell's 'Frognal Gardens set'. So he made a virtue of being a solitary. At the first meeting he had with the Trade Union Group Wilson emphasized that he would be accessible to all but would have no 'political friends'. Anyone who wanted to see him had only to ask his PPS, Joe Slater, the Durham ex-miner, whom he had inherited from Hugh Gaitskell. This was found to be 'extraordinary' by Charles Pannell, who had been one of Gaitskell's few working-class friends. But most trade-union MPs found it a refreshing change from the 'Hampstead set' and other middle-class Labour MPs who had prior access to Gaitskell's ear. 'I don't have political friends as such,' Wilson pretended to Kenneth Harris of the *Observer*, conveniently forgetting Crossman, Balogh and Shore. 'I have plenty of personal friends, family friends, but not political friends. And it would be impossible to have any now, even if I wanted to. Politically, I've been too much on my own and perhaps it had a lot to do with becoming a Minister very young.' 'I never have led much of a social life. I've never cared for cocktail parties and dinner parties, or for entertaining generally. I don't really enjoy it. Nor does my wife. If I've got any time to spare, I'd rather be sitting at home with my slippers on and my feet up.'[145] What could be homelier than that?

## MARY'S NEW ROLE – AND MARCIA'S BATTLE
It was piquant that Wilson won the Leadership on Valentine's Day because it meant that Mary Wilson finally had to give up her old dream. She had been told that she would have to 'play the game' of a political leader's wife. The moment Wilson was elected the media would try to transform him from a man into a superman, and his whole family, particularly his wife, would be involved.

However, Mary seemed determined not to emerge from her Hamp-stead Garden Suburb refuge merely as a pallid suburban helpmate. A week or two after Harold had won the Leader's post she submitted her pro-CND poem, 'After the Bomb', to an exhibition of the work of MPs' wives. It effectively made clear that she was a 'unilateralist', unlike her husband, and also made more difficult her husband's effort to depict himself as a moderate.

For her part Mary Wilson helped create an image of the Wilsons as a comprehensible suburban family with slightly exceptional talents. 'I love it when the house is alive, when Harold has just made a speech and is relaxed and in the mood to give you anything,' she told the *Daily Express*, 'when Robin's playing hymns on the harmonium, when Giles is feeding his stick insects and the cat comes back after winning one more fight.' Added Giles disarmingly: 'I don't suppose I could go down Downing Street on my soapbox on wheels.'[146]

Meanwhile in Westminster the 'office wife' was not doing so well, as indications of her pugnacious personality leaked out for the first time. The problem emerged over whether or not he would retain Mrs Beryl Skelly, who had served as senior secretary to both Attlee and Gaitskell.

'My future depends on the new leader,' she told inquiring newsmen. 'But Mr Wilson thinks very highly of his present secretary, Mrs Marcia Williams, who has been with him for seven years. She lives in Golders Green, not far from Mr Wilson.'[147] Mrs Skelly had been very loyal to Gaitskell. 'In the days when Mr Wilson challenged Mr Gaitskell's leadership of the party,' the *Daily Express* recounted, 'the coolness between the two men spread quite naturally to their two staffs. Lobby gossip at the time held that Mrs Skelly, a homely woman in her forties, and [Mrs] Williams refused to speak to each other.' Mrs Williams was confident if not too forthcoming: 'There is a problem over this secretary business. I think I will almost certainly stay as Mr Wilson's secretary.'[148]

Within a few days Marcia had her way. Initially Wilson asked Mrs Skelly to continue working for him alongside Mrs Williams. He suggested that neither be boss and that they should share the work, with Marcia, a history graduate, doing some of his research and newspaper reading. This lasted for a few days before Mrs Skelly was frozen out. Within a week Mrs Skelly was out and Marcia Williams was in charge. This development was to give the Conservatives a handle for some black propaganda within a few months – after the Profumo case exploded on the scene.

In the meantime Wilson put in a few arduous months proclaiming his radical-democratic image. He felt he had to do this, although he interpreted a speech by Macmillan to the Young Conservatives on 16 February as hinting at a later rather than an earlier general election. But he decided to get through three of the four pending by-elections as soon as possible. This was because he did not want the Conservatives to benefit from the expected tax cuts in the Budget being prepared by the expansionist Chancellor, Reginald Maudling.

At his Cardiff speech on 22 February he pledged the repeal of the Tories' 1957 Rent Act and the return of rent tribunals to establish fair rents and to protect tenants 'against unreasonable rents' and to provide 'security of tenure'. 'I enjoy watching "Coronation Street" because they are real people,' he told his Cardiff audience. 'But there are no baths in "Coronation Street" or in thousands of other "Coronation Streets" all over Britain.' He also promised Wales its first Secretary of State who would, he half-promised, be a Welshman.[149]

The next night, in Cross Keys, he demanded that the Prime Minister name the 'faceless paymasters' of the Tories. 'As First Lord of the Treasury he can explain why all the industrial interests who have waited with their begging bowls outside the Treasury – and not waited in vain – should be given all these doles without the State insisting, as any private investor would have insisted, on taking a share in the control of profits.'

He demanded 'the establishing of State-owned factories in development areas producing equipment for Commonwealth development programmes'.[150]

In his first party political broadcast as Leader on 27 February he said: 'We want to create a society in which useful people are given precedence in our system ... What is wrong today is people who *make* money are rated so much higher than those who *earn* money ... Yes, we *shall* have to expand publicly-owned industry. We are going to renationalize steel so that particular industry can concentrate on production.... Of course, our opponents will misrepresent us. They are old hands at that. They will spend millions of anonymously contributed money on their propaganda.'[151] That telecast drew the biggest TV audience up to that time – being seen in 9,793,000 homes, beating even 'Coronation Street'.

Despite his attacks on Macmillan Wilson was one of the greatest admirers of 'Super-Mac' (as cartoonist 'Vicky' had tagged him).Just as Macmillan had talked Right to move the Tories to the Centre in post-Suez days, Wilson was talking Left to move Labour back to Centre. He also wanted to emulate Macmillan as an international fixer-diplomat. Wilson was sure that Macmillan had won the 1959 general election by a combination of 'You never had it so good' at home and play-acting on the international scene, with Ike's arm around him on one pre-election occasion and photographs of 'Super-Mac' in Moscow in a white fur hat on another. Therefore he quickly set about arranging, first, the trip to Washington he had missed because of Gaitskell's illness and death, and then the trip to Moscow which Gaitskell had agreed on but had been forced to cancel. By going to Washington first Wilson made sure that he would not be attacked as being too pro-Russian.

There was eagerness and wariness on both sides when Wilson took off for his four-day trip at the end of March. He was anxious to be accepted by the Americans both as a strong supporter of NATO and the Anglo-American alliance and as an admirer of the Kennedy dynamic, which he wanted to copy. He felt he had much more in common with the Kennedy approach than Macmillan had, both because he was virtually the same age as Kennedy and because, like the Americans, he did not think Britain could finance an independent nuclear role. The Americans were wary about him because, after a previous trip to Washington, he had told Parliament that not a single highly-placed American believed in the British deterrent. He continued this line in Washington. In his address to the National Press Club he said a Labour Government would phase out Britain's independent nuclear deterrent just as the Kennedy regime was on the point of announcing it would sell the Macmillan Government the promised 100 Polaris missiles. While in Washington Wilson was delighted to receive the full red carpet treatment. He stayed with the British Ambassador, Sir David Ormsby-Gore (later Lord Harlech); he was received by the President for almost an hour and also conferred with Secretary of State Dean Rusk and Defence Secretary Robert McNamara, among others. The British press corps in Washington thought he scored very well: 'Like the little ball in a pinball machine,' summarized Henry Brandon in the *Sunday Times*, 'he hit every pin that would touch off a light, and his score was high.'[152] Wilson could achieve this because, among other preparations, he had read all 163 pages of Robert McNamara's testimony to the House Armed Service Committee before seeing the US Defence Secretary.

He remained very careful about the way in which his 'image' could be endangered. In July 1963 he managed to avoid attending a banquet for the King and Queen of Greece – who were very unpopular in left-wing circles – by pleading a 'longstanding private appointment'; he sent Patrick Gordon Walker in his place.

## PROFUMO ON A PLATE

Wilson's chance of denting the reputation of his most difficult opponent, the wily Macmillan, fell on to his plate in the shape of War Minister John Profumo and his playmate Christine Keeler, together with her friends Dr Stephen Ward and Commander Ivanov. It was a fantastic tale in which fact far surpassed fiction. Wilson himself was not the first to get the scent, even though Stephen Ward, osteopath/artist/pimp to the famous, had written to Wilson on 1 November 1962 – when Wilson was still shadow foreign affairs spokesman – to claim 'I was the intermediary' between the Russians and the British during the October 1962 Cuban crisis. Wilson sent a routine reply, Marcia filed Ward's letter, and both forgot it.[153]

It was Wilson's big-nosed, big-eared intelligence agent, Lt-Col. George Wigg, who first got wind of the Profumo–Keeler–Ivanov scandal. As we have seen, Wigg was predisposed to be suspicious about Profumo because the playboy-turned-War Minister had played him for a sucker over the July 1961 Kuwait operation. He had first been tipped off about Profumo on 11 November 1962, and it was in January 1963 that John Lewis, a former Labour MP, informed him that Christine Keeler had told him of serving as the mistress of both Profumo and the Soviet Naval Attaché, Commander Ivanov, who, she alleged, had asked her to get military secrets from Profumo. Initially Wigg was inclined to discount the lurid tale. More information accumulated in the next three weeks before the police, the Solicitor-General, Sir Peter Rawlinson, and John Wyndham, private secretary to Harold Macmillan, began to get wind of the scandal.

During February when the eyes of the political world were on

Wilson's bid for the Leadership, the behind-the-scenes manoeuvres in the Conservative Government and in Fleet Street concerned whether or not Christine Keeler's story was true, whether it would emerge in print, and if so, where. John Profumo had told all his inquiring colleagues that his relationship with Christine Keeler had been completely innocent. So anxious were they to believe him that they never seemed to ask what sort of relationship was likely between a rich middle-aged politician and a former topless dancer.

While the strange and sordid tale was struggling to come out from the undergrowth its appearance in the public press was inhibited by the menacing manoeuvres between the Macmillan Government and the press. Although the press was preponderantly pro-Conservative it was alienated from the Government because of the clash over the Vassall affair. This involved a Navy clerk whose homosexuality had been discovered by the Russians in Moscow and used to turn him into an agent for them. The press had been very hard on the Civil Lord of the Admiralty, Thomas Galbraith, alleging that he had been more familiar with Vassall than he should have been. To save the Government's skin Macmillan had abruptly jettisoned Galbraith and then, when he turned out to be innocent, instituted the Vassall Tribunal. Its inquiry resulted in the jailing of a *Daily Sketch* reporter, Reginald Foster, for three months and a *Daily Mail* reporter, Brendan Mulholland, for six months for refusing to disclose their sources. These jail sentences in February 1963 made the press both willing to believe the worst about the Macmillan Government and loath to print it for fear of seeming vindictive.

It was in this situation that I became the first to print, in my *Westminster Confidential* newsletter, a version of the Profumo-Keeler story. Its main source was a right-wing Tory MP, a former MI 6 man, but its outline had been confirmed by a representative of Tass. It told of the Profumo letter to Christine Keeler which Miss Keeler was trying to sell to a newspaper, and quoted a Conservative MP as saying: 'That is certain to bring down the Government!'[154] A copy of the newsletter was rushed by the Chief Whip to the Prime Minister, who consulted the Attorney-General. His view was that the newsletter's circulation was too limited to warrant either a libel action or an occasion to quash rumours.

When, the following Sunday, two of the newspapers which had delved into the Profumo-Keeler story still had not published as expected, George Wigg went to see Wilson. Wigg, worried about the security aspect of the Profumo-Ivanov link, wanted to raise the question during the approaching Army Estimates debate. Wilson was against this, but told Wigg he could not hinder him. Apart from the important security question this was, a course, a subject of crucial importance to the position of the Tory party in the country. If it emerged that a rich Tory MP with a responsibility for security had been guilty of a serious indiscretion, it would document Wilson's allegations more vividly than tens of thousands of words. But if Wilson or the Labour Party were thought to be smearing a Minister for a moral dereliction, of interest only to his wife, it would rebound against them. This is why it was not until 21 March that Wigg, Crossman and Barbara Castle – all close to Wilson – raised the question of the flight of Miss Keeler to Spain when she was due in court to testify about a shot fired in her flat by a West Indian boyfriend, and her possible connection with a still-unnamed 'Minister'.

The Attorney-General, Sir John Hobson, the Solicitor-General, Sir Peter Rawlinson, and the Chief Whip, Martin (later Lord) Redmayne – all of whom knew the 'Minister's' identity – went into conference. They decided that Profumo had to be called back to the Commons in the middle of the night to be persuaded to make a personal statement first thing next morning, Friday. Meanwhile, in the Commons the Home Secretary, Henry (later Lord) Brooke, urged that Wigg and company should not raise their 'rumours' and 'insinuations' under 'a cloak of privilege' which kept them safe from libel actions. Wilson, who had not been present during the debate, charged Brooke with being incapable of seeing 'however broad or vital a principle' without reducing it 'to a narrower issue'.[155]

Wilson was not present next morning when John Profumo, flanked by the Prime Minister, the Attorney General, and the Leader of the House, Iain Macleod, rose to make a 'personal statement' – one that cannot be interrupted or challenged in the Commons. He conceded that his name had been 'connected with the rumours about the disappearance of Miss Keeler'. He correctly stigmatized these as 'wholly and completely untrue'. He said that he had met her and Ivanov at a party at Cliveden in July 1961 and met her several times at Dr Ward's flat. 'There was no impropriety whatsoever in my acquaintanceship with Miss Keeler,' he said, adding: 'I shall not hesitate to issue writs for libel and slander if scandalous allegations are made or repeated outside the House.'[156]

This effort by Profumo and the Tory leadership to kill the rumours failed, partly because of the kinky people involved. Dr Stephen Ward went to see Wigg at the Commons and told him part of his involvement with Profumo, Ivanov and Keeler. After Wigg had told Wilson of Ward's mention of a letter to Wilson on 1 November, Marcia Williams went to find it. Next day, 27 March, Wilson saw the Prime Minister and gave Ward's letter to him. Next day he flew off to Washington to see President Kennedy, for the first time as Labour's Leader. On his return he sent to Macmillan, on 9 April, a Wigg memorandum covering what

Ward had told him, with his own expurgated comments. Macmillan took a week to reply, which Wilson considered 'symptomatic of the Prime Minister's indolent nonchalance'. In fact the Prime Minister had handed the information over to the security services. And the story could not die because another of Miss Keeler's boyfriends attacked her on the street and was tried.

Wilson decided to sting Macmillan into action. Dr Ward had already called Profumo a liar in a number of communications: to the Prime Minister through his Principal Private Secretary, Timothy Bligh, to the Home Secretary, Henry Brooke, and to the press. Wilson asked for an appointment with Macmillan on 24 May – the day his friend Ben Parkin put down a question on Dr Ward and 'expensive call-girl organizations'. On 27 May, when he saw Macmillan, Wilson pointed out that when he had informed Prime Minister Attlee that his Parliamentary Secretary, John Belcher, had received gifts beyond the call of duty, Attlee had immediately notified the Lord Chancellor and instituted a brutal investigation by the police, although there was no question of a threat to security. Although Belcher's gifts turned out to be quite trivial he had been crucified. Macmillan said he would look into it again. Two days later he heard from the Head of the Security Service a 123-day-old report that Miss Keeler had been asked by Ward to get secrets from Profumo. Macmillan asked the Lord Chancellor to look into the security aspect and duly informed Wilson before going on a Scottish holiday. Wilson asked him to announce the inquiry at all costs, but without success.

Wilson was determined to concentrate on the security aspect of the problem. He asked Ben Parkin to withdraw his question about Miss Keeler and Dr Ward and an 'expensive call-girl organization'. Instead he wanted former Home Secretary Chuter Ede, an upright elder statesman, to submit a question. Wilson drafted it and handed it to Chuter Ede, who showed it to George Wigg just as they were both going off to Epsom Downs (which were in Ede's home area) to watch the Coronation Cup. Wigg, long an enthusiastic follower of horses, accidentally stuffed the question in his pocket without looking at it. At Epsom Wilson had to tannoy Wigg to let him know that the Ede question had not been allowed and would have to be re-drafted. The original question had inadmissibly referred to police matters. Now the redrafted question read: 'to ask the Secretary of State for the Home Department what information he has received from Dr Stephen Ward about a Ministerial statement made to the House on 22nd March 1963 and what action he proposes to take thereupon.' This question and the knowledge that he would be cross-examined by the heavy-handed Lord Chancellor, Lord Dilhorne, formerly Sir Reginald Manningham-Buller, weighed on

Profumo as he went off to Venice for a Whitsun holiday with his wife, ex-actress Valerie Hobson. Profumo first confessed to his wife in Venice and then, on their return, to the Prime Minister's Principal Private Secretary, Timothy Bligh, and the Chief Whip, Martin Redmayne. Bligh telephoned the Prime Minister about Profumo's confession and resignation.

For a moment it looked as though Profumo's confession would bring crashing the Cabinet that had believed his protestations of innocence. The possibility of a Powell resignation from the Cabinet probably figured more highly in the press than in reality, because it had been fed to the press, probably by Nigel Birch. But all Conservative Ministers knew that they had to hang together or hang separately, because a general election in the wake of the Profumo scandal would produce a slaughter of Tories. Unfortunately for Wilson he could not begin planning that strategy immediately because he was in Moscow with Patrick Gordon Walker, his foreign affairs spokesman, when the Profumo confession broke.

It was a nail-biting time to be absent from Britain, but Wilson did what he could to keep things on the boil while he was away, without destroying the purpose of his Moscow trip. 'I think the whole situation makes it clear beyond doubt that there was a security risk,' he said at London airport before flying out.[157]

In Moscow he tried to give the impression that he might be able to clear up the Soviet–American 'misunderstanding' on nuclear inspection. But he shied away from the suggestion that he had his own 'plan' to put before Soviet leader Krushchev. 'No, I do not think an Opposition can negotiate with a Government,' he said with punctilious correctness, knowing how quickly the Prime Minister would shoot him down for straying over the line. There was no doubting Macmillan's irritation that Wilson was such a good student of his own pre-election visits in 1959. The fact that Wilson was able to see Krushchev made it even more galling. When Wilson and his party went to the Kremlin to meet Krushchev and foreign Minister Gromyko, the Labour Leader introduced Patrick Gordon Walker, his PPS, Joseph Slater ('also a miner' like Krushchev), and Mrs Marcia Williams.

Wilson used the front steps of the Kremlin so to speak, to demonstrate that he had been right in arguing for keeping Germany's finger off the nuclear trigger. Krushchev, he said, had warned that if Germany became a nuclear Power 'this would cause a fundamental change in East–West relationships.' The Soviet leader had described French and British nuclear bomber forces as of 'no military significance', Wilson added. Wilson said he had been told that the Russians had stopped making strategic bombers or surface vessels because of their 'total vulnerability'. He emphasized that there had been a wide gap between himself and Krushchev over Berlin. He showed his calculated gullibility after a meeting with the Soviet Minister for Foreign Trade, N. S. Patolichev. He said there was the chance for British firms to sell the Russians a £100m oil refinery on the scale of Fawley. But, however overoptimistic he pretended to be on Soviet trade, resident British correspondents found his assessments of the power relationships in the Soviet hierarchy very shrewd.

Back home he naturally tried to make the most of these encounters. 'My meetings in Moscow with Mr Krushchev and almost every other top Soviet leader were the first real exchange of views between a British party leader and the Russians for a long time.... My two meetings with Mr Krushchev showed beyond all doubt that he still is completely in charge. Rumours a few weeks ago that he was down and out, weary and out of touch could not be further from the truth.... I was as frank with him as he was with me, and he can be in no doubt of our position.' He left Krushchev with a Gannex raincoat as a present – a curious one since its manufacturer, Joseph Kagan, had once been in a Soviet labour camp. Wilson had secured Krushchev's measurements from Madam Tussaud's in London. [158]

It was frustrating to be in Moscow for eight of the ten days between Profumo's resignation and the subsequent Commons debate on it. This frustration was reflected in the way he gobbled up the London newspapers as they arrived with new visitors. He spent part of his time in Moscow preparing the dossier for his return. The main advantage of being away was that it was easier to maintain a dignified and statesmanlike silence at such a distance.

When he opened proceedings on 17 June he put in a controlled and restrained performance, leaving out completely his usual leavening of wit. His main theme was that either the Prime Minister and his colleagues had been dangerously incompetent in handling this threat to security or that they had cruelly misled the House of Commons, and he doubted the latter. He asked five probing questions. When Ivanov's activities had been detected, why had he not been declared *persona non grata*? When had a 'full security watch' been placed on Dr Ward's flat? When had Macmillan first heard the rumours of the Profumo–Keeler–Ivanov involvement? Who told him? Had he instructed the Security Services to check Profumo's early statements with Miss Keeler? He ridiculed a Security Service which had spent £60m during Macmillan's stay in office but had to rely on the *News of the World* for information. He limited his moralizing to a few telling shafts: 'There is something utterly nauseating about a system of society which pays a harlot twenty-five times as much as it pays its Prime Minister,

250 times as much as it pays its Members of Parliament, and 500 times as much as it pays some of its ministers of religion.' But, he wound up, 'The sickness of an unrepresentative sector of our society should not detract from the robust ability of our people as a whole to face the challenge of the future.'

Macmillan's rather pitiful reply hinged on his having been misled by Profumo: 'I do not remember in the whole of my life, or even in the political history of the past, a case of a Minister of the Crown who has told a deliberate lie to his wife, to his legal advisers, to his Ministerial colleagues, not once but over and over again, who has then repeated this lie to the House of Commons as a personal statement ... and has subsequently taken legal action and recovered damages on the basis of a falsehood.'[159] The Profumo case was as decisive in finishing Macmillan off politically as his prostate operation was in finishing him off physically four months later. It was the prostate which provided him with the excuse, but it was the Profumo case which demonstrated that he had so far lost his grip that Wilson, with Wigg as his 'Security Service', was better informed than the Prime Minister. Macmillan was determined to stay in office. 'I will not be brought down by that girl!' he told intimates. But the misjudgment he had shown over Profumo had come on top of his July 1962 sacking of a third of his Cabinet, including Chancellor Selwyn Lloyd, and his failure to secure entry to the Common Market in January 1963.

While trying to divide and discredit the Tories over Profumo Wilson managed to keep his own side united. A possible danger point came in April when the Conservatives adopted the Beeching Plan to prune the railways, involving the loss of 75,000 railwaymen's jobs. The unions' reaction was to urge a three-day strike. However, Wilson invited union leaders to meet him in his Commons room, where he urged them to leave protests to the politicians; a railway strike would only help the Tories and delay the return of a Labour Government pledged to an integrated transport system. They heeded his advice.

When Ernest Marples, the Transport Minister, presented the Beeching Plan in the Commons on 30 April he pointed out that the 5,000 miles of railway to be cut carried under 1 per cent of traffic. He promised to take a personal interest in every appeal against closure. Wilson deftly punctured Marples's position. He asked how Marples could reconcile this 'semi-judicial position' with his Ministerial position to close 5,000 miles of track. Next day Wilson received an enthusiastic reception from Labour MPs when he went on to talk of an integrated transport system.[160]

Wilson also managed to keep Labour's ranks united on the subject of rebellious left-wingers, hitherto a sore subject. The issue of the Putney

Labour Party, which had officially taken part in the Aldermaston March of 'unilateralists', came before the National Executive Committee on 22 May. Wilson took the initiative of calling for a truce alike from the right-wing Campaign for Democratic Socialism (CDS) and from the left-wing Victory for Socialism (VFS). Hugh Jenkins, Putney's left-wing candidate, had his candidacy endorsed. There was also some discussion about readmitting the 'Rebel Five' who had lost the Whip two years before.    These unifying moves, very important in the event of an early election, began to produce results. Victory for Socialism decided to suspend its activities until after the next general election. On 29 May, after they had given assurances acceptable to the PLP, the 'Rebel Five' had the Whip restored. When factional right-winger George Jeger proposed that a decision be deferred for twelve months Wilson persuaded him to withdraw his motion in the interests of party unity. 'Mr Wilson's personal contribution to the continuing harmony has been considerable,' agreed *The Times*. 'He came to the Leadership of a party that had just been painfully rescued from futility and schism by his predecessor; and he is far too shrewd to have thrown away that advantage.'[161]

With a united Labour Party and a Conservative Party disrupted and discredited by the Profumo affair Wilson felt that Labour was unbeatable, and he was thirsting for the contest. 'Before the Government scandal broke,' he told a Sheffield audience on 22 June, 'Labour was clearly established with an increasing lead in by-elections and public opinion polls. Our lead in the Gallup Poll was the highest any party had had in the twenty-five years of public opinion polls in this country.'[162]

He continued to maintain his posture as a reforming spokesman for ordinary people. In a party-political broadcast on 8 May the Wilsons were presented as normal folks: 'My wife and I are buying our house on a ninety per cent mortgage. It will be ours in another fifteen years.' When he was not invited to the royal wedding of Princess Alexandra and the Hon. Angus Ogilvy on 24 April he pretended that there were many other more important things going on; but he did go to the ball at Windsor, to which he was invited.

## WILSON MOVES IN FOR THE – SCIENTIFIC – KILL

Although the abstention of two dozen Tories in the Profumo debate raised Wilson's hopes that an election might be just around the corner, Macmillan set about slowly restoring a semblance of control. Party Chairman Lord Poole warned Conservatives that if they threw out 'or seem to have thrown out, the Prime Minister as a direct result of the Profumo affair, there will be such a revulsion of feeling in the country as a whole that they will not need to speculate much about the result of the next General Election, or perhaps the one after that.'[163] A week later, Macmillan, speaking in Enoch Powell's Wolverhampton constituency, said: 'All being well, if I keep my health and strength, I hope to lead the party into the election.'[164]

By that time Wilson knew it was too late for a summer election. He had to kindle enthusiasm for a Labour victory at a possible autumn election. His major springboard would inevitably be his annual party conference. He had long since decided that his theme would be science. 'I believe socialism will come through applying the scientific revolution to our country,' he told Jocelyn Stevens well before the party conference. 'Take the trained scientists. Why do they go to America? Of nine Ph.Ds qualified this year in one of our scientific colleges, seven are going to America. I once talked this over with a group of British scientists in America. They said they had not left primarily because of the higher pay abroad, but because they had better chances of promotion. In Britain they were waiting for dead men's shoes. This is our problem in relation to the apathy and cynicism about the future.'[165]

Behind this interview lay not only Wilson's own more technological background – through his factory chemist father – but also other developments. Wilson had given Crossman the task of mobilizing the scientific community. He had brought back into Labour activity the Nobel Prize-winner, Professor Patrick (later Lord) Blackett of Imperial College. A left-winger, Professor Blackett had had a strained relationship with Hugh Gaitskell. When Gaitskell set up the Taylor Committee to report on Higher Education without a single scientist on it, Blackett and his panel of Labour-supporting scientists sent him a note which amounted to a collective resignation in the latter part of 1962. When approached by Crossman, whom he had known as a contributor to the *New Statesman*, Professor Blackett was enthusiastic. Between them they set up committees to work out a new programme for the elevation of science and technology. One committee was headed by Blackett himself, another by Noel (later Lord) Annan, Provost of King's College, Cambridge, another by Dr Vivian (later Lord) Bowden, and another by Robert Maxwell, the rich and plausible scientific publisher and Labour candidate for Buckingham.

Wilson was pushed in these directions – completely outside the range of normal Labour controversies – because he felt that virtually nothing could be done by him to tamper with his inherited Labour team. 'I am trying to run a Bolshevik Revolution with a Csarist Cabinet,' is the way he phrased it on one occasion.[166] He was hesitant about changing things because, particularly after the Profumo case, he expected an early general election, probably in October 1963 or, at latest, May 1964. As a result he did not want to disturb the team he had inherited. He was not at all happy with the economic knowledge of Jim Callaghan, with whom Gaitskell had replaced Wilson as 'Shadow Chancellor'. He feared that if Labour won power in October 1963 the Treasury mandarins would mould Callaghan like soft clay, keeping the economy in the 'stop–go' posture so typical of Treasury thinking. In July 1963 Wilson began to think of rejigging Labour's economic leadership, with Brown as a Minister of Production either on a level with Callaghan or above him. Word leaked out that Brown was urging Wilson to tell Callaghan of his impending demotion. When this was raised indirectly at the PLP Wilson expressed astonishment that anybody could imagine he would ever do anything to complicate the Callaghan–Brown relationship. A leading Wilson-backer leaned towards a neighbour and whispered: 'Isn't it wonderful, now, for a change, to have a Leader who can lie?'[167]

In politics, of course, it is sometimes thought to be clever tactics to give an impression the reverse of your real intention. In the summer of 1963 it must have looked to most people as if Wilson's main aim was to force the Tories to jettison Harold Macmillan, whom he had so fiercely indicted for his apparent negligence over the Profumo affair. In fact, this was the reverse of Wilson's intent. He preferred to keep Macmillan there as a target of infinite opportunity. In this way he could return to the attack when Philby was confirmed as 'the Third Man' (after Burgess and Maclean) in July 1963, long after he had been exposed as such by Marcus Lipton, a Labour MP. Wilson warned Macmillan against laughing off the Philby affair, since it had been he who, as Foreign Secretary, had cleared Philby eight years earlier. Wilson pointed out that Philby had been appointed originally by a Tory, Sir Anthony Eden, and sacked by a Labour Foreign Secretary, Herbert Morrison. Wilson was probably turning the knife so savagely because Macmillan, a few days before, had refused him any opportunity to meet President Kennedy during the latter's brief visit to London. Wilson had suggested, through the American Ambassador, that it might be mutually useful to meet since he could pass on to Kennedy his personal impressions of his talks with Krushchev.

Despite such hurtful pinpricks Wilson wanted to keep Macmillan at Number 10. It was better to have a discredited Tory leader as his opponent, especially one who, during the previous two years, had lost his spark. After the Profumo case exploded in June Macmillan seemed like an elderly sleep-walker. 'My spirit is not broken, but my zest is gone,' Macmillan confessed on the day of the Profumo debate.[168] Wilson tried to keep his sagging adversary on his feet by predicting that Macmillan's Tory supporters would throw in the towel for him. On the eve of President Kennedy's arrival Wilson predicted: 'At this moment of time, we read of the 1922 Committee engaging like a group of aboriginal savages in a frenzied ritual dance with only one end in view – to obtain the Prime Minister's head as a sacrificial offering to expiate the collective anxieties of the Conservative Party.'[169]

Wilson was worried that the Conservatives might turn to a younger, tougher, more cunning politician like Iain Macleod. But this was ruled out by Macleod's participation in the overnight conference which had helped Profumo cook up his lying 'personal statement'. He felt less threatened by the other possible successors to Macmillan then under discussion. He was sure he could make mincemeat of Lord Hailsham if the latter gave up his peerage – as became possible in July 1963. He did not think R. A. Butler dynamic enough, dismissing him as a possible 'churchwarden turned caretaker'. Of the two younger men in the race, Heath and Maudling, he dismissed Heath because of his failure to secure Britain's EEC entry and thought Maudling 'not nasty enough' for the Tories to last long as leader. He preferred to retain Macmillan as the toothless devil he knew. He was delighted when the newspapers headlined their summaries of the Denning Report on the Profumo case 'PREMIER FAILED' and 'MAC BLAMED'[170] in the week before the Labour conference opened at Scarborough.

## HAPPY TRIANGLES
As the Conservatives approached their period of greatest uproar Wilson settled more firmly into his two triangles. Dick Crossman and Tommy Balogh remained his closest political advisers, though he never entertained them at home. Although Mary still barred politicians from her doorstep she did play the agreed role of the Leader's wife; it was likely that she might soon be converted into the wife of a Labour Prime Minister. This event came to be so widely accepted that there was some press resentment expressed that Number 10, then redecorated, should have had its furnishings selected by Lady Dorothy Macmillan on her own without consulting Mary Wilson. Mary began going to a few big meetings with Harold, something she had avoided for years. At the first of these after he was elected leader she was photographed dancing with him. On 18 July Mary gave a tea party for the wives of 150 Labour MPs in the Members' dining room of the House of Commons, with the support of Mrs George Brown and Mrs Herbert Bowden. This was a revival of a custom that had been initiated by Mrs Clement Attlee.

As the political secretary of the leader Marcia Williams was gradually strengthening her position. She was helping Wilson not only with the greatly expanded work of his office but also with two books he was writing, one a collection of his speeches due for publication by Weidenfeld, his longstanding publisher. It was taken for granted that on working trips, like that to Moscow, Marcia would be introduced as more like a *chef du cabinet* than a political secretary. Her brother and sister often helped in the office.

The closeness of the relationship between Harold Wilson and Marcia Williams began at attract gossip, some of it malicious, particularly in Westminster. Mrs Williams, always thin-skinned and quick to strike out in defence either of her own position or that of Wilson, had stepped on quite a lot of sensitive toes in Westminster in her seven years there. Some people were prepared to think the worst of a young and attractive woman. This was particularly true after her husband, who had never been much in evidence, completely disappeared from the scene. It gradually emerged that he had gone to North America, and after a long while it turned out that a divorce had taken place some time before. In fact, of course, Marcia's divorce had become final on 7 April 1961, over two years earlier. Security on this information had been very tight, so tight that several Conservative newspapers tried to exploit the situation right up to the October 1964 general election. When an *Evening Standard* reporter was sent to ask Mrs Williams about the breakdown of her marriage, an agitated Marcia called in Harold, who sent the reporter off with a flea in her ear. In the run-up to the October 1964 general election another newspaper considered urging Ed Williams to return to Britain to divorce his wife, only to discover belatedly that he was already divorced. Mr Williams manfully stood by his agreement and disregarded all Fleet Street blandishments.

A number of Labour enthusiasts privy to these whispers were very concerned lest it blow up into something which the Conservatives could exploit in a general election run-up. At the time when Profumo had first been under fire a number of Conservative MPs had considered the War Minister's dereliction purely a sexual peccadillo which Labour was exploiting for political purposes. They had made it clear they considered this a violation of the 'Gentlemen's Code' and would revenge themselves if any Labour front-bencher stepped out of line.

## ELECTION FEVER

Wilson was at Brighton for his debut as Labour's leader. He was concerned about establishing a better relationship with trade-union leaders on several levels. He needed their support if there was to be an early general election because trade unions were normally generous in their contributions to Labour Party funds on such occasions. More important, he sought an understanding with them on wage restraint, without which any hope of industrial investment under a Labour Government would be hopeless. He had set out his thinking (formed in part by his adviser Dr Balogh) during his speech to the Transport Workers at their Scarborough annual conference on 8 July 1963: 'We shall have to ask for restraint in the matter of incomes ... all incomes, not only wages and salaries but profits, especially monopoly profits and distributed dividends ... Yes and rents as well.'[171]

He was not always careful to avoid stepping on the long toes of trade-union leaders. He was worried that IPC were fairly shortly going to scrap the Labour-supporting *Daily Herald* and replace it by a less political *Sun*, despite Cecil King's promise to keep going for seven years. Wilson appealed to King, who brought to Brighton assurances that the *Daily Herald* would last until after the election at least. Printing union chief Robert Willis criticized Wilson for intervening without consulting the print unions. This omission on Wilson's part may have helped in Wilson's defeat at the Brighton TUC conference. Boilermaker chief Ted Hill steered through a resolution opposing 'wage restraint in any form', although he later explained that this would not apply to a Labour Government which restrained all incomes equitably. ·

After his first weeks of fearing too early a general election Wilson switched to wanting one as soon as possible. With Labour way ahead in the polls he tended to interpret all signs as tending towards an early election. At the beginning of September 1963 he warned Transport House against letting down its guard. He thought that there might be a Tory back-bench revolt against Macmillan, particularly if the Denning Report on the Profumo case were critical. He tried to provoke Macmillan by a strong attack at Lydney on 14 September. Macmillan, he charged, had debauched Britain's public life 'by preaching a selfish, materialist hedonism which has won elections at the cost of Britain's strength and independence'. 'We have seen standards which would have been unthinkable in Lord Attlee's administration, or indeed in any previous Conservative Government.'[172] When he spent 115 minutes reading the full 50,000 words of the Denning Report on the Profumo case in Admiralty House on 17 September, the question of whether the criticism in it of Macmillan would force the Prime Minister's resignation was uppermost in his mind.

When he was putting the finishing touches on his speeches for Labour's conference he was still hopeful that these would provide the launching pad for an election campaign. He tried to keep up the pressure on the Tories by continuing to accuse them of incompetence in the field of security, despite charges of 'McCarthyism' from Tory Minister Joseph Godber.

By the week before the 1963 Labour Conference at Scarborough it was public knowledge that science and technology would be Wilson's chief themes in his main speech at his first Conference as leader. He was hoping to bring to the fore the ideas produced by the half-dozen committees which had been discussing the subject. Ideas were still fluid.

Crossman wanted a Ministry of Science and Higher Education to rank equally with the Ministry of Education. However, there were problems involving personalities: Washington had intimated that US confidence would be damaged if Professor Blackett were brought too much to the fore. He had been a persistent left-wing critic of US nuclear defence policies since Hiroshima.

Wilson reached new heights at Scarborough, not just in one speech but in three. He inspired both his long-time supporters and those who had been either sceptical or antagonistic. In fact the enthusiasm he aroused that week at Scarborough was never again to be activated so powerfully.

Wilson's speech to the eve-of-conference rally evoked the possibility of a new Britain in a new world. It was realistically hopeful, lacking the Walter Mitty element, and also politically clever. He claimed credit for having concentrated attention on the security lapses just confirmed in the Denning Report on the Profumo case. He predicted, incorrectly, that the Tories would 'now seek a sacrifice, on whom all their ills can be blamed, and they have selected the man in whose shadow they climbed to and held on to power.' He predicted a 'massive campaign of de-Stalinization, of de-Macmillanization, which would make the achievement of Mr Krushchev at the 20th Congress look like the efforts of a well-intentioned amateur.'

Wilson contrasted his own vision of the world with that of the tired Macmillan. He rejected as 'grovelling defeatism' and a 'doctrine of humiliating impotence' Macmillan's insistence that Britain would become weaker unless it joined the EEC. He envisaged Britain not so much being linked with EEC as a customs union dominated by right-wing Governments but rather as benefiting from the 'great socialist breakthrough' about to happen: 'We are moving out of the age of Adenauer into the age of Willy Brandt.' This change would make it possible to reject the 'tired contrivances of mix-manned forces and all the [other nuclear] paraphernalia of the Adenauer age'. It would be easier to make a further 'breakthrough' in nuclear and conventional disarmament in the context of this new Europe. Moreover, the problems of Africa, he insisted, 'can now be dealt with only by a Government in this country whose hands are clean.'[173]

Wilson showed his ability next day to use subtle 'leaking' as well as rousing oratory. He used a Fabian tea meeting on the afternoon of Monday, 30 September, to indicate his forward planning, some elements of which had been embarrassingly disclosed by George Brown. In an interview with Henry Brandon of the *Sunday Times*, published two weeks before, Brown had confirmed that he and Wilson had been talking of a Ministry for economic planning – before Jim Callaghan, the

Chancellor-designate, had been informed.[174] Wilson, after discussing Brown's ham-handed 'leak', decided to explain his ideas more fully. At the Fabian meeting he emphasized his desire to end the 'stop-go cycle' which, under the Tories, meant three stops for every go. More purposive physical intervention was needed instead of the Tories' reliance on monetary and tax incentives. To do this one needed a Ministry to carry out planning. A country's economic strength did not depend on its monetary situation. 'The pound is strong if and only if the economy is strong.' He also told of his plans for a Ministry of Overseas Development and a Minister for Disarmament. He wanted too to raise the level of representation at the UN. He wanted to improve decision-making in 10 Downing Street by upgrading the Cabinet Secretary and his staff. He would continue 'Neddy' – the National Economic Development Council – which the TUC liked, but 'we still have to decide what its role is.' He would continue to see the Lobby – the secret group of Westminster political correspondents – rather than rely on open Presidential-style press conferences.[175]

Wilson reached his peak next day, 1 October, with his 'Labour and the Scientific Revolution', a speech which astonished his admirers and impressed his sharpest critics, including Colin Welch of the *Daily Telegraph*. Wilson rejected 'nostalgic illusions' and the 'nuclear posturings' of the Tories with their 'old-boy network approach to life' which convinced them that 'we can always rely on a special relationship with someone or other to bail us out. From now on Britain will have just as much influence in the world as we can earn, as we can deserve.'

Real progress could only be achieved if a fully equipped Britain jumped aboard the automation bandwagon. 'There is no room for Luddites in the Socialist Party,' he announced bravely. He then told a story which would have made Luddites out of the whole United Auto Workers of America: 'Already in the engineering and automobile industries in the United States they have reached a point where a programme-controlled machine tool line can produce an entire motor car – and I mean an American motor car, with all the gimmicks on it – without the application of human skill or effort.'

To cope with this prospect Britain had to do four things: 'First, we must produce more scientists. Secondly, having produced them we must be a great deal more successful in keeping them in this country. Thirdly, having trained them and kept them here, we must make more intelligent use of them when they are trained than we do with those we have got. Fourthly, we must organize British industry so that it applies the results of scientific research more purposively to our national production effort.' This meant, too, an end to selective education, 'this system of educational apartheid.... We cannot afford to cut off three-quarters or more of our children from virtually any chance of higher education. The Russians do not, the Germans do not, the Americans do not, and the Japanese do not, and we cannot afford to either.'

He managed to link Labour's peaceful and Puritan instincts together: 'Until very recently over half our trained scientists were engaged in defence projects or so-called defence projects. Real defence, of course, is essential. But so many of our scientists were employed on purely prestige projects that never left the drawing board, and many more scientists are deployed, not on projects that are going to increase Britain's productive power, but on some new gimmick or additive to some consumer product which will enable the advertising managers to rush to the television screen to tell us all to buy a little more of something we did not even know we wanted in the first place. . . . What we should be doing is to be developing the means of mass producing simple tractors and ploughs to increase food production.'

Only Labour could bring about this scientific revolution, he insisted. 'For the commanding heights of British industry to be controlled today by men whose only claim is their aristocratic connections or the power of inherited wealth or speculative finance is as irrelevant to the twentieth century as would be the continued purchase of commissions in the armed forces by lordly amateurs.' At the end of this forty-eight-minute speech, which he had burnished until 3 a.m. that morning, he received a rapturous reception. Suppressed for the moment were doubts about his wholesale embrace of automation and his reference to the need to create 10 million new jobs by the mid-1970s.[176]

Unfortunately for Wilson he was not able to transform these Scarborough dreams into Downing Street realities by walking straight into a general election against Harold Macmillan. The wounded old fox he had hunted so successfully withdrew with a painful prostate. Quite unexpectedly the Tories fielded a much more aristocratic and seemingly less shrewd opponent in the shape of the little-known Lord Home. This left Wilson on the starting line for a whole year, expecting the starter's pistol to sound at any moment, but to no avail.

Like everyone else Wilson was taken by surprise by Macmillan's sudden retirement. His immediate reaction was to telephone 10 Downing Street to express his sympathy and good wishes for Macmillan's swift recovery. As a man of undoubted kindness who had a real admiration for his adversary – especially in pre-Profumo days – there was no disputing his good wishes. However, he was relieved that the Tories did not pick as Macmillan's replacement a tough and aggressive opponent like Iain Macleod. When Lord Home was designated he did not think the choice was as derisory as he had done when Macmillan had chosen him as Foreign Secretary and Wilson had disparaged him as 'the 14th Earl' – only to be tagged 'the 14th Mr Wilson' by Lord Home. If he had any doubts that the aura of Profumo guilt would evaporate with the passing of Macmillan, the polls made it quite clear as they showed the Labour–Tory gap narrowing.

After the new Douglas-Home Cabinet had been established Wilson was asked on BBC-TV on 22 October why he thought the Tories were making a comeback in the polls. He replied that, as a result of their dramatic Blackpool conference, they had 'been more in the public eye' and were now 'less of a bore' than before. Knowing that a new leader has several months of 'honeymoon', Wilson was kind to Douglas-Home in this interview. Asked about the 'legal snags' which appeared to be bedevilling Lord Home's efforts to become Sir Alec Douglas-Home and MP for Kinross, Wilson replied: 'As the captain of one team in the Cup Final, so to speak, I don't want to see the captain of the other side disqualified because of some trouble about his transfer.' He freely admitted that some of the new Cabinet arrangements – such as the strengthening of the Board of Trade under Edward Heath – were a good idea, though 'whether he is going to be able to achieve it without substantial changes in policy, which will be anathema to Conservative thinking, is another question.'

He even managed to be restrained about the Old Etonian's aristocratic background. 'I think that a peer has just as much right to be considered for the leadership of his party or the Prime Ministership as anyone else. Again, I would say that, whatever his school background, everyone should have an equal chance. But they shouldn't have a flying start. I think it is rather a serious thing that the Conservatives felt that for their last three Prime Ministers they have had to go to the products of one school. There are 40,000 schools in this country. I don't see why one of them' – Eton was not named – 'should regularly fill up half the places in the Conservative Cabinet.'[177] He was much tougher in the Commons two days later, debating the Tories' decision to put off the new Parliamentary session by a fortnight to give the new Cabinet a breathing-space. He ragged the Tories for having had to go to the Lords for a Prime Minister for the first time in sixty years. Wilson did not seem to be able to settle on how to handle Sir Alec. Initially he promised him that he would be playing 'the ball and not the man', although he would have liked an early dissolution and a general election. But he could not avoid irony when he congratulated the new Prime Minister on his pledge to modernize. 'I never undervalue the power of repentance, but it has taken a very long time ... Imitation is certainly the sincerest form of political desperation.'[178]

Wilson was launching on a year-long ordeal of keeping the Labour coalition on a moderate, previously agreed course, inspiring the would-be reformers without frightening others. In the steel constituency of Connah's Quay in North Wales he confirmed that Labour would renationalize steel if they were returned to power: 'That was Hugh Gaitskell's policy. It is my policy and the policy of the whole Labour movement'.[179] At the same time he was reassuring insurance tycoons that they would not be nationalized. He told them he was after speculators. In their field he wanted fair competition from state pensions and the investment of insurance funds in selected industrial projects.

When President Kennedy was assassinated he mourned his loss both personally and politically. 'Not only was he a good friend to this country,' he wrote five days after the assassination. 'His vigorous new approach both to domestic and to international problems brought a fresh wind to the whole conduct of world affairs.' Wilson, who seemed to have a need for models, had begun to model himself on Kennedy's purposive style. He sang the 'Battle Hymn of the Republic' at a hastily-organized memorial service in Westminster Abbey and flew off to attend the Washington funeral services.

Even before he left he had warned his colleagues that Labour's lead over the Tories might shrink even more considerably than it had already. In the wake of Kennedy's death and the resultant uncertainty people might cling conservatively to the familiar Government in office. Moreover, it was easier for the Tories to arouse patriotism over the possession of nuclear weapons than for Labour to show it was a hollow pretence.

A new reason for sagging popularity rose on the horizon. George Brown had gone to Rediffusion's TV studios in London's Kingsway to discuss the impact of Kennedy's death in a tired and distraught frame of mind. This almost led to fisticuffs with a pro-Kennedy American actor, Eli Wallach, who had the effrontery not to know George's friend, Ted (later Lord) Willis, the playwright. Brown's maudlin performance on TV affronted many viewers, who had complained to Labour MPs. Wilson found himself looking again at the question he had so often posed to colleagues: 'What shall we do about George?' On this occasion he and Chief Whip Bert Bowden saw Brown as soon as he came back from a trip to Germany on 28 November. They told him of the many complaints aroused by his 'emotional' behaviour. Brown offered to make a brief personal statement of contrition that night at the normal weekly meeting of the Parliamentary Labour Party. By early December the Tories were almost neck-and-neck in the Gallup Poll and had caught up with Labour in the *Daily Express* Poll.

## WILSON PICKS A MARCH ELECTION
Wilson decided in December 1963 that the Tories could now afford to

have a general election in March, and began planning on that basis. He found it difficult to believe that they would let the election go all the way to October 1964, the point at which the five-year period was up. He also felt sure that Chancellor Reginald Maudling, who had been appointed by Macmillan in 1962 to reflate the economy, would now be warning that economic difficulties could be expected in the autumn of 1964.

Having decided what the Tory strategy must be Wilson decided on his own. He would launch six major speeches, beginning in Birmingham on 19 January 1964 and winding up in March, just before the general election on which he was counting. He was working under fairly difficult circumstances. After a warning to the effect that he would be 'assassinated before 9 p.m. on Saturday', 7 December, a round-the-clock guard was placed on his home; a mentally disturbed man was detained by the police, but the guard was kept, much to the annoyance of Mary Wilson. Marcia Williams, too, was irritated by clinging press photographers, anxious to justify their existence by catching Wilson in an embarrassing off-guard position. When a photographer snapped him smoking a cigar at a private dinner Wilson asked him politely not to print it. 'Why?' 'It would give the wrong impression,' replied Marcia, knowing he did not want to be portrayed as a cigar-smoking tycoon.

Wilson had already decided to end the 'honeymoon' and start lashing out at the new Prime Minister in January 1964 when he received a bonus from an unexpected direction. At the end of December 1963 Randolph Churchill had published *The Struggle for the Tory Leadership*, a Macmillan's-eye-view of how Douglas-Home had succeeded to Number 10. This infuriated Iain Macleod, by now Editor of the *Spectator* (together with Enoch Powell, he had refused to serve under Douglas-Home). In a bitter review of the book which stretched to 4,500 words he told all about how Macmillan had manipulated the battle for the succession to ensure that R. A. Butler did not win out. Macmillan had originally hoped to hand over to the new generation represented by Maudling, Heath or Macleod, but he became convinced that only Hailsham could stop Butler succeeding. When Hailsham threw his opportunity away he turned to Lord Home in desperation. The whole of the 'magic circle' of Old Etonians and the Whips' Office had been used to ensure that Lord Home 'emerged'. People like Maudling and Macleod – who was Leader of the Commons and Joint Chairman of the Conservative Party – were kept in ignorance because they were outside the 'magic circle'.[180] Perhaps because he enjoyed the sight of Tories savaging each other, Wilson did not exploit these disclosures overmuch.

Wilson also felt the Tories were working for him when Sir Alec agreed to let Edward Heath try to abolish Resale Price Maintenance. He himself had tried it over a dozen years before when he was President of the Board of Trade, but the retailers had been too powerful. They were particularly powerful among Tory activists, and Wilson attributed this mistake to the fact that the by-passed Butler was not giving his advice.

Wilson underestimated Sir Alec. In January he suggested that the Prime Minister and he have secret talks on defence. If the Prime Minister accepted, Wilson felt, he would be acknowledging him as his possible successor. If he refused it would look as though he was spurning an effort to take defence out of politics. But the Tories suspected a trap, since neither Churchill not Attlee had agreed to such secret briefings.

When Wilson baited the Prime Minister on 16 January 1964 by asking whether he believed the US would supply the UK with Polaris missiles 'for us to engage in a war to which the United States are opposed' Sir Alec turned the tables on him. He asked about Wilson's pledge to give up Polaris: 'Are you not giving our power away and not getting anything in return?' He also asked why Wilson had told the press about wanting secret defence talks but had not told him. 'Why did you not come to see me?' 'If you feel different from previous Opposition Leaders, of course I will talk to you about it.' Wilson spoke very lengthily, raising laughter with his oft-repeated 'so-called independent, so-called British, so-called deterrent'. But he had few new ideas except for the one planted by George Wigg that Defence Secretary Peter Thorneycroft was scraping the bottom of his Reserves.[181]

Wilson began to show other signs of failing nerves. In a BBC-TV interview in the second week of January he said he favoured bringing in outsiders into a new Ministry. In the old Ministries, he feared, civil servants might fear the newcomers would pinch their jobs. 'This would almost certainly be the wrong recipe,' pointed out the *Economist*. 'Outside recruits might succeed if they could act as a leaven within existing departments. But if a gaggle of what will be called "long-haired socialist intellectuals" are cloistered away in some separate isolated new departments ... traditional Whitehall is very liable to unite against them. In those circumstances traditional Whitehall is generally likely to win (and not necessarily always rightly) unless the political Minister is a quite extraordinarily forceful personality in the Cabinet.'[182]

When Wilson went on his January–March campaign of six big speeches in the country he was anxious to establish the difference between the Labour and Tory mentalities. His 19 January speech at Birmingham Town Hall was an attack on the 'grouse-moor mentality' of

Britain's 'Edwardian Establishment', tags designed to link Sir Alec with Harold Macmillan. It was ridiculous, he said, to choose political leaders on the basis of 'who his father was, or what school he went to, or who his friends are'.[183] Six days later at Swansea he tagged Sir Alec 'Little Sir Echo' because he had already adopted £1,800m worth of Labour-suggested projects to try to win back voters' favour in an election year.[184] He made very practical suggestions – which the *Economist* found 'remarkably orthodox' – to get the economy moving again. These included a two-tier interest system and apprentice training to increase skilled manpower.[185] At Leeds on 8 February he numbed an audience by reading to them a twenty-page speech which described Britain as the 'Effluent Society' because in industrial towns one-third of families had no bathrooms. 'Over half of our primary schools ... were built in the nineteenth century.' He carried forward the demand for a scientific revolution in a BBC party political broadcast on 11 February 1964 and two days later in the Commons. 'Britain has got the brains' but 'nearly one in eight of our yearly output of highly qualified scientists and a far bigger figure of the younger scientists are going as well. ... It has been estimated that it costs the country £20,000 to train each Ph.D. – then we lose him.'[186] Wilson was running into the danger of deafening, if not blinding, his listeners with science.

As the Conservatives stretched out the election campaign for an extra six months and then a further six months to October 1964 Wilson's performance remained on a fairly high level, but at the end he carried less conviction than at the beginning.

There was the charge that he was a 'one-man band', always pushing himself to the fore. In fact he dominated Labour no more than Gaitskell had. Although Gaitskell had had quite a number of friends who shared his own middle-class background, this had not stopped him from rejecting quite brutally their pro-EEC ideas when he stepped out at Brighton in October 1962 as a fiery critic of the European Community. Wilson turned on his friends on much lesser, tactical issues. One of these concerned a study group under Dick Crossman. Its conclusion on how to solve the teacher shortage was to have children under six go to school for only half a day. When this aroused an adverse reaction among teachers and Labour MPs Wilson curtly repudiated the proposals of the Crossman group.

It was not the firmness of his leadership which led Wilson to be considered a 'one-man band', despite the efforts of pro-Conservative newspapers to exaggerate this. Rather it was the enthusiasm with which he played the different tunes in his wide-ranging repertoire. On one occasion he played 'The Super Civil Servant'. He told Dr Norman Hunt – later Lord Crowther-Hunt – that he would institute a strong

Cabinet Secretariat, as in Churchill's and Attlee's time, to give the
Prime Minister the basis for a more independent judgment. On another
occasion he played 'Stars and Stripes Forever', even before his trip to
Washington to see the new President. He displayed in the Opposition
Leader's room a framed picture of himself with Lyndon B. Johnson at
Kennedy's funeral, inscribed by Johnson, 'In appreciation of your
kindness and personal sympathy.' His visit, including his 50-minute talk
with the new President – with Mary Wilson and Giles in attendance –
might have been overlooked had it not been for the misreporting of a
clever Wilson idea to dramatize his emphasis on conventional forces. In
a speech at Bridgeport University he suggested that the Royal Navy and
some of Britain's forces in Germany be used as the core of a UN police
force, if NATO agreed. When an oversimplification by an American
news agency enabled Tory newspapers to pretend his offer was to
'give away' the Royal Navy, he immediately called a press conference at the British Embassy. He felt compelled to do the same at
Transport House on his return: 'I said if we concentrate on our
non-nuclear and conventional world role we would be available for ad
hoc United Nations operations when it was appropriate.'[187]

A couple of months later he announced his decision to see Soviet
leader Krushchev again in June. The Tories, realizing he was imitating
Macmillan's 1959 tactics, denounced this trip as 'pure electioneering'.
But Wilson insisted his object was to 'recapture the peace initiative'. He
felt that the impetus had been lost, particularly on non-proliferation,
since the test-ban agreement. In private he claimed that the willingness
of Krushchev to see him showed that he considered him to be the next
British Prime Minister.

The role he played in both Washington and Moscow was 'Wilson the
Conventional Armer'. Interviewed by Robin Day a week after his return
from Washington he insisted he would give up the Polaris agreement
and convert Polaris submarines to non-missile use.[188] Another theme
which recurred was 'Wilson the Commonwealth Man'. Sometimes his
defence of the old Commonwealth verged on a defence of imperialism.
He was not only firmly on the side of defending Malaysia against
Indonesia. On one occasion he said: 'Aden is worth holding.' He was
cautious on the Simonstown base, insisting that he could not make up
his mind on naval relations with South Africa until he gained office.
Often his fervency for the Commonwealth was the reason given for his
opposition to the EEC. On 9 May 1964 at Weymouth he again
denounced the terms on which Heath had attempted EEC entry as 'a
humiliation for Britain and a betrayal of the Commonwealth'.[189] Two
weeks later, when beef was short, Wilson urged 'long-term guarantees to
British farmers' and 'long-term contracts to Commonwealth suppliers
for some years ahead'.[190]

Sometimes he played the role of 'Wilson the Strike-Settler'. This happened in July 1964, when 3,500 TV technicians struck. Wilson had gone to see a film about Aneurin Bevan with George Wigg. Arnold Goodman (then called 'Mr X') and Jack Hylton urged him to intervene. Wilson spent four days on it. Finally he produced a settlement with George Elvin, the trade unionist, and Bernard Floud, the ITV companies' labour relations chief who was then still the Labour candidate for Acton.

## MISJUDGING THE ELECTION

There was one subject on which he could not preen himself: his ability to tell when the Tories would hold the general election. He had been sure they would call it in the spring and not leave it to the autumn. When it became clear at the beginning of April that there would be no spring election he took off his gloves in his 5 April speech in the Albert Hall. 'We meet at the end of an eventful week,' he cried jubilantly. 'We have had the county council elections. We have had Sir Alec fail his GLC, and we have had the unedifying spectacle of the Prime Minister publicly canvassing his supporters on whether they would prefer to be defeated now or later in the year.' He was at that point still seven per cent ahead in the Gallup Poll. It was frustrating, after Labour had won the by-election on 4 June at marginal Faversham, for Wilson to realize that he would have won a general election at any time that spring. Because he had misjudged the Tories' election strategy he had to fill in time for an extra six months, taking the risk of either overselling himself boringly or of making a blunder in the meantime.

It was not wholly surprising that he blundered in predicting the date of the general election because he was more in tune with the minds of front-bench Conservative MPs of his own generation rather than with the party functionaries in Smith Square. From his own contacts in the Ministries he could discover that the civil servants had persuaded Reginald Maudling and Sir Edward Boyle that there should and must be an election in the spring. This was rejected at Smith Square by Lord Poole, the shrewd and cynical City tycoon who was the real power at Conservative Central Office. Harold Wilson dismissed him as 'the Tory Weygand', because he was brought in to save the Tories from their disasters. But Lord Poole shrewdly concluded that the Tories would benefit by a few more months in office: 'A lot of Ministers got unduly influenced by civil servants who told them the Government couldn't be properly carried on. It was bloody silly; if civil servants don't want to do the job, then you sack them and get some others who can. I made [Viscount] Blakenham [then Chairman of the Conservative Party Organization] bang the table and say he'd walk out if Home had an election in June.'[191] Poole also made Wilson sound repetitious.

An example of 'saturation' selling was his second trip to see Krushchev since he became Leader. Although he was again imitating Macmillan he had none of the former Prime Minister's style. But Wilson had good news sense. He returned to his Soviet hosts a Red Army banner captured by British interventionists in Archangel in 1919. The Russians rolled out the red carpet for him, taking him to *Swan Lake* for the seventeenth time. He showed himself ultra-careful to protect his flanks: 'You can be sure that I shall make it abundantly clear what the British position is on Aden.' 'No, we keep all the domestic political conflicts for the floor of the House of Commons.' Speaking to Soviet journalists he said: 'We are members of an alliance and we are loyal to our allies as you are to yours – though I understand that some of them' – a reference to the Chinese – 'are proving a little unmanageable at the moment.' At this even the Soviet journalists laughed. Wilson could claim to have had two hours with Krushchev and two hours with his other top aides. He could claim to have put forward President Johnson's two proposals – for a freeze on existing missiles and a bonfire of certain obsolete bombers. But while he was presenting his ideas Sir Alec punctured his proposal for annual Summits by pointing out that a poorly pre-planned Summit like that between Kennedy and Krushchev could be worse than none: 'The defect of the abortive meeting in Paris was disastrous.'[192] Wilson felt he was chalking up a major prestige advance in talking again to the Soviet leader – who was then within months of being forcefully retired.

The 'one-man show' accusation by Tories against Wilson was also felt within Labour ranks. An argument within Transport House arose about how to run the party political broadcasts. A broadcasting advisory committee chaired by Anthony Wedgwood Benn, with professional advice from Ted Willis, Christopher Mayhew, James Cameron and George Ffitch, constantly found itself divided. The professionals wanted to use film for the party political broadcasts. The politicians tended to want to be broadcast live, claiming that their faces were not as well known as those of the Tories. The politicians won. Because of past attacks as a 'one-man band' Wilson held himself back and allowed his lieutenants to appear instead.

His tendency to pat himself on the back now began to surface. In an interview with *The Times* he explained how, almost single-handed, he had settled the electricity supply dispute. Almost reluctantly he admitted that he had consulted the TUC's General Secretary, George Woodcock.[193]

His tendency to preen was also reflected in his authorized biography by Leslie Smith, which made its appearance in June 1964. Smith, a BBC broadcaster, lived with his Huddersfield-born wife in Hampstead

Garden Suberb, near to Wilson. The book's main strength was the fact that it was based on long taped interviews with Wilson, who went quite far to disclose his own version of his family and personal history. Partly because Smith was over-indulged by those close to and admiring of Wilson the result was rather uncritical. Some critics thought it depicted Wilson too much as the suburban goody-goody.

Despite the long delay in the timing of the election there was comparatively little polishing done on the Labour Manifesto, possibly because Wilson feared a 'leak' if it came out too early. Most of the Manifesto was written by Peter Shore, then head of the Research Department, with opening and closing paragraphs by Hugh (later Lord) Cudlipp, *Daily Mirror* Group executive. The defence section was rewritten by Wilson. Apart from them, only George Brown, Dick Crossman and Labour's General Secretary, Len Williams, had seen it when, on 8 September, it was shown briefly to the National Executive and the Shadow Cabinet. Both bodies were given half an hour to read it before discussing it. It had to be sent off to the printers that evening. Such fast approval speeded Wilson's chance of changing the party image from one of ethical indignation to one of progressive social engineering. The Manifesto was aimed more against high mortgages and high rents – which affected junior executives and skilled workingmen – rather than at clearing slums. Wilson was trying to attract the votes of those who manned industry, both white-collar and blue-collar.

He also wanted to keep a fairly free hand in limiting the number of firms to be nationalized. He had devised the term 'commanding heights' in order to satisfy full-blown socialists verbally without committing Labour too formally. In a series of luncheons and dinners, which gathered momentum in 1964, Wilson reassured leading tycoons that Labour's targets would be highly selective. In mid-April he lunched with ICI directors. His long-time critic, Tory MP Sir Cyril Osborne, suggested that he had made a 'secret bargain' not to nationalize ICI.[194] A fortnight later he lunched with Colonel Charles Clark, Chairman of Alfred Herbert, Britain's biggest machine-tool group, which required Government aid to survive a decade later. At that time Wilson told the Chairman that Labour would aim to build up majority shareholdings in several big machine-tool companies. 'Naturally, I was most interested', said Colonel Clark. 'We were threatened by the late Hugh Gaitskell, but Harold Wilson's official attitude has always been very vague.'[195]

Although President Johnson was by now well in the saddle Wilson made it clear that he would try to emulate the late John Kennedy in having '100 days of dynamic action' at the beginning of his adminis-tration. This emerged in a party political broadcast on 15 July 1964. After listing all the problems facing Britain he said: 'We are going to have to tackle all these problems pretty well at once. What we are going to need is something like what President Kennedy had after years of stagnation – the programme of 100 days of dynamic action.'[196]

A fortnight later he fell into an almost Trappist silence on the Scilly Isles. He had been persuaded that he was 'over-exposed' because of the many and repeated roles he had played as a result of wrongly forecasting when the Tories would call a general election. He expected that the Labour lead in the opinion polls would sag in August, once the political heat was turned off during the Parliamentary recess. This had happened before, in March, causing some Tories to try to persuade Sir Alec to have a June election. But once the GLC elections took place Labour's lead reasserted itself.

He still felt sure enough of his impending victory to start constructing his Cabinet. Frank Cousins, the left-winger whose succession to the post of General Secretary of the Transport Workers in 1956 had altered the balance of power in the trade-union world, vacationed in Cornwall that month. He and his wife quietly paid a visit to the Wilsons on the Scilly Isles. It was on this occasion that Wilson tentatively offered him a Cabinet post, which Cousins tentatively accepted. Both decided to say nothing until after a Labour victory.

## AFTER A SUNNY SUMMER

The election finally got under way in mid-September. A long hot summer and more than a year of Maudling's reflation had produced euphoria and melted Labour's lead in the polls. The *Daily Mail*'s NOP Poll showed the Tories' nose just ahead of Labour by under 1 percent but it was the first time they had been in front since 1961. This aroused doubts about Wilson among some of his rivals, who blamed Labour's slump on his 'one-man band' tendency. 'It's not just other people he won't have on posters. He won't have policy ideas either ... He's even eased Dick Crossman out; he wanted to write the Manifesto and wasn't allowed to.'[197]

The launching of Labour's campaign at the Empire Pool, Wembley, did not enhance Wilson's reputation. His speech, though competent, was a repetition of themes he had been hammering away at for eighteen months: 'On the one hand, you have a tired Administration which has no longer anything to offer the country, no objectives, no horizons, no heights to conquer: a party which has no more vision of the future than a desire to keep things as they are, to preserve the status quo, to conserve ... On the other hand, we in the Labour Party think Britain can do better.' Certainly George Brown could do better. Unlike Wilson he did not need the stimulus of heckling to arouse an audience with his inner fire.[198] During the campaign Wilson was at his best when heckled, as at Glasgow on 4 October and at Newcastle.

His long-held fear that George Brown would drop a clanger in his exuberance was realized on 26 September in Brown's own constituency of Belper. Asked about mortgages Brown said: 'What we propose to do is to have immediate discussions with building societies, local authorities and other interested parties about reducing the mortgage rate; we shall try to get it down immediately for new mortgages. We have something in mind to the order of 3 per cent, though we are not committed to that figure.'

*Sunday Express* reporter Roy Assersohn, who had been trailing Brown, phoned it to his paper, which splashed it as 'BROWN'S BOMBSHELL – 3 P.C. HOME LOANS'. It described as a 'sensational promise' the suggestion by Labour's Deputy Leader that the party 'was thinking of reducing new mortgages to around 3 percent, compared with the 6 percent now charged by most building societies.'[199] Initially Wilson was annoyed, recalling Gaitskell's rash promises in the 1959 campaign and Douglas-Home's jibe in the current campaign that Labour's programme was 'a menu without prices'.[200] At his press conference next day at Transport House he tried to deflate what he called a 'rather typical *Sunday Express* stunt'. This was clever because no other newspaper wanted to write about news that had appeared exclusively in the *Sunday Express*, not even to disparage it.[201] But even Wilson and others in Transport House soon realized that the 'brick' Brown had dropped had turned golden. As Tories attacked Brown for his mortgage-cutting they seemed to be saying they were against cutting mortgages at all. So Brown and Wilson were able to allege, as Brown did at Ilford on 29 September: 'Some of ... the Conservative leaders ... would not know the difference between a mortgage and the back end of a camel.'[202] Wilson was able to point out to hecklers that he himself was paying off his home on a 6 percent mortgage.[203]

This picture of the Wilsons as a suburban family was one he wanted to emphasize, so that the increasing number of suburbanites would identify with him. He certainly made this pitch when he chatted on train journeys with Anthony Howard and Richard West, who were compiling a book on *The Making of the Prime Minister*, their attempt to imitate Theodore White's chronicles of the US Presidential contests. When he set out on his trip north on 14 September Mary Wilson was with him. She sat beside him in the window seat, reading Edna O'Brien's *A Prologue of Love*, staring out of the window or asking questions – but never about politics. 'Did you know that Giles had got his "A" level?' she asked. 'Yes,' Harold replied, 'he just scraped through. He isn't the brightest scholar in the family.' He added that he had helped him with his Latin. Over high tea he asked for Worcester sauce for his lamb chops but got HP Sauce instead, commenting: 'It's the *Sunday Times* that's responsible.' This was a reference to their quoting Mary as having said: 'If Harold has a fault, it is that he will drown everything with HP Sauce.' Then, to show his memory, Harold recited the quotation in French on the HP Sauce bottle. As the train approached Liverpool Mary Wilson complained: 'Do I have to wear a hat?' as she donned a red hat. 'Red doesn't suit me.' Harold was firm: 'Yes, you'll have to do that, otherwise they'll think you're a Tory because of the blue suit.'[204]

Wilson tended to go down better with Northern or working-class audiences in the London marginals, where he could launch into his stock speech denouncing Rachman and the property profiteers: 'Thirteen years of Tory rule have left Britain with a million families without homes of their own, at least a million slums, and two and a half million other houses lacking such elementary amenities as fixed baths, piped hot water or indoor sanitation.' He also had fixed jokes, like: 'This is a whistle-stop tour with a difference. We've all been reading about some others: they are all whistle and no stop.'[205]

It was a clean campaign except perhaps for two incidents, one provoked by Wilson, the other directed against him. The first was Wilson's effort to rebut the truthful allegation by Julian Amery, Minister for Aviation and MP for the marginal seat of Preston North, that Labour would cancel the TSR-2. This aeroplane, originally constructed as a hedge-hopping battlefield reconnaissance craft, had been 'stretched' at enormous expense to enable it to fly *one way* to Moscow with a nuclear bomb. This British equivalent of the Second World War Japanese 'kamikaze' mission had been supported by Minister of Defence Peter Thorneycroft and Julian Amery, successively Secretary of State for Air and Minister for Aviation, to give Britain a way of keeping up with the Americans and the Russians.

Wilson was against such a suicidal, first-strike weapon, but he did not dare attack the TSR-2 for two reasons. First, he knew that being a 'nuclear Power' still had an appeal to British nationalism, already badly bruised from loss of Empire and the rapid decline from being the world's No. 1 Power. Second, he knew that there were a lot of Labour supporters among skilled workers and junior executives in marginal seats like Preston. 'Mr Amery, the Minister of Aviation and MP for Preston North, is always spreading rumours that Labour will cancel it,' said Wilson. 'I repudiate these rumours. . . . If it works and does what is expected of it at reasonable cost we shall want it, though not for a nuclear role.'[206] By the time he said this he knew the 'plane had been made over-heavy and overly expensive following its conversion to a nuclear role.

The dirty trick played on Wilson was the decision by someone in Conservative Central Office, or one of its allied organizations, to play 'the Marcia card'. A certain amount of effort had been put into assembling information earlier. This was alluded to by H. B. Boyne, then chief Political Correspondent of the *Daily Telegraph*, who wrote of 'some rather unworthy attempts to find skeletons in Mr Wilson's personal cupboard.... As far as I know, there are none; and I fancy I know him a little better than some of the Conservative MPs who have whispered in my ear.' Although Boyne – later knighted by Harold Wilson – wrote that these efforts 'seem to have failed',[207] the people making them did not give up that easily.

On one weekend in June 1964, suddenly, at key spots all over the country, men turned up in pubs talking about an alleged intimate relationship between Marcia Williams and Harold Wilson. The following Monday, Labour MPs converged on Westminster to discuss the outbreak of what some thought was Conservative-inspired 'black propaganda'. This theory received tentative support from a source who telephoned me to claim he had been part of a team recruited to spread the story; but he did not turn up to provide details at the subsequent meeting arranged. There was no follow-up to the campaign, in the sense of a deliberate planting of the story, although ripples continued to radiate. Recollection of this smear campaign may have added special fervour to the libel action brought by Wilson and Mrs Williams when, over three years later, a columnist in the Paris-based *Herald-Tribune* returned to the same allegation.[208]

Despite a heavy cold – a frequent characteristic of autumn campaigns – Wilson did not let up until the very end. He still had his usual press conference on the morning of the day before polling, Wednesday 14 October, as well as on polling day, in the hope of making an impact on the 1 o'clock news bulletin as well as the evening newspapers. On 14 October he was dismissing the previous night's telecast by Sir Alec as 'utterly negative'; this was part of his effort to cast Labour in the image of the constructive, go-ahead party, in contrast to the tired, cynical, grouse-shooting clique led by a left-over laird.[209].

The campaign wound up heatedly after the Wilsons and Marcia Williams had travelled the 200 miles to Liverpool for the eve-of-poll meeting at St Hearge's Hall. A tumbler was thrown which hit a woman standing near Wilson. He was separated from his wife, for whom he looked anxiously. 'I was worried about Mary,' he said.[210]

## NAIL-BITING END

Partly because momentum appeared to go out of the Labour campaign at the end, partly because of stoppages on the London Underground, the October 1964 election had a nail-biting finish. The momentum was lost partly because Wilson had always planned to be in his constituency area for the last thirty hours before close of poll. He made a lot of long rambling, self-praising speeches which his constituents lapped up but which provided no copy for the national press. This enabled Sir Alec to dominate the TV on Tuesday night and the morning newspapers on Wednesday morning. Wilson's own live appearance on TV on Wednesday night, from his Liverpool eve-of-poll meeting, showed what a heavy toll the campaign and his cold had taken on his copious energy.

Election day, 15 October 1964, was like a toboggan run for Wilson. He started at the top with both major opinion polls indicating a Labour victory, partly because neither had sampled opinion during the last few days. News was also good in Huyton where he toured committee rooms; by midday it was clear he would secure an unprecedentedly high majority. Saying 'I'm not worried at all' to a friend, he went off for a sleep in his suite at the Adelphi Hotel. When he woke in the early evening the position seemed much more uncertain, partly owing to heavy polling in Liberal areas. 'Quintin is silly,' Wilson mused about the rumbustious broadcast by Quintin Hogg in which, among other things, he had said that anyone who voted Labour must be 'stark staring bonkers'.

While waiting for more signs Wilson joined in discussions about the Krushchev resignation, which Wilson seemed reluctant to believe was a serious switch of Soviet opinion. 'It may have been a stroke, in which case they'll have to have Mikoyan, who's a safe man.' As usual, to cover his disappointment at having failed to anticipate this change he fell back on jokes. If Krushchev had not been deposed, why had *Izvestia* failed to appear?, he was asked. 'The newspaper may be on strike,' quipped Wilson, 'or perhaps Roy Thomson's made a takeover bid!' Later, when Kosygin's name surfaced, Wilson claimed: 'I knew him very well. He's very tough, very able, very efficient.' He showed no sign of recognizing that the deposing of Krushchev was a reflection of a Soviet decision to compete more effectively with the Americans in terms of armaments in the wake of their Cuban humiliation two years before.

The journalists accompanying Wilson, most of whom expected Labour to win easily, began to receive strong hints of his growing uncertainty. Asked if his father would appear on TV with him, Wilson answered: 'We'll let the old man on if it's a landslide.' He began to be uncertain about when he would return to London: 'We'll be going to London on the 8.15 train, if we win.' Wilson had been informed of a belt of rain in the south-east in the evening, when the main Labour vote would be registered. 'If we lose,' he added, 'we'll have all the time in the world.'

In Suite 100 of the Adelphi Wilson settled down to watch and listen to the results. His party included Mary Wilson, his father Herbert Wilson, Marcia Williams and her brother, Tony Field, who had served as his driver, John (later Lord) Harris, then Transport House's press spokesman, John Allen, a Labour Party researcher and later boyfriend of Marcia's, Tommy Balogh, and two secretaries, Brenda Dew and Sandra Gluck. While the others consumed fish and chips and watched TV Wilson was busy on the 'phone to Transport House and regional party headquarters.

The first sign that there was by no means to be a landslide came when the Tories held Billericay, the enormous Essex constituency thought to be marginal. The first good sign came when Lena Jeger recaptured London's Holborn and St Pancras, which she had lost to Geoffrey Johnson Smith, Tory TV interviewer, in 1959. As Wilson drove to Huyton, six miles away, for his own result he was cheered by news of victories in Northern marginals – in Liverpool, Bolton, Stockport and Bradford. Marcia's brother, Tony, took a wrong turning while listening to the results, bringing them late to the Huyton count.

The growing tension began to tell on the party, causing them to behave like manic-depressives. At first Wilson lost his composure. When they were caught up in the enthusiastic crowd they became separated, and Wilson began shouting: 'Is my wife there?' In the hall, just before midnight, the news of the loss of Smethwick by Patrick Gordon Walker, the 'Shadow' Foreign Secretary, to a racialist Tory burst upon them. Marcia burst into tears. 'I was convinced we had lost,' she later confided.[211] John Harris yelled 'You bloody, bloody fool!' at Tommy Balogh who was laughing, apparently at a previous Labour victory. Wilson went white.

His mood changed a few minutes later when he received private word that his majority had trebled to almost 20,000. He began an Indian-style victory dance and then held his hands over his head, boxer-fashion. When the official announcement was made in front of TV and other cameramen fifteen minutes later Wilson thanked his agent and party workers and gave two hearty kisses, the second for the benefit of press photographers, to Mary, who had been clutching a giant toy panda, Victor, all evening. 'This is the Labour victory,' exploded Balogh with Hungarian exuberance, 'and that is the man who won – the man with the intellectual quality and emotional fervour to capture the country.'

Wilson was not as sure as the surrounding crowds that his own landslide was typical of the country. 'I feel moderately happy with the result,' he told a TV interviewer. Asked whether he felt like a Prime Minister Wilson replied: 'Quite frankly, I feel like a drink.' But when he had one later the faithful Alf Richman shielded him with his body from being photographed. The need for 'Dutch courage' increased. As results came in from the Midlands it became clear that Smethwick was not so much of a freak as thought; the swing to Labour had been minimal, with Rugby going the other way. Wilson was increasingly unsure, but at 3.10 he told a press officer: 'We're going – the 8.15 train,' which made it seem as though he thought he would win. He attended a premature victory party in the room of Peter Jenkins of the *Guardian*, but the champagne did not do as much for him as the Labour gain at Gravesend – a crucial marginal – did at 4.15 a.m.

After a couple of hours sleep a worried Wilson awoke to the crucial day. Revived by a bath, a shave and black coffee, he and his party left the Adelphi just before 8 a.m. to travel to nearby Lime Street station. Wilson, wearing the characteristic Gannex coat, waved as railwaymen shouted 'Good old Harold'. Red-hatted Mary, still hugging panda Victor, climbed into the special compartment with Herbert, Marcia Williams, John Harris and John Allen. After a breakfast of bacon, sausages, sauté potatoes and HP sauce, Wilson began to grow restless about the absence of adequate figures on the election. So long as they were in the train none of their transistor radios worked. Provided with roughly accurate regional figures by one of the journalists, Wilson got to work with his slide-rule. Finally he looked up and said with a rueful grin: 'It's no good. We shan't make it. I've checked with the slide-rule. We've lost by one seat.' Not even the news, picked up at the Nuneaton stop, that Labour had won its first-ever Sussex seat at Kemptown, Brighton, shifted his pall of depression. He snapped at a photographer who asked him if he would order a drink: 'I'm not a performing seal. I've made it quite clear that I'm not going to be photographed eating or drinking.' He refused facilities for a German TV team. 'This is for press photographers only!'

'It's still too early to comment on the result,' he told a press conference at Transport House when he arrived there from Euston station with General Secretary Len Williams. He had refused to make a statement to waiting TV teams at Euston, simply waving to a crowd of 200 that had waited for him. 'It's getting more like the Kennedy story all along,' he commented to a journalist aware of the hair's-breadth presidential result in 1960. 'We'll get the result from Cook County soon.' This, however, was an irrelevant analogy because the Daley-controlled Cook County vote swung the whole electoral vote of Illinois, which gave Kennedy his majority under the completely different system operating in the US.

Wilson was waiting, in fact, for the crucial marginals, which now began to come through. Southeast Derbyshire was won by left-winger

Trevor Park by 873 votes. At 2.45 p.m. came the crucial news that Meriden had been won after a recount, leaving Labour just one short of the needed 315 seats. Three minutes later the last seat needed, Brecon and Radnor, again fell to Labour. This marked the end of thirteen years of Conservative rule. But the Tories still declined to concede. Instead, at 3.23, almost three-quarters of an hour later, Sir Alec Douglas-Home emerged from 10 Downing Street in tails and top hat, announcing 'I'm going to see the Queen.' He meant, of course, that he was handing over the seals of office. By then the staff of Transport House had already laid out the striped trousers, black jacket and morning coat that Wilson would need for his subsequent trip to Buckingham Palace.[212]

Curiously enough, Wilson's victory was symbolized not so much by the Queen's transfer of the seals of office as by the discreet action of two plainclothes detectives. As Sir Alec emerged from Number 10 his two personal bodyguards detached themselves and made their way to Transport House in nearby Smith Square. They slipped in almost unnoticed among the jostling crowd of excited party workers, journalists and well-wishers. They were in place before the long-awaited telephone call came at 3.50. 'Would it be convenient for you to come round and see Her Majesty?' the Queen's secretary, Sir Michael Adeane, had asked Wilson.

By this time he had shed the crumpled clothes of an election barnstormer. He decided against the morning coat as being too 'Conservative' and donned instead the black jacket and striped trousers, putting a red rose in his button-hole. Finally the lookout posted outside the building reported the arrival of the official car a few minutes before Sir Alec arrived at Conservative Central Office opposite in a vast black Daimler. Harold Wilson set off for the Palace in the official Humber with Mary beside him and Robin between them. A second car came behind, bearing his father Herbert – who had shouted to friends 'We've done it at last!' a few minutes before – and his sister Marjorie.

After the half-hour's ceremonial at the Palace Wilson and family went to 10 Downing Street, where he began interviewing the senior members of his Cabinet. For almost an hour this went on while Sir Alec was packing to leave by the rear entrance in a tweed suit.

Inside Number 10 that evening it looked as though not only the Wilsons but the Fields – Marcia's family – had taken over the seat of power. Harold Wilson quipped 'Nice place we've got here' while his father gazed around with a triumphant and proprietary air. Mary Wilson had more mixed feelings. At midday, while waiting at the Crossman house in Vincent Square, she had said to Dick: 'All I have ever wanted is a nice little house in North Oxford and a don for a husband.' Crossman reassured her that life as the wife of the Prime Minister would not be too bad and that she could make a great contribution by keeping a refuge for him in the family flat over the office at Number 10.

Marcia Williams's attitude towards Number 10 was quite different. To her this hair's-breadth victory was the fulfilment of all the hopes she had built up for the victory of her boss since she had joined his staff eight years before. The civil servants at Number 10 had shown that they appreciated her importance, although not necessarily her own or Harold Wilson's evaluation of it. 'Some considerable time before the 1964 election, I had been taken to dinner and lunch several times by the late Sir Timothy Bligh, who was Principal Private Secretary to Sir Alec Douglas-Home, as he had previously been to Harold Macmillan ... These meetings were arranged so that I should learn something about the Downing Street setup in case Labour won. Tim Bligh made it clear during these meetings that the Civil Service considered that there was no place for me, or my office colleagues, at Number 10 ... They knew I had been running Harold's Private Office in Opposition, and if he succeeded in capturing power in 1964, they wanted to make certain that they captured him.' [213] So Marcia entered 10 Downing Street on 16 October 1964 ready to do battle. She won immediate support from Harold Wilson, who told his new Principal Private Secretary, Derek Mitchell: 'Let Marcia have the waiting room for her office.'[214] Marcia also had family support that day. The first meal at Number 10 was cooked by her father, Harry Field.

The Wilsons did not stay that first night, returning to Hampstead Garden Suburb. This was an early reflection of Mary Wilson's reluctance to live 'over the shop'. She continued to resent it, forcing her husband to buy 5 Lord North Street for her before his second stay in office from 1974 to 1976. But, curiously enough, Mrs Wilson became a public 'success' at the job she loathed – that of being the Prime Minister's wife. She became a public heroine. For *Private Eye* satirists she became the imaginary authoress of 'Mrs Wilson's Diary'. For the public at large she became the living demonstration that a suburban housewife could cope with the top job such a wife might have – and write poetry too.

Marcia, in contrast, attracted unfavourable publicity from the outset whilst working hard to keep her master in the job she had striven so faithfully to help him secure. This unpopularity derived partly from her abrasive loyalty, which led her to consider as hostile anyone – such as the BBC, for example – who did not fully share her enthusiasm for Wilson. In part it derived from her belief that her identification with

Wilson entitled her to involve herself in political and governmental decisions for which she had no mandate. She also felt herself entitled to take risks which involved Wilson's reputation.

In short, for Wilson winning power meant putting both his real wife and his 'office wife' under the same roof. This meant that the resultant tensions could now spill over the whole field of his private and public affairs.

## EPILOGUE: WILSON'S 'CONSISTENT INCONSISTENCY'

Wilson's private consistency thereafter tended to blot out his public inconsistency. In public affairs he aped the Macmillan technique of talking in one direction in order to move in the reverse. In Opposition he talked anti-Market, while in office he moved towards the EEC. In 1972 he embraced the idea of a referendum, which was so widely considered to be an anti-Market move that it produced the resignations of Roy Jenkins and other Marketeers; in fact, of course, the two-to-one victory for the Market in the June 1975 plebiscite virtually riveted Britain into the EEC. For his achievement in settling the issue without splitting the party Wilson emerged with credit neither from committed Marketeers nor from anti-Marketeers.

Wilson showed the same 'consistent inconsistency' in his relations with the trade unions. He covered himself by naming in his Cabinet first right-wing trade-union leader Ray Gunter and then left-wing trade-union leader Frank Cousins. He lost Frank Cousins in 1966 after privately promising him free collective bargaining but publicly bringing in a wage freeze. He lost Ray Gunter in 1968 after he began trying to discipline the trade unions while helping them through Barbara Castle's 'In Place of Strife' legislation. Wilson refused to listen to the relevant warnings of James Callaghan in 1968–69, thereby losing the 1970 general election when trade-union militants abstained. Wilson learned from that lesson. When he regained office in March 1974, he promoted Michael Foot to the Cabinet as Employment Secretary; Foot was the favourite politician of Jack Jones, the responsible-Left leader of the mammoth Transport Workers Union. But the significance of this Wilsonian move to cement the trade-union movement to the Labour Party was largely ignored or underestimated, partly because he was considered to be ambivalent or inconsistent in his views on the trade unions and their role.

There never was any doubt about the consistent attention demanded by his able if demanding political secretary, Marcia Williams. In 1974 he put his own reputation at risk by the vehemence of his defence of Marcia's brother, Tony Field, whose activities in 'land reclamation' near Wigan the *Daily Mail* had tried to link to Wilson by exploiting a

forged letter. When Wilson astonished everyone by retiring at the age
of sixty in March 1976, widespread acclamation for his deftness turned
sour as people attacked a handful of peerages and knighthoods bestowed on Marcia's friends.

Sir Harold could claim that unwarranted criticism was a result of the
anti-Labour bias of the bulk of the British press. But knowing that
bias, was it necessary to make available so many juicy titbits? Sir
Harold had long had a reputation for great personal kindness. But was
it not overdoing it to use fully £60,000 of the over £215,000 earned
from his book on *The Labour Government, 1964–70* to set up a trust for
Marcia's two children by Walter Terry?

In the end he paid the price. When he announced his resignation in
March 1976, under the surface admiration floated the recurrent ques-
tion, 'What is Harold up to?' But after the Marcia-backed names on his
Resignation Honours List 'leaked', the recurrent question became
'What is her hold over him?'

# Reference Notes

**CHAPTER I**

1. 17 March 1976.
2. *Sunday Times*, 4 April 1976.
3. *Guardian*, 17 March 1976.
4. *Guardian, Irish Independent*, 17 March 1976.
5. *Observer*, 21 March 1976.
6. *Evening Gazette*, 17 December 1975.
7. *Scotsman*, 19 December 1975.
8. *Daily Mail*, 7 January 1976.
9. 17 March 1976.
10. *Daily Mail*, 6 April 1976.
11. Official text of his speech, 16 March 1976.
12. *Daily Mail*, 6 April 1976.
13. *Irish Independent*, 17 March 1976.
14. *Sunday Times*, 4 April 1976.
15. *Ibid.*
16. *Guardian*, 17 March 1976.
17. *Irish Independent*, 17 March 1976.
18. *Daily Mirror*, 17 March 1976.
19. *Hansard*, 16 March 1976, Vol. 907 Col. 1123.
20. *Ibid.*, 16 March 1976, Vol. 907 Col. 1127.
21. *Ibid.*, 16 March 1976, Vol. 907 Col. 1128.
22. 17 March 1976.
23. Vincent Mulchrone in the *Daily Mail*, 2 April 1976.
24. *Ibid.*
25. *Hansard*, 30 March 1976, Vol. 908 Col. 1099; *Birmingham Post*, 31 March 1976.
26. *Yorkshire Post*, 5 April 1976.
27. From the Transport House text, 5 April 1976.

**CHAPTER II**

1. *The Times*, 10 July 1976.
2. *The Times*, 19 June 1976.
3. Editorial, 27 May 1976.
4. Joe Haines, *The Politics of Power*, Jonathan Cape, London, 1977, p. 206.
5. *Op. cit.*, p. 156.
6. Haines has a version of this, *op. cit.*, p. 156.
7. Sir Harold's press handout, 2 June 1976.
8. 31 May 1976.
9. 30 May 1976.
10. *The Times*, 29 May 1976.
11. *The Times*, 2 June 1976.

12. *Daily Express*, 7 June 1976.
13. 17 February 1977.
14. *Sun*, 2 February 1977.
15. Lord Wigg, *George Wigg*, Michael Joseph, London, 1972, pp. 352–3.
16. Lord Beaverbrook, *The Decline and Fall of Lloyd George*, Collins, London, 1963, p. 203; Frank Owen, *Tempestuous Journey*, p. 664.
17. 27 May 1976.
18. *Sunday Times*, 23 May 1976.
19. Andrew Roth, *The Business Background of MPs*, Parliamentary Profiles, 1962, pp. ix–xi.
20. *Daily Mail*, 18 February 1977.
21. *Op. cit.*, p. 81.
22. Haines, *op. cit.*, pp. 81–2.
23. *Sunday Telegraph*, 20 February 1977.
24. *Hansard*, House of Commons, 12 February 1976, Vol. 905 Cols. 611–12.
25. Andrew Roth, *Enoch Powell: Tory Tribune*, Macdonald, 1970, pp. 362–70.
26. *Daily Mail*, 18 February 1977.
27. *Daily Telegraph*, 18 February 1977.
28. *Daily Mail*, 18 February 1977.
29. *Daily Telegraph*, 19 February 1977.
30. Andrew Roth, *The Business Background of MPs*, Parliamentary Profiles, London, 1972, pp. i–ii.
31. *Daily Mail*, 18 February 1977.
32. *Sunday Times*, 23 May 1976.
33. *Daily Mirror*, 1 November 1976.
34. Haines, *op. cit.*, pp. 193–201.
35. *Hansard*, House of Commons, 8 April 1974, Vol. 872 Cols 28–33.
36. Joe Haines, *op. cit.*, p. 206.
37. *Observer*, 20 February 1977.
38. *Times*, 4 November 1976.
39. *Evening Standard*, 27 May 1976.
40. 27 May 1976.
41. *The Times*, 3 June 1976.
42. *Daily Telegraph*, 8 February 1977.
43. *Hansard*, House of Commons, 8 March 1977, Vol. 927 Col. 502

## CHAPTER III

1. *Evening News*, 9 February 1977.
2. *Evening News*, 18 October 1976.
3. R. H. S. Crossman, *Diaries of a Cabinet Minister*, Vol. II, Hamish Hamilton and Jonathan Cape, London, 1976, p. 782.
4. W. B. Saunders, Philadelphia and London, 1963, pp. 55–6.
5. Jonathan Cape, London, 1974, pp. 202–3.
6. Official text of statement to Cabinet, 16 March 1976.
7. Released 5 April 1976.
8. Leslie Smith, *Harold Wilson*, Fontana, London, 1964, p. 116.
9. From an interview with Mr Hamling. See his letters in the *Liverpool Daily Post*, for example.
10. R. H. S. Crossman, *op. cit.*, pp. 166, 580.
11. 'The Secret Life of Walter Mitty', from *My World and Welcome To It*, reprinted in *The Thurber Carnival*, Penguin Books, London, 1945, p. 42.
12. Weidenfeld and Nicolson, London, 1965.

13. *Daily Mail*, 17 March 1976.
14. Harold Wilson, *The Labour Government, 1964–1970*, Weidenfeld and Michael Joseph, London, 1971, pp. 47–50.
15. *Ibid.*, pp. 79–80.
16. *Guardian*, 22 June 1965.
17. *Ibid.*
18. *The Labour Government*, p. 122.
19. Official text, as distributed, 15 June 1966.
20. 19 June 1966.
21. Secker and Warburg, London 1970, pp. 23–24.
22. *Human Aggression*, Allen Lane, London, 1968, p. 78.
23. *Sunday Express*, 4 July 1948.
24. *Daily Telegraph*, 5 July 1948.
25. *Daily Telegraph*, 8 July 1948.
26. *Liverpool Daily Post*, 8 July 1948.
27. Leslie Smith, *op. cit.*, p. 16.
28. *Yorkshire Evening Post*, 14 February 1963.
29. *Sunday Telegraph*, 23 January 1966.
30. *Sunday Times*, 9 February 1964.
31. *Liverpool Echo*, 15 February 1963.
32. Leslie Smith, *op. cit.*, p. 63.
33. Leslie Smith, *op. cit.*, pp. 70–1.
34. *Sunday Times*, 9 February 1964.
35. Kenneth Harris, *Conversations*, Hodder and Stoughton, London, 1967, p. 268.
36. Interview with Brian Connell, *The Times*, 2 August 1976.
37. Interview with Dr McCullum and David Ayerst, *History of the Guardian*, Collins, 1971, p. 555.
38. *Liverpool Daily Post*, 14 May 1938.
39. *New Statesman*, 22 March 1963.
40. Harris, *Conversations*, pp. 272–3.
41. Beveridge Memorial Lecture, 18 November 1966.
42. *Ibid.*
43. Lord Beveridge, *Power and Influence*, Hodder and Stoughton, 1953, London, p. 267.
44. *Sunday Times*, 4 September 1966.
45. Beveridge Memorial Lecture.
46. Beveridge, *op. cit.*, pp. 271, 276.
47. *Ibid.*, pp. 279–82.
48. Interview with Lord Fulton.
49. J. Harold Wilson, Presidential Address to the Royal Statistical Society, 15 November 1972.
50. J. Harold Wilson, *New Deal for Coal*, Contact Books, London, 1945, pp. 46–50.
51. RSS Presidential Address, 15 November 1972.
52. *Ibid.*
53. Hugh Dalton, *The Fateful Years*, Frederick Muller, London, 1957, p. 389.
54. Entry for 3 March 1942.
55. Entries for 17, 20 April, 8 May 1942.
56. *New Deal*, p. 58.
57. *Ibid.*, p. 59.
58. Dalton diaries, entries for 23, 24, 27, 28, April 1942.
59. *New Deal*, p. 59.
60. Dalton diaries, entry for 6 May 1942.

61. *New Deal*, p. 59.
62. 1 May 1942.
63. Dalton diaries, entries for 12, 19, 22 May 1942.
64. Entry for 11 May 1942.
65. *New Deal*, p. 67.
66. RSS Presidential Address.
67. Harris, *Conversations*, p. 270.
68. *New Deal*, p. 62.
69. Harris, *Conversations*, p. 270.
70. RSS Presidential Address.
71. Beveridge Memorial Lecture.
72. *Op. cit.*, pp. 55–6.

**CHAPTER IV**

1. Samuel French, London, 1949, pp. 5–6, 13.
2. *Guardian*, 15 October 1976.
3. *Observer*, 9 June 1963.
4. *Sunday Times*, 2 August 1964.
5. *Daily Telegraph*, 9 November 1971.
6. *Observer*, 25 January 1950; *Sunday Telegraph*, 17 February 1963.
7. Harris, *Conversations*, pp. 266–7.
8. Harris, *Conversations*, pp. 266–7.
9. *Evening Standard*, 12 September 1972.
10. *Evening Standard*, 15 February 1963.
11. 'New Roydsian', 1966.
12. *Daily Mail*, 15 February 1963.
13. *New Statesman*, 11 April 1959.
14. *Yorkshire Evening Post*, 14 February 1963.
15. BBC interview, *The Listener*, 29 October 1964.
16. Harris, *Conversations*, p. 266.
17. Paul Foot, *The Politics of Harold Wilson*, Penguin, London, 1968, pp. 28–32.
18. Quoted by Godfrey Smith, *Sunday Times*, 9 February 1964.
19. BBC interview, *The Listener*, 29 October 1964.
20. *Isis*, 19 October 1938.
21. *Sunday Times*, 9 February 1954.
22. G. D. H. Cole, *The Machinery of Socialist Planning*, Hogarth Press, 1938, cited in Paul Foot, *op. cit.*, p. 9.
23. *Daily Express*, 9 December 1967.
24. *Ormskirk Advertiser*, 21 June 1945.
25. *Liverpool Daily Post*, 14 June 1945.
26. *Liverpool Daily Post*, 6, 18 June 1945; *Ormskirk Advertiser*, 1, 21 June 1945.
27. Bernard Donoughue and G. W. Jones, *Herbert Morrison, Portrait of a Politician*, Weidenfeld and Nicolson, London, 1973, pp. 339–48; Hugh Dalton, *The Fateful Years*, Muller, London, 1957, pp. 467–8; Hugh Dalton, *High Tide and After*, Muller, London, 1962, pp. 8–14.
28. Dalton, *The Fateful Years*, pp. 476–7; Leslie Smith, *op. cit.*, p. 100.
29. Emanuel Shinwell, *Conflict Without Malice*, Odhams, London, 1955, p. 170.
30. Leslie Smith, *op. cit.*, p. 102; Fred Blackburn, *George Tomlinson*, Heinemann, London, 1954, p. 154.
31. 14 October 1944.
32. *Newsweek*, 15 April 1963; *Observer*, 17 February 1963.

33. *Hansard*, 9 October 1945, Vol. 414 Cols. 186–91.
34. Leslie Smith, *op. cit.*, pp. 102–5.
35. *Hansard*, 3 December 1945, Vol. 416 Cols 2023–4.
36. Michael Foot, *Aneurin Bevan*, Vol. I (1897–1945), Paladin, London, 1975, p. 493.
37. Michael Foot, *Aneurin Bevan*, Vol. II (1945–60), Paladin, London, 1975, pp. 58–61.
38. *Hansard*, 25 March 1946, Vol. 421 Cols 140–56.
39. *Liverpool Echo*, 13 June 1946.
40. Leslie Smith, *op. cit.*, pp. 108–9.
41. 'London Letter', *Liverpool Daily Post*, 20 January 1947.
42. *Hansard*, 6 February 1947, Vol. 432 Cols 1986–98.
43. 6 March 1947.
44. L. Smith, *op. cit.*, p. 114.
45. Harris, *Conversations*, p. 271.
46. *Liverpool Daily Post*, 31 March 1947.
47. *Liverpool Daily Post*, 18 April 1947.
48. Leslie Smith, *op. cit.*, p. 115.
49. *Observer*, 25 January 1950.
50. 16 July 1947.
51. *Liverpool Echo*, 26 July 1947.
52. 25 January 1950.
53. *Liverpool Daily Post*, 9 August 1947.
54. Leslie Smith, *op. cit.*, pp. 122–4.
55. Interview with Jocelyn Stevens, *Queen*, 25 September 1963.
56. Leslie Smith, *op. cit.*, pp. 126–7.
57. 4 October 1947.
58. 11 October 1947.
59. *Liverpool Daily Post*, 4, 8 October 1947.
60. *The Times*, 24 January 1948.
61. *Liverpool Daily Post*, 15 December 1947.
62. *Hansard*, 2 March 1948, Vol. 448 Cols 218–31, 317–45.
63. *Birmingham Guardian*, 9 May 1948.
64. *Economist*, 31 May 1947.
65. *Liverpool Daily Post*, 6 May 1948.
66. 10 May 1948.
67. *Liverpool Echo*, 15 June 1948.
68. *Daily Telegraph*, 8 July 1948.
69. *Sunday Express*, 4 July 1948.
70. *New Statesman, Economist*, 10 July 1948.
71. John Cross, 'The Lynskey Tribunal', *Age of Austerity*, edited by Michael Sissons and Philip French, Hodder and Stoughton, 1963, Penguin, 1964, pp. 266–86; Leslie Smith, *op. cit.*, pp. 142–4.
72. Speech by Harold Wilson to Film Industry Seminar, Cumberland Hotel, London, 30 March 1976.
73. 19 July 1950.
74. 'J Arthur Rank and the Shrinking Screen', by Peter Forster, in *Age of Austerity*, pp. 295–6.
75. *Liverpool Daily Post*, 3 February 1949.
76. Film Industry Seminar, 30 March 1976.
77. *Ibid.*

78. *Guardian*, 15 October 1976.
79. Dalton diary, entry for 15 June 1949, vol. 37, cited in Donoughue and Jones, p. 634.
80. Dalton's diary, entry for 12 September 1949, vol. 37, cited in Donoughue and Jones, p. 438.
81. Douglas Jay, 'Civil Servant and Minister', in *Hugh Gaitskell, 1906–1963*, edited by W. T. Rodgers, MP, Thames and Hudson, London, 1964, p. 95.
82. Leslie Smith, *op. cit.*, p. 149.
83. *The Times*, 12 September 1972.
84. *Hansard*, 28 September 1949, Vol. 468 Cols 184–94.
85. *Liverpool Daily Post*, 9 September 1949.
86. Undated, probably around June 1949.
87. *Liverpool Daily Post*, 1 February 1950.
88. *Liverpool Echo*, 10 February 1950; *Liverpool Daily Post*, 15, 20 February 1950.
89. *Liverpool Echo*, 15 February 1963.
90. Michael Foot, *Aneurin Bevan*, Vol. II (1945–60), pp. 290–1.
91. Herbert Morrison, *An Autobiography*, London, 1960, p. 267.
92. This paragraph is based on interviews with Sir Harold, a memorandum he prepared for Jennie Lee, and Foot, *Aneurin Bevan* (1949–50), pp. 290–2.
93. John Strachey, *Sunday Times*, 20 January 1963.
94. Foot, *Bevan*, Vol. II, pp. 293–4.
95. *Liverpool Daily Post*, 25 August 1950.
96. Keep Left Group confidential *Minutes* for 18 July 1950.
97. Entry for 30 November 1950, Vol. 38.
98. *Liverpool Daily Post*, 21 October 1950.
99. *The Times, Daily Worker*, 14 December 1950.
100. *New York Times*, 21 December 1950.
101. Wilson memorandum prepared for Jennie Lee.
102. Foot, *Bevan*, Vol. II, p. 311.
103. George Brown, *Spectator*, 24 January 1964.
104. *Hansard*, 15 February 1951, Vol. 484 Cols 728–40.
105. Dalton's unpublished diary, entry for 22 March 1951.
106. *News-Chronicle*, 4 April 1951.
107. Leslie Smith, *op. cit.*, p. 153.
108. Dalton's unpublished diary, entry for 6 April 1951.
109. Dalton's unpublished diary, entries for 6, 8 April 1951.
110. Foot, *Bevan*, Vol. II, p. 321; Frank Pakenham (Lord Longford), *Five Lives*, Hutchinson, London, 1964, p. 187.
111. Foot, *Bevan*, Vol. II, pp. 326–7.
112. *Tribune*, 20 April 1951; Foot, *Bevan*, Vol. II, pp. 327–8; Dalton, diary entry for 19 April 1951.
113. Leslie Smith, *op cit.*, pp. 157–8.
114. *Hansard*, 23 April 1951, Vol. 487 Cols 34–43.
115. *Hansard*, 24 April 1951, Vol. 487 Cols 228–31.
116. Leslie Smith, *op. cit.*, pp. 162–3.

## CHAPTER V

1. Confidential *Minutes* of 'Keep Left' Group, 30 November, 12 December 1950.
2. *Minutes*, 26 April 1951; Foot, *op cit.*, p. 336n; Dalton, unpublished diary, entry for 30 November 1951.
3. *Minutes*, 3 May 1951.
4. *Liverpool Daily Post*, 7, 14 May 1951; *Daily Express*, 8 May 1951.

5. Subsequent interview with Arthur Waite.
6. *Liverpool Daily Post*, 17 May 1951.
7. 29 April 1951.
8. *Liverpool Daily Post*, 30 July 1951.
9. 4 August 1951.
10. *New Statesman*, 18 August 1951.
11. *New Statesman*, 25 August 1951.
12. Confidential *Minutes* of 10 May 1951 meeting in Commons.
13. *Liverpool Echo*, 10 May 1951.
14. *Minutes*, 5 June 1951.
15. *Minutes*, 12 June 1951.
16. 10 July 1951.
17. Cited, *Tribune*, 13 July 1951.
18. *Observer*, 29 July 1951.
19. 17 July 1951.
20. *The Times*, 16 August 1951.
21. 25 August 1951.
22. *Minutes*, 17 July 1951.
23. Group Paper No. 12, 'Plan for Mutual Aid', undated, but probably between 24 July and early September 1951.
24. *Guardian*, 24 July 1951.
25. *Observer*, 26 August 1951.
26. Foot, *op. cit.*, p. 348; Conference Proceedings, p. 122.
27. *The Times*, 3 October 1951; Foot, *op. cit.*, pp. 350–1.
28. *Liverpool Daily Post*, 17 October 1951.
29. Dudley Smith, *op. cit.*, pp. 134–5.
30. Interview with Lord Hale; Leslie Smith, *op. cit.*, p. 166.
31. *The Times*, *Liverpool Daily Post*, 8 October 1951.
32. *Hansard*, 6 December 1951, Vol. 494 Col. 2602.
33. Wilson memorandum for Jennie Lee, written around 1961.
34. Confidential *Minutes*, 30 October 1951.
35. Crossman's *Diary*, entry for 30 October 1951.
36. Confidential *Minutes*, 6 November 1951.
37. Unpublished diary of Hugh Dalton, entry for 30 November 1951, cited Foot, *op. cit.*, p. 356.
38. Confidential *Minutes*, 6 November, 4 December 1951.
39. *Diary* entry, 17 December 1951.
40. *Liverpool Daily Post*, 5 November 1951.
41. Those and next comments, from the confidential *Minutes* for November 1951.
42. Confidential *Minutes* of Buscot Conference, 14–15 December 1951.
43. *The Times*, 4 January 1952.
44. *Daily Worker*, 17 January 1952.
45. *The Times*, 11 January 1952.
46. Confidential *Minutes*, 26 January 1952; Crossman *Diary*, 28 January 1952.
47. *News-Chronicle*, 29 January 1952.
48. *Hansard*, 26 February 1952, Vol. 496 Cols 945–63, Foot, *op. cit.*, p. 359.
49. *The Times*, 12 February 1952.
50. Confidential Group Paper No. 27, 27–28 February 1952.
51. *News-Chronicle*, 10 March 1952.
52. *Ibid.*
53. *Evening Standard*, 10 March 1952.
54. Crossman *Diary*, entry for 10 March 1952.

55. Crossman *Diary*, entry for 11 March 1952; Foot, *op. cit.*, pp. 362–4; *The Times*, *Guardian*, 12 March 1952.
56. Crossman *Diary*, entry for 19 March 1952; Foot, *op. cit.*, pp. 369–70; *Daily Express*, 20 March 1952.
57. Crossman *Diary*, entries for 5, 17 December 1951, cited Foot, *op. cit.*, pp. 370–1.
58. Crossman *Diary*, entry for 10 April 1952.
59. Confidential *Minutes*, Group Paper 31, assigned to Wilson on 8 April 1952, discussed on 10 April 1952.
60. Crossman *Diary*, entry for 19 March 1952.
61. Confidential *Minutes*, entry for 22 April 1952.
62. Confidential *Minutes*, memo attached to 22 April 1952 meeting.
63. Confidential *Minutes*, Group Paper 34, 23 April 1952.
64. Confidential *Minutes*, 29 April 1952.
65. Confidential *Minutes*, Group Paper 31, ordered on 8 April 1952 and appended to Minutes of 10 April 1952.
66. Crossman *Diary*, 17 June 1952; Confidential *Minutes*, 17 June 1952.
67. Confidential *Minutes*, 24 June 1952.
68. Crossman *Diary*, 23 July 1952, referring to talks about 20 June.
69. Crossman *Diary*, 24 July 1952.
70. Crossman *Diary*, 1 August 1952; *Daily Telegraph*, 25 July 1952; Confidential *Minutes*, 29 July 1952.
72. 'In Place of Dollars', by Harold Wilson, published by *Tribune*, September 1952.
73. *Daily Express*, September 1952.
74. *The Times*, 1 October 1952.
75. Leslie Smith, *op. cit.*, p. 168.
76. Interview with Lord Williamson, cited Donoughue and Jones. *op. cit.*, p. 520.
77. This account from *Report* of the 51st Annual Conference, Morecambe, 1952.
78. *Diary*, entry for 1 October 1952.
79. Foot, *op. cit.*, p. 379.
80. *Daily Telegraph*, *The Times*, 6 October 1952.
81. Cited Foot, *op. cit.*, pp. 381–2.
82. Crossman *Diary*, 13 October 1952.
83. Crossman *Diary*, entry for 15 October 1952.
84. Crossman *Diary*, 30 October 1952.
85. Crossman *Diary*, 26 November 1952.
86. Crossman *Diary*, 3 December 1952.
87. Crossman *Diary*, 28 October 1952.
88. Crossman *Diary*, 26 November 1952.
89. Crossman *Diary*, 15 December 1952.
90. Crossman *Diary*, 2 January 1953, cited Foot, *op. cit.*, pp. 389–91.
91. Crossman *Diary*, 4 February 1953.
92. Crossman *Diary*, 19 February, 3, 27 March 1953.
93. *Daily Express*, 17 April 1953; *Hansard*, 16 April 1953, Vol. 514 cols 292–413, 418–30.
94. Crossman *Diary*, 18 April 1953.
95. *Daily Express*, 30 September 1953.
96. *Observer*, 17 January 1965.
97. Party political broadcast, 15 December 1951, cited Stephen Haseler, *The Gaitskellites*, Macmillan, London, 1969, p. 127.
98. Hugh Dalton, *High Tide and After*, p. 392.
99. Hugh Dalton, *High Tide and After*, pp. 394–6.

100. Crossman *Diary*, 3 December 1953, cited Foot, *op. cit.*, p. 410.
101. *Hansard*, 25 February 1954, Vol. 524 Cols 574–692.
102. *Hansard*, 25 February 1954, Vol. 524 Col. 600.
103. *Hansard*, 13 April 1954, Vol.526 Col. 971; Foot; *op. cit.*, pp. 425–7.
104. Crossman *Diary*, summarized in Foot, *op. cit.*, pp. 427–31.
105. *Guardian*, 29 April 1954.
106. *New Statesman*, 1 May 1954.
107. W. T. Rodgers, Editor, *Hugh Gaitskell*, Thames and Hudson, London, 1964, p. 110.
108. *Observer*, 26 September 1954.
109. Quoted, A. J. P. Taylor, *Beaverbrook*, p. 635.
110. *Daily Express*, 13 December 1955.
111. Emrys Hughes, *Sydney Silverman*, Charles Skilton, London, 1969, pp. 128–38.
112. Crossman *Diary*, cited Foot, *op. cit.*, pp. 450–1.
113. *Hansard*, 1, 2 March 1955, Vol. 537 Cols 1893–2200; Foot, *op. cit.*, pp. 450–62; Leslie Hunter, *The Road to Brighton Pier*, Arthur Barker, London, 1959, pp. 83–93.
114. *Hansard*, 24 February 1955, Vol. 537 Cols 1464–1584.
115. *Derby Evening Telegraph*, cited Foot, *op. cit.*, p. 462.
116. Crossman's unpublished diary, March 1955, cited. Foot, *op. cit.*, p. 471.
117. L. Hunter, *op. cit.*, pp. 94–6; Foot, *op. cit.*, pp. 462–3.
118. Foot, *op cit.*, p. 464.
119. L. Hunter, *op cit.*, p. 98.
120. *News-Chronicle*, 19 March 1955.
121. *Sunday Times, Observer*, 20 March 1955.
122. *Guardian*, 21 March 1955.
123. 20 March 1955.
124. Crossman's unpublished diary, cited Foot, pp. 479–81.
125. 1 July 1955.

## CHAPTER VI

1. Joe Haines, *op. cit.*, p. 157.
2. *Ibid.*, p. 161, and numerous other sources, all oral.
3. Letter to *The Times*, 21 February 1977.
4. Joe Haines, *op. cit.*, p. 159.
5. *Sun*, 23 February 1977.
6. Crossman, *The Diaries of a Cabinet Minister*, Vol. 1, p. 480.
7. *Observer*, 17 January 1965, Kenneth Harris interview.
8. *Daily Telegraph*, 15 February 1963.
9. *Daily Mirror*, 5 June 1970.
10. *Observer*, 17 January 1965.
11. *Daily Telegraph*, 15 February 1963; *Sunday Times*, 27 December 1964.
12. *Daily Record*, 24 March 1966.
13. *Evening News*, 11 December 1964.
14. 'The Train', *Selected Poems*, by Mary Wilson, Hutchinson, London, 1970, p. 21.
15. 'Winter Parting', *ibid.*, p. 18.
16. *Ibid.*, Preface, p. 11.
17. *Observer*, 17 January 1965.
18. 13 September 1947.
19. *Daily Express*, 30 September 1947.
20. Leslie Smith, *op. cit.*, pp. 127–8.

21. Lewis Broad, *The Women of Number 10*, Leslie Frewin, London, p. 2.
22. *Observer*, 17 January 1965.
23. *Evening News*, 11 December 1964.
24. Eric Kay, *Pragmatic Premier*, Leslie Frewin, London, 1967, p. 66.
25. *Evening News*, 11 December 1964.
26. *Sunday Times*, 9 February 1964.
27. *Evening News*, 11 December 1964.
28. *Evening Standard*, 5 October 1955.
29. *Report* of Annual Conference, Margate, 1955, pp. 137, 151–2.
30. 2 October 1955.
31. *New Statesman*, 15 October 1955.
32. *Hansard*, 13 December 1955, Vol. 547 Cols 1090–2.
33. 21 February 1956.
34. 25 February 1956.
35. 10 March 1956.
36. *Hansard*, 18 April 1956, Vol. 551 Cols 1014–35; *Guardian* 19 April 1956.
37. *Daily Telegraph*, 19 April 1956.
38. *Daily Express*, 8 November 1962.
39. BBC, Radio 4, 9 March 1959, 'Subject for Sunday', interview with Leslie Smith.
40. *Hansard*, 20 June 1956, Vol. 554 Col. 1444–59; *Guardian*, 21 June 1956.
41. 22 November 1956.
42. *Guardian*, 5 November 1956.
43. *Hansard*, 12 February 1957, Vol. 564 Cols 1087–1105; *Guardian*, 13 February 1957.
44. Paul Foot, *The Politics of Harold Wilson*, Penguin, London 1968, p. 127.
45. 11 April 1957.
46. *Hansard*, 10 April 1957, Vol. 568 Cols 1135–56; *Guardian*, 11 April 1957.
47. 21 April 1957.
48. 17 April 1957.
49. *Guardian*, 29 April 1957.
50. *News-Chronicle*, 3 April 1957.
51. Speech at Reading, 5 May 1957, *Guardian*, 6 May 1957.
52. 5 July 1957.
53. Quoted by him in *The Times*, 9 May 1959.
54. Labour Party Annual Conference *Report*, Brighton, September–October 1957.
55. *Hansard*, 3 February 1958, Vol. 581 Cols 815–58.
56. 9 February 1958.
57. *Spectator*, 7 February 1958.
58. *Sunday Express*, 16 March 1958.
59. 17 April 1958.
60. 8 June 1958.
61. *Daily Express*, 30 June 1958.
62. *Guardian*, 20 July 1958.
63. 28 July 1958.
64. *The Times*, 4 November 1958; *Hansard*, 3 November 1958, Vol. 594 Cols 614–30.
65. 7 December 1958.
66. 11 September 1958.
67. 13 December 1958.
68. 25 January 1959.

69. *France-Observateur*, 24 February 1959.
70. *Hansard*, 8 April 1959, Vol. 603 Cols 207–30; *News-Chronicle*, 9 April 1959; *News of the World*, 12 April 1959.
71. *Daily Express*, 25 April 1959.
72. *Guardian*, 4 May 1959.
73. *Guardian*, 15 June 1959.
74. *Daily Express, Guardian*, 30 June 1959; *Hansard*, 29 June 1959, Vol. 608 Cols 34–164.
75. *The Times*, 22 September, 2 October 1959.
76. W. T. Rodgers, *Hugh Gaitskell*, pp. 125–6.
77. *Daily Telegraph*, 24 October 1959.
78. *Sunday Express*, 8 November 1959.
79. Woodrow Wyatt, *Turn Again Westminster*, p. 100.
80. *Ibid.*, p. 103.
81. 2 December 1959.
82. *Daily Telegraph, Guardian*, 4 December 1959.
83. 10 November 1959.
84. 1 November 1959.
85. *Daily Telegraph*, 28 December 1959.
86. 7 December 1959.
87. 6 December 1959.
88. *Daily Telegraph*, 28 December 1959.
89. Foot, *op. cit.*
90. 31 January 1960.
91. *Guardian, Daily Telegraph*, 11 February 1960.
92. 14 February 1960.
93. *New Statesman*, 5 March 1960.
94. Stephen Haseler, *op. cit.*, pp. 167–9; Paul Foot, *Wilson*, p. 130.
95. *Sunday Express*, 20 March 1960.
96. *Hansard*, 5 April 1960, Vol. 621 Cols 204–26; *Guardian*, 5 April 1960; *Daily Telegraph*, 6 April 1960.
97. 13 March 1960.
98. *Evening Standard*, 12 April 1960.
99. *Hansard*, 27 April 1960, Vol. 622 Cols 317–30; *Guardian*, 28 April 1960.
100. *Guardian*, 4 May 1960.
101. 5 May 1960.
102. *Hansard*, 27 April 1960, Vol. 622 Cols 228, 329.
103. Leeds speech, *The Times*, 2 May 1960.
104. Kenneth Harris, *Conversations*, pp. 280–1.
105. Labour Party Annual Conference *Report*, Scarborough, 1960, pp. 133–52.
106. *Sunday Pictorial*.
107. Labour Party Annual Conference *Report*, Scarborough, 1960, pp. 133–52.
108. *Ibid.*
109. E. Kay, *op cit.*, pp. 113–14.
110. Kay, *op. cit.*, p. 114.
111. *The Times, Daily Telegraph*, 22 October 1960.
112. Sunday Times, 9 February 1964.
113. Kenneth Harris, *Conversations*, pp. 280–1 (also *Observer*, 16 June 1963).
114. *Daily Mail*, 26 February 1963.
115. *Economist*, 8 October 1960, 12 November 1960.
116. *Tribune*, 31 March 1961.
117. 19 December 1960.

118. *Sunday Times*, 26 February 1961.
119. *New Statesman*, 30 June 1961.
120. *This Week*, 3 October 1961.
121. *Hansard*, 14 December 1961, Vol. 651 Cols 634–72.
122. *Hansard*, 20 December 1961, Vol. 651 Cols 1464–78.
123. *Hansard*, 4 July 1962, Vol. 662 Cols 779–91.
124. *Hansard*, 8 May 1962, Vol. 659 Cols 229–30; 15 May 1962, Vol. 659 Cols 1147–51.
125. Labour Party Annual Conference *Report*, Brighton, October 1962, pp. 240–1, recalled in Harris, *Conversations*, p. 281.
126. *Sunday Times*, 4 November 1962.
127. 2 November 1962.
128. *The Times*, 9 November 1962.
129. *Daily Mirror*, 10 January 1963; *Guardian*, 11 January 1963; *New Statesman*, 13 January 1963.
130. Anthony Howard, Richard West, *The Making of the Prime Minister*, Jonathan Cape, London, 1965, pp. 9–11.
131. *Evening Standard*, 19 January 1963.
132. Crossman's unpublished diary, 25 January 1963; Howard and West, *op. cit.*, pp. 15–16; *Observer*, 17 February 1963.
133. *Guardian*, 4 October 1963.
134. *Daily Mail*, 21, 22, 23 January 1963; *Daily Telegraph*, 23 January 1963; *Daily Express*, 24 January 1963; *Derby Evening Telegraph*, 23 January 1963; *Observer*, 17 February 1963; Howard and West, *op. cit.*, pp. 18–21.
135. *Sunday Telegraph*, 27 January 1963.
136. *Daily Telegraph*, *Guardian*, 17 February 1963.
137. 13 January 1963.
138. *Hansard*, 31 January 1963, Vol. 670 Cols 1236–50.
139. *Hansard*, 7 February 1963, Vol. 671 Cols 689–708.
140. Howard and West, *op. cit.*, p. 28.
141. *Observer*, 17 February 1963.
142. *Guardian*, 15 February 1963.
143. *Daily Telegraph*, 22 February 1963.
144. *Daily Mail*, 23 February 1963.
145. *Observer*, January 1965; Harris, *op. cit.*, p. 274.
146. 15 February 1963.
147. *Sunday Times*, 17 February 1963.
148. *Daily Express*, 18 February 1963.
149. *Daily Mail*, 23 February 1963.
150. *Observer*, 24 February 1963.
151. *Daily Express*, 28 February 1963.
152. 7 April 1963.
153. Clive Irving, Ron Hall and Jerome Wallington, *Scandal '63*, Heinemann, London, 1963, p. 66.
154. *Westminster Confidential*, 4 March 1963.
155. *Scandal '63*, *op. cit.*, pp. 100–3.
156. *Hansard*, 22 March 1963, Vol. 674 Cols 763–71.
157. *Evening Standard*, 8 June 1963.
158. *Sunday Times, Sunday Telegraph, Observer*, 9 June 1963; *Daily Express, Guardian, Daily Mail*, 11, 12, 13, 14 June 1963; *Sunday Mirror, Sunday Citizen*, 16 June 1963; *Daily Express*, 17 June 1963.
159. *Hansard*, 17 June 1963, Vol. 679 Cols 34–170.

160. *Hansard*, 30 April 1963, Vol. 676 Cols 907–23 and 1021–2; *Guardian*, 3 May 1963; *Daily Mail*, 1 May 1963.
161. 30 May 1963.
162. *Observer*, 23 June 1963.
163. *Guardian*, 24 April 1963.
164. *Observer*, 23 June 1963.
165. *Queen*, 25 September 1963.
166. *Daily Mail*, 11 December 1963.
167. *Observer*, 6 October 1963.
168. Howard and West, *op. cit.*, p. 51.
169. Howard and West, *op. cit.*, p. 52.
170. *Daily Telegraph*, *Daily Sketch*, 25 September 1963; Howard and West, *op. cit.*, pp. 59–61.
171. *Daily Express*, *Guardian*, *Daily Telegraph*, 9 July 1963.
172. *Evening Standard*, 14 September; *Observer*, 15 September 1963.
173. My notes and text.
174. 15 September 1963.
175. My notes; *Daily Express*, 1 October 1963.
176. Text; my notes; *Evening Standard*, 1 October 1963; *The Times*, *Daily Telegraph*, 2 October 1963.
177. *The Times*, *Daily Telegraph*, *Daily Express*, *Daily Mail*, 23 October 1963.
178. *Hansard*, 12 November 1963, Vol. 684 Cols 108–39; *The Times*, 13 November 1963.
179. *Daily Express*, 23 November 1963.
180. *Spectator*, 17 January 1964; Andrew Roth, *Enoch Powell: Tory Tribune*, *op. cit.*, pp. 303–4; Howard and West, *op. cit.*, pp. 113–14.
181. *Hansard*, 16 January 1964; *The Times*, 17 January 1964.
182. 11 January 1964.
183. *Guardian*, 20 January 1964.
184. Text; *Observer*, 26 January 1964.
185. *Economist*, 1 February 1964.
186. *Guardian*, 12 February 1964; *Evening Standard*, 13 February 1964.
187. *Guardian*, *Daily Express*, 2 March 1964.
188. *Guardian*, 10 March 1964.
189. *The Times*, 10 May 1964.
190. Text, Inverness, 23 May 1964.
191. Howard and West, *op. cit.*, pp. 134–5.
192. *Daily Express*, 2, 3 June 1964; *New Statesman*, 5 June 1964.
193. *Sunday Telegraph*, 19 April 1964.
194. *Sunday Telegraph*, 19 April 1964.
195. *Evening Standard*, 4 May 1964.
196. *The Times*, 16 July 1964.
197. Howard and West, *op. cit.*, p. 144.
198. *Observer*, *Sunday Times*, *Sunday Telegraph*, 13 September 1976.
199. 27 September 1964.
200. *Sunday Telegraph*, 13 September 1964.
201. Howard and West, *op. cit.*, pp. 167–8.
202. *Daily Express*, *Guardian*, 30 September 1964.
203. *Guardian*, 1 October 1964.
204. Howard and West, *op. cit.*, pp. 145–9.
205. *Ibid.*, p. 157.
206. Text, 19 June 1964.

207. *Daily Telegraph*, 18 January 1964.
208. *Herald-Tribune*, 12 October 1967; *Daily Telegraph*, 2 January 1968.
209. *Guardian*, 15 October 1964.
210. *Daily Telegraph*, 15 October 1964.
211. *Inside Number 10*, Weidenfeld and Nicolson, London, 1972, p. 1.
212. Howard and West, *op. cit.*, pp. 225–37.
213. *Inside Number 10*, *op. cit.*, p. 20.
214. *Ibid.*, p. 22.

# Index

*Forward* 219, 241
Foster, Reginald 278
France 51, 68, 152, 182, 281
Franco, Gen. Francisco 145
Franks, Oliver (later Lord) 97
Freeman, John 92, 134–5, 139, 143, 144, 150,
  152, 158, 165, 170, 171, 181, 186, 207,
  227, 251
*Friends Apart* 83
Frognal Gardens, Hampstead 233, 263, 273
Fromm, Dr Erich 46, 66, 75
Frost, David 13, 16, 26–7
Fuel and Power, Min. of 71, 93, 100
Fulton, John (later Lord) 32, 63, 68, 69

Gaitskell, Baroness (Dora) 32
Gaitskell, Hugh 2, 70, 71, 74, 77, 92, 100, 105,
  121–2, 124, 127–8, 129, 130, 131, 132,
  133, 134, 135–6, 138, 139, 142, 143, 145,
  152, 153, 154, 155, 165, 169, 170, 172,
  174, 175, 177, 178, 181–2, 183, 187, 190,
  192, 195, 210, 211, 212, 213, 214, 218,
  226, 227, 228, 231, 232, 233, 234, 235,
  237, 238, 239, 241, 245, 246, 247, 248,
  249, 250, 251, 252, 253, 254, 255, 256,
  257, 260, 261, 262, 263–4, 265, 269, 271,
  276, 285, 294, 301, 303
Gaitskellites 234, 235, 239, 240, 241, 243,
  244, 247, 249, 252, 264, 266, 267,
  272
Galbraith, John Kenneth 257
Gale, George, 183
Gallup Poll 220, 268, 284, 294
Gan 53
Gannex raincoats 43, 237, 282, 308
Gardiner, Lord (Gerald) 31
Gatt (International Trade Organization) 105,
  107, 112, 122
General Elections (1923) 80, (1931) 83, (1945)
  89–90, (1950) 124–6, (1951) 148–9, (1955)
  190, 191, 208, (1966) 23, 196, (1974
  February) 40, 196
*General Theory* (J. M. Keynes) 61
Geneva Agreement, 1954 182
George VI 91, 113, 146–7, 149, 156, 205
George-Brown, Lord (*see* Brown, George)
Germany 27, 47, 65, 132, 162, 177, 178–9, 184,
  243, 259, 273, 281
Gladstone, Wm. E. 60–1, 89, 204, 217, 228
Gladstone Memorial Prize 60
Gledhill, Raymond 82
Glenamara, Lord (*see* Short, Edward)
Gluck, Sandra 307
Godber, Joseph 289
'Going Our Way' 148
Goldsmith, Sir James 6, 23, 42–3, 44
Gollancz, Victor 163

Goodman, Arnold (later Lord) 8, 12, 24, 35,
  36, 40, 299
Gordon, Sydney 125
Gordon-Walker, Patrick (later Lord) 52, 86–7,
  88, 159, 165, 206, 212, 233, 257, 266, 268,
  272, 277, 281, 307
Grade, Lord (Lew) 21, 42
Grayson, Victor 80
Greater London Council (GLC) 299
Greene, Lord 72
Greenwood, Anthony (later Lord) 210, 220,
  250, 251, 253, 259
Greenwood, Arthur 181
Grenfell, Dai 73
Griffiths, James 72, 132, 147, 167, 173, 188,
  212, 233, 242
Griffiths, Will 139, 162, 188
Gromyko, Andrei 281
*Guardian, The* 40, 62, 144, 163, 207, 213, 214,
  217, 225, 229, 241, 264, 268, 308
Gunter, Ray 247

H-bomb 185, 186, 187, 218, 220, 221, 251
Hailsham, Lord (*see* Hogg, Quintin)
Haines, J. T. W. (Joe) 1, 5, 6, 10, 12, 14, 17,
  21, 22, 23, 27, 28, 38, 39–40, 41, 42–3, 44,
  194
Hale, Leslie (later Lord) 139, 140, 148–9, 155,
  156, 163, 184
Hamilton, William 30
Hamling, Will 48
Hampstead 194, 226, 265, 273
Hampstead Garden Suburb 115, 143, 176, 194,
  202, 204, 206, 215, 250, 256, 273, 274, 301
Handler, Arieh 35, 36
Hankinson, A. B. 141
Hanson, Sir James 27, 42
Hardie, Keir 20
Harmsworth, Hon. Vere 40
Harris, John (later Lord) 38, 266, 307
Harris, Kenneth 274
Harris, Reader 187
Harrod, Roy 48, 87
Hathaway, Rev. David 28
Hay, Ian 77
Hayday, Fred 266
Healey, Denis 10, 15, 16, 84, 142, 248, 254,
  256, 267, 272
Health Charges Bill 134
Health, Min. of 95, 96, 255
Heath, Edward 3, 18, 19, 34, 36, 41, 42, 48, 84,
  258, 269, 287, 293, 295, 296, 298
Heathcoat-Amory, Derick (later Lord Amory)
  228, 230, 242, 246
Heenan, Cardinal 148
Heffer, Eric 247
*Herald-Tribune* allegation 305